AF839412

PUBLIC BUDGETING AND FINANCIAL MANAGEMENT

It is no secret that public budgeting courses can feel dry, technical, and overwhelming for students. Exploring real financial and budgeting situations in the public sector to engage students more actively in their learning, *Public Budgeting and Financial Management: A Casebook* applies budgeting and public finance course concepts in context to help students transform abstract concepts into practical applications.

Each chapter of this book begins with a brief introduction to a foundational budgeting concept, including definitions, basic steps, and optional further reading, to provide an overview of and context for each concept. The case studies that then follow are organized by topic, designed to help students reflect, make connections, and analyze budgeting situations within and across settings. The cases demonstrate strategies in system implementation, policy formulation, and financial management for different levels of government, with international, federal, state, county, and local cases included. Each case study concludes with questions for discussion, and teaching notes are woven thoughtfully throughout this book, offering instructors guidance on how the case studies can be implemented effectively in a classroom setting.

Public Budgeting and Financial Management: A Casebook is a detailed, indispensable guide for all public budgeting students, as well as early career faculty as they prepare to teach the course for what may be the first time, as well as for more senior faculty looking to improve the learning experience of students in the classroom.

Natalia Ermasova is a Professor and an MPA Program Director at Governors State University, Illinois, USA. She is an Adjunct Professor in the MPPA Program at Northwestern University. She was a Fulbright Specialist at Matej Bel University, Slovakia, in 2025, a Fulbright Visiting Professor at the National University of Public Service, Budapest, Hungary, in 2023, and a DAAD Visiting Professor at Ludwigsburg Academy for Civil Services, Germany. She is the co-author (with Tatyana Guzman) of *Municipal Fiscal Stress, Bankruptcies, and Other Financial Emergencies* (Routledge, 2023).

Tatyana Guzman is an Associate Professor in Public Budgeting and Finance at the Levin College of Public Affairs and Education at Cleveland State University, Ohio, USA. She joined Levin College faculty in 2013, where she teaches government budgeting and finance, economics, statistics, and research methods courses to college students and government officials outside of academia. She is the co-author (with Natalia Ermasova) of *Municipal Fiscal Stress, Bankruptcies, and Other Financial Emergencies* (Routledge, 2023). She is active with the Association for Budgeting and Financial Management (ABFM), serving on the Executive Board and on several other ABFM committees.

Routledge Public Budgeting and Finance

Editor: Bruce D. Mcdonald III

Professor of Public Budgeting and Finance. and Director of the School of Public Service

Old Dominion University, Norfolk VA

Public budgeting is a core function of public administration. Regardless of the level of government, size of government, type of management, or the socio-economic and political characteristics of the government, the execution of policies and programs requires the expenditure of resources, and important funding decisions must be made. Yet public officials are faced with policy and program implementation in an environment of limited resources. The Routledge Public Budgeting and Finance series explores issues related to effective, ethical, and equitable budgeting and financial management in the context of public administration. Topics of interest to the series include, but are not limited to:

- Budgeting for times of uncertainty
- Sales taxes
- Budget and revenue forecasting
- Management of local government debt
- Public pensions
- Financial analysis of public budgets
- Social equity budgeting
- Financing of subgovernment structures
- Financials of economic development
- Law enforcement budgeting
- Managing and organizing budget offices
- Transportation and infrastructure finance

Authors interested in discussing book project ideas on these and other public budgeting topics are encouraged to contact series general editor Bruce D. McDonald, III, Old Dominion University, at bmcdonal@odu.edu.

Recently Published Books

Public Budgeting and Financial Management
A Casebook
Natalia Ermasova and Tatyana Guzman

PUBLIC BUDGETING AND FINANCIAL MANAGEMENT

A Casebook

Natalia Ermasova and Tatyana Guzman

Routledge
Taylor & Francis Group
NEW YORK AND LONDON

Designed cover image: © Getty Images

First published 2027
by Routledge
605 Third Avenue, New York, NY 10158

and by Routledge
4 Park Square, Milton Park, Abingdon, Oxon OX14 4RN

Routledge is an imprint of the Taylor & Francis Group, an informa business

Library of Congress Cataloging-in-Publication Data
Names: Ermasova, Natalia author | Guzman, Tatyana S. author
Title: Public budgeting and financial management : a casebook / Natalia Ermasova and Tatyana Guzman.
Description: New York, NY : Routledge, 2026. | Series: Routledge public budgeting and finance | Includes bibliographical references and index.
Identifiers: LCCN 2026011605 | ISBN 9781032999425 hardback | ISBN 9781032999418 paperback | ISBN 9781003606833 ebook
Subjects: LCSH: Budget—United States—States | Finance, Public—United States—States | LCGFT: Case studies
Classification: LCC HJ2053.A1 E76 2026 | DDC 352.4/82130973—dc23/eng/20260515
LC record available at https://lccn.loc.gov/2026011605

ISBN: 978-1-032-99942-5 (hbk)
ISBN: 978-1-032-99941-8 (pbk)
ISBN: 978-1-003-60683-3 (ebk)

DOI:10.4324/9781003606833

Typeset in Times New Roman
by codeMantra

Access the Support Material: www.routledge.com/9781032999418

CONTENTS

FIGURES

TABLES

ACKNOWLEDGMENTS

This book would not have been possible without the help and encouragement of many people. First and foremost, we express our deepest appreciation to our families, Polina, Evgenia, Sergey, Ilya, David for their love, patience, and understanding that supported us throughout the long process of research and writing this book. We would like to express our deepest gratitude to our parents, Lyudmila and Sergey, Roza and Boris, for their love, support, encouragement, and belief in our work. This book would not have been possible without their continuous inspiration and love. We are sincerely grateful to our student assistants Cleira Henderson and Libby R Warren for their help with data collection, editing this book and preparing it for production. And we are grateful for the Cleveland State University Faculty Scholarship Initiative grant that helped us pay for student support and some other relevant expenses.

We would also like to thank reviewers and the editorial team for their feedback and constructive suggestions. Their guidance helped refine our arguments and improve the clarity and impact of the manuscript.

INTRODUCTION

Abstract

This is an introduction to the book that provides an explanation for why it was written and how it is organized. The first part of this chapter discusses case studies, their importance, and their role in teaching methodology. Six types of case studies and their applications are explored: narrative case studies, descriptive multiple-case studies, decision-forcing case studies, embedded cases, budget simulation games, and cross-case analyses. Approaching education through these types of case studies promotes higher-order learning outcomes, encourages critical thinking, and supports the development of applied competencies in public budgeting. This chapter then proceeds into an overview of each case study within the book, the sum of which collectively addresses issues of budget preparation, revenue and expenditure management, green budgeting, internal controls, capital and debt management, fiscal emergencies, and economic development. By presenting real-world and simulation-based cases, this book seeks to deepen students' practical understanding of public budgeting and finance, preparing them to analyze complex fiscal environments, evaluate trade-offs, and make informed decisions as public administrators.

Introduction

It is no secret that public budgeting courses can feel dry, technical, and often overwhelming for students. From information overload to unengaging instructors, there are many reasons why students might struggle to understand the

DOI: 10.4324/9781003606833-1

applicability and complexity of the subject. A handful of teaching methods can be applied to public budgeting courses, with each one exhibiting different levels of effectiveness. *Traditional lectures* allow instructors to organize and present materials and essential theories while students listen, typically in a passive and noninteractive fashion. But lectures alone do not demonstrate if students truly understand and internalize the material and are able to apply knowledge to real-world settings. Indeed, the traditional components of lecture-based teaching do not produce direct evidence of student learning, comprehension, or the ability to apply course content to practical decision-making. This issue has become even more prevalent with the growing use of artificial intelligence (AI) in education, as traditional methods of learning assessment, such as exams and homework assignments, are increasingly completed with AI assistance.

Experiential learning provides a powerful complement to traditional lecture-based instruction by shifting students from passive consumption of information to active participation in the learning process. Rather than emphasizing memorization or recall, experiential approaches require students to engage with realistic problems, exercise judgment, and reflect on the consequences of their decisions, which generates observable evidence of learning (Kolb, 2014; Maister, 1981; Sullivan & Ruyle, 1997; Yin, 2004). In public budgeting education, experiential learning helps students navigate ambiguity, competing priorities, and institutional constraints that cannot be fully conveyed through traditional lectures or homework assignments. By engaging students in applied tasks, experiential learning reduces reliance on AI-generated outputs and emphasizes process, reasoning, and interpretation (Svinicki & McKeachie, 2014). As a result, this method not only deepens understanding but also restores the instructor's ability to assess genuine student comprehension and competence.

This book showcases one of the powerful forms of experiential learning: case studies. *Case studies* help students master the material at the highest levels of Bloom's taxonomy, enhancing learning outcomes. They directly connect course content to real-world problems and challenges and prepare students to analyze, interpret, and make informed decisions in public sector environments (Austin, 1993; Guzman & Ermasova, 2025; Svinicki & McKeachie, 2014). Yin (2009, 2014) defines a case study as a "craftwork" and an empirical inquiry that investigates a phenomenon in its real-life context. Priya (2021) similarly notes that a case study involves "a detailed study of the concerned unit of analysis within its natural setting" (p. 95). Jordan and McDonald III (2022) emphasize that "Incorporating a case study approach to teaching public budgeting and financial management reminds the students of the public administration context of budgets and financial documents" (p. 257). Overall, case studies can help students:

- Identify relevance to real financial and budgeting situations in the public sector and engage students more actively in their learning

- Apply budgeting and public finance course concepts in context
- Transform abstract concepts into practical applications
- Develop valuable skills of reflecting on topics, making connections, and analyzing budgeting situations in specific settings.

Case study classification

Case studies can be classified along multiple dimensions. First, they can be real-world or fictional. As the names suggest, *real-world cases* are grounded in actual events, organizations, and data, while *fictional cases* are based on hypothetical situations designed to highlight certain concepts. This book presents only real-world cases. While hypothetical cases offer flexibility and control, real-world case studies are particularly valuable in public administration and public budgeting education because they expose students to institutional constraints, political dynamics, and ambiguity inherent in practice.

From a design perspective, case studies can also be classified as single case, multiple case, embedded, and cross case (Yin, 2009). In a *single-case study,* a solo case is examined in-depth and often from several perspectives, enabling theory development. Most cases in this book, including the cases on participatory budgeting (PB) in New York City (NYC), the Shore-to-Core-to-Shore (SCS) Tax Increment Financing (TIF) District in Cleveland, OH, blue laws in South Holland, IL, or budgeting for vacancies case in Cuyahoga County, OH, are single-case studies that focus on a specific budgeting issue in a specific municipality.

Multiple-case studies compare multiple real-world cases to identify similarities, differences, and best practices. This involves studying multiple cases, either simultaneously or sequentially, to explore a broader phenomenon. Multiple-case studies allow students to compare and contrast several cases, which among other benefits helps improve generalizability, and they are "generally considered more compelling and robust, and worthy of undertaking" (Priya, 2021, p. 100). Agranoff and Radin (1991) argue that a successful comparative case study explores the empirical knowledge in the theories used to make observations, classify phenomena, understand and interpret cases, and recognize the role of a pattern of inference. An example of a multiple-case study in this book is a comparative analysis of universal free school meal programs across nine states: Colorado, California, Maine, Massachusetts, Michigan, Minnesota, New Mexico, New York, and Vermont. In this case study, students utilize a comparative policy framework to develop a memo of evidence-based recommendations addressed to a legislator.

The case of universal free school meal programs is also an example of an embedded case study. An *embedded case study* is a case study that includes multiple units of analysis within a single setting (Yin, 2009, 2014). For example, in this book, the universal free school meal programs case evaluates the program at the state and local levels. Many other cases are also characterized by an embedded analysis: the case of closing schools in Jefferson County, CO, studies the issue from the perspective of a state and a school district; the "welcome stranger" case in California evaluates the property tax rates in California from the state, municipal, and school district views; the revenue diversification case in Matteson, IL, offers a simulation exercise at the village and department levels; the Moffett, OK bankruptcy case studies local and state revenue limitations; and lastly, the case of accounting basis in Cuyahoga County, OH, discusses fiscal relationships and policies at the federal and local levels.

In a *cross-case study*, two or more cases experiencing similar events or phenomena are studied individually. Then, data obtained from different cases are compared to derive generalizable conclusions (Yin, 2014). Examples of cross-case studies in this book include the case of congestion pricing in NYC and in London; internal control violations in Clark County, OH, Nelsonville, OH, and Dixon, IL; and fiscal emergency in Milwaukee, WI, and East Cleveland, OH.

Case studies can also be narrative and decision-forcing. The purpose of *narrative case studies* is to explain why and how certain situations occurred, what decisions were made, and the consequences of those decisions and events. By presenting a full story with facts, contextual details, and events, narrative case studies provide students with the adequate knowledge to interpret the situation and draw informed conclusions. Examples of narrative case studies in this book include the case of economic development incentives and revenue impacts in South Holland, IL, the recovery of Illinois credit ratings, Mozambique's "hidden debt scandal" and lessons for international financial accountability, and green budgeting on the federal level in the United States, among others.

Decision-forcing case studies combine storytelling with simulation, where the narrative is intentionally left unfinished. A decision-forcing case describes the dilemma and the available options for resolution, placing students in positions of responsibility where they must weigh options and make a policy or financial decision. This book includes four decision-forcing case studies: (1) a simulation on economic incentives and revenue diversification in the village of Matteson, IL, where students take the roles of board members and community stakeholders debating fiscal alternatives, (2) a school board public hearing simulation in Jefferson County, CO, in which students review fiscal and demographic data to determine school closure proposals, (3) a budgeting for vacancies simulation in Cuyahoga County, OH, where students act as county officials to determine how to treat staffing vacancies in the budgeting process, and (4) capital investments in the infrastructure at the federal level simulation where students decide how to distribute $1.2 trillion in capital funding to cover $9.1 trillion in capital infrastructure needs. These exercises place students in the shoes of a municipal government official faced with a budgeting problem that requires action and provide them with the unique challenge of interpreting incomplete information, considering trade-offs, and defending decisions under political, fiscal, and administrative pressures.

The layout of this book

Every section of this book starts with a short chapter that provides a brief discussion of a budgeting concept. For example, the chapter on capital budgeting discusses what capital budgeting is, how it works on a federal, state, and local level, who is responsible for what, and what the major challenges are. The PB chapter, in a similar fashion, covers what PB is, its history, process, challenges, and advantages. Readers are also provided with supplemental materials related to the chapter's topic. In the capital budgeting chapter, there is an overview of capital investments at different levels of government. In the PB chapter, readers have access to a table with links and a short description of PB efforts in the 150 largest cities in the United States. These chapters are not intended to replace an in-depth discussion of public budgeting and finance concepts offered in traditional budgeting textbooks, but rather to provide an overview or a general understanding of the budgetary issue as the foundation of the discussion of the case studies.

Each chapter is followed by the case studies on the topic. Throughout this book, the cases are organized by the topical area. Below is the general reference to all cases by the level of governance and a short description of each case study.

International cases

- Congestion and Low Emission Zones in London (Case study 11)

London's policymakers introduced several policies to reduce vehicle usage in central London and to limit the most polluting vehicles across Greater London. In February 2003, the city introduced the London Congestion Charge, the city's first congestion pricing system. The Low Emission Zone was implemented in 2008 to target the most polluting heavy vehicles. The Ultra Low Emission Zone was implemented in 2019 to extend stricter standards to a wider range of vehicles. These three policies combine economic incentives with regulatory restrictions to influence travel behavior, reduce emissions, and generate revenues for public transportation investments. The study provides an overview of London's transportation and environmental challenges, outlines the policy frameworks for congestion pricing and emission control, and evaluates their impact on efficiency, equity, and stakeholder engagement.

- Mozambique: Lessons from "the hidden debt scandal" (Case study 20)

This case focuses on the greatest corruption scandal in the history of Mozambique, commonly known as "the hidden debts scandal." State-owned enterprises accumulated over $2 billion in debt from the undisclosed borrowing without parliamentary approval. This resulted in multiple negative consequences, such as fiscal and economic crises, suspensions of International Monetary Fund support, downgrading by credit-rating agencies, political conflict, high inflation, and an increase in poverty. The case exposes key failures in public financial management, the role of international financial institutions, and subsequent reform efforts by the Mozambican government and its development partners, including the World Bank. Such analysis offers critical insights for policymakers, practitioners, and students of public administration on the risks of opaque fiscal practices and the importance of public budgeting and debt management.

U.S. Federal level cases

- Federal green budgeting and the "forever chemicals" challenge: Protecting U.S. drinking water systems (Case study 9)

Per- and polyfluoroalkyl substances (PFAS), commonly referred to as "forever chemicals," have emerged as a global concern due to their persistent and bioaccumulative characteristics and the associated adverse health effects. This extensive class of over 4,000 chemical compounds has been widely utilized for decades across various industrial and consumer applications, valued for their unique properties, including resistance to heat, water, and oil. However, growing evidence shows that PFAS poses risks to human health, including cancers, liver and heart impacts, as well as immune and developmental damage to infants and children. In addition to an explanation of what PFASs are and how they have raised significant public health and environmental concerns, this case study describes the green budgeting and regulation of these forever chemicals in drinking water in the United States. The lessons from the case study underscore the importance of green budgeting, enhanced regulatory guidance, increased financial support, and a strategic plan to safeguard public health and promote environmental sustainability.

- Critical needs of capital investments at the federal level in the United States (Case study 16)

This case study examines the financing challenges facing the United States' surface transportation system, especially the fiscal sustainability of the Highway Trust Fund. Federal investment in highways and mass transit has historically relied on a user-pay financing model, primarily supported by motor fuel and truck-related excise taxes. However, revenues from these sources have failed to keep pace with growing infrastructure needs. The federal gasoline tax has lost nearly half of its real value since it was last increased in 1993, contributing to a widening gap between revenues and expenditures. The case study demonstrates the magnitude and persistence of this funding shortfall and examines implications for intergovernmental finance and capital budgeting. Alternative financing strategies designed to address the declining productivity of fuel tax revenues are examined, with a particular focus on vehicle-miles-traveled fees as a potential long-term solution.

State-level cases

- Comparative analysis of universal free school meals programs at the state level in the USA (Case study 5)

The National School Lunch Program has long provided free or reduced-price meals based on household income eligibility. The introduction of the Community Eligibility Provision in 2010 allowed high-poverty schools to offer meals to all students without requiring individual applications. In recent years, several states have expanded this approach by adopting statewide universal free school meal policies that extend access to all students regardless of income. This multi-case comparative study examines the implementation, funding structures, policy goals, and outcomes of universal free school meal programs in nine states: Colorado, California, Maine, Massachusetts, Michigan, Minnesota, New Mexico, New York, and Vermont. This case study highlights similarities and differences in program design, explores the fiscal and administrative implications for school districts, and evaluates potential effects on student nutrition, equity, and educational outcomes. The study also identifies emerging best practices and policy considerations relevant for states and districts contemplating the expansion of universal school meal programs.

- The recovery of Illinois credit ratings – an institutional and fiscal analysis (Case study 21)

This case study evaluates historical trends in Illinois' credit ratings. From October 2015 to May 2022, the State of Illinois maintained one of the lowest credit ratings among the 50 U.S. states. In 2020, Illinois had BBB (Fitch and S&P Global Inc. credit ratings) and Baa3 (Moody's rating). In June 2021, Illinois received its first credit-rating upgrade from Baa3 to Baa2 (Moody's rating). Altogether, the state received nine credit upgrades from 2021 to 2025. By 2023, S&P Global Inc. had upgraded Illinois to A- and Moody's to A3. This case study critically examines the historical trajectory of Illinois' credit ratings, identifies the economic, managerial, and political determinants influencing its downgrade period, and evaluates the policy shifts that led to subsequent improvements in the following credit rating.

- Revenue windfall from Illinois cannabis taxes, societal benefit, and negative consequences (Case study 2)

This case study examines the revenue generated from adult-use cannabis taxation in Illinois and evaluates its fiscal, social, and policy implications. In FY 2025, approximately $2.1 billion worth of cannabis products were sold through 253 dispensaries statewide, and cannabis tax revenues exceeded $474 million. The revenues collected are distributed through the Cannabis Regulation Fund and allocated to multiple state agencies responsible for public health, criminal justice, community development, and regulatory oversight. These funds have supported a range of social welfare initiatives, including the purchase of opioid reversal medications, investments in behavioral health services, violence prevention programs, and anti-human trafficking efforts. While cannabis taxation has generated significant fiscal revenue and contributed to community-based social benefit programs, it has also raised concerns regarding negative consequences on public health. This case presents an opportunity to evaluate the role of earmarked revenue in achieving social policy objectives and to examine negative consequences associated with "sin tax" revenue streams for public programs.

- "Welcome stranger" system and its impacts on revenues in California (Case study 3)

In 1978, California introduced Proposition 13, a property tax reform that, among other tasks, established an acquisition-based value for property tax assessment purposes. With substantial increase in property values in California since 1978, homeowners who have owned their property for many years pay much lower taxes based on older property values, while newer homeowners pay significantly higher taxes based on current market prices. The system basically "welcomes" new homeowners to subsidize local government revenues. For this analogy, the policy was nicknamed "welcome stranger." While Proposition 13 successfully stabilized property taxes and provided predictability for long-term homeowners, it also produced significant negative consequences, including disparities in tax burdens among property owners with comparable properties, revenue losses for local governments and school districts, and fiscal stress. The case highlights the legal, fiscal, and equity challenges of a "welcome stranger" system.

- Revenue volatility and forecasting error: Navigating budget instability in California (Case study 1)

The State of California experienced fiscal challenges from 2023 to 2025, driven by forecasting errors and heavy reliance on volatile capital gains tax revenue. The state's highly progressive tax structure led to significant revenue fluctuations during a period of economic uncertainty. In response to a projected budget shortfall of over $58 billion in FY 2023–2024, lawmakers deployed a combination of spending reductions, revenue measures, deferrals, and reserve withdrawals.

This case examines the policy tools state governments may use to manage fiscal volatility and highlights key questions related to long-term budget sustainability, equity, and tax reforms.

County-level cases

- Budgeting for vacancies, OH (Case study 7)

This case study analyzes the budgeting decisions of Armond Budish, Cuyahoga County's executive, who made an ultimate call to cut costs by eliminating most unfilled vacant positions in the 2022–2023 biennial budget. Budish received backlash from the county council, bringing attention to the political and administrative pressures of budgeting policy. This case provokes discussion about the challenges of budgeting for vacancies and asks students to advocate for or against vacancy budgeting during a hypothetical county council meeting.

- Accounting basis and budgeting during the COVID-19 Pandemic: Lessons from Cuyahoga County, Ohio (Case study 8)

This case study discusses budgeting strategies and practices in Cuyahoga County, OH, during the COVID-19 pandemic and the use of the federal American Rescue Plan Act (ARPA) funds. It describes how the county took advantage of the timing of receipts and expenses (on a modified accrual accounting basis) to maximize the receipts of ARPA funding and increase flexibility of its use.

- The embezzlement of funds in Clark County, OH (Case study 13)

This case study examines a major embezzlement scheme that transpired in Clark County, OH, involving former Director of Fiscal Services, Robert Vanderhorst. Vanderhorst misappropriated county funds to cover more than $750,000 in credit card payments, over $100,000 each in mortgage and timeshare expenses, as well as payments for luxury catering events, home improvements, and other personal expenditures. The fraud went undetected for years due to weaknesses in internal controls, oversight, and accountability procedures. In 2022, Vanderhorst was convicted and sentenced to seven years in prison and ordered to pay $1,873,979 in restitution. This case underscores the critical importance of adequate financial oversight, segregation of duties, regular auditing practices, and ethical leadership in protecting public resources and maintaining public trust in local government financial administration.

- Benefit-cost analysis RT-30 Ohio (Case study 18)

This case study invites students to use benefit-cost and fiscal impact analyses to evaluate the proposed expansion of U.S. Route 30 (RT-30) in Stark, Carroll, and Columbiana counties in eastern Ohio. Approximately 35 miles of RT-30 remain largely unimproved, operating as a two-lane roadway. The proposed expansion would upgrade this segment to a four-lane freeway.

City- and village-level cases

- Congestion pricing in New York City (Case study 10)

On January 5, 2025, NYC became the first municipality in the United States to implement congestion pricing, commonly known as the Congestion Relief Zone program. This case explores the environmental, fiscal, and social objectives of the program, early performance data, political opposition, implementation, and funding challenges. An evaluation of the program illustrates the complex interplay between urban transportation policy, federal-state authority, and equitable access to public transit. Evidence from the first months of the Congestion Relief Zone indicates reduced traffic volumes, improved travel speeds, lower emissions, and revenue generation for critical Metropolitan Transportation Authority infrastructure projects. The case study presents an opportunity for students to examine real-world public finance and budgeting challenges and the policy responses to congestion pricing programs, encourages students to think critically about fiscal policy tools, revenue stability, political negotiations, and structural reform, and allows instructors to engage students in exploring the intersection of environmental sustainability, fiscal innovation, and political strategy.

- Participatory budgeting in New York City (Case study 12)

This case study helps students learn about PB on the example of NYC (PBNYC), which is the largest and most sustained PB experiment in the United States. It was launched in fiscal year 2013 by four City Council members. By 2024, PBNYC expanded to include 24 of 51 council districts and tens of millions of dollars in capital funding. The process allows residents to propose, deliberate, and vote on how a portion of their council member's discretionary capital funds are spent. While PBNYC has been praised for broadening participation among immigrants, youth, and other historically marginalized groups, it has also generated debate about whether it alters public spending priorities or reshapes how small-scale capital projects are pursued.

- Revenue today, costs tomorrow: A public finance perspective on the Chicago Skyway 99-year lease (Case study 19)

This case study examines the 99-year lease of the Chicago Skyway, a 7.8-mile toll bridge spanning the Chicago River and connecting Chicago and Indiana. As the first long-term lease of an existing toll road in the United States, Chicago's 2005 decision to privatize the Skyway for $1.83 billion holds fiscal, political, and ethical significance. When evaluated using a 3% discount rate, the $1.83 billion lease price at the end of a 99-year lease is reduced to approximately $98 million in present-value terms, illustrating the significant impact of discounting over extended time horizons. The long-term lease of the Chicago Skyway provides a valuable illustration of the implications of discounting for the valuation of an upfront payment. Using toll rate data from 2005 to 2025, the case demonstrates how privatization shifted financial risk to private investors but led to substantial increases in the toll rates and declining traffic volumes. This case offers recommendations for monetizing public assets and mitigating negative consequences.

- When Revenue Disappears: Case of Moffett, Oklahoma (Case study 4)

This case study investigates the municipal bankruptcy of Moffett, OK, which underwent Chapter 9 proceedings in 2009. It examines the fiscal, administrative, and structural factors that contributed to the town's financial insolvency, as well as the challenges encountered by local officials before and during the municipal bankruptcy. A thorough analysis suggests that Moffett's fiscal crisis was primarily the result of an excessive dependence on traffic fine revenues, which accounted for approximately 85% of its total budget, creating an unstable and unsustainable revenue structure vulnerable to policy and enforcement changes. After the Oklahoma Legislature passed a bill prohibiting Moffett from issuing speeding tickets along a four-mile stretch of U.S. Highway 64, the town filed for bankruptcy. Confronted with both the sudden loss of its primary revenue source and significant undisclosed debts, Moffett faced not only bankruptcy but also the prospect of disincorporation.

- Fiscal emergency in East Cleveland, OH (Case study 23)

The city of East Cleveland, OH, has spent nearly 30 of the last 37 years under state-declared fiscal emergency. Structural economic decline, institutional failure, administrative turnover, and corruption undermined the city's ability to achieve financial recovery despite decades of state oversight. The case of East Cleveland illustrates how fiscal-emergency frameworks can falter when local governments lack the political stability and administrative capacity necessary to implement recovery plans.

- Fiscal crisis and recovery in the City of Milwaukee, WI (Case study 22)

This case presents an analysis of fiscal crisis and recovery in the city of Milwaukee. Rising pension obligations, declining state-shared revenues, and state-imposed limitations on local taxation served as the primary reasons for the city's financial turmoil. Examining the various approaches Milwaukee employed to improve its financial position between 2023 and 2024, this case describes the collaborative recovery process and highlights the policy tools and strategic decisions that helped Milwaukee avoid bankruptcy and restore financial stability. The collaborative process resulted in a comprehensive, multi-year recovery strategy that incorporated innovative budgeting reforms, diversification of the city's revenue base, and strategic restructuring of pension and employee benefit systems.

- Economic incentives and revenue diversification in the Village of Matteson, IL (Case study 26)

This budget simulation game is based on the fiscal and operational challenges faced by the Village of Matteson, IL, and examines the approaches used by the local government to improve its financial position between 2009 and 2024. Students are assigned the roles of the village's Board of Trustees' members, department chairs, and residents and participate in a simulation of a budget meeting. This case study replicates the budget hearing process and invites students to discuss cost saving and revenue-generating options such as "stretching the budget," creating business districts and TIFs, implementing new taxes such as municipal hotel tax, installing traffic-light cameras on heavy traffic roads, collecting higher service charges and permit fees, improving budgeting practices, achieving Home Rule status, and providing financial incentives to businesses to support economic development.

- Economic Development and Revenue Impact: Case of Village of Bradley, IL (Case study 27)

The Village of Bradley, IL, used economic development tools and revenue-side budgeting strategies to improve its fiscal health between 2013 and 2025. The case illustrates how local governments can recover from fiscal stress, diversify their revenue base, and enhance long-term sustainability through economic development and strategic planning.

- Economic development incentives and limitations and their impacts on revenues: Case of South Holland, IL (Case study 24)

This case presents an analysis of economic development incentives and limitations, including changes to blue laws (Sunday store-closing laws) in South Holland, IL. Between 2009 and 2015, South Holland's blue law evolved from a strict retail closure policy into a modern ordinance focusing on residential peace and selective professional activity. This change reflects the village's balance between honoring its historic Sunday traditions and responding to the economic and social needs of the community. South Holland has implemented a variety of programs and incentives aimed at fostering business development and promoting the long-term economic vitality and community well-being. These initiatives are designed to attract private investment, strengthen the village's commercial corridors, and encourage sustainable growth through strategic collaboration between local government and the private sector.

- Case study of a mega Shore-to-Core-to-Shore TIF District in Cleveland, OH (Case study 25)

In 2024, the City of Cleveland approved a 42-year citywide TIF district as part of its Shore-to-Core-to-Shore initiative (SCS TIF). This ambitious redevelopment plan seeks to connect Cleveland's lakefront, downtown, and riverfront through multimodal transportation, public space improvements, and mixed-use development. The initiative is projected to generate between $3.3 and $7.5 billion in incremental tax revenue over 42 years. In addition to the SCS TIF, Cleveland extended five TIF districts in 2024 for a period of 30 years. In 2027, Cleveland will create a 45-year Bedrock Project TIF. This case study examines the use of citywide nested TIFs as an innovative local economic development tool, exploring both its potential benefits and risks. Students will assess whether Cleveland's strategy serves as a model for urban redevelopment or constitutes a high-risk investment in long-term economic growth.

- Municipal fraud and whistleblowing in City of Dixon, IL (Case study 15)

This case presents an analysis of financial misconduct, whistleblowing, and the oversight system in Dixon, IL, a small town notorious for the largest municipal fraud case in U.S. history. Rita A. Crundwell, Dixon's comptroller and treasurer from 1983 to 2011, embezzled $53.7 million from the city coffers for her personal expenditures between 1990 and 2011. She used the funds to maintain a luxurious lifestyle and establish one of the nation's leading quarter horse breeding empires, all while forcing staff cuts, slashing police budgets, and neglecting public infrastructure. Crundwell's ability to embezzle so much money over such an extended period indicated the presence of significant vulnerabilities in the city of Dixon's financial management and oversight system. The Dixon case highlights the critical importance of internal controls, transparency, and oversight in public financial management.

- The internal control violations in the City of Nelsonville, OH (Case study 14)

This case discusses internal control violations and embezzlement of funds in the City of Nelsonville, OH, by its former payroll clerk and the income tax administrator, Stephanie Wilson. In the city with a median household income of $38,458, Wilson managed to embezzle close to $300,000 in seven years in the elaborate payroll and income tax return fraud schemes before she was caught.

School district case

- Fiscal stress and closing schools in Jefferson County, Colorado (Public hearing simulation) (Case study 6)

This case study presents a public hearing simulation focused on school closure and reorganization decisions in the Jefferson County Public School (Jeffco) district in Colorado. Between AY 2021–2022 and AY 2023–2024, the Board of Education closed a total of 19 elementary schools in response to declining enrollment and significant fiscal pressures. As of 2024, the district enrolled approximately 69,000 students but maintains facilities with a capacity for 96,000, contributing to operational inefficiencies during a fiscal crisis ($543.3 million deficit for FY 2024). This simulation engages students in a public hearing process, where they assume roles of district administrators, Board of Education committee members, district accountability representatives, state accountability officials, parents, teachers, and nonprofit community advocates. Participants analyze demographic, financial, and educational data, articulate stakeholder concerns, and develop alternative policy proposals. The simulation concludes with a formal presentation of recommendations on school closures and a committee vote on a district reorganization plan. Through this exercise, students practice collaborative decision-making, conflict negotiation, stakeholder communication, and applied fiscal problem-solving in both politically charged and educational environment.

References

Agranoff, R., & Radin, B. A. (1991). The comparative case study approach in public administration. *Research in Public Administration, 1*(1), 203–221.

Austin, J. E. (1993). *Teaching notes: Communicating the teacher's wisdom.* Harvard Business School, Harvard University (5–793-105).

Guzman, T., & Ermasova, N. (2025). Causes and exit strategies from municipal fiscal stress and bankruptcy: A taxonomy. *Journal of Urban Affairs*, 1–30. https://doi.org/10.1080/07352166.2025.2548829

Jordan, M., & McDonald III, B. (2022). *Case studies and service learning in public budgeting and finance*. (Eds. McDonald III, B.& Jordan, M.) Teaching Public Budgeting and Finance. A Practical Guide. Routledge.

Kolb, D. A. (2014). *Experiential learning: Experience as the source of learning and development*. Prentice Hall.
Maister, D. H. (1981). *Preparing for class*. Harvard Business School, Harvard University (9–682-014).
Priya, A. (2021). Case study methodology of qualitative research: Key attributes and navigating the conundrums in its application. *Sociological Bulletin, 70*(1), 94–110.
Sullivan, R., & Ruyle, K. (1997). Case studies: An essential training tool. *Technical and Skills Training, 1*(1), 27–29.
Svinicki, M. D., & McKeachie, W. J. (2014). *McKeachie's teaching tips: Strategies, research, and theory for college and university teachers* (14th ed.). Wadsworth, Cengage Learning.
Yin, R. (2004). *The case study anthology*. Sage Publications.
Yin, R. (2009). *Case study research: Design and methods* (4th ed.). Sage Publications.
Yin, R. (2014). *Case study research and applications: Design and methods* (6th ed.). Sage Publications.

1

REVENUE BUDGETING IN PRACTICE

Abstract

Public finance is fundamentally concerned with how governments raise revenues, allocate resources, and pursue economic and social objectives. This chapter examines the structure, evolution, and current performance of public revenue systems, especially in the United States. At the subnational level, this chapter examines the composition and distribution of state and local revenues, highlighting the roles of income, sales, and property taxes, as well as the significance of intergovernmental transfers in mitigating vertical fiscal imbalances. By integrating historical perspective, empirical revenue trends, and policy analysis, this chapter provides a comprehensive background for understanding public revenue budgeting in the United States, focusing on the institutional framework, revenue forecasting, administrative processes, intergovernmental considerations, and practical challenges faced by public managers.

Introduction

Revenue budgeting refers to the process by which governments estimate, plan, and authorize financial resources necessary to support public programs and services during a fiscal period. Overly optimistic revenue forecasts can lead to midyear budget shortfalls, service cuts, or emergency borrowing, while overly conservative estimates may constrain program capacity and undermine policy objectives. Revenue budgeting is embedded in institutional arrangements that reflect constitutional requirements, statutory tax authority, economic conditions, and political priorities.

DOI: 10.4324/9781003606833-2

In the United States, the revenues collected by the federal government accounted for 64% of total receipts, while state governments collected 21% and local governments collected 15%, excluding intergovernmental transfers (U.S. Treasury, 2025). Fiscal federalism in the United States is characterized by extensive intergovernmental transfers that redistribute resources across various levels of government. The federal government transfers approximately 19% of its revenues annually to state and local governments through grants and shared programs. These transfers support education, healthcare, transportation, and income assistance and play a critical role in equalizing fiscal capacity across jurisdictions.

Revenue budgeting involves multiple institutional actors, including executive budget offices, revenue departments, legislative fiscal staff, and independent forecasting bodies. At the federal level, agencies such as the Office of Management and Budget and the Congressional Budget Office play central roles. At the state and local levels, responsibilities are often shared among departments of revenue, comptrollers, treasurers, and legislative analysts (Guzman and Ermasova, 2024, 2026).

Sources of tax and non-tax revenues

Public financial structure of federal, state, and local governments relies mainly on tax revenues. The three major tax revenue sources are income, consumption, and property taxes.

Income tax includes personal income tax (PIT), payroll taxes, and corporate income tax.

- *PIT* is the tax on income, such as salaries and wages, interest, dividends, pensions, rent, royalties, capital gains, farm income, and business income from proprietorships and partnerships of individuals and unincorporated businesses.
- *Payroll tax* is the tax on wages that is usually paid by both employers and employees and that is used to fund social programs, such as Social Security, Medicare, and unemployment insurance.
- Finally, *corporate income tax* is the tax on corporate profits.

Consumption taxes include:

- *General sales tax (GST),* or retail sales tax (RST), is the general consumption tax that is collected mainly in the United States and Canada on any general sales, such as clothes, shoes, electronic devices, certain food items, and often restaurant meals, prescription (less often), and non-prescription (more often) drugs;

- *Value-added tax (VAT)* is the tax on value added in production; the tax is similar to RST but is collected in stages during the production-consumption process rather than at the point of the final sale, as with RST. Most countries around the world rely on VATs rather than RST.
- *Gross receipts tax (GRT)* is also collected in stages, but this tax is on gross receipts of a producer, rather than value added as VAT. So, the tax creates pyramiding, when the same receipts are taxed over and over again as the product moves along the production process. Gross receipts include gross sales (total quantity multiplied by total price) and non-sales income such as interest, dividends, and donations. GRT is similar to RST in the fact that both tax transactions. But RST is paid by consumers, while GRT is paid by producers.
- *Selective excise* is the tax on certain goods or services with a much narrower base. These include gasoline excises, excises on alcohol and tobacco sales, hotel excises, taxes on admission to sports and music events, and others.
- Finally, *use tax* is the tax on goods or services purchased outside of the state. Usually, the rates are the same as an in-state RST.

The major source of revenue for local governments is the property tax, or the tax on real (not personal) property, which includes real estate or land and improvements on that land.

Some other tax revenues that generate much lower revenues for federal, state, and local governments are the

- *Severance tax* – a tax on weight or volume of extracted natural non-renewable resources;
- *Estate tax* – the tax on the right to transfer property at death;
- *Gift tax* – a tax on gifts from one living person to another;
- *Wealth tax* – a tax on net wealth of individuals or households, including real estate, financial assets, and business equity, collected by some countries, like Spain, Switzerland, or France, but not in the United States;
- Many others.

Government entities also collect revenues from non-tax sources, such as fees and licenses, charges, penalties, government-run utilities, revenues from government-run liquor stores, and from state-run lotteries and off-track betting.

Federal government sources of revenue

The structure of federal revenue in the United States has undergone substantial changes over the past century. In 1915, nearly one-half of total federal revenue was generated by excise taxes, particularly taxes imposed on products such as liquor and tobacco. Customs duties, or tariffs on imported goods, accounted for an additional 30.1% of federal revenue (Greenberg, 2015). At that time, federal financing depended primarily on taxes on consumption and international trade, reflecting the limited role of income taxation. Currently, the federal government relies on a diversified set of revenue instruments, with a strong emphasis on income-based taxation. In fiscal year (FY) 2024, the federal government collected approximately $4.9 trillion in total revenues and $5.23 trillion in 2025 (U.S. Treasury, 2025). The individual income tax was the major revenue source, accounting for 49% of total federal revenues in 2024.

Payroll taxes were the second-largest source of federal revenue, accounting for 35% of the total in 2024 (The White House, Office of Management and Budget, n.d., Table 2.2). Payroll taxes are a relatively new revenue source. They gained prominence with creation of Medicare in 1965 and subsequent increases in Social Security tax rates. Payroll tax revenues increased from 1.6% of gross domestic product (GDP) in 1950 to 6% or more of GDP since 1980 (The White House, Office of Management and Budget, n.d., Table 2.3). This growth reflects both demographic changes and policy choices that favored social insurance financing. As a result, payroll taxes have become one of the most stable components of the federal tax system. These taxes finance major social insurance programs, including Social Security and Medicare Hospital Insurance, and are levied on the wages and salaries of most workers. Payroll taxes also support unemployment insurance, railroad retirement programs, and federal employee pensions.

Corporate income taxes contributed approximately 11% of total federal revenues in 2024, while the remaining share came from excise taxes, estate and gift taxes, customs duties, and miscellaneous receipts (The White House, Office of Management and Budget, n.d., Table 2.2). The reliance on excise taxes has steadily diminished, falling from nearly 3% of GDP in 1950 to about 0.5% in recent years (The White House, Office of Management and Budget, n.d., Table 2.3).

The U.S. tax system differs from other countries in several important ways. Over the past 50 years, federal revenue has averaged 17.4% of GDP, with a high of 20.0% in 2000 and a low of 14.6% during the Great Recession (2009–2010). Member countries of the Organisation for Economic Co-operation and Development (OECD) collect, on average, revenues equal to approximately 35% of GDP. The United States imposes lighter taxes on goods and services than most developed countries. While consumption taxes account for 31% of total tax revenue across OECD countries, the U.S. share is significantly lower. For comparison, Mexico collected approximately 60% of its total tax revenue from consumption taxes in 2008. The United States is the only OECD country without a national VAT and the only OECD country without federal GST in general. Of the consumption taxes, the U.S. federal government collects only excises that have much more narrow tax base.

State government revenue sources

State constitutions define the taxing powers of state governments and often impose limitations, such as tax and expenditure limits.

State governments collected approximately $2.3 trillion in general revenues in 2020. Taxes accounted for 46% of state revenues, while fees, including tolls, tuition at public universities, and hospital payments, added up to about 11% of the total. The federal transfers accounted for 37% of state revenues in 2020, a historically high share, primarily driven by COVID-19 relief funding. Total State General Fund revenue amounted to $1.23 trillion in FY 2024 and $1.28 trillion in FY 2025, with projections indicating an increase to $1.29 trillion in FY 2026 (National Association of State Budget Officers, 2025).

State-level revenue structure is dominated by income and consumption taxes. PITs constitute the largest single source of General Fund revenue, accounting for 42.8% of total General Fund revenue and underscoring the central role of individual income taxation in subnational fiscal systems. State PIT revenues increased from $356,945 million in FY 2025 to $370,531 million in FY 2025 (Urban Institute, 2025).

Corporate income taxes contribute a more modest share, at 9.3%, reflecting both the narrower tax base and income volatility associated with corporate profits (National Association of State Budget Officers, 2025). This limited reliance also reflects competitive pressures among jurisdictions and the mobility of capital, which constrain states' ability to raise significant revenues from corporate taxation. State corporate income tax revenues declined from $93.34 billion in FY 2024 to $88.42 billion in FY 2025, a 5.3% decrease (Urban Institute, 2025).

Sales and use taxes are the second-largest revenue source, accounting for 30.1% of General Fund revenues. These taxes provide a relatively stable and administratively efficient source of funding but are often characterized as regressive, raising important equity concerns. State sales tax revenues declined from $343.78 billion in FY 2024 to $339.78 billion in FY 2025, representing a 1.2% decrease. This reduction may reflect shifts in consumer spending patterns.

While property tax remains the major source of revenue for local governments, 37 state governments, such as Illinois, Maryland, Michigan, Arizona, Nevada, and others, collect some of their revenues from property taxes, although for none of the states property tax serves as a major source of revenue. Overall, state property tax revenues increased from $18,327 million in FY 2024 to $18,525 million in FY 2025, an increase of 1.1% (Urban Institute, 2025).

Finally, all other smaller revenue sources collectively account for 17.8% of General Fund revenues (National Association of State Budget Officers, 2025). This category typically includes excise taxes, fees, licenses, and other miscellaneous revenues that, while individually smaller, provide diversification and flexibility within the overall revenue portfolio.

Local government revenue sources

Taxes accounted for 42% of local revenues, with property taxes serving as the primary source (National Association of State Budget Officers, 2025). Most local governments rely heavily on property taxes, which tend to respond relatively slowly to changes in property values. Since the COVID-19 pandemic, commercial property values, particularly for office spaces, have declined, negatively impacting local property tax collections despite rising residential property values. Charges, including sewage, parking, and service fees, accounted for 18% (Urban Institute, 2025). Approximately 35% of local revenues originated from higher levels of government, including 4% from direct federal transfers and 30% from state transfers.

In 2025, local government revenues exhibited stronger growth. Local major tax revenues increased from $753,717 million in FY 2024 to $778,138 million in FY 2025, representing a 3.2% increase. This growth was driven primarily by income and property taxes. Local PIT revenues rose from $32,587 million in FY 2024 to $33,286 million in FY 2025, an increase of 2.1%. Meanwhile, local corporate income tax revenues increased sharply, from $8,527 million to $9,479 million, an 11.2% increase (Urban Institute, 2025).

Local sales tax revenues declined from $90,405 million in FY 2024 to $89,633 million in FY 2025, a 0.9% decrease, mirroring the decline at the state level. By contrast, local property tax revenues increased significantly, rising from $622,198 million in FY 2024 to $645,740 million in FY 2025, a 3.8% increase (Urban Institute, 2025). Given the central role of property taxes in local government finance, this growth reinforces the importance of property tax as a stable and predictable revenue source.

Conclusions

The U.S. revenue system reflects a distinctive balance of income-based taxation, decentralized fiscal authority, and extensive intergovernmental transfers. While federal revenues are comparatively low by international standards, the system generates substantial resources through individual income and payroll taxes.

The composition of government revenues has shifted substantially over time, reflecting changes in economic structure, public policy, and institutional arrangements. At the federal level, revenue reliance has moved away from excise taxes and customs duties toward individual income and payroll taxes. This transition has increased the elasticity of federal revenues with respect to economic growth, but it has also increased volatility to business cycle fluctuations and raised concerns about equity, particularly in the case of payroll taxation. The historical evolution of federal revenues underscores the importance of aligning revenue instruments with both expenditures and broader economic conditions.

The United States remains a comparatively low-tax country by international standards, particularly when measured as a share of GDP. This characteristic reflects policy choices that favor limited consumption taxation and the absence of a national VAT. It constrains revenue capacity and places greater pressure on subnational governments to finance public services through narrower, and in many cases more regressive, tax bases.

Federal revenues are primarily based on income taxes, while state governments rely on a combination of income and sales taxes, and local governments heavily depend on property taxes. Intergovernmental transfers play a critical role in redistributing fiscal resources across levels of government, accounting for a substantial share of state and local revenues. These transfers are not only essential for addressing vertical fiscal imbalances but also introduce uncertainty and dependence on federal policy decisions. State revenues are constrained by declining sales tax collections and volatile corporate income tax revenues. Sales and excise taxes offer administrative simplicity and relatively stable revenue streams, but they impose disproportionate burdens on lower-income households. Income taxes provide greater progressivity and responsiveness to economic growth. They are stable and well-suited revenue sources to local governments. But they raise concerns related to taxpayer acceptability and uneven impacts across jurisdictions and income groups (Guzman and Ermasova, 2024, 2026).

The following four case studies are from Illinois, California, and Oklahoma. The first case study, "Revenue volatility and forecasting error: Navigating budget instability in California," explores the fiscal challenges the State of California faced from 2023 to 2025, driven by forecasting errors. The main reasons for this situation were heavy reliance on volatile capital gains tax revenue, the state's highly progressive tax structure, and significant revenue fluctuations during a period of economic uncertainty.

The second case study, "Revenue Windfall from Illinois Cannabis Taxes, Societal Benefit, and Negative Consequences," examines the revenue generated by Illinois's adult-use cannabis taxation and evaluates its fiscal, social, and policy implications.

The third case study, ""Welcome stranger" system and its impacts on revenues in California," presents an analysis of Proposition 13, under which long-term homeowners pay lower property taxes based on historical assessed values, while newer homeowners pay significantly higher taxes based on current market values. While Proposition 13 successfully stabilized property taxes and provided long-term homeowners with predictability, it also produced significant negative consequences, including disparities in tax burdens among property owners with comparable properties, revenue losses for local governments and school districts, and fiscal stress.

The fourth case study, "When Revenue Disappears: Case of Moffett, Oklahoma," examines the 2009 Chapter 9 municipal bankruptcy of Moffett,

Oklahoma, focusing on the fiscal, administrative, and structural conditions that led to the town's financial insolvency and the challenges faced by local officials before and during the bankruptcy process. The analysis demonstrates that Moffett's crisis was the result of an unsustainable reliance on traffic fine revenues (approximately 85% of its budget).

References

Greenberg, S. (2015). *How has federal revenue changed over time? Tax foundation.* https://taxfoundation.org/data/all/federal/how-has-federal-revenue-changed-over-time/

National Association of State Budget Officers. (2025). *Fiscal survey of States.* https://higherlogicdownload.s3.amazonaws.com/NASBO/9d2d2db1-c943-4f1b-b750-0fca152d64c2/UploadedImages/Fiscal%20Survey/Fall_2025_Fiscal_Survey_S.pdf

Urban Institute. (2025). The state tax and economic review. *The Urban Institute's State and Local Finance Initiative.* https://www.urban.org/sites/default/files/2025-08/STER_2025Q1.pdf

U.S. Treasury. (2025). *The latest data on federal revenue, spending, deficit, and the national debt.* https://fiscaldata.treasury.gov/americas-finance-guide/

The White House, Office of Management and Budget. (n.d.). Historical tables. https://www.whitehouse.gov/omb/information-resources/budget/historical-tables/

CASE STUDY 1

Revenue volatility and forecasting error: navigating budget instability in California

Abstract

This case study explores the fiscal challenges faced by the State of California from 2023 to 2025, driven by forecasting errors and heavy reliance on volatile capital gains tax revenue. The state's highly progressive tax structure led to significant revenue fluctuations during a period of economic uncertainty. In response to a projected budget shortfall of over $58 billion in FY 2023–2024, lawmakers deployed a combination of spending reductions, revenue measures, deferrals, and reserve withdrawals. This case serves as an examination of the policy tools available to state governments in managing fiscal volatility and highlights key questions around long-term budget sustainability, equity, and tax reform.

Topics

State Government; Revenue; Forecasting; Public Finance; Fiscal Stress

Background

After the COVID-19 pandemic, California's economy experienced a rapid rebound, supported significantly by substantial infusions of federal relief funding. This convergence of factors led to a temporary surge in state revenues, which exceeded $200 billion per year. In 2022, Governor Newsom declared that the state enjoyed a $97.5 billion budget surplus (Walters, 2024). Relying on this atypical revenue spike, the Newsom administration projected in 2022 that PIT, corporate income tax, and sales tax – the state's three primary revenue sources – would collectively continue to generate over $210 billion annually (Walters, 2024).

However, in contrast to forecasts by the state's administration, receipts from the major revenue sources have fallen below the $200 billion threshold in 2023. As acknowledged in Governor Newsom's revised FY 2024–2025 budget proposal, cumulative revenue projections over the four-year period have been downgraded by an extraordinary $165 billion compared to the estimates made two years earlier (California Budget & Policy Center, 2024). The deficit emerged as a result of a combination of volatile stock market earnings, delayed tax filings following severe winter storms, and ambitious spending commitments based on overly optimistic revenue projections.

Governor Newsom's administration estimated the shortfall at around $38 billion for FY 2023–2024 (California Budget & Policy Center, 2024). At the same time, Legislative Analyst's Office (2023) predicted a $68 billion budget deficit. To address the problem over a two-year period, lawmakers enacted cost-cutting and revenue-generating actions totaling more than $58 billion, including reserve withdrawals, spending cuts, revenue shifts, and deferrals (California Budget & Policy Center, 2024).

Revenue volatility and forecast

There is a high degree of uncertainty in forecasting future revenues in California (California Budget & Policy Center, 2025b). A large share of state's revenues comes from PIT and GRT, both very sensitive to economic cycles and difficult to accurately forecast. PIT is California's largest revenue source, expected to contribute around 58.3% of the General Fund revenues in FY 2025–2026 (The State of California Department of Finance, 2025b).

Another revenue source, the capital gains tax, has been very volatile too. In 2021, capital gains reached an unprecedented 11.6% of total personal income, surpassing 8.4% in 2007 and exceeding the 2000 peak of 10.4% (The State of California Department of Finance, 2025a). When the stock market underperformed in FY 2022–2023, General Fund revenues dropped quickly. In 2022, capital gains declined sharply to 5.2% of personal income, with further reductions to 4.5% in 2023. This represents an approximate 59% decline over a two-year period. The capital gains revenues totaled $14.4 billion in 2019, soared to a historic high of $36 billion in 2021, and fell to $14 billion in 2023. The volatility of this revenue source created dramatic fluctuations in General Fund contributions.

Given these fluctuations, revenues could easily end up above or below estimates by astonishing $30 billion from FY 2026–2027 to FY 2028–2029 (Legislative Analyst's Office, 2024b).

Navigating budget volatility

To navigate the uncertainty with revenue estimates and bridge the budget shortfall, the state enacted approximately $16 billion in cuts and deferred more than $5 billion in planned expenditures (Koseff, 2024).

Cutback management strategies

In FY 2023–2024, California enacted approximately $16 billion in spending cuts:

- A 7.95% cut across state departments (around $3.7 billion);
- An additional $358 million cut in the California Department of Corrections and Rehabilitation;
- Budget cuts of affordable housing programs ($1.1 billion);
- A $746 million reduction in healthcare workforce development programs;
- A $500 million cut to student housing grants
- An annual $110 million reduction to the middle-class scholarship program.

In addition, the minimum wage increases for healthcare workers, set to take effect in 2024, were postponed until 2025.

Deferred spending heavily impacted education. While base funding under Proposition 98 that guarantees a minimum funding to K-12 public schools and community colleges was largely protected from cuts, $5.5 billion was delayed for future years (Koseff, 2024). The state also deferred $275 million in planned support for the University of California and California State University systems, promising repayment in 2026 (California Budget & Policy Center, 2025a). The administration preserved initiatives like transitional kindergarten, universal free school meal expansions, and behavioral health initiatives for youth. However, some discretionary spending for colleges and scholarships was decreased or delayed.

Overall, approximately $3.1 billion in planned expenditures were paused or delayed. In addition to education, such delays included a two-year postponement of the planned expansion of food assistance to undocumented residents and a six-month delay in scheduled wage increases for service providers supporting individuals with intellectual and developmental disabilities. About $2.1 billion in obligations were deferred to future FYs, including the rescheduling of one month's payroll expenses for state employees from June 2025 (FY 2024–2025) to July 2025 (FY 2025–2026).

Revenue measures

An estimated $13.6 billion was generated through a combination of temporary revenue increases and internal borrowing from State Special Funds, providing short-term liquidity. As part of the 2024–2025 budget, the State of California enacted temporary measures to increase corporate income tax revenues by imposing targeted limitations on tax benefits. According to California Budget & Policy Center (2024), the enacted budget for tax years 2024 through 2026 includes two key provisions: (1) a $5 million annual cap on the amount of tax credits that businesses may utilize and (2) a suspension of net operating loss deductions for businesses reporting at least $1 million in annual profits. The statute provides the Department of Finance with discretionary authority to suspend these limitations should fiscal conditions improve sufficiently. However, current fiscal projections indicate that the budget does not have the capacity to support such a suspension. Consequently, it is assumed that the restrictions will remain in effect throughout the designated period (Legislative Analyst's Office, 2024b).

These provisions are expected to generate approximately $5.95 billion in additional revenue in FY 2024–2025, $5.5 billion in 2025–2026, and $3.4 billion in 2026–2027 (California Budget & Policy Center, 2024). The budget agreement also incorporates mechanisms to compensate businesses for these temporary limitations in future years. Beginning in FY 2027–2028, the state will allow affected businesses to recover the deferred tax benefits, potentially reducing state revenues by several billion dollars annually. Notably, businesses subject to the tax credit cap will be permitted to claim the disallowed credits above the $5 million threshold as refundable credits, disbursed over a five-year period following the end of the limitation.

Use of reserves and fiscal tools

California withdrew approximately $12 billion from the Budget Stabilization Account (BSA) (Rainy Day Fund), $4.9 billion in 2024, and another $7.1 billion planned for 2025, leaving about $10.5 billion available for future years. As required by the State of California Constitution, the Governor signed a proclamation on June 26, 2025, declaring a budget emergency in order to allow the withdrawal of funds from the BSA. In addition to BSA, the State withdrew $900 million from the Safety Net Reserve, a secondary state's Rainy Day Fund, and $8.4 billion from the Public School System Stabilization Account (PSSSA) in FY 2023–2024. California made a $1.1 billion discretionary deposit to PSSSA in FY 2024–2025, which brought reserve balance to about $17 billion to guard against future shocks.

Altogether, budget stabilization decisions included about $11 billion in spending-related actions and $15 billion in all other solutions, including $5.5 billion in temporary revenue increases and a $7 billion withdrawal from the state's Rainy Day Fund in 2025. After these actions, the spending plan assumed the 2025–2026 budget would be balanced (Legislative Analyst's Office, 2024b).

California's budget in FY 2025–2026

On January 10, 2025, Governor Gavin Newsom released his proposed FY 2025–2026 state budget, projecting a small positive balance of $35.146 million in FY 2024–2025 after two years of state budget deficits (The State of California Department of Finance, 2025b). Table 1.1 demonstrates General Fund budget summary in FY 2024–2025 and FY 2025–2026.

According to the State of California Department of Finance (2025b), total revenues are projected at $296.7 billion, a decrease of $10.5 billion compared to FY 2024–2025. The majority of the revenue ($215.7 billion) comes from the General Fund, with Special Funds contributing $81.0 billion. The largest revenue source remains the PIT at $129.6 billion (43.6% of total revenues), although it experienced a decline of $456 million from the previous year. Corporate income tax also saw a notable decline of $6.1 billion. Sales and use tax, in contrast, increased by $1.6 billion (Table 1.2). Other categories, such as Motor Vehicle Fees and Insurance Tax, showed modest increases, while revenue from "Other" sources fell by $6.1 billion. A $7.1 billion transfer from the BSA helped maintain the total revenue figure (The State of California Department of Finance, 2025b).

According to the Legislative Analyst's Office (2024b), total annual expenditure growth between FY 2025–2026 and FY 2028–2029 is estimated to average 5.8%, which is notably higher than the historical average of 3.5% observed in prior fiscal outlooks. The underlying structural imbalance between revenues and expenditures is likely to persist, with revenue growth proving insufficient to match the pace of ongoing and anticipated spending commitments (Hubler, 2024; Legislative Analyst's Office, 2024a). Table 1.3 demonstrates total state expenditures by agency in FY 2025–2026.

TABLE 1.1 General Fund Budget Summary ($ Millions)

	FY 2024–2025	*FY 2025–2026*
Prior Year Balance	$41,978	$35,146
Revenues and Transfers	$226,745	$215,733
Total Resources Available	$268,723	$250,879
Non-Proposition 98 Expenditures	$147,866	$147,628
Proposition 98 Expenditures	$85,711	$80,738
Total Expenditures	$233,577	$228,366
Fund Balance	$35,146	$22,513
Reserve for Liquidation of Encumbrances	$18,001	$18,001
Special Fund for Economic Uncertainties	$17,145	$4,513
Public School System Stabilization Account	$455	$0
Safety Net Reserve	$0	$0
Budget Stabilization Account/Rainy Day Fund	$18,291	$11,191

Source: Created by authors based on State of California Department of Finance (2025b, p. 8).

TABLE 1.2 2025–2026 Revenue Sources ($ Millions)

	General Fund	*Special Funds*	*Total*	*Changes from FY 2024–2025*
Personal income tax	$125,962	$3,634	$129,596	−$456
Sales and use tax	$34,862	$15,770	$50,632	$1,629
Corporate income tax	$35,613	-	$35,613	−$6,083
Highway users taxes	-	$9,571	$9,571	$60
Insurance tax	$4,359	-	$4,359	$182
Alcoholic Beverage taxes and fees	$421	-	$421	$4
Cigarette tax	$35	$1,131	$1,166	−$47
Motor vehicle fees	$46	$12,826	$12,872	$331
Other	$7,335	$45,136	$52,471	−$6,111
Subtotal	$208,633	$88,068	$296,701	−$10,491
Transfer from the Budget Stabilization Account/Rainy Day Fund	$7,100	−$7,100	-	
Total	$215,733	$80,968	$296,701	−$10,491

Source: Created by authors based on State of California Department of Finance (2025b, p. 10).

TABLE 1.3 Total State Expenditures by Agency in FY 2025–2026 ($ Millions)

Agency	*General Fund*	*Special Funds*	*Bond Funds*	*Totals*
Legislative, Judicial, Executive	$8,558	$4,469	$263	$13,290
Business, Consumer Services & Housing	$924	$1,338	$522	$2,785
Transportation	$728	$17,141	$97	$17,966
Natural Resources	$4,440	$2,981	$459	$7,879
Environmental Protection	$136	$4,107	$13	$4,257
Health and Human Services	$87,140	$45,021	$450	$132,611
Corrections and Rehabilitation	$13,427	$4,089	$-	$17,516
K-12 Education	$80,334	$105	$1,517	$81,956
Higher Education	$22,729	$176	$551	$23,456
Labor and Workforce Development	$958	$1,221	$-	$2,179
Government Operations	$2,715	$185	$12	$2,912
Non-Agency Departments	$1,308	$2,128	$2	$3,437
Tax Relief/Local Government	$63	$3,727	$-	$4,362
Statewide Expenditures	$4,333	$2,111	$1	$6,445
Total	$228,366	$88,799	$3,886	$321,050

Source: Created by authors based on State of California Department of Finance (2025b, p. 9).

According to the State of California Department of Finance (2025b), the FY 2025–2026 California's budget allocates a total of $321.1 billion in expenditures across various agencies. The largest portion is funded by the General Fund ($228.4 billion), followed by Special Funds ($88.8 billion) and Bond Funds ($3.9 billion). Health and Human Services accounts for the largest share of total spending at $132.6 billion, representing over 40% of the budget. K-12 Education ($82.0 billion) and Higher Education ($23.5 billion) also represent major expenditures. Transportation receives a total of $18.0 billion, largely funded through Special Funds. Other main expenditures include Corrections and Rehabilitation ($17.5 billion), Legislative, Judicial, and Executive agencies ($13.3 billion), and Natural Resources ($7.9 billion). This distribution reflects the state's prioritization of health, education, and infrastructure in its fiscal planning (Legislative Analyst's Office, 2024a).

In 2025, Governor Newsom proposed increasing the Rainy Day Fund cap from 10% to 20% of General Fund revenues and exempting deposits from the state's Gann Limit (constitutional cap on state and local government spending in California) (The State of California Department of Finance, 2025a). The governor allowed the state to set aside a larger portion of state revenues in the Rainy Day Fund during periods of strong revenue growth (California Budget & Policy Center, 2025b). Despite a relatively stable fiscal outlook for the upcoming FY, projections indicate that the State of California is likely to experience substantial structural deficits in the medium term. The primary cause of this imbalance stems from the divergence between spending and revenue growth rates over the forecast horizon.

Conclusions

California's fiscal outlook illustrates the inherent risk of overdependence on capital gains and PIT revenues derived from high-income earners. While the FY 2024–2025 budget avoided catastrophic shortfalls through the use of reserves and temporary fiscal tools, structural weaknesses in the state's tax system remain. California's fiscal structure remains vulnerable due to the heavy dependence on a narrow and unpredictable tax base. Such reliance exacerbates revenue instability and complicates efforts to implement sustainable, long-term budgetary planning. The state needs to set a path to long-term fiscal stability by addressing the revenue shortfall and strengthening budget resilience. The budget fell short of delivering progressive tax reforms or new investments in housing and economic equity. The budget "fails to advance equitable tax policies to invest in Californians and protect against federal threats" (California Budget & Policy Center, 2025b).

Addressing these issues will require long-term reforms aimed at enhancing revenue stability, ensuring fiscal resilience, and maintaining equitable access to public services. This case study offers a multidimensional perspective on forecasting and public budgeting under the pressure of fiscal stress. It highlights the practical challenges of forecasting, managing fiscal stress, and implementing politically viable and equitable solutions. It is beneficial for encouraging students to connect theoretical knowledge about public finance and budgeting with the realities of governing in a complex, uncertain environment.

Discussion questions

1 How did California's reliance on capital gains taxation contribute to its budget shortfall?
2 What are the trade-offs between using reserve funds and implementing spending cuts?
3 Should California pursue more progressive tax policies to stabilize future revenue?
4 Which agencies receive the largest share of funding from the General Fund, and what does this suggest about the state's priorities?
5 What are the major challenges in forecasting revenues that directly impact the accuracy of expenditure planning?
6 How does reliance on income tax and capital gains create volatility in budget forecasts? What strategies might mitigate this?
7 What role should budget reserves like the Rainy Day Fund play in long-term forecasting and fiscal stability?
8 If revenue shortfalls persist beyond the current year, which expenditure categories should be protected and which might be reduced? Why?
9 In what ways can structural tax reform reduce volatility in California's revenue stream and make the state's tax system more equitable?
10 How should California balance affordability and equity when enacting future spending cuts? What populations are most vulnerable to spending cuts?

References

California Budget & Policy Center. (2024). *The 2024–25 California state budget explained budget: Agreement protects many critical services, may constrain progress in future years*. https://calbudgetcenter.org/resources/the-2024-25-california-state-budget-explained/

California Budget & Policy Center. (2025a). *What does the budget shortfall mean for California?* https://calbudgetcenter.org/resources/qa-what-does-the-budget-shortfall-mean-for-california/

California Budget & Policy Center. (2025b). *Understanding the Governor's 2025–26 State Budget proposal*. https://calbudgetcenter.org/resources/understanding-the-governors-2025-26-state-budget-proposal/

Guzman, T., & Ermasova, N. (2024). *Municipal fiscal stress, bankruptcies, and other financial emergencies*. Routledge.

Guzman, T., & Ermasova, N. (2026). *Causes and exit strategies from municipal fiscal stress and bankruptcy: A taxonomy*. Urban Affairs.

Hubler, S. (2024, June 22). California narrowly dodges a budget shortfall. *The New York Times*. https://www.nytimes.com/2024/06/13/us/california-budget-explainer.html

Koseff, A. (2024, June 22). What you need to know about the California budget deal. *CalMatters*. https://calmatters.org/politics/2024/06/california-budget-deal-4

Legislative Analyst's Office. (2023). *The 2024–25 budget: California's fiscal outlook*. https://lao.ca.gov/Publications/Report/4819

Legislative Analyst's Office. (2024a). *The 2024–25 budget deficit update*. https://lao.ca.gov/Publications/Report/4850

Legislative Analyst's Office. (2024b). *The 2025–26 budget California's fiscal outlook*. https://lao.ca.gov/Publications/Report/4939

The State of California Department of Finance. (2025a). *Governor's budget summary 2025–26. State of California*. https://ebudget.ca.gov/2025-26/pdf/BudgetSummary/FullBudgetSummary.pdf

The State of California Department of Finance. (2025b). 2025–26 state budget. Enacted on June 27, 2025. https://ebudget.ca.gov/budget/2025-26EN/#/Home

Walters, D. (2024, June 25). *California's self-inflicted fiscal crisis produces a budget full of gimmicks and favors. California's self-inflicted fiscal crisis produces a budget full of gimmicks and favors. Calmatters*. https://calmatters.org/commentary/2024/06/california-budget-deficit-deal-gimmicks/

CASE STUDY 2

Revenue Windfall from Illinois cannabis taxes, societal benefit, and negative consequences

Abstract

This case study examines the revenue generated from adult-use cannabis taxation in Illinois and evaluates its fiscal, social, and policy implications. In FY 2025, approximately $2.1 billion worth of cannabis products were sold through 253 dispensaries statewide. In FY 2025, cannabis tax revenues exceeded $474 million. The tax revenues collected are distributed through the Cannabis Regulation Fund and allocated to multiple state agencies responsible for public health, criminal justice, community development, and regulatory oversight. These funds have supported a range of social welfare initiatives, including the purchase of opioid reversal medications, investments in behavioral health services, violence prevention programs, and anti-human trafficking efforts. While cannabis taxation has generated significant fiscal revenue and contributed to community-based social benefit programs, it has also raised concerns regarding negative consequences on public health. This case presents an opportunity to evaluate the role of earmarked revenue in achieving social policy objectives and to examine negative consequences associated with "sin tax" revenue streams for public programs.

Topics

Local Government; Revenue; Sin Taxes; Public Finance; Cannabis Taxes; Societal Benefit

Background

Sin taxes are designed to discourage specific behaviors deemed harmful to society.

Decriminalizing marijuana for medical and recreational use and creating state-licensed dispensaries creates additional revenue sources for the state and imposes a tax on what society views as a negative externality. According to Ekins and Henchman (2016), "a mature marijuana industry could generate up to $28 billion in tax revenues for federal, state, and local governments, including $7 billion in federal revenue: $5.5 billion from business taxes and $1.5 billion from income and payroll taxes" (p. 3). In many cases, tax burden is transferred to consumers in the form of higher retail prices. Similar to alcohol and tobacco, marijuana exhibits relatively inelastic demand, meaning that consumption is not highly responsive to price changes (Dorsey, 2010; Ermasova, 2020). Consequently, tax increase is likely to be reflected directly in consumer prices.

The program first started with the Compassionate Use of Medical Cannabis Program Act in 2014. In August 2018, Public Act 100–1114, the Alternative to Opioids Act of 2018, was signed, making changes to the Compassionate Use of Medical Cannabis Pilot Program Act. The public act created the Opioid Alternative Pilot Program (OAPP), which allows access to medical cannabis for individuals who have a prescription for opioids or have a condition for which an opioid otherwise would be prescribed, as certified by a registered healthcare provider. On January 31, 2019, the Illinois Department of Public Health officially launched the OAPP. To qualify for OAPP, patients must be at least 21 years old and be residents of the State of Illinois. Licensed physicians must certify that the qualifying patients have a medical condition for which an opioid has been or could be prescribed based on generally accepted standards of care. As of June 30, 2024, the number of active patients in Medical Cannabis Patient Program (MCPP) was 141,189, including 1,274 minors (Illinois Department of Public Health, 2024, p. 73).

Pursuant to the CRTA 410 ILCS 705, cannabis became legal for adult use in Illinois on January 1, 2020. Illinois became the 11th state to legalize adult-use recreational cannabis. Municipal Cannabis Retailers' Occupation Tax and County Cannabis Retailers' Occupation Tax rates took effect from ordinances received by the Illinois Department of Revenue (IDOR) on or before April 1, 2023.

States employ a variety of approaches to cannabis taxation. Some levy taxes based on weight, others on price, and still others on Tetrahydrocannabinol (THC) content. Ad valorem taxes, calculated as a percentage of price, are simpler to administer but tend to produce more volatile revenues and do not specifically address the components that cause harm. Quantity-based (ad quantum) taxes on weight or volume provide more stable revenue and better target the harmful element, though they do not consider potency. In contrast, ad quantum taxes based on THC content most directly address the harm-causing component (Hoffer & Macumber-Rosin, 2025).

Illinois imposes several state and local taxes on cannabis sales and cultivation (Illinois Department of Revenue, n.d.). The first group of cannabis taxes is cultivation taxes:

1 Cannabis Cultivation Privilege Tax: 7% of the gross receipts from a cultivator's first sale of cannabis.
2 Medical Cannabis Cultivation Privilege Tax: 7% of the sales price per ounce of medical cannabis.

Second, Illinois adopted a potency-based tax model, meaning cannabis products with higher levels of THC face higher tax rates on Purchaser Excise Taxes:

1 10% on cannabis with THC ≤ 35%.
2 25% on cannabis with THC > 35%.
3 20% on cannabis-infused products (excluding concentrates and vape products, which are taxed based on THC content).

Third, Illinois imposes sales taxes on cannabis: 7% on Wholesale Gross Receipts; 10% on Retail Sales of cannabis products with ≤35% THC; 20% on Retail Sales of cannabis-infused products like edibles; and 25% on Retail Sales of any product with a THC concentration >35%. Medical cannabis: taxed at the reduced "qualifying food and drug" rate (Hoffer & Macumber-Rosin, 2025). Municipalities and counties may impose additional cannabis retailers' occupation taxes, collected by the IDOR.

Revenue Windfall from Illinois cannabis taxes

In 2022, approximately $1.5 billion worth of cannabis products were sold through 113 dispensaries statewide. In 2023, there were 177 licensed adult-use dispensaries. According to the Illinois Department of Financial and Professional Regulation (2024), FY 2024 was a year of rapid growth in the cannabis industry. In total, 82 new dispensaries were opened that year (a total of 220 dispensaries), and total sales in Illinois reached $2 billion. By June 2025, a total of 253 dispensaries were licensed across Illinois, generating a combined $2.1 billion in medical and adult-use cannabis sales during the FY. Monthly adult-use sales have stabilized between $130 million and $150 million, while revenues from medical cannabis continue to decline. In FY 2025, cannabis tax revenues surpassed $474 million, with a substantial portion directed toward reinvestment in communities disproportionately affected by prior drug enforcement policies

(Swartz et al., 2025). Despite the industry's continued growth, it is estimated that nearly half of the cannabis consumed in Illinois still originates from the underground economy.

In FY 2024, the IDOR collected "$457.3 million in tax and assessment payments from adult-use cannabis cultivators, craft growers and dispensaries, and disbursed $149.7 million in cannabis revenues to local governments" (p. 80). Total revenue from adult-use cannabis amounted to $466,816,883 in FY 2022 and $451,868,765 in FY 2023 (Illinois Department of Revenue, 2024, p. 83).

Pursuant to Section 6z–112 of the Illinois Compiled Statutes (30 ILCS 105/6z–112), the Cannabis Regulation Fund was established as a dedicated account within the State Treasury (Illinois General Assembly, n.d.). The statute mandates that all revenues generated under the CRTA, including taxes, license fees, and other related charges, be deposited into this fund. The resources of the Cannabis Regulation Fund are subject to legislative appropriation, ensuring that all proceeds from the regulation and taxation of cannabis are managed and allocated through this designated state fund.

Combined transfers from the Cannabis Regulation Fund in FY 2024 totaled $256,314,994 and $253,896,171 in FY 2025 (Table 1.4). Cannabis taxes

TABLE 1.4 Transfers from the Cannabis Regulation Fund in FY 2025

Receiving Fund	*Description*	*Total Transferred Out (FY 2025)*
Budget Stabilization Fund	State "rainy day" budget stabilization fund	$25,098,917
Cannabis Expungement Fund	Supports expungement of eligible cannabis-related offenses	$2,815,000
Criminal Justice Information Projects Fund	Supports criminal justice research and information systems	$62,747,292
DHS Community Services Fund	Funds community services administered by the Department of Human Services	$50,197,834
Drug Treatment Fund	Supports substance use treatment and prevention programs	$5,019,783
General Revenue Fund	The main operating fund	$87,846,210
Local Government Distributive Fund	Distributes revenues to local governments	$20,079,133
Professional Services Fund	Funds professional or consulting services	$39,900
Workers' Compensation Revolving Fund	Pays workers' compensation claims	$52,100

Source: Created by authors based on the Illinois Department of Revenues, 2025.

generate significant revenue that can be reinvested in public services, including education, healthcare, and substance abuse prevention programs. The majority of transfers were distributed to the General Revenue Fund, the Criminal Justice Information Project Fund, the Department of Human Services (DHS) Community Service Fund, and the Budget Stabilization Fund (Illinois Department of Revenues, 2025). The administrative expenditure of the Cannabis Regulation Fund was $27,471,980 in FY 2025. Table 1.4 demonstrates transfers from the Cannabis Regulation Fund in FY 2025.

Societal benefits

Historical evidence indicates that cannabis possesses both therapeutic benefits and associated costs. It has been reported to alleviate pain, address certain neurological disorders, stimulate appetite, and enhance sleep quality. Records from various ancient civilizations document the use of marijuana for the treatment of a wide range of ailments. During the 19th and early 20th centuries in the United States, marijuana was commonly incorporated as a principal ingredient in over-the-counter medications, which were widely distributed through mail-order catalogs and by traveling peddlers. Table 1.5 presents the main medical conditions for receiving medical marijuana.

A majority (85.9%) of Illinois residents ages 16–64 who indicated they had ever used and received a prescription for cannabis indicated they had used cannabis to manage mental health symptoms, such as anxiety (66.6%), depression (48.2%), and Post-traumatic stress disorder (PTSD)/Trauma (31.8%) (Illinois Department of Financial and Professional Regulation, 2023). In 2024, enrollment in the State Medical Cannabis Patient Program and OAPP has declined as more individuals shift to adult-use channels (Swartz et al., 2025).

The CRTA allows for expungement, which is the elimination of a person's public record related to low-level cannabis offenses, such as the possession, manufacture, delivery, or intent of delivery of under 30 grams of cannabis that did not result in conviction (Illinois Cannabis Regulation Oversight Officer, n.d.). As of January 17, 2023, the Illinois State Police have expunged over 780,000 charges for

TABLE 1.5 Nature of the Five Main Debilitating Medical Conditions of the Qualifying Patients under MCPP in FY 2024 in Illinois

Nature of the Debilitating Medical Conditions	*Number of Patients*	*Percentage*
Chronic pain	19,283	36.39
Post-traumatic stress disorder (PTSD)	8,232	15.54
Migraines	5,428	10.24
Osteoarthritis	4,195	7.92
Cancer	2,502	4.72

Source: Illinois Department of Public Health (2024, p. 74).

minor cannabis offenses that occurred since July 2019. Minor cannabis offenses that resulted in a conviction, where the person pled guilty or was found guilty by a court, may be pardoned by the Governor, which also expunges the record and removes the record from public databases. As of January 17, 2023, the Governor has pardoned 11,430 conviction records for minor cannabis offenses since July 2019. As of January 17, 2023, 23,097 conviction records for minor cannabis offenses that occurred since July 2019 have been eliminated (Illinois Cannabis Regulation Oversight Officer, n.d.). The majority of the expungements have been in Cook County (over 488,000 records). In 2024, cannabis-related arrests and prison admissions have declined substantially since legalization was adopted, achieving one of the central goals of the CRTA. However, racial disparities in arrests and incarceration persist, particularly in Chicago (Swartz et al., 2025).

Illinois is supporting minority-owned cannabis businesses. The Illinois Department of Commerce and Economic Opportunity (DCEO) established the Cannabis Social Equity Loan Program, which provides direct, forgivable loans to qualified social equity licensees for start-up and operating expenses (Illinois Department of Commerce and Economic Opportunity, n.d.). The Cannabis Regulation & Tax Act (CRTA) 410 ILCS 705 defines Social Equity Applicants where at least 51% of the business is owned and controlled by individuals who meet one of the following criteria:

- Have lived for at least five of the past ten years in a Disproportionately Impacted Area (DIA – geographic area that has been significantly affected by war on drugs) or, at the time of license application, owned and controlled at least 51% of the business and lived for five of the past ten years in a DIA.
- Have a personal arrest, conviction, or juvenile adjudication for cannabis-related offenses eligible for expungement, including possession up to 500 grams or intent to deliver up to 30 grams.
- Have a parent, child, or spouse with a qualifying cannabis-related offense eligible for expungement.

Businesses with more than ten full-time employees must have over half of their staff who either:

- Live in a DIA,
- Have a qualifying personal cannabis offense, or
- Have a parent, child, or spouse with a qualifying cannabis offense.

This framework ensures that ownership and workforce participation prioritize individuals and communities historically affected by cannabis criminalization. $12 million support for the program in 2025 was provided by the State of Illinois. The program provided loans of up to $240,000 to qualified, licensed social equity dispensaries (Illinois Department of Commerce and Economic Opportunity, n.d.). The Disparity Study found that the CRTA significantly increased license ownership diversity for each license type with new licenses over the study period. Dispensary licenses went to 59% minority- or women-owned businesses compared to 21% for the medical cannabis market. Additionally, minority- or women-owned businesses held 63% of craft growers, 61% of infusers, and 74% of transporters. In total, around 84% of the State's Direct Forgivable Loans went to minority- or women-owned businesses (Illinois Cannabis Regulation Oversight Officer, 2025). These demographics make Illinois the most diverse cannabis industry in the nation.

Negative consequences of cannabis

Marijuana was a contributing factor to much higher addiction rates prior to the passage of the 1914 Harrison Act, and the 1937 Marijuana Tax Act prohibited any further medical research into the drug. Due to the longstanding legal restrictions on marijuana research and use, comparatively fewer studies have examined its effects on the respiratory system than those conducted on tobacco. However, marijuana users are more likely to be poly-drug consumers, thereby making the drug's long-term effects harder to isolate (Chen et al., 2008; Hall & Degenhardt, 2009; Vick, 2011).

Kempker et al. (2015) show negative respiratory effects of long-term marijuana use. Smoking marijuana can lead to lung-related diseases similar to tobacco uses, such as bronchial irritation and bronchitis, inflammation of the lung tissue, reduced lung capacity, and development of pre-cancerous cells. Marijuana produces four times the amount of tar that is found in one tobacco cigarette, a leading contributor to lung and/or oral cancers, chronic obstructive pulmonary disease, and other respiratory diseases (Vick, 2011). Marijuana depresses the immune system. It reduces the body's ability to fight off bacteria, fungi, or tumor cells. HIV/AIDS patients are at a higher risk of infection that can outweigh the benefits of marijuana consumption. Same is true for persons battling cancer who are undergoing chemotherapy or radiation treatment and for persons suffering from mental health illnesses who consume marijuana for symptom control.

Many scholars have suggested that marijuana use can increase the risk of addiction, as THC binds to cannabinoid receptors in the brain (Hall & Degenhardt, 2009; Lachenmeier & Rehm, 2015; Vick, 2011). Marijuana use can also reduce cognitive skills, coordination, and perception. Some negative effects include difficulties with attention, judgment, and balance, as well as impacts on the immune system.

In Illinois, cannabis use during pregnancy remains a public health concern, with approximately 7% of pregnant women reporting use in 2024. Among Illinois high school students, state-level data indicate a modest rebound in initiation rates among youth aged 12–17 (Swartz et al., 2025). Early initiation is associated with a higher likelihood of developing cannabis use disorder and other negative behavioral and health outcomes. Peers and siblings continue to be the most common sources of cannabis supply among adolescents.

Based on the report (from July 2024 to June 2025) by the Illinois DHS, Division of Behavioral Health & Recovery, which evaluates the public health impacts of legalized adult-use cannabis, Black and multiracial respondents report higher rates of cannabis use and cannabis use disorders compared to White and Hispanic respondents (Swartz et al., 2025). Individuals experiencing serious mental illness exhibit substantially elevated levels of use and dependence, highlighting the strong correlation between mental health challenges and cannabis consumption. Additionally, those living below the federal poverty line report disproportionately higher rates of cannabis use and cannabis use disorder, underscoring the socioeconomic disparities associated with substance use patterns.

While the drug's proponents claim marijuana reduces anxiety and negative impact of various mental illnesses, long-term marijuana consumption is listed as a separate mental illness in the American Psychiatric Association's The Diagnostic and Statistical Manual of Mental Illnesses (DSM-5) (First et al., 2022). The short-term psychological effects of marijuana include impaired perception, slowed cognitive processing, and short-term memory deficits. Two key components of marijuana addiction are tolerance and withdrawal. Individuals addicted to marijuana often develop an increased tolerance, necessitating greater amounts to achieve the desired effect. They may take extraordinary measures to avoid withdrawal symptoms while continuing to experience a persistent desire to reduce or cease consumption. Despite experiencing recurrent physical or psychological problems related to marijuana use, affected individuals frequently neglect important social, occupational, or recreational activities (Pacula et al., 2001, 2002; Vick, 2011).

Persons addicted or abusing marijuana to treat existing mental health conditions often find that the symptoms of preexisting conditions are exacerbated when THC is consumed. Pedersen et al. (2015) examined the association between mental health symptoms and marijuana expectancies on marijuana use and consequences for youth involved in the juvenile court system. They found that "stronger positive expectancies and weaker negative expectancies were both associated with increased marijuana use. Youth who reported more symptoms of both anxiety and depression, and stronger positive expectancies for marijuana, also reported more consequences" (p. 151). This is especially relevant for individuals diagnosed with bipolar disorder, borderline personality disorder, major depressive disorder, or schizophrenia. Even in the absence of preexisting mental health conditions, THC consumption can induce panic attacks, flashbacks, delusions, hallucinations, paranoia, profound lethargy, and episodes of uncontrolled aggression (Williams et al., 2004; Vick, 2011).

Based on the 2025 Annual Cannabis Report by the Health Advisory Committee, cannabis-related poisonings, Emergency Medical Services (EMS) runs, and poison center calls have increased, particularly among children exposed to edibles. Cannabis-related fatalities remain rare but have grown modestly and usually occur with additional substances present in the toxicology report. In the area of traffic safety, more fatal crash victims test positive for cannabis (Swartz et al., 2025). The enforcement findings underscore the continued prevalence of illicit cannabis activity and impaired driving in Illinois, reinforcing public health data that nearly half of cannabis consumed in the state is obtained from illegal sources despite ongoing legalization and regulation efforts. The Illinois State Police seized approximately 12 tons of illicit cannabis, including 1,725 cannabis plants, with an estimated street value of $63.7 million (Illinois State Police, 2024, p. 47). In FY 2024, Division of Patrol filed 424 DUI cannabis-related charges, reported 16 crashes involving cannabis, and seized 565 unlawful possessions in vehicles (p. 60).

Miron (2001) suggests that sin taxation, subsidized treatment, medicalization, and the use of public education campaigns are some of the other methods that can be used to reduce the negative effects of drug use.

Taxes on marijuana

Snowdon (2012) described sin taxes as instruments of social engineering that function as "blunt tools" which often fail to influence the intended behavioral change. Instead, they may generate unintended consequences, including adverse health effects, increased criminal activity, and, beyond a certain point, reductions in government tax revenue. Snowdon (2012) concluded that sin taxes are a costly and inefficient mechanism for modifying consumer behavior. These taxes disproportionately burden lower-income populations, as wealthier individuals are better positioned to absorb higher costs (Ermasova, 2020; Snowdon, 2012).

This distributional pattern is also evident in the context of marijuana taxation. Before the passage of the Controlled Substances Act, marijuana was widely portrayed as a substance primarily used by racial minorities and lower-income communities. Davenport and Caulkins (2016) found that 19% of marijuana use in 2012–2013 occurred among adults without a high school diploma. Additionally, approximately 29% of all marijuana use was associated with individuals living in households earning less than $20,000 annually, compared to 27% of cigarette consumption and 13% of alcohol consumption. Their study also noted that 15% of marijuana users allocate roughly one-quarter of their income to marijuana purchases, underscoring the regressive impact of cannabis taxation.

Discussion questions

1 In what ways do cannabis tax revenues benefit society? Provide examples of programs or services that could be funded.
2 What negative consequences might arise from cannabis legalization, and how can policymakers mitigate these risks?

3 How effective are Illinois's Social Equity Applicant provisions in addressing historical injustices related to cannabis criminalization?
4 If Illinois' cannabis revenues continue to grow, what strategies should state policymakers consider to balance economic benefits with public health and safety concerns?
5 Compare and contrast ad valorem taxes and ad quantum taxes in terms of revenue stability and targeting harm-causing elements. Which approach would you recommend for Illinois, and why?
6 How should Illinois balance increase adult access with concerns about youth use?
7 How can sin taxes contribute to or eliminate black markets? Keep the consumer safe?

References

Chen, A. L., Chen, T. J., Braverman, E. R., Acuri, V., Kerner, M., Varshavkiy, M., Barverman, D., Downs, W., Blum, S. H., Cassel, K., & Blum, K. (2008). Hypothesizing that marijuana smokers are at significantly lower risk of carcinogenicity relative to tobacco-non-marijuana smokers: Evidence based on statistical reevaluation of current literature. *Journal of Psychoactive Drugs, 40*(3), 263–273.

Davenport, S., & Caulkins, J. P. (2016). Evolution of the United States marijuana market in the decade of liberalization before full legalization. *Journal of Drug Issues*, *46*(4), 411–427.

Dorsey, R. (2010). In defense of "sin taxes": Tax policy, virtue ethics, and behavioral economics. *Southern Law Journal*, *20*(1), 53–67.

Ekins, G., & Henchman, J. (2016). Marijuana legalization and taxes: Federal revenue impact. *Tax Foundation*. https://taxfoundation.org/marijuana-tax-legalization-federal-revenue/

Ermasova, N. (2020). Fiscal and health effects of U.S. marijuana legislation at the state level. *Journal of Social, Political and Economic Studies*, *45*(1–2), 151–177.

First, M. B., Yousif, L. H., Clarke, D. E., Wang, P. S., Gogtay, N., & Appelbaum, P. S. (2022). DSM-5-TR: Overview of what's new and what's changed. *World Psychiatry*, *21*(2), 218–219. https://doi.org/10.1002/wps.20989

Hall, W., & Degenhardt, L. (2009). Adverse health effects of non-medical cannabis use. *The Lancet*, *374*(9698), 1383–1391.

Hoffer, A., & Macumber-Rosin, J. (2025). Recreational marijuana taxes by state, 2025. *Tax Foundation*. https://taxfoundation.org/data/all/state/recreational-marijuana-taxes/

Illinois Cannabis Regulation Oversight Officer. (2025). Disparity study. https://cannabis.illinois.gov/legal-and-enforcement/disparity-study.html

Illinois Cannabis Regulation Oversight Officer. (n.d.). *Expungement*. https://cannabis.illinois.gov/legal-and-enforcement/expungement.html

Illinois Department of Commerce and Economic Opportunity. (n.d.). *Cannabis social equity program*. https://dceo.illinois.gov/oe3/cannabisequity.htm

Illinois Department of Financial and Professional Regulation. (2023). 2023 Annual Cannabis Report.

Illinois Department of Financial and Professional Regulation. (2024). 2024 Annual Cannabis Report. https://idfpr.illinois.gov/content/dam/soi/en/web/idfpr/forms/auc/compiled-cannabis-annual-report-2024.pdf

Illinois Department of Public Health. (2024). *2024 Annual Cannabis Report.* https://idfpr.illinois.gov/content/dam/soi/en/web/idfpr/forms/auc/compiled-cannabis-annual-report-2024.pdf

Illinois Department of Revenue. (2024). *2024 Annual Cannabis Report.* https://idfpr.illinois.gov/content/dam/soi/en/web/idfpr/forms/auc/compiled-cannabis-annual-report-2024.pdf

Illinois Department of Revenue. (2025). Cannabis regulation fund. https://tax.illinois.gov/content/dam/soi/en/web/tax/research/taxstats/cannabisregulationfund/documents/cannabisregulationfundfy2026.pdf

Illinois Department of Revenue. (n.d.). Cannabis taxes. https://tax.illinois.gov/research/taxinformation/other/cannabis-taxes.html

Illinois State Police. (2024). 2024 Annual Cannabis Report. https://idfpr.illinois.gov/content/dam/soi/en/web/idfpr/forms/auc/compiled-cannabis-annual-report-2024.pdf

Illinois General Assembly. (n.d). 30 ILCS 105/6z 112). <source>Sec. 6z–112. The Cannabis Regulation Fund</source>. https://www.ilga.gov/documents/legislation/ilcs/documents/003001050K6z-112.htm

Kempker, J., Honig, E., & Martin, G. (2015). The effects of marijuana exposure on expiratory airflow: A study of adults who participated in the U.S. National Health and Nutrition Examination Study. *Annals of the American Thoracic Society*, *12*(2), 135–141.

Lachenmeier, D. W., & Rehm, J. (2015). Comparative Risk Assessment of Alcohol, Tobacco, Cannabis and other Illicit Drugs using the Margin of Exposure Approach. *Scientific Reports*, 5, Article 8126, 1–7. https://www.nature.com/articles/srep08126.pdf https://doi.org/10.1038/srep08126

Miron, J. (2001). The economics of drug prohibition and drug legalization. *Social Research*, *68*(3), 835–855.

Pacula, R. L., Grossman, M., Chaloupka, F. J., O'Malley, P., Johnston, L. D., & Farrelly, M. C. (2001). Marijuana and youth. In J. Gruber (Ed.), *Risky behavior among youth: An economic analysis* (pp. 271–326). National Bureau of Economic Research.

Pacula, R. L., Chriqui, J. F., Reichmann, D. A., & Terry-McElrath, Y. M. (2002). State medical marijuana laws: Understanding the laws and their limitations. *Journal of Public Health Policy*, *23*(4), 413–439.

Pedersen, E., Miles, N., Osilla, K., Ewing, B., Hunter, S., & D'Amico, E. (2015). The effects of mental health symptoms and marijuana expectancies on marijuana use and consequences among at-risk adolescents. *Journal of Drug Issues*, *45*(2), 151–165.

Snowdon, C. (2012). The wages of sin taxes. *Adam Smith Institute*. https://cei.org/wp-content/uploads/2013/02/Christopher-Snowdon-The-Wages-of-Sin-Taxes.pdf

Swartz, J. A., Franceschini, D., Giangrande, E., Han, Y., Falso, P., & Schwartz, R. (September 2025). *2025 Illinois Adult Use Cannabis Health Advisory Committee Annual Report*. Illinois Department of Human Services, Division of Behavioral Health & Recovery.

Vick, D. (2011). *Drugs and alcohol in the 21st century*. Jones and Bartlett Publishers.

Williams, J., Pacula, R., Chaloupka, F. J., & Wechsler, H. (2004). Alcohol and marijuana use among college students: Economic complements or substitutes? *Health Economics, 13*(9), 825–843.

CASE STUDY 3

"Welcome stranger" system and its impacts on revenues in California

Abstract

This case study evaluates the impacts of Proposition 13, also known as "welcome stranger" system, on revenues in California. In 1978, California introduced Proposition 13, a property tax reform that, among other tasks, established an acquisition-based value for property tax assessment purposes. With a substantial increase in property values in California since 1978, homeowners who have owned their property for many years pay much lower taxes based on older property values, while newer homeowners pay significantly higher taxes based on current market prices. The system basically "welcomes" new homeowners to subsidize local government revenues. For this analogy, the system was nicknamed "welcome stranger." While Proposition 13 successfully stabilized property tax revenues and provided long-term homeowners with predictability, it also produced significant negative consequences, including disparities in tax burdens among property owners with comparable properties, revenue losses for local governments and school districts, and fiscal stress. The case highlights the legal, fiscal, and equity challenges of a "welcome stranger" system.

Topics

Revenue Generation; Limitations on Revenue Generation; Proposition 13; Property Tax; Local Government; Fiscal Policy; Public Finance

Background

Proposition 13 followed many years of rapidly rising real property taxes in California. From FY 1967–1968 to FY 1971–1972, revenues from property taxes increased on average by 11.5% per year (Nordlinger v. Hahn, 505 U.S. 1, 1992). The median price of an existing home doubled from $31,530 in 1973 to $62,430 in 1977. As a result, tax levies continued to rise because of sharply increasing assessment values. Some homeowners saw their tax bills double or triple during this period, well outpacing any growth in their income and ability to pay.

By 1978, property tax relief had emerged as a major political issue in California. The campaign "The People's Initiative to Limit Property Taxation" was organized in response to resulting increases in property taxes and marketed as a protection for homeowners, particularly those on fixed incomes (Nichols, 2018). The idea is that homeowners should not be taxed on unrealized increases in property value or "paper gains." In only one month, tax relief advocates collected over 1.2 million signatures to qualify Proposition 13 for the June 1978 ballot (Nordlinger v. Hahn, 505 U.S. 1, 1992). On election day, Proposition 13 received a statewide favorable vote of 64.8% and was supported in 55 of the state's 58 counties.

In 1978, California voters approved Proposition 13, a constitutional amendment designed to limit the state's property tax rates and control rising tax burdens. The policy combines a 1% ceiling on the property tax rate with a 2% cap on annual increases in assessed valuations. The assessment limitation, however, is subject to the exception that new construction or a change of ownership triggers a reassessment up to the current appraised value. Exemptions from the reassessment provision include two specific categories of property transfers: (1) exchanges of principal residences involving individuals over the age of 55 and (2) transfers of property between parents and their children. Proposition 13 requires a two-thirds vote to pass new tax rates (California State Board of Equalization, 2018).

California's property tax system is based on the principle that taxes should reflect the original purchase price of a property, rather than its current market value. This system was intended to protect long-term homeowners from being taxed out of their homes due to rapidly rising property values. Proposition 13 has been labeled by some as a "welcome stranger" system; the newcomers to an established community are "welcome" in anticipation that they will contribute a larger percentage of support for local government than a settled neighbor who owns a comparable home.

Challenges of "welcome stranger" system

Since 1978, this "welcome stranger" system has led to substantial differences in property taxes paid among owners of similar homes. Homeowners who have owned their property for many years pay lower taxes based on older property values, while newer homeowners pay much higher taxes based on current market prices. Over time, the law produced significant disparities in the property tax system, especially between longtime homeowners and new buyers. By 1989, 44% of California homeowners who had owned their homes since the enactment of Proposition 13 in 1978 carried only 25% of the more than $4 billion in residential property taxes paid by homeowners statewide (JUSTIA US Supreme Court, n.d.).

A family moving from a home in which its members have resided for a number of years would be faced with a substantially higher tax burden in a new home, even if they purchase a house that has exactly the same current market value, only because the house is purchased later. For example, consider two homes that were each worth $100,000 in 1995. One home has frequent turnovers, while the other remains in the same ownership. If home prices increase by 7% per year, the transferred house would have a taxable value of more than $750,000 by 2025. The assessed value of the other house, increasing at only 2%, is going to be about $180,000 (JUSTIA US Supreme Court, n.d.). Proposition 13 may discourage people from buying and selling real estate.

Amerkhanian et al. (2023) found that California's residential parcels had average market values that were 2.4 times their assessed values, and, in San Mateo, market values for residential parcels were 4.3 times their assessed value. In San Francisco, one of the famous Painted Lady homes sold in 2020 for $3.55 million and was assessed at $3.7 million in 2023, resulting in a property tax bill of about $44,000. In contrast, a nearly identical Painted Lady, owned by the same family since 1974, was assessed at only $94,000 and owed just $1,100 in property taxes, despite its market value being around $1.7 million (Stiefel, 2025). Similar disparities appear elsewhere in California. For example, in Santa Clara County, Proposition 13 saved homeowners an average of $7,700 in property taxes in 2023, and, in the Loyola neighborhood, average savings reached $20,000 (Stiefel, 2025). Substantial differences occur even among property owners of similar ages, incomes, and wealth. California Legislative Analyst's Office (2016) found significant variation among 45–55-year-old homeowners with homes worth $575,000–$625,000 and incomes of $80,000–$90,000; property tax payments in 2014 ranged from $1,350 to $7,500 in the Bay Area. These examples illustrate how Proposition 13 creates substantial differences in property tax burdens among homeowners. California Legislative Analyst's Office (2016) found that "higher-income Californians own more homes and own homes of higher value and, therefore, receive the majority of the total dollars of tax relief provided to homeowners by Proposition 13" (p. 9).

According to JUSTIA US Supreme Court (n.d.), the petitioner had bought a home in Los Angeles and sued the county and the tax assessor, claiming that Proposition 13 violated the Equal Protection clause because the system treated similar taxpayers unequally. The petitioner was paying about five times more taxes than some of her neighbors who had owned comparable homes within the same residential development since 1975. According to the petitioner, her total property taxes over the first ten years in her home will approach $19,000, while any neighbor who bought a comparable home in 1975 will pay just $4,100 (JUSTIA US Supreme Court, n.d.). The County Superior Court dismissed the case, and the State Court of Appeal agreed with that decision. The court concluded that Proposition 13's acquisition-value system was constitutional and did not violate the Equal Protection Clause (JUSTIA US Supreme Court, n.d.). The California Court of Appeals explained that the "welcome stranger" system, which bases taxes on the purchase price of a property rather than its current market value, is Constitutional and it serves two main purposes: it prevents taxes from suddenly increasing when property values rise sharply, and it allows homeowners to predict their future tax bills with confidence.

While Proposition 13 helped protect homeowners from rapid property tax increases, it also created new challenges for local and state governments in balancing their budgets and maintaining service levels. Before Proposition 13 passed, California's average property tax rate was about 2.7% (California Legislative Analyst's Office, 2016). By the 2023–2024 FY, that rate had dropped to approximately 1.2%. The property tax revenues as a share of California's GDP decreased from 4% in 1978 to 2% in 1980 and 2018 (Figure 1.1).

Local governments were the primary losers under Proposition 13, as their budgets had heavily relied on local property taxes. Its immediate impact was a reduction of more than 50% of their revenue, forcing them to seek alternative sources of funding (California Budget Project, 1997). Counties' own-source revenues declined by more than a third (35%) in inflation- and population-adjusted terms between 1977–1978 and 1993–1994. Total county revenues, adjusted for population and inflation, declined by 10% between 1977–1978 and 1993–1994 (California Budget Project, 1997).

Counties responded to limited resources by reducing spending for general governmental functions and public assistance. At the county level, real per capita spending on public assistance, including both the state and county shares of welfare and county costs for General Assistance, declined by 6%. County spending for health and sanitation, on the other hand, increased by 15% between 1977–1978 and 1993–1994 (California Budget Project, 1997).

In 1979, the legislature passed Assembly Bill 8 (AB 8) to address the distribution of sharply reduced local property tax revenues by providing local governments with a more predictable revenue source. AB 8 aimed to offer fiscal stability and reduce the need for ongoing state aid. Known as "the bailout," the bill redirected approximately $2.7 billion in property tax revenues from schools to cities, counties, and special districts. This shift lessened schools' dependence on property taxes while helping local governments manage their budgets.

FIGURE 1.1 California

Source: Picture provided by the authors

In exchange, the state assumed a larger role in funding education. As a result of Proposition 13 and AB 8, the state's share of funding for K-12 schools and community colleges nearly doubled, rising from 36% in 1977–1978 to 65% in 1979–1980 (California Budget Project, 1997). California's school districts experienced a centralization of finance that made them dependent on state funds instead of the former method of reliance on local property tax revenues.

The AB 8 system remained in place for over a decade. However, in response to the state's repeated budget crises in the early 1990s, the legislature moved to "reverse the AB 8 bailout" by shifting property tax dollars from local government back to schools first in 1992 and again in 1993. Revenues transferred from local governments were used to offset the amount of state assistance provided to schools and community colleges on a dollar-for-dollar basis. Over two years, local governments lost $3.6 billion in property tax revenues (California Budget Project, 1997). These shifts strained the finances of local governments, already burdened by the effects of the recession. With few options open to replace lost revenues, most local governments reduced services.

Proposition 13 had a negative impact on California schools' budgets as well. The largest shift in post-Proposition 13 spending patterns occurred in the funding of K-12 education. Per capita school revenues generated from local property tax declined by 52% between 1977–1978 and 1993–1994 in inflation-adjusted dollars (Legislative Analyst's Office, n.d.). Increased state and federal aid made up for part of this decline. However, the total of school funding provided by state, local, federal, and miscellaneous dollars still dropped by 14% over the same period when adjusted for inflation and population growth (Amerkhanian et al., 2023). Catterall and Brizendine (1985) estimated a net loss of 20% in real resources per student and a 25% lower budget for schools in 1983 compared to 1978. The reduced budget for school districts forced most schools to cut staffing, support services, and school materials, leading to larger and fewer sections of classes and decreasing students' scheduling options. Nearly every district reported cutting course offerings or class periods to adjust for decreased staff and resources. The most commonly reduced courses included performing arts, driver education, social science electives, and honors classes.

Proposition 13 separates the benefits of public services from the burdens of paying for them because some residents receive the same public benefits at a lower cost, while newer residents carry a heavier tax load (O'Sullivan et al., 1995). Additionally, future homeowners have no voice in current tax policy decisions, despite being affected by them later.

California policymakers and taxpayers should examine ways to mitigate the growing inequality in property tax burdens among similar properties. Possible solutions include modifying the property tax system to eliminate reassessments upon the sale of newer properties, thereby gradually reducing existing tax disparities. Another potential approach involves reexamining Proposition 13 in its entirety to develop a more equitable and sustainable framework for property taxation in California.

Discussion questions

1 What were the positive impacts created by Proposition 13?
2 What were the main fiscal and political outcomes of Proposition 13 for California's school districts, state, and local governments?
3 In what ways does Proposition 13 influence housing market behavior, such as homeownership decisions, property turnover, and residential mobility?

4 How has Proposition 13 affected local government revenues and their ability to provide essential public services such as education, infrastructure, and safety?
5 How did Proposition 13 alter the fairness of California's property tax system? Who benefits most, and who bears the most significant burden?
6 Should California reform or repeal Proposition 13? What economic, political, and social factors should policymakers consider before doing so?
7 What alternative property tax policies could balance the goals of revenue stability, taxpayer predictability, and intergenerational fairness?
8 How does Proposition 13 illustrate the trade-offs between horizontal equity (taxpayers in similar situations should pay similar taxes) and vertical equity (taxes should be based on ability to pay)?

References

Amerkhanian, P., Zhang, M., & Hawkins, J. (2023). A reexamination of Proposition 13 using parcel-level data. *Berkeley Institute for Young Americans*. https://youngamericans.berkeley.edu/wp-content/uploads/2023/02/Report_A-Reexamination-of-Proposition-13-Using-Parcel-Level-Data_final.pdf

California Budget Project. (1997). *Proposition 13: Its impact on California and implications*. https://calbudgetcenter.org/app/uploads/2018/09/Issue-Brief_Proposition-13-Its-Impact-on-California-and-Implications_04.1997.pdf

California Legislative Analyst's Office. (2016). *Common claims about Proposition 13*. https://lao.ca.gov/publications/report/3497

California State Board of Equalization. (2018). California property tax: An overview (Publication 29). https://www.boe.ca.gov/proptaxes/pdf/pub29.pdf

Catterall, J., & Brizendine, E. (1985). Proposition 13: Effects on High School Curricula, 1978–1983. *American Journal of Education*, *93*(3), 327–351.

JUSTIA US Supreme Court. (n.d.) Nordlinger v. Hahn, 505 U.S. 1 (1992). https://supreme.justia.com/cases/federal/us/505/1/

Legislative Analyst's Office. (n.d.). State spending plan. https://lao.ca.gov/publications?productid=15

Nichols, C. (2018, October). Taxpayers revolt: Forty years ago California voters passed Prop. 13 and reshaped the California dream for generations. CalMatters, KPBS, KPCC, KQED and Capital Public Radio. https://projects.scpr.org/prop-13/history/.

O'Sullivan, A., Sexton, T. A., & Sheffrin, S. M. (1995). *Property taxes and tax revolts: The legacy of Proposition 13*. Taylor & Francis.

Stiefel, E. (2025). California property tax map: How much homeowners in every ZIP code are saving due to Prop 13. https://www.sfchronicle.com/projects/2025/prop-13-subsidy-california/

CASE STUDY 4

When revenue disappears: case of Moffett, Oklahoma

Abstract

This case study investigates the municipal bankruptcy of Moffett, Oklahoma, which filed for Chapter 9 bankruptcy protection in 2009. The case examines fiscal, administrative, and structural factors that contributed to the town's financial insolvency, as well as the challenges encountered by local officials before and during municipal bankruptcy. The analysis indicates that Moffett's fiscal crisis was primarily the result of an excessive dependence on traffic fine revenues, which accounted for approximately 85% of its total budget, creating an unstable and unsustainable revenue structure vulnerable to policy and enforcement changes. After the Oklahoma Legislature passed a bill prohibiting Moffett from issuing speeding tickets along a four-mile stretch of U.S. Highway 64, the town filed for bankruptcy. Confronted with both the sudden loss of its primary source of revenue and significant undisclosed debts, Moffett faced not only bankruptcy but also the prospect of disincorporation.

Topics

Municipal Bankruptcy; Revenue; Revenue Diversification; Tax Policy

Background

Moffett, Oklahoma, a town with a population of 178, filed for Chapter 9 bankruptcy protection in November 2009. In the case of Moffett, Oklahoma, the town's fiscal crisis was directly linked to its heavy reliance on traffic fine revenues. Just weeks after the Oklahoma Legislature passed a bill prohibiting Moffett from issuing speeding tickets along a four-mile stretch of U.S. Highway 64, the town filed for bankruptcy (CNBC, 2013). For years, Moffett generated approximately 85% of all municipal revenues from issuing speeding tickets on a four-mile stretch of U.S. Highway 64 (Thornton & Stogsdill, 2007). In 2009, State Attorney General and Department of Public Safety declared speed trap illegal (In re Town of Moffett, Case No. 09–81814. Bankr. E.D. Oklahoma. 2009).

When the Oklahoma Legislature passed a bill prohibiting the town from issuing citations on that roadway, Moffett's municipal revenue base collapsed almost overnight. With approximately $200,000 in outstanding debt and only $43,000 in assets, the town was unable to meet its obligations and sought bankruptcy protection (CNBC, 2013). The Town of Moffett, Case No. 09–81814, was filed in the U.S. Bankruptcy Court for the Eastern District of Oklahoma on October 22, 2009. After multiple time extensions, the Debtor filed a plan and disclosure statement on September 1, 2011. The plan was two pages long and merely identified the classes and stated their treatment. The plan was confirmed on December 9, 2011, and a final decree was entered on April 23, 2012. The Town of Moffett, Oklahoma, serves as an illustration of the risks associated with overreliance on a single, volatile revenue source.

Fiscal dependence on traffic fines

Moffett functioned essentially as a "speed trap town." The highway passing through its jurisdiction provided a steady flow of non-resident motorists whose speeding tickets subsidized the town's revenue base. This arrangement allowed the town to avoid building a broad or sustainable residential sales or property tax base. The town's fiscal stability was largely contingent upon the state's discretionary authority. Consequently, its reliance on traffic fines as a primary source of revenue washes out the fine line between legitimate public safety enforcement and revenue generation.

The dependence on traffic fines created three critical vulnerabilities:

1 Revenue instability
2 Lack of revenue diversification
3 Ethical and legal tensions.

Once the legislature intervened to curb predatory enforcement, the town's fiscal structure collapsed instantly.

After municipal bankruptcy

Moffett's population declined sharply from 178 in 2009 to 128 in 2022. By 2024, Moffett's population had declined to 32 residents. In 2025, the average household income in Moffett was $29,600 with a poverty rate of 51.43% (World Population Review, 2025). The median age in Moffett was 32.8 years: 30.5 years for males, and 34.3 years for females.

With such a diminished population and limited tax base, the town was unable to sustain the costs of local governance or maintain essential public services. In response, the Oklahoma Department of Commerce and other state agencies convened meetings with residents to discuss the community's future, to consider:

- Whether Moffett revenues could be restructured,
- Whether services could be outsourced or regionalized,
- Or whether the town should disincorporate and be absorbed into county administration.

Confronted with both the sudden loss of its primary revenue source and significant undisclosed debts, Moffett faced not only bankruptcy but also the prospect of disincorporation.

Conclusions

The decision-making process becomes especially critical during periods of fiscal crisis or municipal bankruptcy, when officials must make difficult choices about restructuring budgets, prioritizing essential services, and managing competing demands amid severe resource constraints. The ability of local leaders to act promptly, transparently, and based on sound evidence often determines whether a municipality can stabilize and recover or fall into deeper fiscal distress. When early warning signs of financial trouble are ignored, fiscal deterioration can accelerate, leading to service disruptions and a decline in community trust (Trussel & Patrick, 2012). Municipal bankruptcy thus represents the most severe manifestation of fiscal stress, a situation in which a community's financial capacity is pushed to its limits, as illustrated by the case of Moffett's bankruptcy.

This case study provides several key lessons for public financial management (Table 1.6).

The case illustrates broader themes in public finance, such as the necessity for revenue diversification, ethical governance, fiscal accountability, and state–local relations. It also raises questions about the sustainability of small town governments with narrow tax bases. The Moffett case provides a platform for analyzing early warning indicators of fiscal distress and exploring strategies for stabilization, regional cooperation, and revenue diversification.

TABLE 1.6 Key Lessons from the Moffett Municipal Bankruptcy

Lesson	*Explanation*
Revenue diversification is critical	Municipalities should rely on multiple stable revenue sources to avoid fiscal collapse when one source of revenue fails.
Policies can change quickly	Local governments must anticipate external risks, including those stemming from state-level regulations.
Ethics and legitimacy matter	Revenue models perceived as predatory are at higher risk of reform and public backlash.

Source: Created by authors.

Discussion questions

1 How did the town's excessive dependence on traffic fine revenues contribute to Moffett's fiscal insolvency and eventual bankruptcy filing in 2009?
2 How might stronger financial oversight or transparency mechanisms have prevented Moffett's fiscal crisis?
3 What role did population decline and economic stagnation play in exacerbating the town's financial instability?
4 Should state governments intervene earlier when municipalities rely heavily on unstable or ethically questionable revenue streams?
5 What strategies could have been implemented to gradually transition Moffett from fine-based revenues to more sustainable local tax structures?
6 How could intergovernmental cooperation, such as shared service agreements or county partnerships, have mitigated Moffett's fiscal stress?
7 What types of early warning indicators could the state or local officials have used to detect fiscal stress in Moffett?
8 Considering Moffett's limited economic base, what realistic pathways exist for recovery or reorganization, such as state assistance, consolidation, or disincorporation, and what are the advantages and drawbacks of each?

References

CNBC (2013, July 19). Detroit joins these towns that have 'gone bust'. https://www.cnbc.com/2013/07/19/Detroit-joins-these-towns-that-have-gone-bust.html

In re Town of Moffett. (2009). Case No. 09–81814. Bankruptcy. E.D. Oklahoma. 2009.

Thornton, T., & Stogsdill, S. (2007, February 2). Moffett seeks bankruptcy protection: Town bears toll of designation as a speed trap and debts incurred by the late mayor. *The Oklahoman*. https://eu.oklahoman.com/story/news/2007/02/02/moffett-bankruptcy-protectionbrspan-classhl2town-bears-designation-speed-debts-incurred-mayorspan/61819216007/

Trussel, J. M., & Patrick, P. A. (2012). A survival analysis of U.S. municipalities in fiscal distress. *International Journal of Public Administration, 35*(9), 620–633. https://doi.org/10.1080/01900692.2012.661189

World Population Review. (2025). Moffett, OK. https://worldpopulationreview.com/us-cities/oklahoma/moffett

2

EXPENDITURE BUDGETING IN PRACTICE

Abstract

This chapter examines institutional, political, and technical aspects of expenditure budgeting at the federal, state, and local levels. It highlights its role as a planning instrument, financial management tool, and a legal mechanism for expenditure control. This chapter addresses the influence of economic conditions, political priorities, and social equity considerations on government spending decisions. This chapter demonstrates that effective expenditure budgeting requires a balance between political negotiation, managerial efficiency, and fiscal responsibility.

Introduction

Expenditure budgeting is the process by which governments determine how limited public resources are allocated across programs, departments, and services. Expenditure budgeting focuses on how funds are spent to achieve policy objectives and deliver public services. Public expenditure budgeting is complex because governments must make decisions under conditions of uncertainty, legal constraints, and political pressure, while ensuring fiscal discipline and maintaining service quality.

Expenditure budgeting also serves as a primary control mechanism by which legislatures and executives oversee the use of public funds. Governments categorize expenditures to enable policymakers and the public to understand spending patterns. Main classification systems include organizational classification (by department or agency), functional classification (by program area such as

DOI: 10.4324/9781003606833-3

health or public safety), economic classification (by type of expense such as personnel or equipment), and program classification (by objective or output). Each classification system serves a distinct analytical purpose, enabling performance evaluation, transparency, and reporting.

The expenditure budgeting process typically follows a structured cycle. Agencies first submit budget requests to the central budget office, justifying increases and explaining operational needs. The executive branch reviews proposals, revises requests, and prepares a proposed budget. The legislative body then holds hearings, amends the budget, and adopts a final appropriation. Throughout this process, negotiation is constant, as agencies compete for limited funds and political leaders weigh public demands. Once adopted, the expenditure budget enters the execution phase. Agencies are responsible for managing expenditures within authorized limits. Budget officers monitor spending through accounting systems, monthly reports, and internal audits. Variances between budgeted and actual expenditures may require corrective action, including spending freezes or midyear adjustments. Budget control mechanisms are essential to prevent overspending and financial mismanagement. These include expenditure ceilings, procurement regulations, internal controls, and external audits by independent auditors. The steps in the process are shown in Figure 2.1.

Economic and fiscal conditions play a major role in shaping expenditure budgets. During economic downturns, governments face revenue declines while demand for public services increases, which can widen budget deficits. As a result, expenditure budgets must adjust through hiring freezes, service reductions, or the use of reserve funds. Strong economic performance can either reduce deficits or even create surpluses if spending remains stable. Governments may intentionally run budget deficits as a tool to stimulate economic activity during periods of recession. During an economic downturn, a government may deliberately reduce its sources of revenue while maintaining or even increasing public expenditures. Investments in areas like infrastructure generate employment, support household income, and strengthen overall demand. Economic growth periods provide opportunities to invest in public service improvements and program expansion.

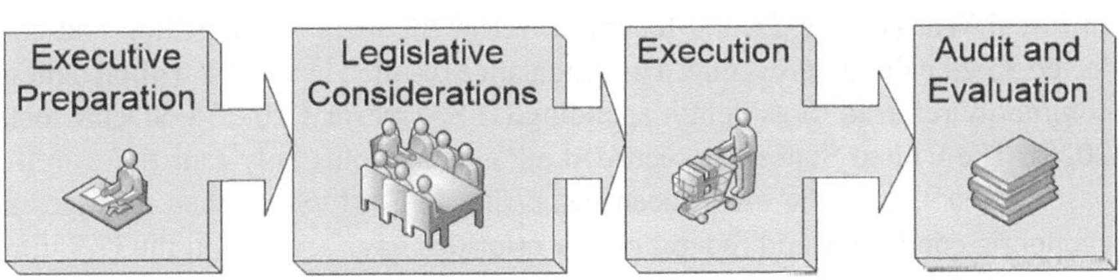

FIGURE 2.1 Steps in the public expenditure (operating) budgeting process

Source: Created by authors

Expenditure budgeting also reflects political values and social priorities. Education, public safety, healthcare, and social services often compete for funding. Changes in political leadership can alter spending patterns. Technology has transformed the practice of expenditure budgeting. Integrated financial systems, data dashboards, and predictive analytics now allow governments to monitor spending more effectively (Ermasova & Guzman, 2024). Technology also increases transparency by enabling open data portals and public reporting (Clark & Guzman, 2017).

Despite all technological innovation, personnel expenditures still represent the largest component of government operating budgets. Personnel spending includes salaries, wages, overtime, health insurance, pensions, and other fringe benefits. Because many public services are labor-intensive, changes in personnel spending have direct implications for service delivery. Personnel costs are often constrained by administrative rules, collective bargaining agreements, and statutory benefit obligations, which limit short-term flexibility and make quick budget adjustments difficult. As a result, governments facing fiscal stress frequently seek to control personnel expenditures through hiring freezes, vacancy savings, overtime restrictions, or benefit adjustments rather than through immediate layoffs.

Besides personnel expenditures, the government spends money on such operating costs as supplies, utilities, fuel, maintenance, information technology, and professional services. In addition to operating costs, capital expenditures that fund such long-term investments as roads, bridges, public buildings, schools, water and sewer systems, and parks represent another major component of public spending. The government also spends on debt service, which includes principal and interest payments on outstanding bonds and loans. And government spends on transfers and intergovernmental payments, such as aid to school districts, payments to other local governments, and contributions to state or federal programs.

Federal budget expenditures

In Fiscal Year (FY) 2025, the federal government spent $7.01 trillion and collected $5.23 trillion in revenue. This imbalance resulted in a $1.78 trillion deficit, commonly referred to as deficit spending (U.S. Treasury, 2025; USDebtClock, 2025). The United States has recorded a FY-end surplus only four times in the past 50 years, with the most recent occurring in 2001. Since then, changes in economic conditions and federal policy priorities have resulted in the U.S. running annual deficits for 25 years (Congressional Budget Office, 2025).

U.S. government spending in FY 2026 is allocated to Medicare (22%), Social Security (19%), defense (15%), and interest payments (13%) (U.S. Treasury, 2025). Income security programs account for 9%, supporting individuals and families through unemployment assistance, nutrition programs, and other safety-net services. Veterans' benefits and services account for 7% of total spending. Education, training, employment, and social services account for 3%, transportation for 2%, and agriculture for 1%. Since 2016, the federal government has experienced a sustained pattern in which growth in spending on Social Security, healthcare programs, and interest on the federal debt has outpaced the growth of federal revenue. This structural imbalance increases the deficit even during periods of economic expansion. In 2024, Medicare remained one of the largest components of the U.S. social insurance system, providing coverage to approximately 67.3 million adults. The program primarily serves older adults, with nearly 90% of beneficiaries aged 65 or older. Overall, roughly one-fifth of the U.S. population was enrolled in Medicare in 2024, underscoring its central role in federal health policy. In 2023, federal expenditures on Medicare totaled $832 billion, accounting for 3.1% of the GDP (Hall, 2025). From FY 2019 to FY 2021, federal spending increased by approximately 50%. Congress enacted large-scale emergency measures to address public health needs, unemployment, business closures, and economic instability.

Expenditure budgeting at the state level

All states except Vermont have statutory requirements to produce balanced budgets (balanced budget requirement), in which spending on operations, excluding pensions and capital projects, is tied to expected revenue (Oxford Analytica, 2025). As a result, states must align expenditures closely with anticipated revenues, making expenditure budgeting both more constrained and more immediately sensitive to economic cycles. Table 2.1 demonstrates states' operating funds spending from FY 2021 to FY 2025.

State operating spending increased from $124.1 billion in FY 2021 to a peak of $132.9 billion in FY 2022, and then gradually declined to $130 billion in FY 2024. All funds spending grew steadily, rising from $222.3 billion in FY 2021 to approximately $237 billion during the period from FY 2022 to FY 2025.

TABLE 2.1 State Operating Funds Spending from FY 2021 to FY 2025 (Billions of dollars; adjusted to FY 2025 dollars)

Fiscal Year	*State Operating Spending*	*All Funds Spending*
2021	$124.1	$222.3
2022	$132.9	$237.1
2023	$131.4	$234.1
2024	$130.0	$237.9
2025	$130.0	$237.0

Source: Fiscal Policy Institute (2025).

Although operating spending declined after 2022, all funds spending continued to increase. This pattern suggests growth in federally supported programs, an expansion of special funds directed toward infrastructure and social services, and a broader funding base that extends beyond the general operating budget.

On average, federal transfers accounted for approximately 34% of total state expenditures in FY 2024 (Kramer, 2025). Of the more than $3 trillion spent by states that year, slightly over $1 trillion was transferred from federal sources. The federal share of state budgets had a historic peak of 36% in FY 2021. Major federal initiatives enacted during the Biden Administration, including the Infrastructure Investment and Jobs Act and the Inflation Reduction Act, continued to direct significant additional resources to states to support implementation of their statutory provisions

State spending is concentrated in education, healthcare, and social services. In FY 2024, total state general fund expenditures amounted to $1,181 billion. K-12 education accounted for the largest share, at 33.6%, of all general fund spending. According to the 2024 State Expenditure Report, Medicaid accounted for 18.7%, while higher education made up 9.4% (NASBO, 2025). Corrections represented 5.6% of spending, and transportation made up 1.8%. Public assistance constituted 0.9% (NASBO, 2025).

Education is another dominant area of state expenditures, encompassing funding for K-12 schools and public higher education systems. State policymakers often rely on education funding not only as a service provision tool but also as an economic development strategy. During fiscal downturns, however, higher education funding is frequently one of the first areas to experience cuts because it is less protected by statutory obligations compared to healthcare and social services (Bruce et al., 2018). In 2025, state lawmakers increasingly directed expenditures toward targeted population groups, including families with children, older adults, and low-income residents. This trend is expected to continue into 2026 as states attempt to balance constituent demands for public services with long-term fiscal sustainability (NCSL, 2025).

Medicaid represents the single most significant expenditure for most states and is highly sensitive to changes in economic conditions and federal policy. During economic downturns, enrollment increases, and state spending expands even as tax revenues decline, creating substantial fiscal stress. Because Medicaid is a jointly funded federal-state program, changes in federal cost-sharing rules or program eligibility can directly affect state spending patterns and budget stability.

Looking ahead to FY 2026, state governments will face a challenging fiscal environment characterized by slower economic growth, declining federal financial support, and labor market uncertainty. These pressures, coupled with rising healthcare costs, are increasing demands on state expenditure systems and forcing policymakers to reassess spending priorities. With federal program funding increasingly constrained, states are assuming greater responsibility for financing education, healthcare, infrastructure, and social services. At the same time, some states are reallocating expenditures to support enforcement and regulatory policy aimed at newly emerging sectors, including digital services and artificial intelligence-driven industries. These strategies reflect a broader shift toward outcome-oriented budgeting, where resources are increasingly allocated based on performance, return on investment, and long-term fiscal impact (NCSL, 2025).

Debt service and pension obligations also exert growing pressure on state budgets. While states generally limit borrowing for operating purposes, long-term obligations related to employee retirement systems have become significant expenditure categories. Underfunded pension systems increase required annual contributions and reduce fiscal flexibility, often forcing difficult tradeoffs between infrastructure, services, and financial reserves.

Expenditure budgeting at the local level

Expenditure budgets at the local level are primarily focused on public safety, education, infrastructure maintenance, utilities, and community services.

County governments in the United States allocate resources across a wide range of functional areas, including utilities, public safety, transportation, education, and other public services. Counties invest nearly $743 billion annually to provide essential services, including public safety, infrastructure, healthcare, and workforce development (NASACT, 2025). The composition and magnitude of these expenditures vary substantially across jurisdictions, reflecting differences in the scope of services provided, statutory and regulatory responsibilities, and local political and institutional contexts. For all counties in the United States, the largest individual expenditure sources are public safety, education, hospitals, and welfare (GFOA, n.d.). Police and fire protection represent core functions for most municipalities and counties, accounting for a large portion of operating expenditures. Because labor costs dominate these services, personnel expenses constitute the majority of local government budgets.

Elementary and secondary education accounts for a substantially larger share of local government direct expenditures than of state-level direct expenditures. Approximately 40% of direct local government spending is devoted to elementary and secondary education, compared with less than 1% of direct state government spending. This apparent disparity in spending responsibility, however, masks the intergovernmental nature of education finance. Although local governments are the primary agents through which these funds are expended, a significant portion of the resources originates from state and federal governments.

Local governments face rising expenditure pressures from aging infrastructure, public safety demands, and compliance with state and federal mandates. Economic conditions directly influence local spending capacity. During economic crises, property values may stagnate or decline, weakening the primary source of revenue for many municipalities. At the same time, demand for services such as housing assistance, social expenditures, and law enforcement may increase. Local governments have limited borrowing capacity for operating expenditures and must frequently respond to fiscal stress by implementing budget cuts, hiring freezes, delaying maintenance, reducing services, or increasing taxes and fees.

State aid and shared revenues often account for a substantial portion of local budgets. Local governments received substantial federal assistance provided through the CARES Act, the American Rescue Plan Act (ARPA), and the Bipartisan Infrastructure Law (NASACT, 2025). Counties with populations exceeding 500,000 received direct allocations, whereas smaller counties relied on state governments to administer and distribute funds. The ARPA created the State and Local Fiscal Recovery Fund, which directed $65.1 billion in direct investment to county governments to support economic recovery, strengthen infrastructure, and sustain essential public services (NASACT, 2025). Over the past four years, counties have strategically utilized these resources to bolster long-term fiscal and administrative capacity, expand and improve public services, and leverage additional public and private investment.

Conclusions

Expenditure budgeting determines how the community's resources will be allocated among essential services, including public safety, infrastructure, economic development, education, and other critical areas, all of which are crucial for a thriving community. It requires balancing financial resources, political objectives, technical efficiency, and fiscal responsibility (GFOA, 2025). Effective expenditure budgeting ensures efficiency, accountability, and sustainability. By allocating fiscal resources, governments signal their policy commitments, values, and responsiveness to social needs. This chapter demonstrates that expenditure budgeting constitutes both a financial management process and a political arena in which competing priorities are negotiated under conditions of limited resources and growing public expectations.

Economic conditions were shown to play a significant role in expenditure decisions. Revenue volatility forces governments to make budget cuts. The periods of economic growth create opportunities for economic development and capital investments that must be managed responsibly. Governments that fail to align expenditure growth with long-term revenue trends risk structural deficits and fiscal stress. Integrating expenditure budgeting with financial forecasting and reserve policies is necessary for long-term stability.

In this chapter, the first case is a comparative analysis of universal free school meals (UFSM) programs in nine states: Colorado, California, Maine,

Massachusetts, Michigan, Minnesota, New Mexico, New York, and Vermont. This case study examines the implementation, funding structures, policy goals, and outcomes of UFSM programs, explores the fiscal and administrative implications for school districts, and evaluates potential effects on student nutrition, equity, and educational outcomes.

The second case study evaluates fiscal stress and closing schools in Jefferson County, Colorado. It presents a public hearing simulation focused on school closure and reorganization decisions in the Jefferson County Public Schools (Jeffco) district.

The third case study discusses the pros and cons of budgeting for vacancies. It examines a revenue shortfall in Cuyahoga County, Ohio, where County Executive Armond Budish chose to reduce costs by eliminating all unfilled vacant positions in the county's 2022–2023 biennial budget, rather than implementing direct program cuts, and analyzes the resulting backlash from the majority of the county council members and on social media.

References

Bruce, M., Ermasova, N., & Mattox, L. (2018). The fiscal disparity and achievement gap between extremely wealthy and poor school districts in Illinois. *Public Organization Review*, *19*(4), 541–565.

Clark, B. Y., & Guzman, T. S. (2017). *Does technologically enabled citizen participation lead to budget adjustments? An investigation of Boston, MA, and San Francisco, CA. The American Review of Public Administration, 47*(8), 945–961. https://doi.org/10.1177/0275074016642568

Congressional Budget Office. (2025). Summary for fiscal year 2024. https://www.cbo.gov/publication/60843/html

Ermasova, N., & Guzman, T. (2024). Assessments of municipalities' fiscal health: Comparative analysis of state online Dashboard systems. *Public Finance & Management*, *22*(2), 112–145.

Fiscal Policy Institute. (2025). Fact sheet: NYS fiscal year 2025 enacted budget. https://fiscalpolicy.org/wp-content/uploads/2024/04/FY 25-Fact-Sheet.pdf

GFOA. (n.d). Local Government Expenditure Sources – Counties. https://www.gfoa.org/expenditure-dashboard-counties

GFOA. (2025). A guide to designing a local budget. https://www.gfoa.org/long-form/a-guide-to-designing-a-local-government-budget

Hall, A. (2025). Medicare statistics and facts In 2025. https://www.forbes.com/advisor/health-insurance/medicare/medicare-statistics/

Kramer, B. (2025, February 28). State budgets in the shadow of federal uncertainty. *MultiState*. https://www.multistate.us/insider/2025/2/28/state-budgets-in-the-shadow-of-federal-uncertainty

NASACT. (2025). State and local fiscal facts. https://www.nasact.org/files/News_and_Publications/White_Papers_Reports/2025_state_and_local_fiscal_facts.pdf

NASBO. (2025). 2024 State Expenditure Report. https://www.nasbo.org/reports-data/state-expenditure-report

NCSL. (2025, November 11). State budgets in transition as revenue slows and surpluses shrink. https://www.ncsl.org/state-legislatures-news/details/state-budgets-in-transition-as-revenue-slows-and-surpluses-shrink

Oxford Analytica. (2025, August 27). US states rein in spending amid revenue concerns. https://www.oxan.com/insights/us-states-rein-in-spending-amid-revenue-concerns/

USDebtClock. (2025, November 20). World debt. https://www.usdebtclock.org/world-debt-clock.html

U.S. Treasury. (2025). How much has the U.S. government spent this year? Fiscal Data U.S. Treasury. https://fiscaldata.treasury.gov/americas-finance-guide/federal-spending/

CASE STUDY 5

Comparative analysis of universal free school meals programs at the state level in the United States

Abstract

Food insecurity continues to affect millions of children in the United States, disproportionately impacting low-income households. While the National School Lunch Program (NSLP) has long provided free or reduced-price meals based on household income eligibility, the introduction of the Community Eligibility Provision (CEP) in 2010 allowed high-poverty schools to offer meals to all students without requiring individual applications. In recent years, several states have expanded this approach by adopting statewide universal free school meal policies that extend access to all students regardless of income. This multi-case comparative study analyzes secondary data to examine the implementation, funding structures, policy goals, and outcomes of universal free school meal programs in nine states: Colorado, California, Maine, Massachusetts, Michigan, Minnesota, New Mexico, New York, and Vermont. The case study highlights similarities and differences in program design, explores the fiscal and administrative implications for school districts, and evaluates the potential effects on student nutrition, equity, and educational engagement. Through cross-state comparisons, the study identifies emerging best practices and policy considerations relevant to states and districts contemplating the expansion of universal school meal programs.

Topics

State Government; Expenditures; Public Finance; Meal Plans; Education Expenditures

Background

Food insecurity remains a persistent challenge across the United States, particularly among low-income households with children. The federal National School Lunch Program (NSLP) has historically served meals to children at reduced or no cost based on household income. However, the Community Eligibility Provision (CEP), introduced in 2010 under the Healthy, Hunger-Free Kids Act, enabled high-poverty schools to serve meals to all students free of charge without collecting individual applications. Building on this, several states have implemented statewide UFSM policies. This case study provides a comparative analysis of UFSM programs across nine states: Colorado, California, Maine, Massachusetts, Michigan, Minnesota, New Mexico, New York, and Vermont.

The objective of the UFSM program is to provide students, regardless of socioeconomic status, with access to free breakfast and lunch during the school day. The primary purpose of UFSMs is to improve educational outcomes and enhance the overall well-being of school students (School Meals for All, 2024). While the traditional school meal eligibility system ensures that children in poverty receive assistance, it also imposes significant barriers. Students receiving free meals often face social stigma, which can deter participation and contribute to feelings of shame or embarrassment. In addition, schools expend significant resources processing income applications and managing eligibility, diverting staff and time away from educational priorities. Many eligible students do not receive free meals due to missed paperwork or reluctance to enroll, creating participation gaps that leave vulnerable children without access to nutritious food. These persistent issues prompted districts and states to consider universal access as a more equitable and efficient alternative.

Colorado, California, Maine, Massachusetts, Michigan, Minnesota, New Mexico, New York, and Vermont have passed legislation mandating free breakfast and lunches to all students, independently of their socioeconomic status (Food Research & Action Center, 2024). California was the first state to implement universally free school meals for the AY 2022–2023, with Maine following the same year. Colorado, Massachusetts, Michigan, New Mexico, Minnesota, and Vermont signed and passed their legislation to start the program in AY 2023–2024, and New York passed their legislation to start the program in AY 2025–2026.

The educational and social impact of universal free school meals

Research indicates that UFSM programs provide several interconnected benefits. The United States Department of Agriculture (2024) highlights that students consuming school lunches exhibit higher overall diet quality compared to those who bring meals from home. Schwartz and Rothbart (2020) demonstrated that universal free meal programs significantly increase meal participation among both low- and middle-income students, removing barriers that traditionally discouraged engagement. The objective of this universally free school meals program is to provide students, independently of their socioeconomic status, access to a free, nutritional breakfast and lunch during the school day. A direct result of healthy eating is children putting more of their focus and energy into their classroom learning. Access to school breakfast and lunch has been associated with improved academic performance, reduced absenteeism, decreased health disparities in the lunchroom, and fewer disciplinary incidents (Anderson et al., 2017; Critch, 2020; Frisvold, 2015; Imberman & Kugler, 2014; Kirksey & Gottfried, 2021; Peterson, 2009, 2011; Roy & Stretch, 2018; Schwartz & Rothbart, 2020; Teboe, 2021; Terry-McElrath et al., 2016; Turner et al., 2016; Wharton et al., 2008; Zuercher et al., 2022). Critch (2020) and Frisvold (2015) found that students with regular access to healthy meals tend to perform better on standardized tests and classroom assignments. Improved nutrition contributes to higher graduation rates and better attendance. Kirksey and Gottfried (2021) observed that older students were more likely to attend school when free breakfast was available as an incentive. Eating breakfast helps students stay focused on the material, rather than wasting instructional time on children who will not retain any information (Teboe, 2021).

These UFSM programs serve as a buffer against food insecurity for families, particularly during times of economic hardship. Food Research & Action Center (2024) emphasizes that universal meals reduce household stress related to food access and support children's capacity to learn and thrive. UFSM programs also address disparities in the lunchroom. Unlike means-tested subsidies that often carry stigma, providing meals to all students regardless of income reduces social stratification and allows children to concentrate on learning rather than hunger (Michigan Department of Education, 2023; Project Bread, n.d.). These findings underscore the economic and educational value of such programs, not only in supporting individual families but also in contributing to broader educational equity.

Comparative analysis of universal free school lunch programs at the state level in the United States

A case study provides a comparative analysis of free school lunch programs in nine U.S. states: California, Colorado, Maine, Massachusetts, Michigan, Minnesota, New Mexico, New York, and Vermont (Figure 2.2).

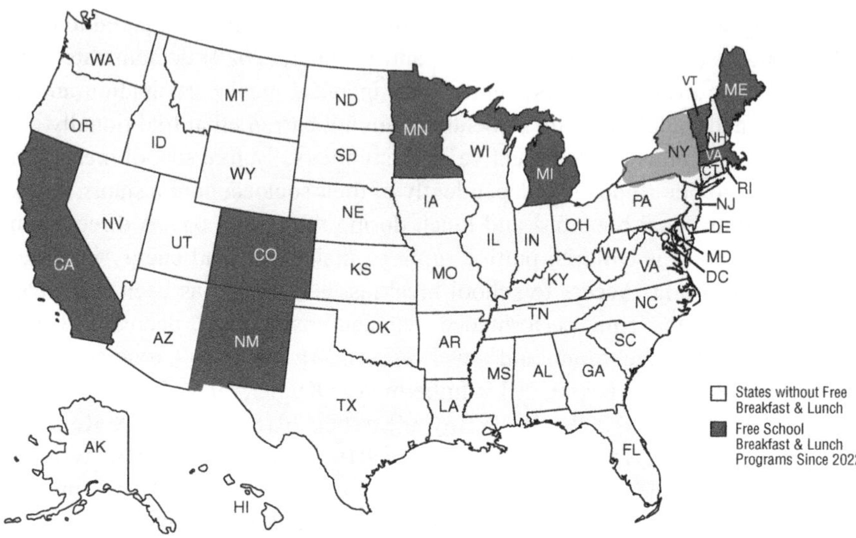

FIGURE 2.2 Selected states for analysis with universal free school lunch programs in the United States in 2025

Source: Created by authors based on Food Research & Action Center (2024) and the State of New York Education Department (2025)

California

California has implemented Healthy School Meals for All (HSMA) policies, offering free breakfast and lunch to all students, regardless of household income, in grades kindergarten through 12th grade at public and charter school institutions in the 2022–2023 academic year (California Legislature, 2021a; Food Research & Action Center, 2024). All schools are required to participate. High-poverty schools must use federal meal provisions (like the Community Eligibility Provision – CEP).

Under California's Universal Meals Program, funding is administered through a reimbursement model, requiring the state to cover all costs associated with meals provided under the U.S. Department of Agriculture's (USDA's) nutrition guidelines (California Legislature, 2021a). This includes financial support for necessary kitchen equipment upgrades, expanded staffing, and implementation logistics. The program mandates the inclusion of an external evaluator to assess its impact and effectiveness (California Legislature, 2021b). According to School Meals for All (2024), the FY 2022–2023 California state budget allocated approximately $2 billion toward improving school food infrastructure, supporting staff training, and increasing access to freshly prepared, locally sourced meals. Of that amount, $596 million was specifically designated for the provision of two free meals per day to all public school students.

This funding not only ensures universal access to nutritious food but also strengthens the school nutrition workforce by supporting new hires and enhancing staff training. The foundation of this legislation stems from the argument that children throughout the state of California do not regularly eat breakfast because their families cannot afford enough food to support this habit (California Legislature, 2021a). This funding is intended to bridge the gap between federal meal reimbursements and the actual costs of providing meals, ensuring that all schools can offer free meals to students without incurring financial burdens.

Colorado

In June 2022, the Colorado General Assembly passed legislation to create the HSMA program, and voters approved Proposition FF, which authorized a dedicated revenue stream to fund the program. The program requires annual appropriations from the Colorado General Assembly to cover any additional costs (Colorado General Assembly, 2022). This program provides public school students with a free breakfast and lunch. School districts have the choice to opt in or out of the program. Colorado has implemented policies that offer school meals to all students at no charge, ensuring all children have the nutrition they need to learn and thrive (Colorado Department of Human Services, n.d.). Additionally, the funding can be used to purchase local food grants and increase wages for staff who prepare and serve lunches (Ballotpedia, 2022). The "school meal authorities are reimbursed by the Colorado Department of Education School Nutrition Unit with state funding" (Ballotpedia, 2022, para. 1). The Program "Healthy School Meals for All" began during the AY 2023–2024. All school districts are eligible to participate, but individual schools cannot choose to participate in the program. School districts are the determining factor in whether schools will provide free meals or not. Colorado implements a progressive tax against the wealthiest tax bracket to fund HSMA (Colorado General Assembly, 2022).

The state funds the program by capping itemized and standard income tax deductions for taxpayers with a federal adjusted gross income of $300,000 or more. Proposition FF created a dedicated funding stream by limiting state tax deductions for Coloradans making more than $300,000 per year ($12,000 in state income tax deductions for single filers and $16,000 for joint filers) and using the difference between the limit and the federal standard deduction amount or federal itemized amount to pay for HSMA (Gutierrez et al., 2024). Colorado uses their federal funds to reimburse schools for their lunches, and tax dollars are used to provide students with healthier meals (Gutierrez et al., 2024). This is inclusive of locally grown fruits and vegetables, as well as healthier food groups within the lunchroom (Food Research & Action Center, 2024). The funding is accessed through a reimbursement program where

> the amount of reimbursement distributed pursuant to the program is equal to the federal free reimbursement rate multiplied by the total number of

meals served minus any other federal or state reimbursement the school food authority receives for providing the meals.

(Ballotpedia, 2022; Campaign, 2022; Colorado General Assembly, 2022, para. 10)

Starting in the AY 2024–2025, the program provides grant funding to school meal providers for several purposes: to purchase Colorado-grown, -raised, and -processed products for school meals; to increase wages or offer stipends to employees who prepare and serve those meals; and to receive training, equipment, and technical assistance to support the preparation of healthy meals using basic, nutritious ingredients and to encourage collaboration among schools, communities, and local food producers. Additionally, the act establishes the Local School Food Purchasing Technical Assistance and Education Grant Program. Through this program, a statewide nonprofit organization distributes grants to help participating school food authorities (SFAs) buy Colorado-grown, -raised, or -processed foods and to support them in preparing meals using basic ingredients instead of processed items. The nonprofit is required to report annually to the department on the program's implementation. (Colorado General Assembly, 2022).

Colorado implemented Summer Electronic Benefits Transfer (EBT), which provides food benefits during summer for students who qualify for free/reduced-price meals (Colorado Department of Human Services, n.d.).

Altogether, Colorado has the following Food Distribution Programs:

- Commodity Supplemental Food Program
- The Emergency Food Assistance Program (TEFAP)
- National School Lunch Program
- Child and Adult Care Food Program (CACFP).

Maine

Maine passed HSMA policies on May 3, 2022, providing free school meals to all students (Maine Department of Education, n.d.). Maine is focused on providing all students with the same opportunities, as this will help them achieve their long-term goals and success. This program was implemented before the end of the COVID-19 pandemic because senators were concerned that families would take on the burden of full-priced meals after the pandemic (Teboe, 2021). Maine's free school lunch program expands access to free school lunches for all students through the Maine Legislature (Maine Legislature, 2022). These meals must fit the requirements of the federal health standards (Maine Legislature, 2022).

The funding began with $10 million in 2022, but later advocacy efforts were successful in securing an estimated $34 million from the general fund (Maine Legislature, 2022). In addition to providing students with free meals, the law directs the Maine Department of Education to collaborate with schools to maximize federal reimbursement, thereby reducing the financial burden of the program on the schools (Maine Legislature, 2022). The program is funded primarily through state appropriations and federal reimbursements (Food Research & Action Center, 2024). Not all students are required to participate; they continue to have the option to bring their own lunches and opt out of the program (Teboe, 2021).

The State of Maine Department of Education administers several USDA-funded nutrition programs. These include the NSLP, the School Breakfast Program (SBP), the After-school Snack Service, the Summer Food Service Program (SFSP), the CACFP, and the Fresh Fruit and Vegetable Program (FFVP) (The State of Maine Department of Education, n.d.). These programs are designed to ensure that children across the State of Maine have access to healthy meals both during the school year and in out-of-school settings. The goals of the federal nutrition programs are to reduce hunger, combat childhood obesity, support schools, childcare centers, and after-school programs in providing nutritious meals and to promote local food sourcing through the Farm and Sea to School initiative. To support these goals, the department provides a range of resources. These include training and webinars for food service professionals, meal planning tools, and culinary education through the Culinary Classroom. The department also offers guidance on program eligibility, the application process, and compliance with federal regulations. In addition to its core programs, the department supports several special initiatives. For example, Maine Harvest of the Month and the Local Foods Fund encourage the use of Maine-grown foods in school meals.

SUN Bucks provide food support during the summer and in emergency situations (State of Maine Department of Health and Human Services, n.d.). The SUN Bucks program, also known as Summer EBT, provides $120 in grocery benefits per eligible child during the summer months when school meals are not available. Children are automatically eligible for the program if they meet certain criteria. These include being certified for free or reduced-price school meals, being between the ages of 6 and 16, and enrolled in programs such as Supplemental Nutrition Assistance Program (SNAP), Temporary Assistance for Needy Families (TANF), The Food Distribution Program on Indian Reservations (FDPIR), or MaineCare (with household income below 185% of the federal poverty level). Children in foster care, experiencing homelessness, or part of migrant agricultural families are also eligible. Most eligible families are automatically enrolled in the program.

Massachusetts

UFSM was implemented in Massachusetts on July 28, 2022, when Governor Baker signed an extension of the federally assisted school lunch program (Food Research & Action Center, 2024). This is to be funded by a new 4% tax on the state's wealthiest residents, which was approved by voters in 2022. The bill ensures all students have access to free breakfast and lunch, regardless of their socioeconomic status (Massachusetts Legislature, 2022). All students are eligible for one breakfast and lunch a day, which includes fruits, vegetables, and whole grains (Massachusetts Department of Elementary and Secondary Education, 2024). Schools could also opt into providing "a la carte" items for a fee, such as milk or an extra serving, but students must pay for this. However, the first meal is always free (Healey & Driscoll, 2023).

Reimbursement for school meals was determined using the federal reimbursement rates established by the USDA under the NSLP and the SBP. These rates vary based on student income eligibility: "free," "reduced-price," and "paid." The "free" rate provides the highest reimbursement per meal, as families are not charged for these meals. The "reduced-price" rate is slightly lower, while the "paid" rate is the lowest (Massachusetts Department of Elementary and Secondary Education, 2024). To support the implementation of UFSMs, all breakfasts and lunches served in schools across Massachusetts were reimbursed at the "free" rate, regardless of a student's income eligibility. Since families were not being charged for any meals, the state provided additional per-meal reimbursement to cover the difference between the "free" rate and both the "reduced-price" and "paid" rates. This approach enabled every meal to be claimed at the highest reimbursement level.

Most of the state funds went toward covering the gap between the "free" and "paid" rates, which represents the largest cost difference. In FY 2023, this amounted to $3.56 per lunch and $2.17 per breakfast (Massachusetts Department of Elementary and Secondary Education, 2024). In FY 2023, a total of 379 school districts received $168.2 million in state reimbursements based on their monthly meal claims. In the FY 2024 budget, the program received $172 million in state funding that is supplemented by federal funds for students eligible for the NSLP. Funds were available to purchase fresh local food from local producers, including but not limited to farmers, food hubs, and fishermen, with all products originating within 400 miles of the school.

Because the state's universal free meal reimbursements only applied to meals originally claimed as "paid" or "reduced-price," districts with the highest number of students in these categories received the most funding. Meals already claimed as "free" were fully reimbursed by the USDA and did not require additional state support. Many school districts receiving this funding were not eligible for the USDA's CEP, which offers federal reimbursement for universal free meals in high-poverty schools. As a result, over 185,000 students eligible for free or reduced-price meals attended schools were, without this state funding, meals would not have been free for all families. The Department of Elementary and Secondary Education offers training, compliance support, and multilingual assistance to ensure equitable access (Massachusetts Department of Elementary and Secondary Education, 2024; Massachusetts Legislature, 2022).

Michigan

Michigan's HSMA Program was implemented during the AY 2023–2024 to provide a no-cost breakfast and lunch program to all public school students. The purpose of this program is to give students "the best, most healthy learning environment" (Michigan Department of Education, 2023). This program is estimated to save families approximately $850 per child a year (Michigan Department of Education, 2023, 2024).

Approximately $160 million was allocated for free school meals in FY 2024 (Food Research & Action Center, 2024). The program is funded through a combination of state and federal resources, with state funds supporting initiatives that operate in partnership with the federally funded NSLP (Michigan Legislature, 2023).

Participation in the program is optional, allowing school districts to opt in based on the needs of their student populations. However, districts that choose to participate receive funding to provide one free breakfast and one free lunch per day to all enrolled students (Michigan Department of Education, 2023). The Michigan Department of Education strongly encourages all districts to participate, emphasizing the program's positive impact on students' academic performance and overall health. In AY 2022–2023, over 1,600 schools were serving free meals. In AY 2023–2024, over 3,300 schools participated. More than 850,000 public school children are choosing to eat lunch at school, and over 474,000 are eating breakfast at school. Michigan's HSMA Program is estimated to save families at least $850 annually (Michigan Department of Education, 2024). School administrators report improvements in students' reading and math scores, as well as enhanced concentration and memory (Michigan Department of Education, 2024).

Minnesota

Governor Tim Walz signed free school meals for Kids into law on March 17, 2023 (Minnesota Department of Education, 2023, 2024). The legislation was introduced in response to rising food costs and growing food insecurity across Minnesota. Lawmakers emphasized that eliminating school meal costs helps reduce the burden on families and has even lessened the need for food shelf visits (Cummings, 2023). The program began on July 1, 2023, and is implemented by the Minnesota Department of Education.

Under this program, schools are reimbursed to provide one free breakfast and one free lunch to all students, regardless of income. Eligibility is based on participation in the NSLP and the SBP, and schools must adhere to USDA nutritional guidelines (Minnesota Legislature, 2023). All traditional public school districts in Minnesota participate in the Minnesota Free School Meals Program, implementing it at the majority of their school sites. Among the state's 181 charter schools, 167 have opted into the program. Additionally, 163 private schools and residential childcare institutions also participated in this program (Minnesota Department of Education, 2024, n.d.). However, because the Minnesota Free School Meals Program operates under federal school nutrition program regulations, not all schools are eligible. Online schools do not qualify for participation.

The estimated cost of this initiative was $388 million over the state's two-year budget cycle (Cummings, 2023). In AY 2023–2024, the funding includes $47.77 million for breakfasts and $220.04 million for lunch costs that were previously not covered prior to the implementation of Minnesota Free School Meals (Minnesota Department of Education, 2024). Per-student funding is calculated based on the cost of full-priced meals, with estimates of $2.25 per breakfast and $3.50 per lunch over a 180-day school year. As more students participate in the program, Minnesota becomes eligible for increased federal reimbursements, potentially up to $550 million toward universal school meals (Cummings, 2023). In AY 2023–2024, breakfast participation grew by 40% and lunch participation grew by 15% compared to AY 2022–2023 (Minnesota Department of Education, 2024). This program saved Minnesota's families around $267.81 million in AY 2023–2024 or $1,000 in savings per student per year. The program also reduces administrative burdens for schools. Staff no longer need to collect meal payments or manage unpaid meal debt. Instead, they can focus on meal quality and student health (Shockman, 2023). With fewer bureaucratic hurdles, schools have more time and resources to upgrade kitchen facilities and train food service personnel.

New Mexico

New Mexico became the fourth state in the nation to implement a UFSM program through the passage of the Healthy Universal School Meals Act (the Hunger-Free Students Bill, SB 4) (New Mexico Legislature, 2023). New Mexico's "Healthy School Meals for All" program, formally known as the "Healthy Hunger-Free Students Bill of Rights Act," was signed into law by Governor Michelle Lujan Grisham in March 2023. It went into effect on July 1, 2023.

Schools that use the CEP or similar programs do not need to collect individual meal applications to provide free meals. The state pays the difference between what the federal government reimburses and the actual cost of providing meals, ensuring schools can offer free meals without financial strain. This program applies to public schools, charter schools, tribally controlled schools, and private schools that participate in federal meal programs.

In AY 2023–2024, the state allocated $30 million to fund the program. This amount supports the initial implementation, with standards being phased in over the next two years to evaluate the program's effectiveness (New Mexico Legislature, 2023). Additionally, $20 million was included in the state budget to upgrade school kitchen infrastructure, ensuring the capacity to serve fresh, nutritious, and homemade meals (Grisham, 2023).

The program encourages schools to participate in the New Mexico Grown Grant Program, which supports the use of locally grown foods in school meals. In addition to providing universal meals during the school year, New Mexico also operates the SFSP through the Early Childhood Education and Care Department (ECECD). This program offers free meals to children ages 1–18 throughout the summer months, further reducing the gap in food access when school is not in session (Sclafani, n.d.).

New York

On May 13, 2025, the UFSM program was implemented in the State of New York. Governor Kathy Hochul announced a historic initiative in her 2025 State of the State address to provide free breakfast and lunch to all 2.7 million students in New York State. The program is expected to save families $165 per child each month. It is supported by $180 million in the FY 2025 budget to expand participation in the CEP.

The 2025–2026 Executive Budget amended New York State Education Law by adding Section 915a UFSMs (The State of New York Education Department, 2025). Beginning in school year 2025–2026, New York State SFAs participating in the federal school lunch and/or breakfast programs are required to provide reimbursable school meals at no cost to all students. The state will reimburse SFAs up to the combined state and federal reimbursement rate for a free meal for each federally reimbursed reduced-price and paid meal claimed. Schools and districts not currently enrolled in federal meal programs must apply to the New York State Education Department, Office of Child Nutrition by July 31, 2025, to participate in the 2025–2026 school year to provide free school meals.

The State of New York has the following federally funded school nutrition programs, including:

- National School Lunch Program
- School Breakfast Program
- Summer Food Service Program
- After-school Snack Program
- Special Milk Program
- Fresh Fruit and Vegetable Program

New York City (NYC) offers a Free Summer Meals Program from June 27 to August 29, 2025. All youth aged 18 and under can receive free meals; no ID or registration is required. Meals are available at select NYC public schools, parks, libraries, community centers, and food trucks located in Manhattan, Brooklyn, and the Bronx.

Vermont

On May 31, 2022, the Vermont Legislature passed a UFSM law, which began on July 1, 2022 (Vermont Legislature, 2022). Although Governor Phil Scott initially opposed the bill due to cost concerns, the legislature passed it without his signature. He later acknowledged the importance of supporting children's health and learning, especially after the disruptions caused by the pandemic (D'Auria, 2023). This law was based on data from the Vermont Agency of Education showing that 38% of students needed free meals during the 2019–2020 school year. Additional research from the National Food Access and COVID Research project found that, during the first year of the pandemic, nearly one-third of Vermont's population experienced hunger. Families with children were five times more likely to face food insecurity, and these levels remained high even after pandemic restrictions were lifted (Vermont Legislature, 2022).

Vermont's Act 64 establishes a permanent universal school meals program, requiring public schools to provide free meals to all students. If schools implement the CEP or Provision 2, the state provides funding to support the program. This funding also extends to state-approved independent schools that offer universal meals through CEP or Provision 2 and serve publicly funded students (State of Vermont Agency of Education, n.d.). The state covers the cost difference between the federal reimbursement for "Paid" and "Free" meal categories. Under this law, all students in public schools and in participating private or charter schools receive free breakfast and lunch. Schools that are not operating under a non-pricing program (like CEP or Provision 2) must still encourage families to submit applications for free and reduced-price meals. Schools must designate a Determining Official to review and approve applications. Schools must also conduct verification of a sample of approved applications each year (State of Vermont Agency of Education, n.d.). Meals are provided through the federal National School Lunch Act and the Child Nutrition Act, making them available free of charge to all students regardless of their income.

A study by the University of Vermont and Hunger Free Vermont reported that universal school meals helped create a more positive school environment by reducing visible financial differences and improving students' ability to learn (Vermont Legislature, 2022). For AY 2023–2024, Vermont allocated $29 million from its education fund to support the program. Public schools are required to participate in federal aid programs to maximize federal reimbursements. The state is also exploring long-term funding solutions to sustain the program in the future. In addition to universal school meals, Vermont offers the Summer EBT (SUN Bucks) program. This provides $120 per eligible child to help families buy groceries during the summer months when school meals are unavailable (Vermont Legislature, 2022). Table 2.2 provides a comparative analysis of free school lunch programs in nine states in the United States.

TABLE 2.2 Comparative Analysis of Free School Lunch Programs in Nine States in the United States

State	*Program Name/ Legislation*	*Participation*	*Eligibility and Enrollment*	*Funding Source*	*Additional Meal Programs*	*Comments*
California	Healthy School Meals for All	All schools are required to participate	All students regardless of income; automatic enrollment in SUN Bucks	State supplements federal funding	Summer EBT (SUN Bucks) included	
Colorado	Universal Free Meals (Various Programs)	Only school districts can opt into Free School Meals	All students	State supplements federal funding and taxes on the wealthiest tax bracket ($300,000 and higher)	Summer EBT available, SNAP, Double Up Food Bucks, The Emergency Food Assistance Program (TEFAP)	Progressive taxation of the wealthiest tax bracket to fund the program
Maine	Healthy School Meals for All	Encouraging all schools to participate	All students, SUN Bucks automatic enrollment for eligible families	State supplements federal funding		Emphasis on local food sourcing (farm and seafood for schools' free meals)
Massachusetts	Universal Free School Meals	Not specified	All public school students	Funding by a new 4% tax on the state's wealthiest residents		Multilingual outreach
Michigan	Universal Free School Meals	Not specified	All students	State supplements federal funding		

(*Continued*)

TABLE 2.2 (Continued)

State	*Program Name/ Legislation*	*Participation*	*Eligibility and Enrollment*	*Funding Source*	*Additional Meal Programs*	*Comments*
Minnesota	Free School Meals for Kids Program (HF 5)	All schools are required to participate	All students in schools under NSLP/SBP; CEP participation is required for some schools	State reimburses costs not covered by federal funds	Meals for all; eliminates stigma; CEP participation required for some	
New Mexico	Healthy Universal School Meals Act (SB 4)	Covers public, charter, tribal, and private schools	All students in participating schools	State supplements federal funding	Summer Food Service Program (SFSP)	Encourages schools to participate in the New Mexico Grown Grant Program, which supports the use of locally grown foods
New York	Free School Meals Statewide (Governor Initiative)	Not specified	All 2.7 million public school students	State supplements federal funding and expands CEP	Summer meals programs	No ID required for meals served in public spaces during summer
Vermont	Universal Meals (Act 64)	Optional for public schools. Private schools can receive funds if they offer Universal Meals	All public school students, automatic SUN Bucks for qualifying families	State covers non-reimbursed costs	Summer meals programs	Schools must designate officials to review applications and conduct annual verifications for schools not operating under universal meal provisions

Source: Created by authors.

Challenges of universal free school meal programs

Implementing UFSM programs presents a range of fiscal and operational challenges. Providing two nutritious meals per day to all students requires strategic coordination across federal, state, and local funding sources. One of the most significant barriers is the funding gap; federal reimbursements often do not cover the full cost of meal production, leaving states and school districts responsible for the remaining expenses. Without sufficient state-level support, program sustainability and meal quality can be compromised.

Disparities in funding and infrastructure across school districts also affect the UFSM program. Some schools may lack adequate kitchen facilities, food preparation equipment, or trained food service staff to meet increased demand. Expanding meal services at scale often requires substantial investments in infrastructure, staffing, and supply chain logistics. Moreover, while universal access promotes equity and reduces stigma, its successful implementation must also address the diverse needs of students. This includes accommodating dietary restrictions, cultural food preferences, and ensuring the overall nutritional value and appeal of meals. Failure to meet these expectations can reduce student participation and diminish the program's intended benefits.

Conclusions

Free school breakfast and lunch in the states of Colorado, California, Maine, Massachusetts, Michigan, Minnesota, New Mexico, New York, and Vermont have successfully been mandated into permanent legislation. The new laws demonstrate a commitment to addressing food insecurity throughout their communities while erasing the stigma of government-assisted meals in the lunchroom. Universal free meal school programs represent a policy tool for advancing child well-being, supporting academic success, and strengthening family stability. Although financial and logistical challenges remain, the evidence from existing programs indicates that the societal and educational benefits outweigh the costs.

States have adopted varying financial strategies to fund their school breakfast and lunch programs. The federal government already provides financial support through the NSLP, which covers free or subsidized meals for lower-income and migrant students (U.S. Department of Agriculture, 2024). States such as Maine, Michigan, Minnesota, and Vermont have designed their programs to maximize these federal funds before contributing state resources (Cummings, 2023; D'Auria, 2023; Maine Legislature, 2022; Michigan Department of Education, 2023). Still, these states have committed significant state funding to cover the cost of meals for students who do not qualify under NSLP, reflecting a strong legislative focus on ensuring that no child goes hungry during the school day.

California, New Mexico, and Massachusetts fund their universal meal programs through general state funds (California Legislature, 2021; Grisham, 2023). Among them, Massachusetts is currently the only state with permanent, dedicated state funding for its program (Healey & Driscoll, 2024). Colorado stands out as the only state to finance universal school meals through a progressive tax on its highest income bracket (Colorado General Assembly, 2022). Most states have avoided progressive taxation and instead rely first on federal funding before supplementing state funds for universal free meal programs.

California, New Mexico, and Massachusetts have prioritized integrating homegrown foods into their school meal programs. These states emphasize serving nutritious, minimally processed meals over fried and heavily processed options. Colorado utilizes federal reimbursements for school lunches, and the state uses additional tax revenue to enhance meal quality, offering healthier options, including locally grown fruits and vegetables and other nutritious food groups (Food Research & Action Center, 2024).

Beyond meal provision, only California and New Mexico include funding for kitchen infrastructure and staffing improvements. California is investing in hiring additional food service workers to ensure the smooth operation of the program and to allow students ample time to eat (California Legislature, 2021). New Mexico, on the other hand, is prioritizing kitchen upgrades to bring infrastructure up to code and enhance meal preparation capacity (Grisham, 2023). Notably, New Mexico is also the only state that has extended universal meal access into the summer months through its SFSP, which ensures continued support for children during school breaks (Sclafani, n.d.).

Discussion questions

1. How do universal free meals school programs address issues of equity and social stigma in school environments?
2. What are the short- and long-term fiscal challenges states face when implementing universal free meals school programs? How should states plan for the sustainability of such programs?
3. Should other states implement income taxation of the wealthiest tax bracket to fund the program, as Colorado did?
4. What are the short-term and long-term social implications of eliminating means-tested school lunch eligibility?
5. What outcomes would you use to evaluate the effectiveness of a universal free meals school program in your state or school district?
6. What logistical challenges might school districts encounter when expanding meal service to all students? How can administrators plan for infrastructure, staffing, and supply chain needs?

7 Can the successes from states like California, Colorado, and Massachusetts be replicated elsewhere?
8 What political, economic, or cultural conditions might affect the scalability of these universal free school lunch programs in other states?

References

Anderson, M. L., Gallagher, J., & Ritchie, E. R. (2017). School lunch quality and academic performance (w23218). *National Bureau of Economic Research.* https://doi.org/10.3386/w23218

Ballotpedia. (2022). Colorado Proposition FF, reduce income tax deduction amounts to fund school meals program measure (2022). https://ballotpedia.org/Colorado_Proposition_FF,_Reduce_Income_Tax_Deduction_Amounts_to_Fund_School_Meals_Program_Measure_(2022)

California Legislature. (2021a). *Assembly Bill No. 130, Chapter 44.* An act to add Section 49501.5 to the Education Code, relating to school meals. *California State Legislature.* https://legiscan.com/CA/text/AB130/id/2424179

California Legislature. (2021b). Assembly Bill No. 558, Chapter 558. An act to add Section 49501.5 to the Education Code, relating to school meals. *California State Legislature.* https://leginfo.legislature.ca.gov/faces/billStatusClient.xhtml?bill_id=202120220AB558

Campaign, C. (2022, May 6). Healthy school meals for all coalition shifts strategy with a new bill. *Colorado Children's Campaign.* https://www.coloradokids.org/healthy-school-meals-for-all-coalition-shifts-strategy-with-a-new-bill/

Colorado Department of Human Service. (n.d.). Food assistance. https://cdhs.colorado.gov/food-assistance

Colorado General Assembly. (2022). *House Bill 22–1414: Concerning the Creation of a Healthy School Meals for All Program.* Colorado General Assembly. https://leg.colorado.gov/bills/hb22-1414

Critch, J. N. (2020). School nutrition: Support for providing healthy food and beverage choices in schools. *Paediatrics & Child Health, 25*(1), 33–38. https://doi.org/10.1093/pch/pxz102

Cummings, C. (2023, February 9). Minnesota House passes "universal" school meals, providing free breakfast, lunch to students. *CBS News.* https://www.cbsnews.com/minnesota/news/minnesota-house-to-approve-universal-school-meals/

D'Auria, P. (2023, June 14). *Free school meals bill becomes law without governor's signature.* VTDigger 15. https://vtdigger.org/2023/06/14/free-school-meals-bill-becomes-law-without-governors-signature/

Food Research & Action Center. (2024). *Raise your hand for healthy school meals for all.* https://frac.org/healthy-school-meals-for-all

Frisvold, D. E. (2015). Nutrition and cognitive achievement: An evaluation of the School Breakfast Program. *Journal of Public Economics, 124*, 91–104. https://doi.org/10.1016/j.jpubeco.2014.12.003

Grisham, M. L. (2023, March 28). Governor signs Senate Bill 4, making universal free and healthy school meals the law of the land. *Office of the Governor.* https://www.governor.state.nm.us/2023/03/28/governor-signs-senate-bill-4-making-universal-free-and-healthy-school-meals-the-law-of-the-land/

Gutierrez, E, Reeves, M., Meltzer, A., Nelson, N., & Terrones, F. (2024). healthy school meals for all in Colorado. *Center on Education Data and Policy*. https://www.urban.org/sites/default/files/2024-12/Healthy_School_Meals_for_All_in_Colorado.pdf

Healey, M., & Driscoll, K. (2023, September 14). *Governor Healey joins legislative leadership to celebrate permanent universal free school meals*. Mass.gov. https://www.mass.gov/news/governor-healey-joins-legislative-leadership-to-celebrate-permanent-universal-free-school-meals

Imberman, S. A., & Kugler, A. D. (2014). The effect of providing breakfast in class on student performance. *Journal of Policy Analysis and Management*, *33*(3), 669–699. https://doi.org/10.1002/pam.21759

Kirksey, J. J., & Gottfried, M. A. (2021). The effect of serving "Breakfast After-the-Bell" meals on school absenteeism: Comparing results from regression discontinuity designs. *Educational Evaluation and Policy Analysis*, *43*(2), 305–328. https://doi.org/10.3102/0162373721991572

Maine Legislature. (2022). *LD 1679, SP 540, Chapter 719, Public Laws of 2021*. https://www.mainelegislature.org/legis/bills/display_ps.asp?ld=1679&PID=1456&snum=130

Massachusetts Legislature. (2022). *Bill S.* 314*: An Act to promote student nutrition*. https://malegislature.gov/Bills/192/S314

Massachusetts Department of Elementary and Secondary Education. (2024). Universal Free School Meals: FY24 Legislative Report. https://www.mass.gov/doc/universal-free-school-mealsfinal070124/download

Michigan Department of Education. (2023, November 1). 1.3 million Michigan students can receive free school breakfast and lunch. DOE – Department of Education. https://www.michigan.gov/mde/news-and-information/press-releases/2023/11/01/michigan-students-can-receive-free-school-breakfast-and-lunch

Michigan Department of Education. (2023, August 4). *Michigan children win healthy school meals for all*. DOE – Department of Education. https://www.michigan.gov/mde/news-and-information/press-releases/2023/08/04/michigan-children-win-with-healthy-school-meals-for-all

Michigan Department of Education. (2024, March 7). *100 percent increase in public school buildings serving meals due to Michigan School Meals Program*. DOE – Department of Education. https://www.michigan.gov/mde/news-and-information/press-releases/2024/03/07/100-percent-increase-in-public-school-buildings-serving-meals-due-to-michigan-school-meals-program

Michigan Legislature. (2023). *SB 500: Healthy School Meals for All*. https://legiscan.com/MI/text/SB0500/2023

Minnesota Department of Education. (2023). *Free school meals for kids program*. DOE – Department of Education. https://education.mn.gov/MDE/dse/FNS/SNP/free/

Minnesota Department of Education. (2024). Minnesota Free School Meals: First Year Preliminary Summary. https://education.mn.gov/mdeprod/idcplg?IdcService=GET_FILE&dDocName=PROD085180&RevisionSelectionMethod=latestReleased&Rendition=primary

Minnesota Department of Education. (n.d.). Free school meals for kids program. https://education.mn.gov/MDE/dse/FNS/SNP/free/

Minnesota Legislature. (2023). *HF 5 – Free school lunch and breakfast for all students*. Office of the Revisor of Statutes. https://www.revisor.mn.gov/bills/bill.php?b=House&f=HF5&ssn=0&y=2023

New Mexico Legislature. (2023). *SB 4 – Free school meals.* 2023 Regular Session. https://www.nmlegis.gov/Legislation/Legislation?Chamber=S&LegType=B&LegNo=4&year=23

Peterson, C. (2009). A comparative cost analysis of commodity foods from the U.S. Department of Agriculture in the National School Lunch Program. *Journal of Policy Analysis and Management, 28*(4), 626–654. https://www.jstor.org/stable/20685145

Peterson, C. (2011). A rotten deal for schools? An assessment of states' success with the National School Lunch Program's in-kind food benefit. *Food Policy, 36*(5), 588–596. https://doi.org/10.1016/j.foodpol.2011.07.006

Project Bread. (N.d.). *Serving Massachusetts school meals.* https://projectbread.org/school-meals-program

Roy, P. G., & Stretch, T. (2018). Position of the Academy of Nutrition and Dietetics: Child and adolescent federally funded nutrition assistance programs. *Journal of the Academy of Nutrition and Dietetics, 118*(8), 1490–1497. https://doi.org/10.1016/j.jand.2018.06.009

School Meals for All. (2024). *Final 2022–2023 State Budget*. Benefits of School Meals for All in California. https://www.schoolmealsforall.org/news/ca2022budget/

Schwartz, A. E., & Rothbart, M. W. (2020). Let them eat lunch: The impact of universal free meals on student performance. *Journal of Policy Analysis and Management, 39*(2), 376–410. https://doi.org/10.1002/pam.22175

Sclafani, J. (n.d.). *Over 600 sites offering meals for New Mexico youth this summer.* New Mexico Early Childhood Education and Care Department. https://www.nmececd.org/2024/05/31/over-600-sites-offering-free-meals-for-new-mexico-youth-this-summer/#:~:text=Michelle%20Lujan%20Grisham%20signing%20the,meals%20during%20the%20academic%20year

Shockman, E. (2023, December 20). Minnesota's push for free school meals proves popular, but costs are climbing. *MPR News*. https://www.mprnews.org/story/2023/12/20/minnesotas-push-for-free-school-meals-proves-popular-but-costs-are-climbing

State of Maine Department of Education. (n.d.). Child Nutrition. https://www.maine.gov/doe/schools/nutrition

State of Maine Department of Health and Human Services. (n.d.). SUN Bucks https://www1.maine.gov/dhhs/ofi/programs-services/food-supplement/sun_bucks

The State of New York Education Department. (2025). New York State Universal Free Meals. https://www.cn.nysed.gov/content/new-york-state-universal-free-meals

State of Vermont Agency of Education. (n.d.). Free and Reduced Meals. https://education.vermont.gov/student-support/nutrition/school-meals/free-and-reduced-meals

Teboe, C. (2021, July 13). *New law will require Maine public schools to provide free meals to all students.* News Center – Maine. https://www.newscentermaine.com/article/news/local/as-seen-on-tv/new-law-requires-free-school-meals-for-all-maine-public-students-regardless-of-family-income-starting-2022-2023/97-4e822474-cd25-4641-958e-c0c8599971c3

Terry-McElrath, Y. M., O'Malley, P. M., & Johnston, L. D. (2016). Foods and beverages offered in US public secondary schools through the National School Lunch Program from 2011–2013: Early evidence of improved nutrition and reduced disparities. *Preventive Medicine*, *78*, 52–58. https://doi.org/10.1016/j.ypmed.2015.07.010

Turner, L., Ohri-Vachaspati, P., Powell, L., & Chaloupka, F. J. (2016). Improvements and disparities in types of foods and milk beverages offered in elementary school lunches, 2006–2007 to 2013–2014. *Preventing Chronic Disease*, *13*. https://doi.org/10.5888/pcd13.150395

United States Department of Agriculture. (2024, June 11). *National School Lunch Program Factsheet.* USDA – Food and Nutrition Service. https://www.fns.usda.gov/nslp/factsheet

Vermont Legislature. (2022). S.100: An act relating to universal school meals. *Vermont General Assembly*. https://legislature.vermont.gov/bill/status/2022/S.100

Wharton, C. M., Long, M., & Schwartz, M. B. (2008). Changing nutrition standards in schools: The emerging impact on school revenue. *The Journal of School Health*, *78*(5), 245–251. https://doi.org/10.1111/j.1746-1561.2008.00296.x

Zuercher, M. D., Cohen, J. F. W., Hecht, C. E., Hecht, K., Ritchie, L. D., & Gosliner, W. (2022). Providing school meals to all students free of charge during the COVID-19 pandemic and beyond: Challenges and benefits reported by school foodservice professionals in California. *Nutrients*, *14*(18), 3855. https://doi.org/10.3390/nu14183855

CASE STUDY 6

Fiscal stress and closing schools in Jefferson County, Colorado (Public hearing simulation)

Abstract

This case study presents a public hearing simulation focused on school closures and reorganization decisions in the Jefferson County Public Schools (Jeffco) district in Colorado. Between AY 2021–2022 and AY 2023–2024, the Board of Education closed 19 elementary schools due to declining enrollment and significant fiscal pressures. As of 2024, the district enrolls approximately 69,000 students but maintains facilities with a capacity for 96,000, contributing to operational inefficiencies during a fiscal crisis ($543.3 million deficit for FY 2024). The Board of Education is now considering restructuring options for middle and high schools in the upcoming academic year. This simulation engages students in a public hearing process, where students assume roles of district administrators, Board of Education committee members, district accountability representatives, state accountability officials, parents, teachers, and nonprofit community advocates. Participants analyze demographic, financial, and educational data, articulate stakeholder concerns, and develop alternative policy proposals. The simulation concludes with a formal presentation of recommendations and a committee vote on a district reorganization plan. Through this exercise, students practice collaborative decision-making, conflict negotiation, stakeholder communication, and applied fiscal problem-solving in a politically contested educational environment.

Topics

Expenditures; School District; Fiscal Stress; Deficit; Closing School

Background

In Jefferson County, Colorado, school-age population peaked in 2001. The highest decline in school-age population happened between 2020 and 2025. As a result of this decline in enrollment, the Jefferson County Public Schools district (Jeffco) has a capacity to educate 96,000 students, which significantly exceeds current enrollment of 69,000 students.

Such sharp decrease in enrollment was one of the contributing factors to a budget deficit that Jeffco experiences. In FY 2023, the budget deficit was $566 million. On June 30, 2024, the deficit was $543.3 million (Jeffco Public Schools District, 2025). The district had a net pension liability of $1,373.6 million in FY 2023 and $1,661.4 million in FY 2024. The district's investments in capital assets for its governmental and business-type activities were $1.16 billion in FY 2023 and $1.17 billion in FY 2024 (net of accumulated depreciation) (Jeffco Public Schools District, 2025).

In FY 2024, general revenues totaled $963.0 million, accounting for 79% of total revenues. Program revenues (including charges for services, grants, and contributions) account for $252.1 million or 21% of total revenues. The total fund balance across all funds is $472.9, inclusive of funds earmarked to debt service, building construction, and other restricted uses. This fund balance is $13.5 million lower than the prior year, primarily due to capital investments and facilities spending. The total unassigned fund balance was $115.7 million, representing approximately 10% of total governmental expenditures of $1.18 billion in FY 2024.

Total outstanding long-term debt was $769,450,761 in FY 2024 (Jeffco Public Schools District, 2025, p. 25). The district maintains an Aa1 credit rating from Moody's and an AAA from Standard & Poor's for senior general obligation debt. State-imposed debt ceiling limits the general obligation debt the district may issue. At the end of the current FY, the legal debt limit was $2,700,606,942, and the legal debt margin (the difference between legal debt limit and outstanding debt) was $1,981,423,769.

In 2022, 49[1] of the district's elementary schools had student populations of under 250 pupils and/or a building utilization of 60% or less (Jeffco Board of Education, 2022). The Jeffco Board of Education made two emergency spring closure decisions: Allendale Elementary School in 2021 and Fitzmorris Elementary School in 2022. On April 7, 2022, the Jeffco Board of Education voted unanimously to direct Superintendent Tracy Dorland to prepare a multi-phase consolidation plan to address two decades of shifting demographics in Jefferson County, which have led to a declining school-age population and subsequent impacts on enrollment. (Jeffco Board of Education, 2022; Jefferson County School District R-1, 2023).

On August 25, 2022, the Jefferson County Public Schools staff made a recommendation to the Board of Education for school closures and consolidations for the 2023–2024 school year (Jeffco Board of Education, 2022). To decide on closing schools, Jeffco Public Schools staff used data from EnrollJeffco about enrollment and capacity of its facilities on August 15, 2022.

According to Jeffco Public School (2024a), the following criteria were used for Phase I elementary school consolidations:

- Had enrollment of less than 220 K-2, K-5, K-6 students OR
- Is using 45% or less of the capacity of its facility AND
- Had an elementary school less than 3.5 miles away that can serve the students from the closing school in the current articulation area.

On November 10, 2022, the Board of Education voted on the recommendation to close 16 elementary schools in the 2023–2024 school year and one school in the 2024–2025 school year.

The following schools were consolidated in the 2023–2024 school year:

- Emory Elementary School → Lasley Elementary School
- Emory Center Program → Rose Stein Elementary School
- Peck Elementary School → Secrest Elementary School
- Thomson Elementary School → Swanson Elementary School
- Peiffer Elementary School → Kendallvue Elementary School
- Colorow Elementary School → Powderhorn Elementary School
- Green Mountain Elementary School → Foothills Elementary School
- Green Mountain Center Program → Belmar Elementary School
- Molholm Elementary School → Lumberg Elementary School
- Glennon Heights Elementary School → Belmar School of Integrated Arts
- Glennon Center Program → Hutchinson Elementary School
- Parr Elementary School → Little Elementary School
- Sheridan Green Elementary School → Ryan Elementary School
- Witt Elementary School → Lukas Elementary School
- New Classical Academy at Vivian Elementary School → Stober Elementary School
- Vivian Center Program → Maple Grove Elementary School
- Wilmore-Davis Elementary School → Stevens Elementary School
- Kullerstrand Elementary School → Prospect Valley Elementary School
- Campbell Elementary School → Fremont Elementary School or Vanderhoof Elementary School or Early Childhood Education (ECE) Center 2023–2024.
- There is existing demand for ECE in the area and no current programs at Fremont or Vanderhoof Elementary Schools.
- Campbell Center Program → Vanderhoof Elementary School
- Campbell Elementary School became an ECE Center in 2023–2024, home to ten Preschool Classrooms.

The following schools were consolidated in the 2024–2025 school year:

- Bergen Meadow Elementary and Preschool K-2 were combined with the Bergen Valley Elementary School to become PK-5.

In November 2024, the Jefferson County Public Schools board approved the sales of three closed schools:

- Glennon Heights Elementary was transformed into a daycare center,
- Thomson Elementary was repurposed as a behavioral health center for autistic students, and
- Vivian Elementary was redeveloped into housing (Brundin, 2023; Jha, 2024).

The sales brought in $9 million for the school district.

These school closures affected nearly 2,500 students and 422 staff members (Jeffco Public Schools, 2024b). The Jeffco School District hired, trained, and managed 17 Enrollment Specialists to provide one-on-one support to the 2,464 impacted students. Overall, 84% of all students affected by the school closures during the 2022–2023 school year re-enrolled in another Jeffco school as of October 2023. As of October 2023, each designated welcoming school received an average of 87 impacted students, representing approximately 54% of all students impacted by reorganization. The schools received anywhere between 31% and 76% of students from the paired schools closed (Jefferson County School District R-1, 2023; Jefferson County School District, 2024b).

The Jeffco district partnered with the City of Edgewater and the Edgewater Collective to conduct a demographic study of the area affected by the closure. The survey results show that

> it was also difficult to separate the enrollment process from the ongoing grief some families felt as a result of their child's school closing. The family survey, while focused on learning about enrollment supports, included a significant number of comments on the process and decision to close schools. This indicates ongoing frustration and anger on the part of some families about the closure of their school.
>
> *(Jeffco Public Schools, 2024b, p. 6)*

Public hearing simulation

This case study is a public hearing simulation for a Board of Education committee in the Jefferson County Public Schools district. The Board of Education closed two elementary schools in AY 2021–2022, 16 elementary schools in AY

2023–2024, and one elementary school in the Jefferson County Public Schools (Jeffco) district. In 2024, the Jefferson County Public Schools district had around 69,000 students. The capacity of district-run schools is 96,000 students. The Jefferson County (Jeffco) district is in a fiscal crisis, with a $543.3 million deficit in FY 2024. After elementary school closures, the Board of Education of the Jefferson County School District are now making their mind about potential middle and high school closures for the next academic year. The public hearing exercise will discuss various opinions and proposals of the Board of Education of the Jefferson County School District. Students will assume the roles of (1) Jefferson County Public Schools staff; (2) members of the Board of Education of Jefferson County School District's Committee; (3) representative from Jeffco district advisory accountability committee; (4) representative from Accountability Clock at Colorado Department of Education; (5) parents of students from closing schools; (6) teachers from closing schools; and (7) representatives from non-for-profit organizations. During the simulation of public hearings, students will create and present their proposals to the Board of Education's committee in the Jefferson County Public Schools district. At the end of the simulation game, the committee will vote on the proposed reorganization plan for the school district configuration.

On May 11, 2023, the Board approved the Regional Opportunities for Thriving Schools Phase II Resolution (Jeffco Public School, 2024a). Phase II focused on thriving K-8 and middle schools to address declining enrollment in the district. The Jefferson County School District Board of Education conducts a public hearing when deciding a course of action for the Jeffco School District on what should be done moving forward after closing 19 elementary schools from 2021 to 2025.

Public hearings, comments, feedback, and testimony submitted before the hearing by parents, community members, local officials, and others are an essential part of the district board's review process (Colorado Department of Education, 2025). The Board of Education seeks input from families, school staff, and community members on accountability hearings. According to the Colorado Department of Education (2023), members of the public may comment on the school's current status and effectiveness and provide input regarding state board-directed actions on what should be done moving forward.

The Jefferson County School District Board of Education studies the affected schools and develops a proposal. The Board of Education posts notice of and convenes public hearings on the proposed plan to collect public comments about the future steps toward K-8, middle, and high schools. Before making these decisions, the District Board of Education meets with affected stakeholders in the Jefferson County School District. After hearings, the committee may make changes to its proposed plan. The committee may reconvene to come up with a new plan.

The head of the committee had meetings with Jefferson County Public Schools district leaders, the Jeffco District Advisory Accountability Committee, the Colorado Department of Education Accountability Clock, and the Jeffco Public Schools staff to discuss different proposals for solving the enrollment decrease, fiscal emergency shortfall, and future reorganization. After these meetings, several proposals were presented to the committee:

- Closing several middle and high schools
- Closing several middle schools, but not closing high schools
- Not closing any schools
- Introducing new taxes and service charges
- Ranking capital projects and improving budgeting and financial management in the school district.

Public hearing simulation roles and proposals

Roles:

- Jefferson County Public Schools leadership
- Members of the Board of Education of Jefferson County School District's Committee
- Representative from the Accountability Clock at the Colorado Department of Education
- Representative from the Jeffco district advisory accountability committee
- Parents of students from the closing schools
- Teachers from the closing schools
- Representatives from nonprofit organizations

The interest groups present the following proposals during Phase II to address low enrollment and budget deficit problem in the Jeffco School District:

- **Introducing the proposal by the Jeffco Board of Education**

  The Jeffco Board of Education identifies that the Jeffco School District is facing a $534 million deficit for the next FY. There is a citizen outcry, and strong disagreement among the Board of Education, parents, teachers, and not-for-profit organizations about which options to pursue. The Jefferson County School District Board of Education suggested that closing K-8 and middle schools is necessary due to unsustainable enrollment. The Board of Education recommended school boundary adjustments aligned with current and projected enrollment, choice patterns and trends, and transportation efficiency and reliability.

The Jeffco Board shared their concerns with the Colorado Department of Education and asked that the department present the council with a proposal that addresses all those considerations. More than 300 residents, teachers from closing schools, and representatives from nonprofit organizations attended that Jefferson County School District Board of Education committee meeting.

- **Introducing the proposal by Jefferson County Public Schools District leaders**

The proposal from this group is to close several middle and high schools based on data from the FCB dashboard. The FCB dashboard[2] was created in June 2022 following the request by the Board of Education. The dashboard includes, among other information, financial, staffing, and enrollment data, and information about buildings and educational programs. From January to April 2023, the dashboard was updated to include secondary, charter, option, and Alternative Education Campus schools. It is a permanent and ongoing source of data available to the public and initiates important community discussions around closing schools in phase II of Regional Opportunities for Thriving Schools.

Jeffco School District leaders understand that school consolidation is complex, difficult, and emotional work. Jeffco Public Schools District has previous experience closing elementary schools from 2022 to 2025.

In the 2023–2024 school year, Coal Creek Canyon K-8 School (Coal Creek K-8) was the lowest-enrolled district-managed Jeffco school, serving fewer than 85 students, which represented a 45% decline in enrollment since 2019. Arvada K-8 School used 60% of its intended capacity and served fewer than 560 students as the district's second-lowest-enrolled K-8 school (Jeffco Public School, 2024a). Enrollment was not projected to increase, and both schools were unsustainable.

The district decided to consolidate elementary schools, aware that its actions would have real implications for students, families, educators, staff, and communities. Once the decision to close schools was made, the district had to focus on "consolidating schools well." By that, the district meant supporting principals, ensuring educators had jobs, helping families enroll in a school that was a good fit for their students, and ensuring students had a positive end-of-school experience while creating connections to their new school. Jeffco hosted a central staffing event for impacted teachers, both probationary and non-probationary, to help match them with a mutually agreed-upon position for the 2023–2024 school year. One hundred forty-eight teachers participated. In total, 700 mini-conferences (interviews) were pre-scheduled and conducted by school teams for 305 open positions (Jeffco Public Schools, 2024b, p. 4). Educators with the longest tenure with the district received the first interview slots of the day.

The Jeffco district anticipated that coaching support would be needed for principals and contracted with an external vendor, Disruptive Partners, to design innovative professional learning, a hybrid group, and one-on-one coaching model to meet the unique needs of school leaders who felt a responsibility to be everything to everybody in their school community (Jefferson County School District R-1, 2023).

Based on this experience, the Jeffco staff established three goals during the closing of middle and high schools: (1) principals feel supported, (2) staff and teachers of closing schools understand career opportunities, and (3) impacted families continue to attend Jeffco schools next year. The district ensured that every student currently enrolled in a closing school, whether they lived in that school's boundary or choice-in, would have a place at the designated welcoming school. This was done in part by absorbing the closing school's boundary into the welcoming school's boundary.

All impacted students attending a closing school received a special level of priority in the choice lottery for all district-managed elementary schools. This special level of priority placed students impacted by closures one step above the "Students who reside in Jefferson County" priority level during Round 1 and Round 2 of the EnrollJeffco process.

- **Introducing the proposal by the Jeffco District Advisory Accountability Committee**

  Due to the dramatic enrollment drop that has led to fiscal stress for the school district, the Jeffco district advisory accountability committee suggested that Jefferson County Public Schools leadership needs to increase revenues and reduce expenditures while avoiding disruptions, especially those related to public safety and health.

  The committee proposes to introduce new taxes and service charges specifically earmarked for school funding in the Jeffco School District:

- Property Tax Increase
- Hotel and Lodging Tax for Education
- Transportation Impact Fee
- Extracurricular Activity Fees
- Facility Rental Fees (increasing or introducing fees for outside organizations using school property for events)
- Parking Fees (implementing or increasing parking permit fees for students and staff who park on school property).

  The committee proposes a long-term solution to fiscal problems, which could be ranking and prioritizing capital projects and improving the maintenance of the capital infrastructure of schools. They proposed the Board to conduct an inventory of equipment, buildings, and facilities of schools. They suggested assessing the status of current capital projects with a focus on the safety of students and staff and starting to prioritize their capital projects. During fiscal stress, it is even more critical than ever for the district to effectively prioritize where limited capital funding should be spent, weighing the costs and benefits of competing capital projects and understanding the implications of deferred construction and maintenance.

The committee suggested to Jefferson County Public Schools leaders that capital investments should be ranked by (1) safety, health, regulatory, security, environmental requirements, or accreditation; (2) upgrading or replacement of major mechanical systems and utility infrastructure; (3) renovation or maintenance of existing school facilities; (4) construction, expansion, or acquiring facilities to meet school program needs; and (5) improving energy efficiency. During fiscal stress, the Jeffco district would then be able to target spending only to high-priority areas. They also suggested the district focuses on repair, renovation, and capital renewal, rather than new construction. However, this proposal may offer a long-term solution, but it would cost money to conduct the current inventory of assets, and it would not remedy the immediate fiscal issues.

- **Introducing the proposal by the Colorado Department of Education Accountability Clock**

The Colorado Department of Education Accountability Clock proposes closing several middle schools and providing a moratorium on considering high school consolidations or closures. This pathway might be selected due to the financial insolvency of the school district, low enrollment, staff turnover, or availability of better educational options for students. Colorado Department of Education staff will work with the district and schools to finalize and implement the plan of closing several middle schools. During the school closure process, there will be flexibility around the schools' incentive structure for staff to stay during the year prior to schools' closure. Incentives may include additional professional development, bonus pay, or other mechanisms to retain staff during school closure.

Jeffco's strategic plan, Jeffco Thrives 2025, named a priority area around "Our People, Our Strength." It will navigate school closures by ensuring employees have the career, emotional, and logistical support needed to make a smooth transition (Jeffco Public Schools, 2024b). Human Resources and Educators from Jeffco Public Schools' Employee Assistance Program Office will provide central workshops to support resume writing. Principals in closing schools will help their teachers with resume reviews, mock interviews, references, and other hiring supports.

Additionally, schools may choose to offer incentive options to students to stay at the school during the year preceding school closure (e.g., concurrent enrollment opportunities). While communication with students, parents, staff, and the surrounding community about the closure process is required, there is flexibility around how communication materials are specialized to fit the local context and different audiences (Colorado Department of Education, 2022).

- **Introducing the proposal from the teachers at the closing schools**

  The teachers recommend that the district place a moratorium on school closures and instead explore innovative strategies to budget improvements, enhancing fiscal responsibility, and preserving educational opportunities for all students. They emphasize that school closures disproportionately affect vulnerable student populations, disrupt educational continuity, and weaken community ties. Instead of closing schools, the district must explore strategic budgeting and financial management improvements to ensure long-term sustainability while maintaining quality education for all students.

  Rather than implementing school closures, the district must adopt a proactive approach to financial management. The teachers from closing schools have proposed the following strategies for improving budgeting and financial management: (1) conduct an independent audit of district finances to identify inefficiencies and reallocate resources more effectively; (2) repurpose under-enrolled schools for community services, adult education, vocational training, or ECE, rather than closing them; (3) explore partnerships with local businesses, grant opportunities, and state or federal funding to supplement district finances; and (4) engage educators, parents, and community members in budgetary decision-making to ensure that fiscal policies align with student needs and educational priorities.

- **Introducing the proposal by students' parents from closing schools**

  Parents of students affected by potential school closures have also proposed a moratorium on closing schools. School closures displace students, separate them from their teachers and peers, and hinder students' academic and social development. The parents emphasize the negative impact the decisions to close schools have on their communities. The parents expressed deep concern, stating that their neighborhood represents a unique and closely knit community that is currently facing fragmentation due to school closure plans. Schools are more than educational institutions; they provide essential services such as meal programs, healthcare, and after-school support. Closing schools destabilizes families and neighborhoods.

  The parents expressed their children's concerns about being separated from their friends if their school is shut down. The student's educational experience has already been marked by significant disruptions, having experienced instability due to the COVID-19 pandemic. Parents are urging the school district to implement policies prioritizing continuity in students' educational journeys, ensuring they can remain within established academic programs. Many also worried about students in welcoming schools and how they might be affected by large enrollment increases.

Parents expressed their opinion: "They are overloading, dilapidating, breaking down schools and revamping other schools. Just invest in the schools you have. Keep them open, keep your students where they want to learn, and let them flourish. Invest in them, help them be the future we all want to see" (Glassman, 2025).

- **Introducing the proposal by Representatives from not-for-profit organizations**

  Representatives from nonprofit organizations propose a moratorium on closing middle and high schools. Schools in historically marginalized communities are disproportionately affected by closures, exacerbating existing educational and socioeconomic disparities. The continuous rise in housing costs, coupled with a shortage of affordable housing, has forced many families to reconsider their ability to remain in their communities. As rents and home prices escalate, long-established Latino and African American residents are increasingly being displaced. Representatives from nonprofit organizations feared that closing schools in these areas would destabilize communities and disrupt the lives of children and families, affecting their safety and security. Meanwhile, new families are moving into these neighborhoods; however, due to school choice policies, they are not obligated to enroll their children in local schools. Consequently, institutions that have historically served students of color are experiencing significant declines in enrollment.

  Nonprofit representatives express concern that school closures will disproportionately impact students of color and immigrant families, who often rely on these institutions not only for education but also for essential services such as meal programs, dental care, and community support. The potential loss of these schools threatens to increase existing inequities, further marginalizing vulnerable populations within the education system. Nearly 90% of Jefferson Jr./Sr. High School students are Hispanic, compared with just under 29% of Wheat Ridge High School students. "A lot of us are minorities," a 12th-grade student said in a breakout session. "If they go to Wheat Ridge, for example, there's a very different demographic. If there's racism here, it can be solved quickly because we have each other. They're not going to get that priority. It's going to be like, 'Well, too bad, suck it up.' So I'm worried about those kids that will not get the community that we have" (Glassman, 2025).

The proposals

Due to the dramatic enrollment drop that has led to fiscal stress for the school district, the Board of Education must choose the Proposal or a combination of Proposals.

PROPOSAL 1: Closing several middle and high schools.

PROPOSAL 2: Closing several middle schools but not closing high schools.

PROPOSAL 3: Moratorium on middle and high schools closing.

PROPOSAL 4: Introduce new taxes and service charges. Implementing the ranking of capital projects.

PROPOSAL 5: Improving budgeting and financial management in the school district.

Simulation schedule

Part 1: the Jefferson County School District (30–40 minutes)

Students will be divided into groups and assigned a role to play (a school board member, parent, teacher, school administrator, etc.). Every group will use the FCB dashboard to assess if any K-8, middle, or high schools should be closed during Phase II, and if yes, which schools should these be: Jeffco middle, high, and multi-level schools at https://app.powerbi.com/view. Students should select two or three indicators from the FCB dashboard for evaluation. Based on their findings, each group should recommend which one of the five proposals or a combination of thereof to recommend to the Board. During their presentation to the Board in the next phase of the game, students should stick with their assigned position but be willing to compromise based on their group's findings.

Part 2: presentations to the Board of Education considerations (30 minutes)

In a role-play, each group will present their proposals to the Members of the Board of Education. In the role-play, stakeholders should raise concerns that the Members of the Board of Education have omitted or that might be too heavily prioritized. The students will have the opportunity to share their opinions on closing 17 elementary schools over two academic years (AY 2023/2024 and AY 2024/2025) and to present their opinion on the proposal to close middle and high schools. Every group is presenting its findings and recommendations for "Regional Opportunities for Thriving Schools Phase II" to all stakeholders for consideration. This section of the simulation game aims to help the Members of the Board of Education develop an actual proposal.

Part 3: proposal of the Board of Education (20 minutes)

The Board will be able to ask questions to any stakeholders for clarification. Board members now have to decide how to handle the enrollment drop and fiscal emergency situation in view of the political and public pressures. The Board members fear for the Jefferson school district's future and realize that this decision is extremely important to the residents and other stakeholders. The Board will vote and decide whether to approve various proposals. The Board can choose the combination of proposals.

Part 4: reflection and discussion (20 minutes)

No longer in role-plays – post-simulation reflections by the students!

Content-related discussion questions

1 What were the main reasons for voting for closing schools?
2 What are the arguments against the closing of school options? Are there equity concerns?
3 What negative and positive long-term implications of closing 17 elementary schools do you see for the Jefferson County, Colorado community? Will there be the same negative and positive long-term implications of closing middle and high schools for the Jefferson County, Colorado community?
4 How do you propose more revenues should be generated in the Jefferson County School District to save schools from closing? What are the options for increasing revenues, and what is the feasibility of each? Does Jefferson County or Colorado need the tax reforms?
5 What expenditures could the school reduce? Which services should be provided, and which services should be cut? Can any services be reduced, and if so, what will the effects of that reduction be?
6 What examples of extreme school closures have you heard from other municipalities or states? Do these examples provide any valuable suggestions for Jefferson County, Colorado?
7 Why do different stakeholders choose different priorities?

Notes

1 In 2025, 72 elementary schools were in the Jefferson County Public Schools district, Jeffco Public Schools (2025). About Jeffco Public Schools. Retrieved from https://www.jeffcopublicschools.org/about.
2 The meaning of FCB abbreviation is never spelled out in Jeffco documents or FCB dashboard.

References

Brundin, J. (2023). What's happening with all the closed school buildings around the state? *CPR News*. November, 13, 2023. https://www.cpr.org/2023/11/13/whats-happening-with-closed-school-buildings/

Colorado Department of Education. (2022). End-of-Clock pathway guidance - School closure. Retrieved from https://www.cde.state.co.us/accountability/pathways_guidance_school_closure

Colorado Department of Education. (2023). State Board Accountability Hearings. https://www.cde.state.co.us/accountability/stateboardaccountabilityactions

Colorado Department of Education. (2025). Accountability pathways. Retrieved from https://www.cde.state.co.us/accountability/accountability_clock

Glassman, S. (2025). 'Why Jefferson? Why Now?' Families fight to save school amid closure plans. *KUNC*. February 28, 2025. https://www.kunc.org/news/2025-02-28/why-jefferson-why-now-families-fight-to-save-school-amid-closure-plans

Jeffco Public Schools District. (2022). Resolution Board of Education Decision on District Recommendation Regional Opportunities for Thriving Schools. November 10, 2022.

Jefferson County School District R-1. (2023). Resolution Board of Education Decision on District Recommendation Regional Opportunities for Thriving Schools Phase II. May 11, 2023. Retrieved from https://www.jeffcopublicschools.org/about/initiatives/regional-opportunities-for-thriving-schools

Jeffco Public Schools. (2024a). Phase I Recommendation. Regional Opportunities for Thriving Schools Phase I. Retrieved from https://www.jeffcopublicschools.org/about/initiatives/regional-opportunities-for-thriving-schools

Jeffco Public Schools. (2024b). Regional Opportunities for Thriving Schools After-Action

Jeffco Public Schools District. (2025). FY 2023-2024 Annual Comprehensive Report (ACFR) https://www.jeffcopublicschools.org/services/financial-services/financial-transparency

Jha, R. (2024, November 14). Jeffco School Board approves sale of three closed schools. 9NEWS. https://www.9news.com/article/news/local/jeffco-schools-approves-sale-of-empty-schools/73-59921ab6-e71c-4d7e-9b95-9c8c5102f1ce

CASE STUDY 7

Budgeting for vacancies

Abstract

This case study discusses the situation when the Cuyahoga County, OH, executive, Armond Budish, made an ultimate decision to cut costs by eliminating most unfilled vacant positions in the 2022–2023 biennial budget and the backlash it received from the County Council. The case discusses the challenges of budgeting for vacancies and asks students to advocate for or against vacancy budgeting during a hypothetical county council meeting. Budget preparation is a complicated process that requires input from multiple players and incorporates various moving parts. Forecasting and estimates of agencies' revenues and expenses are fundamentals of budgeting. When forecasts and estimates are made, the budget is put together. To balance the budget, entities may try to look for new ways to raise additional funds and tackle operating inefficiencies. Additionally, decisions must be made about services or functions that need to be cut or kept balancing the budget. One of such decisions that are the central to this case study is how to budget for unfilled positions.

Topics

Budget Preparation; Balanced Budget; Vacancies; Expenditures

Background

Cuyahoga County (pronounced kai-uh-how-guh) is the second most populous county in Ohio located in the northeastern part of the state. The name "Cuyahoga" comes from Native American (Iroquoian) meaning "crooked river."

The "crooked" Cuyahoga River divides the county's largest city of Cleveland into east and west and feeds into Lake Erie. The city of Cleveland was established by Moses Cleaveland in 1796. From the end of the 19th century to the beginning of the 20th century, Cleveland was considered the richest city in the world with most wealth concentrated on the stretch of the city's Euclid Ave, known then as "Millionaires' Row," home to John D. Rockefeller, George Worthington, Marcus Hanna, and other ultra-rich individuals of that time. Now, 1,264,817 people reside in Cuyahoga County according to the 2020 Decennial census (U.S. Census Bureau, 2020). The county includes 38 cities, 19 villages, 2 townships, 36 school districts, 9 library systems, a port authority, a regional sewer district, and a park district (Cuyahoga County, n.d.). The county is headed by an executive and an 11-member council.

Budgeting for vacancies

Budget preparation is a complicated process that requires input from multiple players and incorporates various moving parts. Forecasting and estimates of agencies' revenues and expenses are fundamentals of budgeting. When forecasts and estimates are made, the budget is put together. To balance the budget, entities may try to look for new ways to raise additional funds and tackle operating

FIGURE 2.3 Wade Lagoon, Cleveland

Source: Picture provided by authors

inefficiencies. Additionally, decisions must be made about services or functions that need to be cut or kept balancing the budget. One of such decisions that is the central to this case study is how to budget for unfilled positions.

Since government entities mainly provide services rather than produce goods, personnel expenses (salaries, wages, benefits, and pensions) are by far the largest line-item in a government expenditure budget. Budgeting for vacancies is a common cost-containment strategy used by governments to manage fiscal pressure without immediately reducing services or eliminating funded programs. By assuming that a certain number of authorized positions will remain unfilled during a budget period, governments can lower projected personnel expenditures while preserving organizational flexibility. Vacancy savings often arise from normal turnover, hiring delays, recruitment challenges, or strategic pauses in filling positions.

While vacancy savings can be politically attractive because this approach avoids explicit layoffs or program cuts, it carries important trade-offs. Persistent or aggressive vacancy budgeting can increase workloads for remaining staff, weaken service delivery, and mask underlying structural imbalances in personnel costs. Over time, reliance on vacancy savings may erode institutional capacity and reduce an organization's ability to respond effectively to public needs, particularly in service-intensive areas such as public safety, health, and social services.

Budgeting for vacancies in Cuyahoga County

To budget revenues and expenses, the County uses the previous year as a baseline and decides what line-items to cut or increase from the previous base. While budgeting for the 2022–2023 biennium, the County found itself in a situation where it was spending as much as before COVID, but its general fund revenues have not bounced back to the pre-COVID level. To satisfy the State's balanced budget requirement, and not run a budget deficit, the administration had to make a hard decision choosing what to cut.

After giving the issue much thought and consideration, the county executive team made a choice to cut the unfilled vacancies, as these would likely result in lesser disruptions than cuts in actual expenses. As it is common with government units that provide services rather than produce goods, personnel is the highest ticketed line-item in the budget. Many people, including social workers, correction officers, and others, left the workforce during COVID, and the county had a hard time filling these vacancies. After numerous recruitment efforts that included information sessions throughout the County, a pay increase for correction officers, sheriff's deputies, detention officers, and others, introduction of tuition reimbursement program to local universities and a community college, and other initiatives, it became clear that it will not be possible to fill all the available positions. In fact, the County had been trying to fill many of these positions for years before COVID. COVID simply exacerbated the problem.

The idea of cutting vacant positions from every county department's budget was announced on October 14, 2021, at the Committee of the Whole Budget meeting by the Cuyahoga County executive, Armond Budish. During the delivery of the executive budget for legislative considerations, Mr Budish said:

> We are presenting a budget that's balanced without using ARPA dollars. But I should point out that to achieve balance we had to reduce expenditures. We chose not to make cuts of people or programs that would harm services to residents in the community. The reduced expenses result from choosing to not budget for vacancies that go unfilled year in and year out. This doesn't mean we are eliminating jobs or job positions. If any department or organization is able to hire personnel to fill allotted spots, or if a department or organization is in need of additional personnel, we will be happy to consider those requests… You may ask why not just budget vacancies in full, and if a department or organization does not spend their budget, the money will just come back to the general fund at the end of the year? Let me give you three answers. First, we don't want to set aside money for a year that most likely won't be spent. That doesn't work, especially in a tight budget. Second, is that this will eliminate audit findings for over appropriations. And third, this enhances Council oversight. In the past some departments and organizations have used unspent funds for unfilled vacancies as a sort of extra fund by which they could move money around within their budget usually with only a minimum Council oversight. That's not a wise fiscal policy and it's not what's contemplated in the Charter.
>
> *(Committee of the Whole Budget meeting, 2021b)*

The Cuyahoga County Budget Director, Walter Parfejewiec, and Fiscal Officer, Michael Chambers, backed the idea. They argued that, by not budgeting for vacancies, the central administration would have a better oversite, accountability, and higher flexibility with how money is spent. This would make the numbers truer. They also seconded Budish's statement that by not budgeting for vacancies the County can get better auditors' reports that consistently noted that the County budgets more for the personnel expenses that it actually spends. In fact, in 2020 alone, the County budgeted over $10 million more for personnel than it spent on a general fund side (Astolfi & Durbin, 2021; Committee of the Whole Budget meeting, 2021a;). The county executive further explained that, by not funding positions that are not expected to be filled, the County would not "lock up money in the budget,"

> If we have to put another $10 million into this budget to pay for people that are not going to be employees of the county, that means I have to give you a budget that cuts other things by $10 million… That might be contracts we can't sign….
>
> *(Committee of the Whole Budget meeting, 2021a)*

During the budget presentation, the County executive reassured the Council that the efforts to hire would not stop. The department heads were promised funds if any vacant positions were filled during the budget year. In addition, the 2022–2023 biennial budget included "$2.2 million for additional Social Workers for the Division of Children and Family Services," "$2.5 for additional Corrections Officers for the County Jail," and "$1.3 million for additional Public Defenders and support staff" (Cuyahoga County 2022–2023 Budget, p. 44).

The call to cut vacancies was not, however, taken easily by the Council and media (see for instance Astolfi & Durbin, 2021). Of the eleven councilmembers, only one, Dale Miller, the Chair of the Budgeting and Finance Committee, agreed with the proposition. Miller said that not budgeting for vacancies "enables us to produce a more accurate budget that's more close to what the actual spending is probably going to look like."

Other council members opposed the proposition mainly due to their beliefs that after eliminating vacant positions departments would have a much harder time hiring new personnel. They also argued that not budgeting for vacant positions is the wrong way to budget in the first place. Councilman Gallagher, the most outspoken opponent of the proposal, claimed that because the County is cutting a vacancy budget "to a bear bone" any future one-by-one departments' hiring requests would not be adequate to fill positions. The councilman called the idea "ridiculous" and said that by eliminating a budget for vacancies the County is "underbudgeting in the most delicate place [such as disability services, prisons, etc]" and it does so "just to look good." Councilwoman Baker was wondering if the money is not budgeted would they be available if an opportunity to hire arrives. Councilwoman Stephens added that when

> positions are removed from a budget then staff is told it's not in the budget and they don't try to hire additional staff… I am concerned that we have the right staffing numbers in health and human services and in the jail, where we have the most liability and the largest risk for loss of life or damage to someone else.

Councilman Schron was asking if departments are paying bonuses from the pot of money left from the unfilled positions, then by taking this money away "are we now going to be paying them below the market rate… or are these folks getting a windfall?" Councilman Tuma added:

> If I have three projects at home that I may or may not get to this year I budget for them. And if I don't do these projects, I have these funds and I decide what to do with them.

Councilwoman Simons simply concluded that "We are not comfortable with this… We've never done this before. If the goal is to achieve a balanced budget, then come back to take care of that in a different way" (Committee of the Whole Budget meeting, 2021a).

The deliberations about budgeting for vacancies and the proper staffing levels continued during several subsequent budget hearings and meetings with the department heads. The 2022–2023 biennial budget was passed on December 7, 2021. In the end, the administration and the council compromised to make cuts in unfilled positions for the larger, but not smaller, agencies. "We were able to reduce our budget by not budgeting for employees we knew we were not going to have" (A. Budish, former Cuyahoga County Executive, personal interview, September 4, 2024).

Simulation game

Naturally, departments and agencies are gaining and losing employees on a regular basis. For this assignment, students are divided into two teams, one siding with administration, and another one with the Council.

Discussion Questions for Post-simulation

Do you agree with the County administration that cutting vacancies would result in a truer accounting for personnel expenses, would prevent the administration from making cuts in real programs, and would enhance accountability and oversight?

Or are you more inclined to agree with the Council that the vacancies should still be budgeted for, as these represent the actual personnel needs in different areas (otherwise it is not a correct way to do budgets), and once a position is cut, it would be hard to reinstate?

By the end of the discussion, independently of what role you were assigned to play, explain your stance on the issue of budgeting for vacancies. What, from your perspective, is the correct way of budgeting for unfilled positions and why?

References

Astolfi, C., & Durbin, K. (2021, October 14). Cuyahoga County Council skeptical of Executive Budish's two-year budget plan. cleveland.com. https://www.cleveland.com/news/2021/10/cuyahoga-county-council-skeptical-of-executive-budishs-two-year-budget-plan.html

Cuyahoga County. (n.d.). 2022–2023 Biennial budget.https://cuyahogacounty.gov/fiscal-officer/departments/office-of-budget-and-management/

Cuyahoga County. (2021a, October 14). Committee of the Whole Budget meeting minutes. https://cuyahogacounty.gov/council/council-event-details/2021/10/14/council/committeeofthewholemeeting-10-14-_104414ce-fa50-44c2-ae60-91b2b16922d9

Cuyahoga County. (2021b, October 14). Statement of Armond Budish. Executive Testimony at the Committee of the Whole Budget meeting https://cuyahogacounty.gov/council/council-event-details/2021/10/14/council/committeeofthewholemeeting-10-14-_104414ce-fa50-44c2-ae60-91b2b16922d9

U.S. Census Bureau (2020). Cuyahoga County. https://www.census.gov/quickfacts/fact/table/cuyahogacountyohio/HEA775224

3

GOVERNMENT ACCOUNTING BASIS

Abstract

This chapter examines the principal accounting basis used in public finance and analyzes their implications for financial reporting, fiscal management, and accountability in the public sector. This chapter outlines cash-based accounting, which recognizes economic events when they are earned or incurred, and accrual accounting, which recognizes economic events when they are earned or incurred and provides a more comprehensive view of an entity's financial position. This chapter explores modified accrual accounting as a hybrid framework predominantly used in governmental fund reporting, balancing short-term fiscal accountability with recognition of incurred liabilities. By comparing these accounting bases, this chapter demonstrates how each serves distinct analytical and managerial purposes and underscores the importance of aligning the choice of accounting basis with the objectives of financial reporting, decision-making, and public accountability.

Accounting basis

The Government Accounting Standards Board (GASB) was established in 1984. It is a counterpart to the Financial Accounting Standards Board, founded in 1973, that sets standards for private-sector accounting organizations. GASB recognizes what is considered generally accepted accounting principles in public accounting and annually publishes a document, called Codification of Government Accounting and Financial Reporting Standards, that establishes government accounting standards. GASB Statement No. 34 "establishes

DOI: 10.4324/9781003606833-4

financial reporting standards for state and local governments, including states, cities, towns, villages, and special-purpose governments such as school districts and public utilities" and requires local governments to use the accrual basis for government-wide reporting and modified accrual for governmental fund reporting (GASB, 1999).

The accounting basis refers to the timing of recognition of revenues and expenditures in the financial statements. The three accounting bases are the accrual, modified accrual, and cash. The cash basis is the most straightforward. Under the cash basis, revenues are recognized when money is received, and expenses are recorded when payments are made. The emphasis of this approach is on liquidity. It shows how much cash flows into and out of an organization. Due to its simplicity, the cash basis is often employed by smaller organizations or nonprofits, and it can be particularly valuable for internal management reports that require a focus on cash availability. However, its most significant limitation is the failure to account for obligations and resources that exist but have not yet been realized in cash. A government that relies on cash accounting may appear solvent even when it has significant unpaid bills or unfunded liabilities.

By contrast, the accrual basis recognizes revenues when they are earned and expenses when they are incurred, regardless of when cash is paid or received. The accrual basis provides the most complete and accurate picture of an organization's financial position, since it includes receivables, payables, and other long-term obligations. The accrual basis is more complex to administer. This approach is, however, important for understanding the long-term financial health of an organization as it captures both current transactions and future commitments. Its drawback is that it obscures short-term liquidity, as a government may appear financially sound on an accrual basis while struggling to meet immediate cash demands.

Modified accrual accounting is a middle ground between cash and accrual basis, and it is particularly important in the public sector, used primarily in governmental fund reporting (such as the general fund or special revenue funds). Modified accrual recognizes revenues when they are both measurable and available to finance expenditures in the current period. Expenditures, by contrast, are generally recognized when liabilities are incurred, except for long-term items like debt service, which are recorded when due. The primary concern of modified accrual basis is whether resources are sufficient to cover obligations in the short term.

The choice of accounting basis

The choice of accounting basis depends on the purpose: the cash basis highlights liquidity, the accrual basis emphasizes long-term financial health, and the modified accrual balances both.

TABLE 3.1 Accounting Bases

Feature	*Cash Basis*	*Accrual Basis*	*Modified Accrual Basis*
Revenue recognition	When cash is received	When earned	When measurable and available
Expense recognition	When cash is paid	When incurred	When incurred, with exceptions (e.g., debt service)
Focus	Cash flows, liquidity	Overall financial position and long-term outlook	Budgetary compliance and short-term accountability
Use	Small organizations, some nonprofits	Private sector, government-wide statements	Governmental funds (e.g., general fund, special revenue funds)

Under the *Cash basis*, revenues and expenses are recorded or recognized when received or paid.

- Revenue recorded when cash is received
- Expenditure recorded when cash payment is completed, a check is written, or money is disbursed

Under the *Accrual basis*, revenues and expenses are recorded or recognized when they are earned or incurred, regardless of whether cash is received or paid.

- Revenue recorded when earned (inflow is recognized when it is known)
- Expenses recorded when liability incurred (when goods or services are used)

A *Modified Accrual basis* is a hybrid between the cash and accrual bases that combines elements of both (Table 3.1).

- Revenues are recorded when they are both measurable and available. Availability means that revenues are already received or will be collected in the short term and available to pay for current liabilities (resembles cash basis).
- Expenditure recorded when fund liability accrued (when a good or service is received) (resembles accrual basis).

Conclusions

The following Cuyahoga County ARPA case demonstrates that effective fiscal recovery depends not only on the availability of federal resources but also on the capacity of local governments to interpret, adapt, and strategically apply accounting bases and financial rules. It offers an example of how accounting frameworks and intergovernmental policy design can either constrain or enable public problem-solving during times of crisis. This Cuyahoga County's experience with ARPA funding demonstrates that fiscal recovery is not determined solely by economic conditions or the magnitude of intergovernmental aid but also by governments' ability to navigate complex regulatory environments, interpret financial rules strategically, and align accounting practices with policy objectives.

Reference

Governmental Accounting Standards Board. (1999). Statement No. 34: Basic financial statements - and management's discussion and analysis - for state and local governments (PDF). https://gasb.org/page/ShowPdf?path=GASBS+34.pdf&title=GASB%20STATEMENT%20NO.%2034,%20BASIC%20FINANCIAL%20STATEMENTS%E2%80%94AND%20MANAGEMENT%27S%20DISCUSSION%20AND%20ANALYSIS%E2%80%94FOR%20STATE%20AND%20LOCAL%20GOVERNMENTS

CASE STUDY 8

Accounting bases and budgeting during the COVID-19 pandemic: lessons from Cuyahoga County, OH

Abstract

This case study discusses budgeting strategies and practices in Cuyahoga County, OH, during the COVID-19 pandemic and the use of the federal ARPA funds. It describes how the county took advantage of the timing of receipts and expenses (on a modified accrual accounting basis) to maximize the receipts of ARPA funding and increase the flexibility of its use.

Topics

Accounting; Budget Execution; ARPA; Federal Grants; Accounting basis; Fiscal Strategy; Opioid Settlement; GASB

Background

Several federal stimulus bills were signed into law to provide relief from the COVID-19 pandemic to local governments. These bills offered trillions of dollars for paycheck assistance, support for public healthcare, new funding for new capital and broadband infrastructure, green energy, and numerous other causes:

1 The Coronavirus Aid, Relief, and Economic Security (CARES) Act (2020), signed into law on March 27, 2020, provided financial assistance not only to workers, their families, small businesses, and industries but also to the largest localities and states.

2 The American Rescue Plan Act (ARPA), the 1.9 trillion-dollar economic stimulus bill signed into law on March 11, 2021. ARPA provided $350 billion to state and local governments to deal with side effects of the pandemic (U.S. Treasury, 2021a).
3 The Infrastructure Investment and Jobs Act (IIJA), signed into law on November 15, 2021, provided $550 billion in new funds for the nation's physical infrastructure. It is the largest investment in roads, bridges, ports, water, and rail in years (CBC News, 2021). IIJA provided $110 billion for roads, bridges, and major projects, $39 billion for public transit, and $66 billion for railways. It also included $65 billion to expand broadband infrastructure and $55 billion for clear water investments.
4 Inflation Reduction Act signed into law on August 16, 2022, and offered $150 billion in clean energy investments, including investments made by local governments.

The funding made possible by the ARPA is the focal point in this case study. In May 2021, the U.S. Department of the Treasury launched the Coronavirus State and Local Fiscal Recovery Funds, established by the ARPA, which provided $350 billion in funding for eligible state, local, territorial, and Tribal governments to respond to the emergency caused by the COVID-19 pandemic and bring back jobs. $65.1 billion of these funds were earmarked for counties (U.S. Treasury, 2021a).

ARPA funding

The ARPA funding was allocated in two tranches, which could be used over a five-year period. On June 14, 2021, Cuyahoga County, OH, received the first advance payment of about $120 million.[1] The money, however, came with many restrictions, offering very little flexibility in how funds could be used. Specifically, the U.S. Treasury's Interim Final Rule identified the following five areas of uses of the Coronavirus State and Local Fiscal Recovery Funds:

- Support public health expenditures by funding COVID-19 mitigation efforts, medical expenses, behavioral healthcare, and certain public health and safety staff;
- Address negative economic impacts caused by the public health emergency, including economic harms to workers, households, small businesses, impacted industries, and the public sector;
- Replace lost public sector revenue, using this funding to provide government services to the extent of the reduction in revenue experienced due to the pandemic;
- Provide premium pay for essential workers, offering additional support to those who have borne and will bear the greatest health risks because of their service in critical infrastructure sectors; and

- Invest in water, sewer, and broadband infrastructure, making necessary investments to improve access to clean drinking water, to support vital wastewater and stormwater infrastructure, and to expand access to broadband internet.

(U.S. Treasury, 2021a, p. 3)

These limitations restricted the county's ability to spend funds in the first place and even more so to spend on high-priority projects and causes.

In the summer and fall of 2021, the Cuyahoga County executive, Armond Budish, and his team were hard at work assembling a list of ideas for what they considered might be the best use of ARPA funding. The next task was to slot these ideas into the approved categories. The defining factor is that money should have been spent on COVID-relief efforts only. Furthermore, the only broad, hence the most attractive category where funds could be used for other, more general purposes, was the revenue loss.

> Sections 602(c)(1)(C) and 603(c)(1)(C) of the Act allow recipients facing budget shortfalls to use payments from the Fiscal Recovery Funds to avoid cuts to government services and, thus, enable State, local, and Tribal governments to continue to provide valuable services and ensure that fiscal austerity measures do not hamper the broader economic recovery.

The Interim Final Rule further specified that

> For purposes of measuring revenue growth in the counterfactual trend, recipients may use a growth adjustment of either 4.1 percent per year or the recipient's average annual revenue growth over the three full fiscal years prior to the COVID-19 public health emergency, whichever is higher.
>
> *(U.S. Treasury, 2021b, p. 57)*

Technically, from the cash accounting basis, the County indeed lost about $40 million in 2020 compared to 2019 due to the COVID-19 pandemic, mainly through necessitated layoffs and furloughs (W. Parfejewiec, Director, Cuyahoga County Office of Budget and Management, personal interview, September 4, 2024). But there was one potential major obstacle. In October 2019, Cuyahoga was one of the two counties in Ohio (alongside Summit) that won a $260 million landmark opioid settlement with Big Pharma.[2] The three distributors – McKesson, Cardinal Health, and AmerisourceBergen – and several pharmaceutical companies were alleged to have engaged in aggressive marketing and sale of opioids while downplaying the risks of long-term use of these highly addictive medications, which contributed to the opioid pandemic. Altogether, Cuyahoga County received over $124 million in opioid settlement receipts; of this amount, about $22 million was received at the end of 2019, while over $95 million was received

FIGURE 3.1 Cleveland script sign—Edgewater Park.

Source: The picture is provided by the authors.

in early 2020. With this settlement, the County did not lose, but substantively gained revenues in 2020 compared to 2019, even though these revenues were a one-time payment and were earmarked to a specific cause – the opioid crisis (W. Parfejewiec, personal interview, September 4, 2024).

Final rule and ARPA funds

In early fall of 2021 in response to the Interim Final Rule from May 17, 2021, and frequently asked questions related to the use of ARPA funds on the U.S. Treasury website, updated in May and June of 2021, Armond Budish sent a seven-page letter with questions and comments related to the use of funds to Janet Yellen, the Secretary of the U.S. Department of Treasury. The document outlined 13 general areas that needed clarification of the county-specific situations. For example, the document asked on whether ARPA funds could be used to subsidize Cleveland Food Bank, a Diversion Center for people with mental and health addictions, the "Say Yes to Education" program for low-income families from Cleveland Metropolitan School District, and other programs supported by the county that for one reason or another did not quite fit the outlined categories of ARPA funds uses. The document also inquired about how to divide time for public health and safety employees between their regular responsibilities and emergency response related to the COVID-19 pandemic and asked other clarification questions (Budish, 2021). Point 5 in the letter inquired specifically about the treatment of the afore-mentioned one-time opioid settlement funding:

> 5. The Interim Final Rule defines the term "general revenue" to include "revenues collected by a recipient and generated from its underlying economy." And further states that revenues "would capture a range of different types of tax revenues, as well as other types of revenue that are available to support government services" (FR pg. 26799). Finally, the Rule states that the definition of Revenue "would exclude refunds and other correcting transactions" and "focuses on sources that are generated from economic activity that are available to fund government services..."
>
> *(FR pg. 26800)*
>
> At the beginning of 2020, our county received a large settlement of our opioid lawsuit against manufacturers and distributors. We want to clarify that the settlement should not be included in revenue for 2020, since that would substantively impact our calculation of revenue loss.
>
> Unlike tax revenues, the settlement funds are not "generated from [our] underlying economy." As soon as we received the settlement, our County Council adopted legislation requiring the funds to be segregated and used only for addressing the opioid crisis. Accordingly, the funds cannot be used to support general government services.
>
> The settlement dollars were based on recovery of prior costs incurred by the county resulting from the opioid crisis. The settlement is more like a one-time refund of prior costs, which is excluded from revenue, rather than regular tax income.
>
> Finally, the Rule states that payment under a settlement agreement should not factor into the calculation of revenue loss (FR pg. 26801). Therefore, the receipt of a settlement also should not factor into the calculation of the base revenue for determining revenue loss.
>
> Please confirm that the "general revenue" would not include our opioid settlement.
>
> *(Budish, 2021, p. 1)*

After several long months of waiting and uncertainty, the Treasury's response to the letter finally came in January of 2022. Page 246 of the Final Rule, a 437-page document, specified the following:

> In response to requests that the definition of general revenue excludes revenue from special assessments, settlements that make the recipient hold

> for past expenditures and one-time revenues, such as revenue from the sale of property, Treasury is maintaining its position in the Final rule that **such revenue is included in general revenue**.
>
> *(U.S. Treasury, 2022, p. 4404)*

The Treasury response provided in the Final Rule was very disappointing for Cuyahoga County, which would now have very little flexibility in spending the $120 million advance ARPA payment that arrived in June of the previous year. In the worst-case scenario, the County could potentially face a situation where it is unable to spend the entire amount because of all the restrictions accompanying the funds, would have to return the unspent balance, and would never receive the second payment. County Law, Finance, and other departments perused through hundreds of pages of the Final Rule, not having much hope, but still brainstorming and trying to find a way to claim additional ARPA funds, until its Executive noticed the following sentence on page 258 of the Final Rule:

> In calculating revenue loss, recipients may use data on a cash, accrual, or modified accrual basis provided that recipients are consistent with their choice of methodology throughout the covered period.
>
> *(U.S. Treasury, 2022, p. 4407)*

Well, the opioid settlement funds on an accrual basis were received by the County in 2019, on a cash basis in 2020.[3] If one proceeds with accrual basis, adds settlement money to the general revenue in 2019, accounts for a 4.1% annual growth rate instructed by the Final rule, and compares the number to 2020, "all of a sudden counting the opioid settlement money worked tremendously to our benefit" (A. Budish, personal interview, September 4, 2024). So much so that the Cuyahoga County ended up receiving $240 million in ARPA funding due to loss of general fund revenues, and, importantly, they had very high flexibility on how these funds could be used. As a result, in the next three years, the ARPA funds were spent on a variety of projects all over the County, including expansion of a food bank building, redesigning of a homeless shelter, construction and expansion of parks, trails, and playgrounds, vacant lots restoration, lead abatement, and numerous other causes.

Conclusions

This case study illustrates how accounting choices and statutory interpretation can significantly affect fiscal outcomes for local governments during periods of uncertainty and fiscal stress. Cuyahoga County's experience with ARPA funding demonstrates that fiscal recovery is not determined solely by economic conditions and the size of intergovernmental aid, but also by governments' ability to navigate complex regulatory environments, interpret financial rules strategically, and align accounting practices with policy objectives.

The success in obtaining funding was so high that other counties contacted Cuyahoga, asking for help with their own situations. For comparison, Cuyahoga County received the second-largest amount of ARPA funding in Ohio after Franklin County, the most populous county and the home to the state's capital, Columbus, which got $255.8 million. Besides Cuyahoga, the other counties in Northeast Ohio received anywhere between $2.9 million (Harrison County) and $105 million (Summit County) in ARPA funds (Ohio Poverty Law Center, n.d.).

Discussion questions

1 In your opinion, which accounting basis (cash, accrual, or modified accrual) should government entities use? Explain why. Should there be a uniform use of a certain government basis for different levels of government (federal, state, and local) and within different local governments (cities, counties, special districts, etc.)?
2 The Case study discussed a situation when the use of accrual versus cash accounting basis turned out very beneficial for the County. In what other situations can the use of one rather than the other accounting basis benefit (or hurt) a local government?
3 Should GASB be stricter with the requirements to use cash or the accrual basis? Explain why.
4 Do you agree with the Treasury decision that one-time payments should not have been counted toward an organization's general revenue? Explain your position. To give more reasoning to the Treasurer's decision, the Final Rule further specified:

> In response to requests that the definition of general revenue exclude revenue from special assessments, settlements that make the recipient whole for past expenditures, and one-time revenues such as revenue from the sale of property, Treasury is maintaining its position in the final rule that such revenue is included in general revenue. While such revenues may be less predictable than other sources of revenue (e.g., property taxes), these are not uncommon sources of revenue for recipients, and their inclusion provides a more complete view of the financial health of a recipient government and is consistent with the Census Bureau methodology. Treasury is also maintaining the exclusion of all payments from the federal government (including payments for services) from general

revenue in order to avoid substantial dilution of the definition of revenue, particularly in light of extraordinary fiscal support provided during the pandemic. Treasury is maintaining the inclusion of intergovernmental transfers other than from the federal government for the reasons provided in the Supplemental Information to the interim final rule; to do otherwise would be to significantly distort the revenue calculations for local governments that regularly receive revenue sharing payments, for example, from their state governments.

(U.S. Treasury, 2022, pp. 4407–4408)

Notes

1 All information in the case, unless cited otherwise, comes from the interview with the former Cuyahoga County executive Armond Budish and Budget Director for the County, Walter Parfejewiec, on September 4, 2024.
2 The total amount of opioid litigation was over $325 million if account for donated products and attorney fees (Principles, 2022).
3 As a sidenote, the County's internally operates on a cash basis, but for auditing and reporting they convert to accrual basis.

References

Budish, A. (2021). The letter to Janet Yellen, the Secretary of the US Department of Treasury. Re: Coronavirus State and Local Fiscal Recovery Funds. Unpublished Letter.

Budish, A., & Parfejewiec, W. (2024, September 4). Interview with former Cuyahoga County Executive Armond Budish and Budget Director Walter Parfejewiec [Personal interview].

CBC News. (2021). Biden signs $1.2 trillion infrastructure bill into law, hailing bipartisan breakthrough, 16 November. www.cbsnews.com/live-updates/infrastructure-bill-biden-signing-ceremony-white-house/

Ohio Poverty Law Center. (n.d.). Ohio ARPA Tracker.https://www.ohiopovertylawcenter.org/ohio-arpa-tracker

Principles, O. L. (2022, October 24). How did Cuyahoga and summit counties spend their litigation money? *Opioid Principles*. https://opioidprinciples.jhsph.edu/how-did-cuyahoga-and-summit-counties-spend-their-litigation-money/

U.S. Treasury. (2021a). FACT SHEET: The Coronavirus State and Local Fiscal Recovery Funds Will Deliver $350 Billion for State, Local, Territorial, and Tribal Governments to Respond to theCOVID-19 Emergency and Bring Back Jobs. https://home.treasury.gov/system/files/136/SLFRP-Fact-Sheet-FINAL1-508A.pdf

U.S. Treasury. (2021b). *Coronavirus state and local fiscal recovery funds*. Interim Final Rule.

U.S. Treasury. (2022, January 2022). Coronavirus state and local fiscal recovery funds. *Final Rule*. https://www.govinfo.gov/content/pkg/FR-2022-01-27/pdf/2022-00292.pdf

4

GREEN BUDGETING

Abstract

This chapter evaluates the evolution of the green budgeting concept across OECD countries, the European Union, low-income developing countries, and international organizations, including UNEP, UNDP, and the World Bank. This chapter introduces the European Union's Green Budgeting Reference Framework as a benchmark to assess coverage, methodology, governance, and transparency and demonstrates how green budgeting is becoming a vital component of modern public financial management and an important tool for supporting countries' commitments to sustainable development and the transition to low-carbon, climate-resilient economies. This chapter uses the European Union's Green Budgeting Reference Framework to evaluate the green budgeting practices in the United States.

Introduction

The Organization for Economic Cooperation and Development (OECD) defines green budgeting as environmentally responsive budgeting: "using the tools of budgetary policymaking to help achieve environmental goals. This includes evaluating the environmental impact of budgetary or fiscal policies and assessing their coherence towards the delivery of national and international commitments" (2018, p. 1). Green budgeting encompasses activities such as "climate/green tagging of budget lines, assessments of the social costs of carbon, cost-benefit analysis in environmental budget policy development, climate public expenditure and institutional reviews, and environment protection programs" (Vinogradova, 2022, p. 385).

DOI: 10.4324/9781003606833-5

Green budgeting relies on such fiscal policy instruments to help achieve climate and environmental objectives as budgetary/fiscal rules, budgetary classification systems, external audits, program or performance-based budgeting, and others. These fiscal policy instruments are important for developing green budget planning and implementation processes.

There are numerous benefits that come with the proper implementation of green budgeting policy. These include climate action transparency, higher awareness about climate spending, increased policy effectiveness in achieving national climate objectives, help in issuing and reporting on green government bonds, help with understanding how fiscal measures impact green objectives, and assistance to countries on meeting international commitments, among many others (Kumar, 2020; Mensah, 2019; OECD, 2020a, 2020b, World Commission on Environment and Development, 1987)). Green budgeting provides support to national governments in achieving their environmental goals by evaluating the environmental impacts of budgetary and fiscal policies and "assessing their coherence towards the delivery of national and international commitments contributing to informed, evidence-based debate and discussion on sustainable growth" (OECD, 2022, p. 2).

History of green budgeting development

Early efforts to "green," the budget cycle include Norway's introduction of an environmental profile for the public budget in 1989, and France's introduction of a mandatory environmental report attached to the annual budget around the same time. Other innovative green budgeting practices emerged in the late 2000s, mainly in developing economies facing serious climate change challenges, with the support and encouragement of development partners. During the One Planet Summit in Paris on December 12, 2017, the OECD launched the Paris Cooperation Initiative on Green Budgeting (OECD, 2022). Many countries are enhancing their commitments to meet the goals of the Paris Agreement by implementing green budgeting.

Over the past few years, integrating green budgeting principles into the budget cycle has gained increasing visibility based on innovative global collaboration platforms. The documents published by the UNEP, the OECD, and the World Bank used terms such as "green economy," "green finance," and "green budgeting" (OECD, 2020a, 2020b, 2020c, 2021a, 2021b; UNDP, 2019; UNEP, 2019; World Bank, 2021). In 2019, The Coalition of Finance Ministers for Climate Action was established to promote a collective commitment to transitioning toward low-carbon and resilient development (The Coalition of Finance Ministers for Climate Action, 2026). Finance ministers, fiscal and economic policymaker from more than 100 countries endorsed the six non-binding principles, which aim to "promote national climate action, in particular through fiscal policy and the use of public finances." Principle 4 "focuses on mainstreaming climate change into macroeconomic policy, fiscal planning, budgeting, public investment management, and public procurement practices." Some of the environmental impacts of fiscal policy are positive, including funding for environmental protection, R&D spending on green technologies, environmental regulation, the collection, monitoring, reporting of environmental data, and research on how to conserve the environment (European Union Commission, 2018; Petrie, 2019). Other environmental impacts of fiscal policies can be negative, such as those from fossil fuel and agriculture subsidies or subsidized water and electricity consumption. According to Petrie (2019), "between 2010 and 2015 direct government expenditure on subsidies for fossil fuels amounted to US$373–617 billion annually across 76 major economies" (p. 1). Many scholars have suggested that adequate environmental funding, strategic programmatic goals, and fiscal-based measures are crucial to environmental protection and the quality of their environmental programs (Hemming, 2013; Nyikos, 2013, 2022; Nyikos & Ermasova, 2021; Nyikos & Kondor, 2022a, 2022b; North, 1991).

Components of green budgeting

The OECD has identified several components of green budgeting that might be included in the annual budget documentation or a separate "Green Budget Statement." These components include:

- The anticipated environmental impacts of existing spending and revenue policies and any new policies or measures being introduced in the budget. These policies include direct spending, grants, loans, guarantees, and other contingent liabilities, taxes, resource royalties, other non-tax revenues, tax expenditures, and the fiscal opportunity cost of measures such as the non-auctioning of rights to pollute.
- An assessment of the use of the tax system to "price" environmental externalities (including carbon emissions).
- A cross-country comparison of selected environmental benchmarks, e.g., progress toward achieving biodiversity targets, the volume of spending on environmental protection, resource management, and fossil fuel tax subsidies, and estimates of the effective carbon price.

Fiscal risks related to climate change include the uncertainty of the costs associated with mitigating climate change and the global transition to a low-carbon economy, including the side effects on the country of measures adopted by other countries or international organizations, the potential costs of adaptation (both prevention and recovery) due to the increased frequency of natural disasters, projected sea-level rise and long-term changes in weather patterns, and the exposure of infrastructure assets to these factors (World Bank Group, 2014).

Macro-fiscal projections and models that consider climate and environmental impacts can inform the preparation of the fiscal strategy and the budget (e.g., Climate Report or Green Reform Project). Green priorities, both on the revenue and expenditure side, should be incorporated at this early stage of the budgeting process. Ex-post evaluation or monitoring of the impact and effectiveness of climate change policies by the government or the country's auditor general should assess whether impacts are consistent with the climate objectives that have been set out in national development plans.

Green budgeting elements can be built into program and performance budgeting processes. Performance audits, which explicitly seek to assess the link between policy outputs/results and the instruments covered by a given policy, may include climate or environmental aspects. Monitoring and reporting on climate-related income and expenditure is also an important part of an effective green budgeting system. Green expenditure tracking should be considered from planning to implementation. In the context of green revenues, it should be noted that fiscal environmental instruments can be either environmentally discouraging (taxes, emissions trading) or environmentally beneficial (tax breaks, subsidies). "Green" taxes include taxation on energy, transport, pollution, and resources. Energy taxes are taxes levied on energy products and electricity used for transport, such as petrol and diesel, and for other purposes, such as heating oil, natural gas, and coal.

The following evaluation criteria could be addressed when analyzing green budgeting:

Coverage:	What kind of environmental objectives of budgetary items and public sector entities are covered by the green budgeting process?
Methodology:	How to assess a contribution to green goals of budgetary policies?
Deliverables:	Where, how, and to whom should the green budgeting information be presented?
Governance:	Who is involved? Who does what? How are responsibilities allocated?
Transparency and accountability:	What ensures that the processes are transparent and open?

In terms of coverage, green budgeting should at least cover mitigation and adaptation at the basic level (level 1), while other objectives can be progressively added at the developed level (level 2) up to full coverage at the advanced level (level 3). The full coverage of budget lines also requires that both positive and negative (environmentally) expenditure and revenue items, as well as positive and negative (environmentally) tax expenditures, are considered. The green budgeting system should cover the public sector; at the basic level, state or central government and social security, at the developed level, local and regional government, and at the advanced level, state-owned enterprises and off-budget funds.

The federal green budgeting systems include a methodology for assessing the consistency of budgetary policies with long-term environmental objectives. At the basic level, it identifies only certain budgetary measures according to their positive or negative environmental impact. At a developed level, a form of green budget labeling, i.e., a methodology for identifying positive or negative items, should be introduced for all budget lines. At the advanced level, it should also include a methodology for implementing impact assessments of budgetary policies. The federal government should assess the greenness of the budget as accurately as possible, considering specific sub-headings of programs and/or measures on the expenditure side and specific revenue items on the revenue side.

With the deliverables of green budgeting, it is expected that the content and timing of the tasks to be carried out in relation to the green content will be detailed in legal or other documents. The presentation of green content can be done in several ways: in targeted documents (annual budget plan and budget implementation reports) as annexes to the annual budget plan and the final accounts at basic level and in related multiannual budget plans, the forecast of green content at the developed level, while at advanced level it is complemented by reports on the expenditure of public enterprises and off-budget funds.

From a governance perspective, the federal green budgeting system should ensure that the roles and responsibilities of the different actors are clearly described and the necessary human and administrative resources are available. Building on current practice, the management of the planning and implementation of the green budget should be entrusted to the authority responsible for coordinating the budget process. The practical solution could be a working group (at the basic level) or a permanent body within the institutional system (at the developed level). The coordinating authority should work with other government actors and non-governmental stakeholders. At an advanced level, a permanent central structure could be supported by a network of "green budget officers" in different departments.

In terms of transparency and accountability, all results should be made public, and the methodology should be evaluated by independent experts (basic level). At the developed level, an independent ex-post evaluation of performance is required, carried out by external experts, and subject to parliamentary scrutiny. The advanced system also includes regular publication of ex-post reviews.

Green budgeting in the United States

In 2021, the United States launched an unprecedented effort to mitigate climate change, reduce pollution, advance environmental justice, build resilience to intensifying climate impacts, protect the economy and financial systems from climate-related financial risks, and plan to deliver 40% of the benefits from federal investments in climate and clean energy to disadvantaged communities to build their economies. At the 2021 United Nations Climate Change Conference, the U.S. Methane Emissions Reduction Action Plan was launched to support the Global Methane Pledge to reduce the world's methane emission levels by 30% by 2030 compared to 2020 levels. To advance the global phasedown of hydrofluorocarbons, the president secured domestic action to reduce emissions of these super pollutants by 85% within 15 years.

According to the Office of Management and Budget (2022), the United States pledged to invest

> more than $65 billion through the Department of Energy to upgrade power infrastructure, facilitate the expansion of renewables and clean energy, and fund new programs to support the development, demonstration, and deployment of cutting-edge clean energy technologies to accelerate our transition to a zero-emission economy.
>
> *(p. 13)*

The green budgeting process involves both the public and private sectors and achieving the environmental goals will require a restructuring and reform of public policies and incentives. On March 21, 2022, the U.S. Securities and Exchange Commission proposed a rule to enhance and standardize climate-related disclosure for investors. The rule would require public issuers to disclose material climate risks, greenhouse gas (GHG) emissions, and, as applicable, emissions reduction targets and transition plans. The relevance of the topic is based on a need to assess and improve the current institutional environment and capacities both in countries that do not have a European Green Budgeting Reference Framework (GBRF) and in countries that already have some green budgeting tools in place compared to the proposed European Union (EU) GBRF (GBRF, 2021).

Since 1970, the United States has spent approximately $4.8 trillion (in 2017 dollars) to clean up surface water pollution and provide clean drinking water (Keiser & Shapiro., 2019). Since 2021, the U.S. government's strategic priorities and objectives relating to the environment and climate are clearly set out to improve green budgeting and fiscal planning. According to the Office of Management and Budget (2022), the U.S. Federal 2023 Budget set out several environmental objectives, priorities, and goals, such as:

1 Reduce GHG pollution 50 to 52% from 2005 levels by 2030.
2 Reduce the world's methane emissions by 30% from 2020 levels by 2030.
3 Reduce emissions of hydrofluorocarbons by 85% from 2020 to 2035.
4 Negotiate the world's first carbon-based arrangement on steel and aluminum trade with the EU.

5 Eliminate carbon pollution from the electricity sector by 2035.
6 50% electric vehicle sales share by 2030.

U.S. has pursued new climate-smart agriculture and forestry initiatives, protections for historical monuments and habitats, and the America the Beautiful initiative to conserve 30% of U.S. lands and waters by 2030 (Office of Management and Budget, 2022).

According to the Office of Management and Budget (2022), the Environmental Protection Agency (EPA) has committed to

> clean-up and clear the backlog of 49 previously unfunded Superfund sites and accelerate clean-up at dozens of other sites across the nation through the Bipartisan Infrastructure Law, the Administration also secured the largest investments ever in the Nation's water infrastructure, power grid, public transit, and resilience.
>
> *(p. 13)*

Climate and other environmental impacts were assessed in the preparation of the budget proposal. The following climate objectives were integrated into budgetary decision-making in the 2023 Federal Budget, including sustainable use of water and marine resources (Chesapeake Bay, Great Lakes, Upper Mississippi, Florida's Everglades, Columbia River, etc.), increased resilience of climate change, adaptation to climate change, and maintaining healthy ecosystems. These strategies and goals will help guide tax and spending decisions to support the achievement of national objectives. The 2023 Federal Budget included $1.7 billion for the Harbor Maintenance Trust Fund. The 2023 Federal Budget invested in programs and projects that would reduce the risk of damage from floods and storms and restore the aquatic ecosystems. The budget also invested in helping local communities identify and address their risks associated with climate change and improve the resilience of infrastructure to climate change.

Methodology of green budgeting in the United States

The United States has developed a methodology for assessing the consistency of budgetary policies with long-term environmental objectives. It identifies specific budgetary measures according to their positive or negative environmental impact. It uses a simplified labeling approach, classifying only certain appropriations by green target and identifying environmentally beneficial expenditures (Congressional Budget Office, 2020).

When Congress considers climate-related legislation, the Congressional Budget Office (CBO) provides estimates of the budgetary effects. The CBO provides information to the House and Senate that can be used to enforce budgetary rules or targets, mostly after a committee has approved legislation. "That information includes estimates of changes in mandatory spending, revenues, and the deficit in the current year and the subsequent ten-year period, as well as estimates of the amounts needed to fund modified or newly created discretionary programs" (Congressional Budget Office, 2020, p. 12). CBO calculates whether the bill is estimated to increase the budget deficit in any of the subsequent four decades.

Many legislative proposals have been made for federal and state programs to mitigate climate change or adapt to it. For example, the federal Pre-Disaster Mitigation Grant Program was created to reduce the adverse consequences of floods and other natural disasters. Some proposals involve increasing the size or scope of existing federal policies or programs, while others involve creating new ones. Such proposals may have important benefits beyond their effects on the budget (Congressional Budget Office, 2021). According to Congressional Budget Office (2021), CBO currently has no basis for estimating the extent to which the upfront costs of environmental policies "might lead to future budgetary savings, because many of the linkages between climate change and the federal budget require additional information and analysis" (p. 7).

Governance of green budgeting in the United States

The Council on Environmental Quality (CEQ) within the Executive Office of the President coordinates the federal government's efforts to improve, preserve, and protect America's public health and environment. CEQ was created in 1969 by the National Environmental Policy Act (NEPA). CEQ advises the president and develops policies on climate change, environmental justice, federal sustainability, public lands, oceans, and wildlife conservation, among other areas. CEQ is responsible for implementing NEPA, focusing particularly on addressing the environmental justice and climate change challenges the nation faces, and works to ensure that environmental reviews for infrastructure projects and federal actions are thorough, efficient, and reflect the input of the public and local communities (Council on Environmental Quality, 2022).

The U.S. Department of Health and Human Services (HHS) is a cabinet-level executive branch department of the U.S. federal government created to protect health of all Americans and provide essential human services (U.S. Environmental Protection Agency, 2020, 2021a, 2021b, 2022a, 2022b). Executive Order 14008, entitled Tackling the Climate Crisis at Home and Abroad (2021), directs federal agencies to develop programs, policies, and activities to address the disproportionate health, environmental, economic, and climate impacts on disadvantaged communities. In 2021, HHS released its Climate Adaptation and Resilience Plan to bolster the resilience of its operations and assets from the accelerating impacts of climate change. The plan identified five priority actions: (1) expand existing climate change-related public health and biomedical research activities; (2) improve responses to the climate crisis; (3) develop climate-resilient grant policies; (4) foster workplace optimization and effective space management for climate resilience; and (5) promote sustainable and climate-resilient operations. The HHS is committed to protecting the health and well-being of all Americans by integrating environmental justice and equity into its work to build a safer, healthier future. The agency has established an Office of Climate Change and Health Equity that serves as a coordinating body to make this goal a reality (U.S. Department of Health and Human Services, 2022).

The Office of Environmental Justice engages all Justice Department bureaus, components, and offices in the collective pursuit of environmental justice. On May 5, 2022, Associate Attorney General Vanita Gupta signed the Comprehensive Environmental Justice Enforcement Strategy. The strategy is grounded in four core principles, which direct attorneys to prioritize cases that will reduce public health and environmental harms to overburdened and underserved communities, make strategic use of all available tools to address environmental justice concerns, engage with impacted communities, and be transparent about environmental justice efforts, as well as the results of those efforts. The Justice Department advances environmental justice in underserved communities that have been historically marginalized and overburdened, including low-income communities, communities of color, and Tribal and Indigenous communities (Office of Environmental Justice, 2022).

For transparency and accountability of green budgeting in the United States, it is important that all results achieved in green budgeting are publicly available and respectively carry out ex-post reviews. According to Hart (2020), "Allocating resources to prioritize transparency and support effective operations to protect public trust in the agency must be a commitment for senior leaders in Congress, the White House, and EPA to achieve success" (p. 44).

Environmental Protection Agency

The creation of the EPA in 1970 ushered in tremendous reforms for environmental and public health protections in the United States. The EPA is responsible for protecting human health and the environment in the United States. Another agency, the U.S. Department of Agriculture's (USDA's) Natural Resources Conservation Service, an agency within the USDA, assists America's farmers, ranchers, and forest landowners in conserving the nation's soil, water, air, and other natural resources. All programs are voluntary and offer science-based solutions that benefit both the landowner and the environment.

In 2023, Federal Budget added $575,948,000 and 534 Full-Time Equivalents (FTEs) relative to 2022 levels to enhance EPA's capacity (Table 4.1).

TABLE 4.1 EPA's Budget Spending and Workforce from 2005 to 2024

Fiscal Year	*Enacted Budget*	*Workforce*
FY 2005	$8,023,483,000	17,495
FY 2006	$7,617,416,000	17,355
FY 2007	$7,725,130,000	17,072
FY 2008	$7,472,324,000	16,916
FY 2009	$7,643,674,000	17,049
FY 2010	$10,297,864,000	17,278
FY 2011	$8,682,117,000	17,359
FY 2012	$8,449,385,000	17,106
FY 2013	$7,901,104,000	15,913
FY 2014	$8,200,000,000	15,408
FY 2015	$8,139,887,000	14,725
FY 2016	$8,139,887,000	14,779
FY 2017	$8,058,488,000	15,408
FY 2018	$8,824,488,000	14,172
FY 2019	$8,849,488,000	14,172
FY 2020	$9,057,401,000	14,172
FY 2021	$9,237,153,000	14,297
FY 2022	$9,559,485,000	14,581
FY 2023	$10,135,433,000	15,115
FY 2024	$9,158,894,000	15,130

Source: Table created by authors based on EPA (2024). EPA's Budget and Spending. https://www.epa.gov/planandbudget/budget.

Increasing staffing capacity would allow the EPA to help cut air, water, and climate pollution and advance environmental justice (Dillon et al., 2018).

Conclusion

Green budgeting has emerged as a crucial tool for integrating environmental and climate considerations into the heart of fiscal policy. Its implementation requires new methodologies and procedures, a modern budget system, and new expertise. Program and performance budgeting systems could provide an opportunity to develop a system for collecting and evaluating the necessary information (Government Accountability Office, 2021). While there are significant differences in country contexts and public financial management systems, there are also common decisions that must be taken in designing any approach to green budget, such as defining what is "green," developing a classification system, and discerning what type of information is needed.

Across the world, governments increasingly recognize that achieving long-term sustainability goals requires more than isolated environmental programs; it demands the systematic alignment of budgets, institutions, and public financial management systems with climate and environmental objectives. As this chapter demonstrates, countries at all income levels are adopting a wide range of green budgeting tools, each reflecting differing administrative capacities, governance structures, and national priorities.

International organizations have played a central role in shaping this shift. The OECD's Paris Collaborative on Green Budgeting, the EU's GBRF, the UNDP's climate budget tagging initiatives, and the World Bank's technical guidance have collectively spurred global action, helping countries integrate environmental objectives into expenditure planning, fiscal risk analysis, and reporting systems. Despite this progress, countries remain at different stages of implementation. Some nations (France, Finland, and the Netherlands) have developed advanced methodologies and integrated climate objectives across budget cycles. Other countries are in the early phases, focusing on identifying environmentally significant expenditures or conducting preliminary environmental impact assessments.

Several common challenges persist for green budgeting. Governments must define what constitutes "green," determine how to assess both positive and negative environmental impacts, and establish transparent reporting mechanisms that enable meaningful scrutiny by legislatures, civil society, and independent experts. Effective green budgeting requires robust performance measurement systems, consistent data, and strong institutional coordination among ministries of finance, environment, planning agencies, and audit institutions. Political support and administrative capacity remain decisive factors for success.

This book covers three case studies related to green budgeting. The first case study, "Federal green budgeting and the 'forever chemicals' challenge: Protecting U.S. drinking water systems," examines "forever chemicals" (Per- and polyfluoroalkyl substances [PFAS]), which are widely used in industrial and consumer products. This case study examines green budgeting and regulatory efforts aimed at addressing PFAS contamination in U.S. drinking water.

The second case study, "Congestion Pricing in NYC," examines New York City's congestion pricing program and its environmental, fiscal, and social goals. It reviews early performance data, political resistance, implementation challenges, and funding issues.

The third case study, "Congestion and Low Emission Zones in London," provides analysis of the London Congestion Charge (LCC), the Low Emission Zone (LEZ), and the Ultra-low Emission Zone (ULEZ). Together, these policies combine economic incentives and regulatory limits to influence travel behavior, lower emissions, and generate revenue for public transportation improvements.

References

Congressional Budget Office (2020). *CBO's Cost Estimates Explained* (February 27, 2020), Retrieved from www.cbo.gov/publication/56166

Congressional Budget Office (2021). Budgetary Effects of Climate Change and of Potential Legislative Responses to It. *Report*. April 27, 2021. Retrieved from https://www.cbo.gov/publication/57019

Council on Environmental Quality (2022). *Council on environmental quality*. https://www.whitehouse.gov/ceq/

Dillon, L., Sellers, C., Underhill, V., Shapiro, N., Ohayon, J. L., Sullivan, M., Brown, P., Harrison, J., & Wylie, S., (2018). The environmental protection agency in the early Trump administration: Prelude to regulatory capture. *American Journal of Public Health, 108*(S2), S89–S94.

European Union Commission (2018). *Action Plan: Financing Sustainable Growth*. 8 March, 2018. https://eur-lex.europa.eu/legal-content/EN/TXT/?uri=CELEX:52018DC0097

GBRF (2021). *Green Budgeting reference framework*. https://economy-finance.ec.europa.eu/document/download/bfd8d6c1-d501-4cf2-873f-811f6453dde8_en?filename=European%20Union%20Green%20Budgeting%20Reference%20Framework.pdf

Government Accountability Office (2021). *High-Risk Series: Dedicated Leadership Needed to Address Limited Progress in Most High-Risk Areas, GAO-21–119SP* (March 2021), pp. 97–102, www.gao.gov/products/GAO-21-119SP.

Hart, N. (2020). *Strengthening Transparency and Accountability at EPA*. Bipartisan Policy Center. Retrieved from https://bipartisanpolicy.org/report/strengthening-transparency-and-accountability-at-epa/

Hemming, R. (2013). The macroeconomic framework for managing public finances. In R. Allen, R. Hemming, & B. Potter (Eds.), *The international handbook of public financial management* (pp. 21–45). Palgrave Macmillan.

Keiser, D. A., & Shapiro, J. S. (2019). *US water pollution regulation over the past half century: Burning waters to crystal springs? Journal of Economic Perspectives, 33*(4), 51–75.

Kumar, A. (2020). The role of green budgeting. *TerraGreen, 13*(1), 12–17.

Mensah, J. (2019). Sustainable development: Meaning, history, principles, pillars, and implications for human action: Literature review. *Cogent Social Sciences, 5*(1), 165–175.

North, D. (1991). Institutions. *Journal of Economic Perspectives, 5*(1), 97–112.

Nyikos, G. (2013). Fiskalregeln als Instrumente für einen nachhaltigen Haushalt in Ungarn. In M. Eckardt, & Z. T. Pállinger (szerk.), *Schuldenregeln als goldener Weg zur Haushaltskonsolidierung in der EU? Fiskalregeln als Instrumente für einen nachhaltigen Haushalt in Ungarn* (pp. 141–156). Nomos.

Nyikos, G., & Ermasova, N. (2021). Public capital infrastructure management: Cases of Germany, Hungary and the USA. *International Journal of Public Administration, 45*(12), 869–893.

Nyikos, G., & Kondor, Z. (2022a). National development banks in Europe – A contribution to sustainable finance. *Central European Public Administration Review, 20*(1), 135–165. ISSN 2591-2240 (print); 2591–2259 (online)

Nyikos, G., & Kondor, Z. (2022b). The involvement of national development banks promoting sustainable finance. *Deturope: The Central European Journal Of Regional Development And Tourism, 14*(1), 147–163. ISSN 1821–2506

Nyikos, G. (2022). *Fenntartható finanszírozás és fejlesztés - Stratégia és szabályozás: átállás a fenntartható finanszírozási modellekre*. Akadémiai Kiadó, ISBN 978 963 454 785 3

OECD (2018). *Paris collaborative on green budgeting.* Retrieved from https://www.oecd.org/environment/green-budgeting/

OECD (2020a). *Green budgeting and tax policy tools to support a green recovery.* OECD Policy Responses to Coronavirus (COVID-19), 9 October 2020. Retrieved from https://www.oecd.org/coronavirus/policy-responses/green-budgeting-and-tax-policy-tools-to-support-a-green-recovery-bd02ea23/

OECD (2020b). *Green budget tagging: Introductory guidance and principles.* Working Draft. Retrieved from https://www.financeministersforclimate.org/events/helsinki-principle-4-workshop-green-budgeting

OECD (2020c). *OECD green budgeting framework* (Highlights). OECD, Retrieved from www.oecd.org/environment/green-budgeting/OECD-Green-Budgeting-Framework-Highlights.pdf.

OECD (2021a). *Green budgeting in OECD countries.* OECD. Retrieved from https://www.oecd.org/publications/green-budgeting-in-oecd-countries-acf5d047-en.htm

OECD (2021b). *Green budget tagging: Introductory guidance & principles.* OECD Publishing. https://doi.org/10.1787/fe7bfcc4-en

OECD (2022). *Paris collaborative on green budgeting.* Retrieved from https://www.oecd.org/environment/green-budgeting/

Office of Environmental Justice (2022). *Environmental justice.* Retrieved from https://www.justice.gov/oej

Office of Management and Budget (2022). *Budget of the U.S. Government. Fiscal Year 2023.* White House. Retrieved from https://www.whitehouse.gov › uploads › 2022/03

Petrie, M. (2019). *High time for green budgeting.* Retrieved from https://blog-Paxton, L. (1993). *Enviro Facts 3: Sustainable development.* Environmental Education Association of Southern Africa.

The Coalition of Finance Ministers for Climate Action (2026). *Coalition of Finance Minister events, reports, tools, and highlights.* https://www.financeministersforclimate.org/

UNDP (2019). *Climate change knowing what you spend. A guidance note for Governments to track climate finance in their budgets.* Climate Change Financing Framework Technical Note Series. https://www.undp.org/content/undp/en/home/librarypage/climate-and-disaster-resilience-/knowing-what-you-spend.html

UNEP (2019). *Environmental rule of law: First global report.* UNEP. https://doi.org/10.1017/s1466046605250056

U.S. Environmental Protection Agency (2020). *EPA proposes first ever rule to improve transparency of guidance.* May 19, 2020. Retrieved from https://www.epa.gov/newsreleases/updated-what-they-are-saying-epa-proposes-first-ever-rule-improve-transparency-guidance

U.S. Environmental Protection Agency (2021a). *U.S. Environmental Protection Agency.* Retrieved from https://www.epa.gov/

U.S. Environmental Protection Agency (2021b). *EPA finalizes rule strengthening transparency in pivotal science underlying significant regulatory actions and influential scientific information.* https://www.epa.gov/newsreleases/epa-finalizes-rule-strengthening-transparency-pivotal-science-underlying-significant

U.S. Environmental Protection Agency (2022a). *EPA's budget and spending.* Retrieved from https://www.epa.gov/planandbudget/budget

U.S. Environmental Protection Agency (US EPA) (2022b). *Certification standards for pesticide applicators*. Retrieved from https://www.epa.gov/pesticide-worker-safety/certification-standards-pesticide-applicators

U.S. Department of Health and Human Services (2022). *HHS Environmental justice strategy and implementation plan*. The United States Department of Health and Human Services Retrieved from https://www.hhs.gov/civil-rights/for-individuals/special-topics/environmental-justice/index.html

Vinogradova, T. (2022). Improving green budget decisions and transparency through public participation: Evidence from Russia. *Public Sector Economics*, *46*(3), 385–401.

World Bank. (2021). *Climate change budget tagging: A review of international experience. Equitable growth, finance and institutions insight*. World Bank.

World Bank Group (2014). *Moving toward climate budgeting*. Policy Note 93383. World Bank.

World Commission on Environment and Development (WCED) (1987). *Our common future: The Brundtland report*. Oxford University Press.

CASE STUDY 9

Federal green budgeting and the "forever chemicals" challenge: protecting U.S. drinking water systems

Abstract

Per- and polyfluoroalkyl substances (PFAS), commonly referred to as "forever chemicals," have emerged as a global concern due to their persistence, bioaccumulation, and associated adverse health effects. This extensive class of over 4,000 chemical compounds has been widely utilized for decades across various industrial and consumer applications and valued for their unique properties, including resistance to heat, water, and oil. However, growing evidence shows that PFAS poses risks to human health, including cancers, liver and heart impacts, as well as immune and developmental damage to infants and children. This case study describes the green budgeting and regulation of "forever chemicals" in drinking water in the United States. It explains what PFASs are and how they have raised significant public health and environmental concerns due to their persistence in the environment and potential toxic effects on humans and wildlife. This case describes the regulation of "forever chemicals" in drinking water in the United States and the technologies available to remove them. It highlights the challenges of green budgeting for "forever chemicals" and federal funding efforts aimed at addressing PFAS contamination. The case study underscores the importance of green budgeting, enhanced regulatory guidance, increased financial support, and a strategic plan to safeguard public health and promote environmental sustainability.

Background

Green budgeting is a financial and policy tool that integrates environmental considerations in the government budgeting process at the federal, state, and local levels. Green budgeting ensures that public funds are allocated to programs that support sustainability (such as renewable energy programs), combat climate change, and are directed at the initiatives that mitigate negative externalities and remediate the aftermath of pollution. One of the aspects of green budgeting efforts discussed in this case study is the control of "forever chemicals," including the transition to safer and more sustainable materials.

"Forever chemicals"

Per- and polyfluoroalkyl substances (PFAS) are known as "forever chemicals" because they break down extremely slowly, some of them persisting for thousands of years. There are nearly 15,000 PFAS according to a chemicals' database (CompTox) maintained by the U.S. Environmental Protection Agency (EPA, 2016, 2024). The Organization for Economic Cooperation and Development (OECD) recognizes over 4,000 PFAS (National Institute for Public Health and the Environment, 2025). PFAS are a group of synthetic chemicals that have raised significant public health and environmental concerns not only due to their persistence in the environment but also due to potential toxic effects on humans and wildlife. Since the 1940s, "forever chemicals" have been widely used in industrial applications and consumer products like nonstick cookware, water-repellent fabrics, food packaging, and firefighting foams. Because the chemicals are nonstick, stain-resistant, and waterproof, they are used in carpets, furniture, takeout containers, dental floss, and makeup. "Forever chemicals" are released into the environment as waste and emissions by factories that make or use the substances (Willige, 2024).

PFAS are not directly linked to food production, but these particles have been found in food and water because of the use and disposal of PFAS-containing products (European Chemical Agency, 2025). As PFAS break down slowly if at all, they accumulate in the environment and the human body. A 2012 report by the National Institute of Environmental Health Sciences (NIEHS) found that 97% of Americans had PFAS in their blood (Lewis et al., 2015). Another NHANES study suggested the level of certain forever chemicals in the blood was reduced after those chemicals were removed from consumer products in the early 2000s (National Institute of Environmental Health Sciences, 2025). However, new PFAS chemicals are created on a regular basis and exposure to them is difficult to assess.

PFAS exposure has been linked to several health issues, including increased risk of certain cancers, immune system suppression, thyroid hormone disruption, liver damage, developmental effects in children, and reduced vaccine response (Willige, 2024). PFAS contamination poses risks in communities where industrial discharge, landfill leachate, or firefighting activities have compromised drinking water sources because "forever chemicals" accumulate in groundwater and drinking water supplies. Wildlife in contaminated areas is also affected, with PFAS detected in the blood and tissues of animals, impacting ecosystems and potentially entering the human.

History of regulation of "forever chemicals" in the United States

The regulation of PFAS in the United States has evolved significantly over the past two decades, reflecting growing scientific understanding and public concern about these persistent chemicals. Initially, all regulatory actions were voluntary. The two PFASs chemicals that were most extensively produced and studied, the perfluorooctanoic acid (PFOA) and the perfluoroctane sulfonate (PFOS), were voluntarily phased out of production in the United States between 2000 and 2002 by its primary manufacturer. Eight other major manufacturers of PFOA and PFOA-related chemicals voluntarily agreed to phase out their global production in 2006 (EPA, 2016, 2024, 2025).

Federal government began regulations of "forever chemicals" in 2009 when the NIEHS and the EPA collaborated to provide a more systematic approach to identifying the sources of PFAS, understanding associated health risks from exposure to forever chemicals, and developing relevant health advisories. EPA's health advisories are non-enforceable and non-regulatory. They provide information to relevant state agencies and health officials on the health effects, analytical methodologies, and treatment technologies associated with drinking water contamination.

Figure 4.1 presents a timeline of U.S. regulatory updates that have influenced the federal response to PFAS contamination and management.

A major regulatory milestone occurred in March 2023, when the EPA proposed legally enforceable maximum contaminant levels (MCLs) for six PFAS in drinking water to protect public health. Through this proposed rule, EPA is leveraging the most recent science and building on existing state efforts to limit PFAS, providing a nationwide, health-protective level for these specific PFAS in drinking water.

Subsequently, in August 2023, the EPA finalized its National Enforcement and Compliance Initiatives for 2024–2027, prioritizing the reduction of PFAS exposure. This initiative focuses on implementing the EPA's PFAS Strategic Roadmap and holding accountable those who manufactured PFAS and/or used PFAS in the manufacturing process, federal facilities that released PFAS, and other industrial parties that significantly contributed to the release of PFAS into the environment (Figure 4.1).

Reinforcing the EPA's regulatory efforts to prevent PFAS releases to the environment, the EPA has taken significant action to reduce PFAS uses in commerce, in coordination with federal partners and complementing

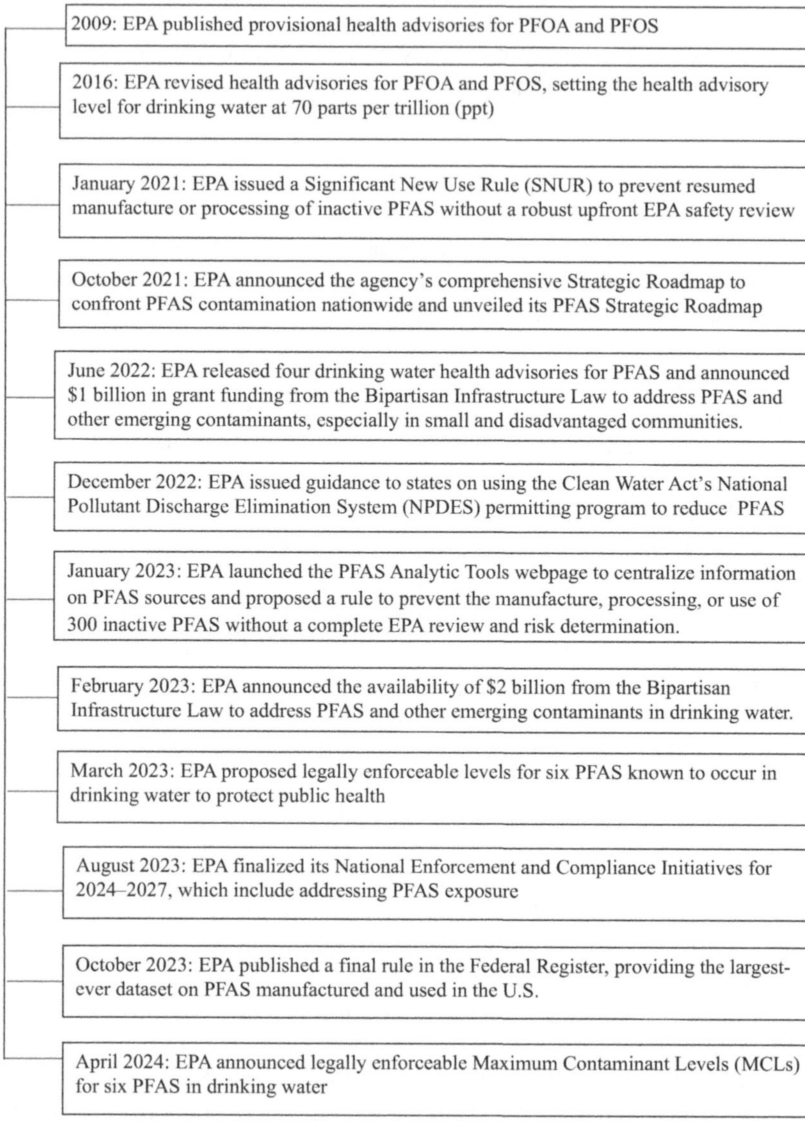

FIGURE 4.1 Timeline of U.S. regulatory updates on PFAS from 2009 to 2024

Source: Created by authors

significant efforts by several states. Following through on Executive Order 14057 on federal sustainability, the EPA has developed and refined a number of online resources to educate purchasers and other users on which ecolabels and sustainability standards restrict or eliminate PFAS from their products. The EPA has ensured that its information and tools focus on removing

PFAS as a class of chemicals rather than only a few chemicals at a time. The EPA has removed PFAS from the Safer Choice program's Safer Chemical Ingredients List and is ensuring that PFAS are not intentionally added to Safer Choice-certified products. The EPA has taken action to remove 12 PFAS from the list of inert ingredients approved for use in nonfood pesticide products.

The roadmap sets timelines by which EPA plans to take specific actions and commits to bolder new policies to safeguard public health, protect the environment, and hold polluters accountable. The actions described in the PFAS Roadmap each represent important and meaningful steps to safeguard communities from PFAS contamination. Cumulatively, these actions will build upon one another and lead to more enduring and protective solutions (EPA, 2025).

Under this roadmap, public water systems must:

- Monitor for these PFAS and complete initial monitoring for the new MCLs by 2027
- Begin providing the public with information on the results from 2027
- Implement solutions to reduce PFAS (if they exceed MCLs) by 2029
- Take action to reduce PFAS and notify the public of any violations of MCLs from 2029.

Starting in April 2029, the EPA will require public water systems to limit specific "forever chemicals" in drinking water.

Federal funding to tackle PFAS contamination

From 2021, the Federal government made several investments available to state and local governments to deal with forever chemicals. The Bipartisan Infrastructure Law (BIL) signed by President Biden on November 15, 2021, allocated over $50 billion to improving the quality of drinking water and clean water systems nationwide. $10 billion of these funds are designated to assist communities and water systems affected by PFAS and other emerging contaminants. Forty percent of the benefits are directed to disadvantaged communities that have been historically marginalized by underinvestment and are disproportionately affected by pollution (EPA, 2024, p. 4).

In February 2023, the EPA allocated an additional $2 billion in BIL funding to states and territories to address PFAS contamination in drinking water (EPA, 2025). This investment became available to communities as grants through EPA's Emerging Contaminants in Small or Disadvantaged Communities grant program. The Trump administration has rolled back the federal regulations and support of PFAS programs and initiatives.

States actions

The regulation of forever chemicals has also recently started on a state level. So far, 15 states, including Alaska, California, Colorado, Connecticut, Hawaii, Illinois, Maine, Maryland, Minnesota, New Hampshire, New Jersey, New York, Rhode Island, Vermont, and Washington, have introduced regulations of PFAS in various consumer products. Colorado, Connecticut, Maine, Minnesota, Rhode Island, and Vermont banned "forever chemicals" in nonstick cookware (such as Teflon).

California has some of the strictest regulations on PFAS chemicals in the nation. The state requires labeling of chemicals in cookware as of January 1, 2024, and bans the use of PFAS in food packaging as of January 1, 2023. Additionally, it prohibits the use of PFAS in any juvenile products as of July 1, 2023, and in cosmetics and most apparel as of January 1, 2025. New York bans PFAS in textile articles (such as bedding, upholstery, and towels) and apparel as of January 1, 2025. Colorado bans PFAS in outdoor apparel for severe wet conditions from January 1, 2025.

There have been several class action lawsuits filed against W.L. Gore & Associates, a prominent producer of Core-Tex fabric, for failing to disclose PFAS chemicals in its waterproof jackets and other apparel, for misleading consumers into believing these apparel items were environmentally friendly, and for contaminating the environment. Maryland's lawsuit asserts that Gore was aware of PFAS's persistence and toxicity for decades but failed to disclose these risks to regulators or the public (Halter et al., 2025). The State of Maryland also sued the company for contaminating the area surrounding its Cherry Hill facility in Elkton, Maryland. In January 2025, the City of Wausau, Wisconsin, sued multiple paper plants, chemical and packaging manufacturers, and a landfill, alleging that PFAS wastewater discharges contaminated groundwater wells and seeking response and remediation costs under the Comprehensive Environmental Response, Compensation, and Liability Act (Halter et al., 2025).

The challenges for green budgeting of "forever chemicals"

The regulation of PFAS contamination has become quite strenuous for state and local governments, water systems, and individuals. According to Gage et al. (2024), widespread concerns exist about whether those managing water systems have been provided with enough information and resources to implement PFAS treatment methods and safely address the resulting contaminated waste at the state and local levels.

Based on the EPA report (2024), most public water system managers needed more information and guidance from EPA about treatment methods, the availability of federal funding, and managing PFAS-contaminated waste. EPA report (2024) highlights that public water systems have the following challenges in green budgeting and regulation of treating water and removing waste from "forever chemicals":

- Communicating with customers about the health risks of high PFAS levels
- Dealing with evolving regulations for waste disposal of "forever chemicals"
- Raising enough revenue or accessing federal funding to cover costs
- Hiring enough qualified engineering staff for operations
- Complying with regulations' deadlines
- Having the capacity to store waste.

EPA report (2024) provides an example of one wastewater treatment manager concerned about legal standards, who said, "Regulations are still being developed while we are trying to determine solutions. Not having a complete regulatory landscape…is challenging in that we do not know what may be expected after we choose and implement solutions" (EPA, 2024). In another example from the EPA report (2024), a survey respondent commented, "We are a small homeowner's association with a community well/water system…In short, our resources are extremely finite as it is. Adding testing and mitigation requirements relative to PFAS is going to most likely be financially crippling for us."

The new EPA standards will prompt water utilities and industries to invest in treatment technologies capable of filtering out PFAS, such as granular activated carbon and reverse osmosis. However, addressing PFAS contamination will require substantial financial investments from federal and local governments, particularly for testing, treatment, and remediation efforts in affected areas.

Conclusions

The case study proves that only through coordinated efforts of federal, state, and local governments can public water systems effectively combat the challenges posed by PFAS. This case study demonstrates that efficient and effective public financial management processes and frameworks should support green budgeting policies to ensure their effective design and implementation. The strategic planning and budgetary framework must consider green priorities and risks.

Green priorities, both on the revenue and expenditure side, should be incorporated at this early stage of the budgeting process. Ex-post evaluation or monitoring of the impact and effectiveness of climate change policies by the government should assess whether impacts are consistent with the climate objectives set out in national development plans.

A green dimension can be built into programmed and performance budgeting processes. Performance audits, which explicitly seek to assess the link between policy outputs/results and the instruments covered by a given policy, may include climate or environmental aspects.

Monitoring and reporting climate-related income and expenditure is also an important part of an effective green budgeting system. Green expenditure tracking (labeling) should be considered throughout the planning and implementation process. To address the challenges of PFAS regulations, public water systems must adopt green budgeting strategies that:

- Leverage federal funding and grants for PFAS mitigation.
- Prioritize transparent communication with stakeholders regarding health risks and cost implications.
- Foster collaboration with regulatory agencies to align treatment solutions with evolving standards.
- Invest in workforce development to recruit and train skilled engineers.

Discussion questions

1. What should be the role of federal, state, and local governments in providing guidance and funding to address PFAS contamination?
2. How might green budgeting principles be applied to prioritize sustainable solutions for PFAS treatment and disposal?
3. How can evolving regulations of "forever chemicals" be effectively communicated to smaller public water systems with limited resources?
4. What strategies could public water systems use to incorporate PFAS treatment costs into their budgets without overburdening taxpayers?
5. What mechanisms could be implemented to ensure equitable access to funding for smaller, under-resourced water systems?
6. How can public administrators foster collaboration between stakeholders, including government agencies, private industries, and local communities, to address PFAS challenges?
7. Who is involved in green budgeting for regulating "forever chemicals"?
8. How are responsibilities allocated in green budgeting for regulating "forever chemicals"?
9. What ensures the processes are transparent and open in green budgeting for regulating "forever chemicals"?

References

EPA (2016). *Fact sheet PFOA & PFOS. Drinking water health advisories*. EPA. Retrieved from https://www.epa.gov/sites/default/files/2016-06/documents/drinkingwaterhealthadvisories_pfoa_pfos_updated_5.31.16.pdf

EPA (2024). *EPA's PFAS strategic roadmap: Three years of progress*. November 2024. EPA.

EPA (2025). *Key EPA actions to address PFAS*. Retrieved from https://www.epa.gov/pfas/key-epa-actions-address-pfas

European Chemical Agency (2025). *Per- and polyfluoroalkyl substances (PFAS).* Retrieved from https://echa.europa.eu/hot-topics/perfluoroalkyl-chemicals-pfas

Gage, G., De Kervenoael, M., Guillet, C. Malarkey, B. & Simeon, B. (2024). Understanding new PFAS regulations in the U.S. and EU. *Rolan Berger*. October 29, 2024. Retrieved from https://www.rolandberger.com/en/Insights/Publications/Opportunities-challenges-in-new-regulations-of-forever-chemicals.html

Halter, A. G., Zarghamee, R., Myers, A., & Marullo, J. (2025, March 13). *Maryland files PFAS suit against downstream manufacturer*. PFAS Navigator. https://pfas.pillsburylaw.com/maryland-pfas-suit-downstream-manufacturer/

Lewis, R. C., Johns, L. E., & Meeker, J. D. (2015). Serum biomarkers of exposure to Perfluoroalkyl substances in relation to serum testosterone and measures of thyroid function among adults and adolescents from NHANES 2011–2012. *International Journal of Environmental Research and Public Health, 12*(6), 6098–6114.

National Institute of Environmental Health Sciences (2025). *Perfluoroalkyl and Polyfluoroalkyl Substances (PFAS)*. Retrieved from https://www.niehs.nih.gov/health/topics/agents/pfc

National Institute for Public Health and the Environment (2025). *PFAS. Ministry of health, welfare, and sport: National institute for public health and the environment, Netherlands.* Retrieved from https://www.rivm.nl/en/pfas

Willige, A. (2024). What are forever chemicals, and why does the EU want to ban them? *World Economic Forum*. March 6 2024. Retrieved from https://www.weforum.org/stories/2024/03/pfas-forever-chemicals-eu-ban/

CASE STUDY 10

Congestion pricing in New York City

Abstract

On January 5, 2025, New York City became the first municipality in the United States to implement congestion pricing. This case examines New York City's congestion pricing program (Congestion Relief Zone). It explores the policy's environmental, fiscal, and social objectives, early performance data, political opposition, implementation, and funding challenges. The evaluation of New York City's congestion pricing program illustrates the complex interplay between urban transportation policy, federal-state authority, and equitable access to public transit. Evidence from the program's initial months indicates that congestion pricing is achieving its intended objectives: reducing traffic volumes, improving travel speeds, lowering emissions, and generating dedicated revenue for Metropolitan Transportation Authority (MTA) infrastructure projects. The case study presents an opportunity for students to examine real-world public finance and budgeting challenges and the policy responses to congesting pricing programs. The case encourages students to think critically about fiscal policy tools, revenue stability, political negotiations, and structural reform. This case allows instructors to engage students in exploring the intersection of environmental sustainability, fiscal innovation, and political strategy.

Topics

Green Budgeting; Congestion Pricing; Sustainability; Fiscal Policy; Revenues

Background

Traffic congestion imposes a range of costs on travelers, including reduced speeds, longer travel times, diminished reliability of travel time, increased fuel consumption and vehicle wear, and the inconvenience associated with rescheduling trips or shifting to alternative modes of transportation. Over the longer term, congestion may also lead to costly residential or employment relocation. Traffic congestion in the United States has a wide range of negative impacts on the economy, environment, and society. In 2023, the total national cost of congestion exceeded $70.4 billion (Pishue, 2024, p. 2). The average U.S. driver loses approximately 42 hours annually due to traffic delays, which is equivalent to a full work week (Pishue, 2024, p. 2). The burden was particularly acute in major metropolitan areas. For example, drivers in Chicago lost 112 hours in congestion, corresponding to a $2,063 cost of congestion per driver; drivers in New York City experienced an average loss of 102 hours, corresponding to a $1,879 cost of congestion per driver; and drivers in Los Angeles lost 87 hours with a $1,602 cost of congestion per driver (Pishue, 2024).

A variety of policies have been adopted or proposed to address traffic congestion. The first approach has been to expand roadway capacity through the construction of new roads, to upgrade existing infrastructure, and to improve the efficiency of the road system (re-timing of traffic lights, metering access to highway entrance ramps, high-occupancy vehicle lanes, and Advanced Traveller Information Systems, among other measures). However, this strategy is now constrained by environmental considerations, limited fiscal resources, and the scarcity of available space (Lindsey & Verhoef, 2000).

The second approach seeks to reduce travel demand, particularly during peak periods, by restricting access to congested areas. Such measures include congestion pricing, permit systems, parking restrictions, bans on commercial vehicles during certain hours, and other demand-management techniques. Vickrey (1969) highlighted the potential of congestion pricing to influence route and mode choice, its implications for land use, and the feasibility of automated toll collection systems. Congestion pricing involves setting tolls that reflect the severity of congestion, requiring variation in charges according to time, location, vehicle type, and prevailing conditions (e.g., accidents or adverse weather). Congestion pricing is a form of Pigouvian tax (Pigou, 1920) designed to limit or reduce vehicular traffic in specific areas. As a prescriptive tax, congestion pricing requires users to pay a fee for driving on public roads during peak travel times or within designated high-traffic zones. By levying a charge, congestion pricing compels travelers to account for the negative externalities associated with their trips, including heightened traffic congestion, increased GHG emissions, and diminished air quality (de Palma & Lindsey, 2011; Lindsey & Santos,

2020; Lou et al., 2011). The specific structure of each system aims to discourage excessive automobile use (de Palma & Lindsey, 2011; Ecola & Light, 2009).

Area-based congestion pricing systems impose charges on vehicles entering and/or exiting a designated zone, typically enforced through restricted checkpoints and automated camera systems. These systems are further subdivided into cordon and zonal models. Cordon area-based congestion pricing systems employ artificially defined boundaries and apply tolls exclusively upon entry and/or exit (de Palma & Lindsey, 2011). Zonal area-based congestion pricing systems are delineated by natural landmarks or geographic features, such as rivers or mountains, and may impose charges for travel within the zone in addition to entry or exit fees (de Palma & Lindsey, 2011). Practical applications of area-based congestion pricing include the London Congestion Charge (LCC), New York's Congestion Relief Zone (CRZ), Singapore's pioneering electronic road pricing system, Scandinavian toll rings, and California's high-occupancy toll lanes.

In some cases, rather than charging drivers directly at the point of access, area-based congestion pricing restricts entry based on vehicle emissions standards. Motorists whose vehicles do not meet these standards must either invest in a more efficient vehicle or choose an alternative mode of transportation. While this approach is less common, it still functions as a Pigouvian mechanism. Drivers must bear a cost, whether through direct payment or through the investment required to comply with emissions standards, thereby reducing traffic and environmental harm.

Congestion pricing in New York City

For several decades, policymakers in New York City have engaged in ongoing debates regarding the adoption of congestion pricing. Congestion pricing was first proposed in the 1950s and was rejected. This proposal was revived unsuccessfully in the early 2000s. The plan finally received federal approval in 2023. On January 5, 2025, New York City implemented the nation's first urban congestion pricing program (Central Business District [CBD] Tolling Program) to alleviate traffic congestion in Manhattan's CRZ, located south of 60th Street. This CBD is not only the largest one in the United States, but it also contains more office space than the next five business districts combined (Plotch, 2025).

This CBD Tolling Program charges motorists a fee to enter the CBD zone, thereby reducing gridlock and generating revenue to fund critical transit infrastructure. About 1.5 million people work in the 8-square-mile tolling zone. While the tolling system records all vehicle entries to Manhattan below 60 Street (CBD), only entries to the CRZ are subject to a toll (MTA, 2025a). Vehicle trips that remain solely on the Excluded Roadways are not subject to a toll.

Vehicles entering the CRZ are subject to tolls that vary according to vehicle classification, time of day, applicable crossing credits, and payment method. Passenger and small commercial vehicles, including sedans, sport utility vehicles, pickup trucks, and small vans, are charged a toll of $9 during peak periods and

FIGURE 4.2 Congestion Relief Zone in New York City

Source: Photo by authors

$2.25 during overnight periods characterized by reduced congestion, contingent upon payment via a valid E-ZPass.

Motorcycles pay tolls of $4.50 during peak hours and $1.05 during the overnight period. These categories of vehicles are tolled once per day (Table 4.2).

Small trucks and certain bus classifications pay tolls of $14.40 during peak hours and $3.60 during overnight periods. Larger vehicles, such as multi-unit trucks and tour buses, face higher tolls of $21.60 during peak times and $5.40 during off-peak hours (MTA, 2025a,b). Eligible trucks and buses are exempted from the daily toll requirement under the current program framework. For taxis and for-hire vehicles licensed by the New York City Taxi & Limousine

TABLE 4.2 Toll Rates by Vehicle Type and Time Period

Vehicle Category	*Peak Hours Toll*	*Overnight Toll*	*Notes*
Passenger and small commercial (sedans, SUVs, pickups, small vans)	$9.00	$2.25	Once per day; E-ZPass required
Motorcycles	$4.50	$1.05	Once per day
Small trucks and certain buses	$14.40	$3.60	Once per day
Large trucks and tour buses	$21.60	$5.40	Once per day
Eligible trucks and buses	Exempt	Exempt	No daily toll
High-volume for-hire vehicles	$1.50/trip	$1.50/trip	Applies to all time periods
Taxis, green cabs, black cars	$0.75/trip	$0.75/trip	Applies to all time periods

Source: Created by authors based on MTA (MTA, 2025b).

Commission, tolling is applied via a per-trip passenger surcharge for trips to, from, within, or passing through the CRZ. The per-trip fee is set at $1.50 for high-volume for-hire vehicles across all time periods. In contrast, taxis, green cabs, and black cars are subject to a reduced per-trip charge of $0.75 (MTA, 2025b). The program incorporates provisions for discounted toll rates applicable to low-income residents, while certain vehicle classes, such as emergency response vehicles and school buses, are granted exemptions.

The Metropolitan Transportation Authority (MTA) is phasing in the congestion toll structure over a six-year horizon, commencing with an initial $9 peak-period toll for passenger vehicles. The toll is scheduled to increase to $12 in 2028 and subsequently to $15 in 2031 (MTA, 2025b).

Benefits of New York's Congestion Relief Zone

The main goals of New York's CRZ were to reduce traffic, improve safety and environmental quality, increase transit ridership, bring economic benefits, and raise dedicated funds for public transit. On July 5, 2025, Governor Kathy Hochul and the MTA announced that, in its first six months of CBD Tolling Program's implementation, "New York City's congestion pricing program has succeeded in reducing traffic and raising revenues to fund transit improvements across the region, while economic activity in New York City has flourished" (Governor of New York State, 2025). MTA's Chair and CEO Janno Lieber acknowledges that congestion pricing "dramatically reduced congestion, bringing reduced traffic and faster travel times, while increasing speeds for buses and emergency vehicles" (MTA, 2025d).

Reduced traffic flow

Since its launch on January 5, 2025, congestion pricing has yielded measurable improvements in traffic flow. The Eno Center for Transportation reports that, since New York's congestion pricing program began, approximately 80,000 fewer vehicles enter the city each day, resulting in a 12% decrease in traffic volume (Plotch, 2025). The Regional Plan Association (2025) reported a 25% reduction in traffic delays within the zone and a 9% decrease across the broader metropolitan area. There was a 10% reduction in traffic delays in Bronx and 14% reduction in Bergen County, New Jersey (Regional Plan Association, 2025). In April 2025, there were 2.3 million fewer cars entering CRZ, which is 12% fewer than would have been expected given historical traffic trends (Badger et al., 2025). According to MTA (2025c), the highest reduction in traffic flow was recorded in June 2025 (Table 4.3).

Cook et al. (2025) found that average traffic speeds in NYC's CBD increased by 15% following the introduction of congestion pricing, with larger effects during the most congested hours. The Eno Center for Transportation reports that traffic speeds on Eighth Avenue, north of Times Square, increased from 7.6 miles to 15.5 miles per hour, while speeds decreased from 3.9 to 1.7 miles per hour on 42nd Street near Grand Central Terminal (Plotch, 2025). Roads commonly traveled on routes to the CBD before the policy have also seen an increase in speed. Overall, these speed changes reduced travel times on trips to and within the CBD by approximately 8%. Commuters have gained back approximately seven minutes per hour previously lost to congestion in 2024, with river crossing travel times improving by 6% to 42% in 2025. The rush hour delays in the Holland Tunnel declined by 65%, and MTA express buses in the Lincoln Tunnel operate nearly 24% faster than in 2024 (Badger et al., 2025; MTA, 2025c).

TABLE 4.3 Reduction in Vehicle Entries in NYC's CBD

Month	*Average Daily Entries*	*Daily Baseline (Historical Average)*	*Change from Baseline*	*Change from Baseline (%)*	*Total Fewer Entries per Month*
January 2025	533,526	580,500	−46,974	−8	−1,268,298
February 2025	541,309	613,900	−72,591	−12	−2,032,548
March 2025	560,255	642,500	−82,245	−13	−2,549,595
April 2025	568,143	644,400	−76,257	−12	−2,287,710
May 2025	580,226	647,200	−66,974	−10	−2,076,194
June 2025	570,329	662,400	−92,071	−14	−2,762,130
July 2025	554,615	616,600	−61,985	−10	−1,921,535

Source: MTA (2025c).

Improved safety and environmental quality

Crashes within the CRZ declined by 14%, and traffic-related injuries dropped by 15%, with pedestrian fatalities in New York City reaching lows comparable to 2018. Noise complaints regarding honking and vehicle sounds decreased by 45% in 2025 (MTA, 2025c). Additionally, the City Department of Health and Mental Hygiene reported steady or declining levels of fine particulate matter (PM2.5) at monitoring sites inside and outside the CRZ (Badger et al., 2025).

Increased transit ridership

Public transit ridership across all MTA modes surged from January to May 2025 compared to the same period in 2024, reaching post-pandemic record highs. Subway ridership rose by 7%, bus ridership increased by 12%, the Long Island Rail Road (LIRR) ridership was higher by 8%, Metro-North by 6%, and Access-A-Ride paratransit services by 21%. Transit service reliability also improved, with subway on-time performance hitting 85.2% in May 2025, the best non-pandemic figure on record, and LIRR and Metro-North have consistently achieved on-time rates near 97–98%. From January to June 2025, average trip times for buses have decreased by 17% at the Lincoln Tunnel and 48% at the Holland Tunnel (Regional Plan Association, 2025). The MTA increased service on eight Express Bus routes in March and expanded local bus service on 14 high-ridership routes in June 2025. The first phase of the Queens Bus Network Redesign was launched in June 2025, improving frequency and connections for 800,000 riders. Commuters save up to 21 minutes each way, translating into annual time savings valued at approximately $1.3 billion (Governor of New York State, 2025). Pedestrian activity in business districts within the CRZ increased by 8.4% year-over-year in May 2025, outperforming districts outside the zone.

Economic benefits

Economically, congestion pricing has reduced the substantial costs of gridlock, which previously accounted for $20 billion annually in lost productivity and wasted time, according to the Partnership for New York City (Governor of New York State, 2025). Other economic indicators in the CRZ also demonstrate strong growth. Broadway achieved record ticket sales of $1.9 billion; retail sales are projected to increase by $900 million in 2025; hotel occupancy rose from 85% to 87% from April 2024 to April 2025; and commercial office leasing grew 11% from Q4 2024 to Q1 2025, representing an 80% increase since early 2024 (Governor of New York State, 2025). New York City's workforce also expanded, reaching nearly 4.86 million jobs in April 2025, a 1.6% increase over the prior year and outpacing national growth (Governor of New York State, 2025).

Raised dedicated funds for public transit

According to a survey by Verhoef et al. (1997a), road users expressed a preference, ranked in descending order, for the use of toll revenues. These are the investments in new road infrastructure, reductions in vehicle ownership taxes, reductions in fuel taxes, investment in public transportation, subsidies for public transportation, investment in carpool facilities, general tax reductions, and expansion of other public expenditures. New York's congestion pricing enables the MTA to finance major transit investments by issuing $15 billion in bonds backed by toll revenues.

Funded projects include the purchase of 435 additional R211 subway cars (including 80 open-gangway models), 44 new dual-mode locomotives for the LIRR, and 300 new M9A railcars for Metro-North and LIRR; signal modernization through Communications-based Train Control upgrades on the A and C subway lines improves service reliability and frequency; and, Americans with Disabilities Act improvements at 23 subway stations, including the installation of new elevators and platform reconstructions, enhance system accessibility (Governor of New York State, 2025; MTA, 2025b).

Legal, political, social, and fiscal challenges of congestion pricing

The implementation of congestion pricing in New York City has recently encountered significant legal, political, social, and fiscal challenges. In early 2025, U.S. Secretary of Transportation Sean Duffy rescinded federal approval, citing concerns over economic impacts on working-class commuters and small businesses. The MTA filed a lawsuit, arguing that the reversal was unlawful and politically motivated (New York City Comptroller, 2025). In May 2025, U.S. District Judge Lewis Liman issued a temporary restraining order preventing the federal government from withholding funding, citing the likelihood of MTA's success on the merits and the risk of "irreparable harm," including diminished bond value and stalled infrastructure improvements. The preliminary injunction in MTA v. Duffy prevented the federal government from rescinding approvals or withholding funding, thereby preserving the program pending further judicial review (New York City Comptroller, 2025). Although this ruling provided temporary stability, the litigation underscores the contentious nature of the policy and the vulnerability of its long-term implementation to judicial outcomes. Legal challenges continue to present substantial hurdles. Lawsuits from the State of New Jersey, a Manhattan resident, New Yorkers Against Congestion Pricing, the United Federation of Teachers, and the Trucking Association of New York have sought to block or delay implementation, citing concerns ranging from health, social, and economic impacts on neighboring jurisdictions to alleged procedural deficiencies in environmental reviews (Anderson, 2025). While courts have thus far upheld the congestion pricing program, the ongoing litigation creates uncertainty and may influence public perception.

In addition to legal disputes, political resistance remains strong among certain constituencies, including drivers, suburban commuters, and business groups concerned about potential declines in commercial activity. Social opposition is fueled by perceptions of unfairness, misinformation about the policy's effects, and broader distrust of government spending priorities. Addressing these challenges will require transparent governance, clear communication of benefits, rigorous accountability for revenue allocation, and a sustained commitment to equity-focused transit improvements.

From a social standpoint, concerns about equity have been central to the public debate. The Community Service Society (CSS), a leading anti-poverty organization in New York City, conducted a comprehensive analysis of the potential impacts of congestion pricing on Manhattan commuters (Community Service Society, 2017). The findings indicate that only 4% of employed residents in the city's outer boroughs (Brooklyn, Queens, the Bronx, and Staten Island) commute to Manhattan by private automobile. In contrast, 56% rely on public transit and would benefit from transportation investments funded by congestion pricing revenues. Notably, only 2% of the city's working poor are projected to incur the congestion fee. This evidence suggests that, if revenues are allocated effectively, congestion pricing could disproportionately benefit lower-income residents by enhancing transit access and improving service quality. Nevertheless, translating potential benefits into tangible outcomes requires targeted and sustained investment in mass transit. Affordable, reliable transportation is essential not only for daily commuting but also for enabling access to employment opportunities, job training, and educational programs. Currently, the high cost of bus and subway fares compounds economic hardship for low-income populations, while persistent underinvestment in the transit system has resulted in frequent delays, service disruptions, and declining reliability.

The threats to withhold federal transit funding, underscores the vulnerability of CBD Tolling Program's funding, even when this program had received prior federal approval. This tension raises broader questions about the stability of transportation financing mechanisms. The MTA projected that the program would generate $1 billion annually, enabling the agency to leverage this revenue through bond financing to support $15 billion in critical capital projects. Congestion pricing is the source in revenue needed for subway construction projects, including crucial accessibility improvements for people with disabilities. Modernizing New York City's aging transit infrastructure, that serves nearly nine million riders daily, is critical to maintaining the city's economic competitiveness and ensuring equitable mobility. Persistent underfunding of the subway and bus systems by policymakers has predictably resulted in frequent service delays, breakdowns, and declining system reliability.

Conclusions

The evaluation of New York City's congestion pricing program illustrates the complex interplay between urban transportation policy, federal-state authority, and equitable access to public transit. New York City's congestion pricing is achieving its early goals: reducing congestion, improving travel speeds, lowering emissions, improving safety and environmental quality, increasing transit ridership, receiving economic benefit, and generating dedicated revenue for critical MTA infrastructure projects. Rolling back the program would risk exacerbating existing service deficiencies, undermining environmental gains, and delaying investments essential to the city's long-term economic vitality. This case study demonstrates that the policy can advance both transportation efficiency and socioeconomic equity, particularly if revenues are earmarked for upgrading transit systems and reducing service disparities. Policymakers should, however, consider targeted mitigation measures for the small proportion of low-income drivers who would be directly impacted. Furthermore, the policy's success will depend on transparent reinvestment of revenues into the public transit system, clear communication of benefits, and consistent monitoring of distributional impacts to ensure that intended equity goals are met. The program serves as a replicable model for other cities confronting similar challenges. Despite the strong economic and environmental rationale for congestion pricing, its implementation has encountered persistent social and political resistance.

Discussion questions

1. What are the primary benefits and drawbacks of congestion pricing from a public policy perspective?
2. What strategies could policymakers use to ensure that congestion pricing revenues are reinvested in ways that directly benefit the communities most reliant on public transit?
3. What strategies might help build public trust and support for congestion pricing in New York City?
4. How might congestion pricing influence long-term patterns of commuting, housing, and job location in New York City?
5. In what ways could congestion pricing exacerbate or alleviate economic and social inequalities among New Yorkers?
6. What lessons could other major cities learn from New York's approach to implementing congestion pricing?

7 What measures should be taken to evaluate the policy's effectiveness over time?
8 What strategies could city officials use to sustain the program amid political opposition?
9 How should policymakers address concerns from groups who feel disproportionately affected?
10 If federal approval were revoked, what alternative funding mechanisms could replace the lost revenue?

References

Anderson (2025, April 18). *Judge in NYC congestion pricing lawsuits dismisses arguments from groups against toll*. NBC New York. https://www.cbsnews.com/newyork/news/nyc-congestion-pricing-judge-dismisses-arguments/

Badger, E., Chen, S., Elkeurti, A., Hu, W., Paris, F., & Singer, E. (2025, May 11). Here is everything that has changed since congestion pricing started in New York: Fewer cars. Faster travel. Less honking. And some questions we still can't answer. *The New York Times*. https://www.nytimes.com/interactive/2025/05/11/upshot/congestion-pricing.html

Community Service Society (2017). *Congestion pricing - A CSS analysis*. https://www.cssny.org/news/entry/congestion-pricing-css-analysis

Cook, C., Kreidieh, A., Vasserman, S., Allcott, H., Arora, N., van Sambeek, F., Tomkins, A., & Turkel, E. (2025, March). The short-run effects of congestion pricing in New York City (NBER Working Paper No. 33584). National Bureau of Economic Research. https://doi.org/10.3386/w33584

de Palma, A., & Lindsey, R. (2011). Traffic congestion pricing methodologies and technologies. *Transportation Research Part C: Emerging Technologies*, *19*(6), 1377–1399. https://doi.org/10.1016/j.trc.2011.02.010

Ecola, L., & Light, T. (2009). *Equity and congestion pricing a review of the evidence sponsored by the environmental defense fund*. https://www.rand.org/publications/

Governor of New York State (2025). Six Months In, Governor Hochul Highlights Success of Congestion Pricing: Traffic Is Down, Business Is Up, and Critical Investments Are Being Made to Improve Transit. https://www.governor.ny.gov/news/six-months-governor-hochul-highlights-success-congestion-pricing-traffic-down-business-and

Lindsey, R., & Santos, G. (2020). Addressing transportation and environmental externalities with economics: Are policy makers listening? *Research in Transportation Economics*, *82*, 100872. https://doi.org/10.1016/j.retrec.2020.100872

Lindsey, C. R., & Verhoef, E. T. (2000). Traffic congestion and congestion pricing (Tinbergen Institute Discussion Paper No. 00–101/3). Tinbergen Institute.

Lou, Y., Yin, Y., & Laval, J. A. (2011). Optimal dynamic pricing strategies for high-occupancy/toll lanes. *Transportation Research Part C: Emerging Technologies*, *19*(1), 64–74. https://doi.org/10.1016/j.trc.2010.03.008

MTA. (2025a). *The most detailed view of NYC traffic (so far)*. https://www.mta.info/article/most-detailed-view-of-nyc-traffic-so-far

MTA (2025b). *Congestion relief zone*. https://congestionreliefzone.mta.info/tolling

MTA (2025c). *Reduction in vehicle entries to the CBD*. https://metrics.mta.info/?cbdtp/vehiclereductions

MTA (2025d). *Statement from MTA chair and CEO Janno Lieber regarding legal filing to continue benefits of congestion relief program.* https://www.mta.info/press-release/statement-mta-chair-and-ceo-janno-lieber-regarding-legal-filing-continue-benefits-of

New York City Comptroller (2025). *NYC comptroller lander & advocates gather to keep congestion pricing on and Trump away from MTA funding.* March 20, 2025. https://comptroller.nyc.gov/newsroom/nyc-comptroller-lander-advocates-gather-to-keep-congestion-pricing-on-and-trump-away-from-mta-funding/

Pigou, A. C. (1920). *Wealth and welfare*. Macmillan.

Pishue, B. (2024, June). 2023 INRIX global traffic scorecard with Q1 2024 update. *INRIX.* https://inrix.com/scorecard/

Plotch, P. (2025). *Has New York's congestion pricing reduced congestion? Eno center for transportation.* April 25, 2025. https://enotrans.org/article/has-new-yorks-congestion-pricing-reduced-congestion/

Regional Plan Association. (2025). *New congestion pricing research shows fewer Traffic Jams and delays across the city and region.* https://rpa.org/news/news-release/new-congestion-pricing-research-shows-fewer-traffic-jams-and-delays-across-the-city-and-region

Verhoef, E. T., Nijkamp, P., & Rietveld, P. (1997a). The social feasibility of road pricing: A case study for the Randstad area. *Journal of Transport Economics and Policy, 31*(3), 255–267.

Vickrey, W. S. (1969). Congestion theory and transport investment. *American Economic Review (Papers and Proceedings), 59*, 251–260.

CASE STUDY 11

Congestion and Low Emission Zones in London

Abstract

London's policymakers pursued congestion pricing to reduce vehicle usage in central London and implemented Low and Ultra-low Emission Zones (LEZ and ULEZ) to limit the most polluting vehicles across Greater London. In February 2003, London introduced the London Congestion Charge (LCC), the city's first congestion pricing system. The LEZ was implemented in 2008 to target the most polluting heavy vehicles. The ULEZ was implemented in 2019 to extend stricter standards to a wider range of vehicles. These three policies combine economic incentives with regulatory restrictions to influence travel behavior, reduce emissions, and generate revenues for public transportation investments. These initiatives were part of a broader urban sustainability strategy aligned with climate action goals. The study provides an overview of London's transportation and environmental challenges, outlines the policy frameworks for congestion pricing and emission control, and evaluates their impacts on efficiency, equity, and stakeholder engagement.

Topics

Green Budgeting; Low Emission Zones; Low Emission Zone; Sustainability

Background

In 1998, drivers in London, including those in the wider metropolitan area, spent approximately 30% of peak travel time at a standstill and more than half of their journeys moving at speeds below 10 miles per hour, highlighting significant productivity losses attributable to congestion (Leape, 2006). By 2002, the situation had worsened, with the all-day average travel speed in central London declining to just 8.6 miles per hour, compared to an uncongested average of about 20 miles per hour (Leape, 2006). The economic cost was substantial. In 2002 alone, time lost to congestion was estimated to cost London between £2 million and £4 million per week (ESCAP, n.d.). The surveys in 1999 identified public transport and traffic congestion as the two most pressing issues requiring government action, prompting the London administration to prioritize congestion management on its policy agenda (Leape, 2006).

By the early 2000s, the main pollutants in London were nitrogen oxides (NOx) where Central London often exceeded the European Union (EU) limit of 40 $\mu g/m^3$ in annual average concentration level, volatile organic compounds, particulate matter (especially PM10) which was increasing at a rate of 3% per year from 2000 to 2002, and carbon monoxide (Croke, 2024; UK Parliament, 2002; University of London, 2003).

Congestion and Low Emission Zones

The Low Emission Zone (LEZ) is a geographically defined area in which access by polluting vehicles is restricted through either pricing or non-pricing mechanisms (Institute for Transportation and Development Policy [ITDP], 2023). LEZs are designed to reduce reliance on high-emission motor vehicles and to promote the adoption of cleaner alternatives, such as electric and hybrid vehicles. In priced LEZs, vehicle access is regulated by imposing fees on drivers, with charges typically scaled according to emission levels – higher-emitting vehicles incur greater costs, while low- or zero-emission vehicles, such as electric cars, may receive exemptions or pay significantly reduced fees (ITDP, 2023). In contrast, non-priced LEZs prohibit the entry of the most polluting vehicles altogether, with substantial fines levied against violators (ITDP, 2023).

LEZs operate as zonal systems with a primary focus on emission reduction rather than traffic volume management and are therefore not classified within the traditional congestion pricing literature. Nonetheless, congestion pricing initiatives are often implemented as part of broader urban governance frameworks, where objectives extend beyond congestion mitigation to encompass GHG reduction, air quality improvement, and the encouragement of active transportation modes (Veitch & Rhodes, 2024).

In 1999, the Greater London Authority Act established the Greater London Authority and granted the mayor broad authority over transportation. The Road Charging Options for London working group published its Report in March 2000. On February 17, 2003, London introduced the London Congestion Charge (LCC), the city's first congestion pricing system, covering a 21-square-kilometer area in the central city (Croci, 2016; Lehe & Devunuri, 2022). The initial charge of £5 per day was for vehicles entering the designated Congestion Charging Zone (CCZ) from 7:00 a.m. to 6:30 p.m., Monday to Friday, excluding public holidays (Leape, 2006). The LCC's capital implementation cost was approximately £160 million, with annual operating costs of about £90 million. The system generated an average gross revenue of £182.5 million per year (Croci, 2016). Although an expansion of the LCC was proposed in 2004, it was ultimately abandoned due to insufficient public support (Lehe & Devunuri, 2022).

In June 2020, to facilitate safer travel during the COVID-19 pandemic, the congestion charge was temporarily increased to £15 per day, with extended hours from 7:00 a.m. to 10:00 p.m., seven days a week (Transport for London, 2020). Currently, the congestion charge involves a daily fee of £15 for vehicles that pay in advance or on the same day, driving within the CCZ from 7:00 a.m. to 6:00 p.m., Monday to Friday; 12:00 p.m. to 6:00 p.m., Saturday, Sunday, and bank holidays. £17.5 is charged to those paying within three days after the travel (Transport for London, n.d.).

Low Emission Zone

London saw quick results after establishing a congestion zone in 2003, but traffic crept back over time as the city's streets became clogged with taxis, ride-hail cars, and delivery trucks (Hu et al., 2023). To further address the air pollution caused by transportation, LEZ was implemented in February 2008 to encourage the most polluting heavy diesel vehicles driving in London to become cleaner (Transport for London, n.d.). The LEZ imposes differentiated emissions standards for vehicles entering the zone, exempting compliant vehicles from the daily charge. These standards have been progressively tightened over time. Vehicles that fail to meet the prescribed requirements are subject to financial penalties (CloudFront, 2020). Specifically, lorries, vans, and specialist heavy vehicles exceeding 3.5 tons gross vehicle weight (GVW), along with buses, minibuses, and coaches over 5 tons GVW, are required to comply with at least the EURO 6 standards for NOx and PM (Transport for London, n.d.). In addition, vans and specialist diesel vehicles with an unladen weight between 1.205 tons and 3.5 tons GVW, as well as minibuses up to 5 tons GVW, must meet at minimum the EURO 3 standard.

Ultra-low Emission Zone

The Ultra-low Emission Zone (ULEZ), introduced in April 2019, established stricter emission standards across a broader spectrum of vehicles with the objective of achieving substantial reductions in NOx and PM emissions (Coggins, 2023). Unlike the LEZ, which primarily targeted heavy-duty vehicles, the ULEZ applies to passenger cars, vans, and motorcycles in addition to heavier vehicles. Initially restricted to a small area of inner London, the ULEZ was expanded on 29 August 2023 to encompass all London boroughs, making it the largest clean air zone in the world (Mayor of London, n.d.). Vehicles that do not comply with ULEZ standards and are not exempt are subject to a daily charge of £12.5. This requirement applies to cars, motorcycles, vans, and specialist vehicles up to 3.5 tons GVW, as well as minibuses up to 5 tons

GVW (Transport for London, n.d.). In contrast, lorries, vans, and specialist heavy vehicles exceeding 3.5 tons GVW, as well as buses, minibuses, and coaches over 5 tons GVW, are subject to the LEZ charge if they fail to meet LEZ standards, rather than the ULEZ charge.

Funding of congestion and Low Emission Zones in London

The congestion charges scheme has generated substantial revenue for the London government. In 2022, net revenues from the Congestion Charge amounted to £307 million, while the ULEZ and LEZ produced net incomes of £111 million and £34 million, respectively (OECD, 2022). Consistent with the Mayor's Transport Strategy, revenues from road user charges are reinvested in improving London's transport system, with the overarching goal of increasing the modal share of walking, cycling, and public transport to 80% of all trips by 2041 (Transport for London, n.d.). The strategy encompasses a wide range of initiatives, including plans for bus network expansion, cycling infrastructure, freight management, safety improvements, and enhanced pedestrian accessibility, all of which emphasize sustainability and inclusivity. Furthermore, the strategy integrates broader urban development goals, such as delivering 65,000 new homes and generating approximately 1.3 million additional jobs by 2041, thereby contributing to improvements in overall quality of life (Transport for London, n.d.).

Benefits of congestion and Low Emission Zones in London

After the introduction of the congestion charge in 2003, there was a significant reduction in congestion by about 30% compared to pre-charging levels in 2002, which was only 8% by 2006 (Transport for London, & Mayor of London, 2008). About 30% of those who previously drove in the western extension zone during charging hours stopped doing so after the introduction of the congestion charge and switched to alternative modes of transport (Transport for London, & Mayor of London, 2008). Additionally, the congestion charge realized a reduction of about 68 car occupant casualties per year within CCZ, representing a drop of 3.4% compared to the prior year (Noland et al., 2008).

The annual CO_2 emissions in the CCZ fell by 11.16% in the first year (2003) of the implementation of the CCS, compared to the emissions in 2002. The Greater London area saw a 1.75% reduction in CO_2 emissions in the same period (Bu, 2013). While the annual methane emissions in the CCZ increased slightly by 0.35% in 2003 compared to 2002, the Greater London area saw a reduction of 7.73% in methane emissions (Bu, 2013).

The congestion charge resulted in modest reductions in NO_2 and PM10 concentrations across Greater London. The annual average NO_2 level in Greater London was reduced by 0.10 $\mu g/m^3$, while within the CCZ the reduction was 0.73 $\mu g/m^3$ from 2003 to 2008 (Tonne et al., 2008). For PM10, the reductions were 0.03 μg/m³ across Greater London and 0.24 micrograms per cubic meter within the CCZ (Tonne et al., 2008). From 2008 to 2013, the CCZ led to a 20% decrease in PM10 emissions in London and indirectly resulted in a 27% reduction in PM2.5 emissions and a 25% decrease in NOx emissions (Mayor of London, 2021). The expansion of ULEZ contributed to the reduction of NO_2. By June 2022, roadside NO_2 concentrations in central London were 35 μg/m³ lower than the estimated "no ULEZ" scenario, with those in inner London 8 μg/m³ lower than the estimated "no ULEZ" scenario, representing a difference of 44% and 20% respectively (Mayor of London, 2022).

Equity concerns for specific groups

Essential workers, including National Health Service (NHS) staff and caregivers, frequently face rigid schedules and critical responsibilities that necessitate driving into Central London. Patients, particularly those with chronic conditions or disabilities, often require regular access to healthcare facilities in the congestion zone. For these groups, congestion charges may impose an undue financial burden. To mitigate such effects, the London government offers reimbursement schemes for eligible NHS staff, patients, and home care workers. For instance, qualifying NHS patients may claim reimbursement of both the Congestion Charge and the ULEZ charge for travel to and from hospital appointments, while NHS staff may receive reimbursement for specific work-related journeys made in personal vehicles (Transport for London, n.d.). To address the equity concern for the disabled, the government established exemptions for blue badge holders in the European Economic Area, which means the qualified individual can enjoy a 100% discount when traveling within the CCZ (Transport for London, n.d.).

In addition to healthcare-related groups, low-income travelers are disproportionately affected (Craik & Balakrishnan, 2023). Empirical evidence indicates that under the congestion charging scheme, low-income travelers reduced their trips into Central London by 25%, including both chargeable and non-chargeable journeys, compared to only a 2% reduction among higher-income groups (Craik & Balakrishnan, 2023). This disparity suggests that low-income individuals face greater constraints in substituting alternative modes of transport or adjusting travel times, reflecting limited access to reliable public transportation. Consequently, congestion charges represent a heavier financial burden for these groups, who typically have less disposable income. Moreover, even when public transit routes are available for occupations commonly held by low-skilled workers, such routes may be inconvenient or inadequate, compelling workers to continue driving and thereby exposing them more acutely to the costs of congestion pricing (Department of Transportation, 2008). For low-income groups, investments in public transportation provide greater commuting options and can help alleviate financial burdens associated with private vehicle use. Additional measures, such as targeted assistance through tax credits or income-based discounts, could provide more direct and effective relief to vulnerable populations, ensuring greater equity in the distribution of costs and benefits under the congestion charging scheme (Craik & Balakrishnan, 2023). The reinvestment of revenues into sustainable transport infrastructure not only advances environmental goals but also provides tangible benefits to disadvantaged groups by improving accessibility and affordability of mobility options. Moreover, targeted exemptions and reimbursement programs for NHS staff, patients, and low-income households further reflect a conscious effort to mitigate the regressive impacts of the charges (Kraft & Furlong, 2024; Rossi et al., 2019).

The LCC involved extensive collaboration among key stakeholders, including the Mayor of London, Transport for London (TfL), the London Assembly, the national government, and local authorities. The funding was through its General Fund and additional funding by the UK government via the Ministry of Transport. Moreover, local authorities utilized video cameras to record license plates; the Department of Transport, local highway authorities, and the Highways Agency collaborated with TfL to install signage indicating the charging zone boundaries (Center for Public Impact, 2016).

In 2023, TfL engaged stakeholders by consulting with motoring organizations, freight and logistics groups, and transport and environmental advocacy groups, co-creating the ULEZ expansion details (Sam Schwartz, 2024). A coalition involving stakeholders such as NHS trusts, unions, professional bodies, advocacy groups for the disabled and elder, local communities, and faith groups was also formed to address air quality and health impacts from traffic congestion (Sam Schwartz, 2024). Then TfL launched a multi-channel integrated campaign to raise awareness about the forthcoming expansion, covering detailed aspects, which achieved a 94% awareness rate among the population. This kind of multi-stakeholder engagement can achieve "collaborative decision-making and planning aspires to resolve potential conflicts" in terms of different interests and, following implementation, ensuring more informed and comprehensive decision-making while defining clearly separate responsibilities (Kraft & Furlong, 2025, p. 410).

Conclusions

London established a congestion zone in 2003 and quickly saw an improvement on its streets. Within a year, the number of vehicles entering the zone dropped 18%, according to city officials. Findings reveal significant reductions in traffic volume, improvements in air quality, and enhanced public transportation investment. Traffic delays were reduced by 30%, and the average speed of vehicles rose to 10 miles an hour from 8.8 miles an hour. Air quality also improved as a result of the lower traffic volume, with a 12% reduction in emissions of NOx and PM from vehicles in the zone. However, equity concerns may exist during the implementation because congestion pricing may disproportionately affect marginalized groups, including disabled people and low-income individuals. Thus, the London government implemented specific discounts and exemptions for disabled people and low-income individuals, followed by re-investing and improving public transportation.

Discussion questions

1. What are the primary benefits and drawbacks of congestion pricing from a public policy perspective?
2. In what ways did the London Congestion Charge and LEZ complement each other in addressing urban transportation challenges?
3. What measures did London take to address equity concerns, and how effective were they?
4. How do congestion charges function as both a revenue-generating tool and a policy instrument for behavior change?
5. What trade-offs between efficiency and equity are most evident in London's congestion and emission zone policies?
6. How should policymakers evaluate the success of congestion pricing schemes – by revenue raised, emissions reduced, congestion alleviated, or equity considerations?
7. In what ways did London's use of revenue reinvestment into public transport contribute to long-term sustainability and social equity?
8. Considering the regressivity of congestion charges, what additional fiscal or policy instruments could governments adopt to protect low-income households?
9. How do stakeholder coalitions (e.g., NHS, unions, advocacy groups, local authorities) influence the political feasibility and legitimacy of congestion pricing policies?
10. What lessons can U.S. cities (e.g., New York, Chicago, Los Angeles) learn from London's phased implementation of congestion and emission zones? How can the revenue generated from congestion pricing be strategically reinvested to maximize public benefit?

References

Bu, L. J. (2013). *The impact of the congestion charging scheme on greenhouse gas and air pollutants emissions in London*. Columbia University. https://academiccommons.columbia.edu/doi/10.7916/D89Z931K

Center for Public Impact. (2016, April 15). *London's congestion charge*. https://www.centreforpublicimpact.org/case-study/demand-management-for-roads-in-london

CloudFront. (2020). *Congestion Charging*. https://d2e1qxpsswcpgz.cloudfront.net/uploads/2020/03/transport-report-evidence-table-congestion-charging.pdf

Coggins, M. (2023, September 22). *ULEZ and its expansion*. Institute for Government. https://www.instituteforgovernment.org.uk/explainer/ulez

Craik, L., & Balakrishnan, H. (2023). Equity impacts of the London congestion charging scheme: An empirical evaluation using synthetic control methods. *Transportation Research Record, 2677*(5), 1017–1029. https://doi.org/10.1177/03611981221138801

Croci, E. (2016). Urban road pricing: A comparative study on the experiences of London, Stockholm and Milan. *Transportation Research Procedia*, *14*, 253–262. https://doi.org/10.1016/j.trpro.2016.05.062

Croke, D. (2024, March 26). Weekly market update: the real cost of highway congestion. *DAT*. https://www.dat.com/blog/weekly-market-update-the-real-cost-of-highway-congestion

de Palma, A., & Lindsey, R. (2011). Traffic congestion pricing methodologies and technologies. *Transportation Research. Part C, Emerging Technologies*, *19*(6), 1377–1399. https://doi.org/10.1016/j.trc.2011.02.010

Department of Transportation. (2006, December). *Congestion pricing: A primer*. https://ops.fhwa.dot.gov/publications/congestionpricing/congestionpricing.pdf

Department of Transportation. (2008). *Income-based equity impacts of congestion pricing: A primer*. https://ops.fhwa.dot.gov/publications/fhwahop08040/fhwahop08040.pdf

Department of Transportation. (2021, March 26). *Pricing, demand, and economic efficiency—A primer*. https://ops.fhwa.dot.gov/publications/fhwahop08041/fhwahop08041.pdf

ESCAP. (n.d.). *London, United Kingdom's congestion charge*. https://www.unescap.org/sites/default/files/30.%20CS-London-United-Kingdom-congestion-charge.pdf

Heller, C.-P., Johnen, J., & Schmitz, S. (2019). Congestion pricing: A mechanism design approach. *Journal of Transport Economics and Policy*, *53*(1), 74–98.

Hu, W., Ley, A., Castle, S., & Anderson, C. (2023, December 2). Congestion pricing's impact on New York? These 3 cities offer a glimpse. *The New York Times*. https://www.nytimes.com/2023/12/02/nyregion/new-york-congestion-pricing-london-stockholm-singapore.html

IPCC. (2022). Emissions trends and drivers, Climate change 2022: Mitigation of climate change. Contribution of Working Group III to the Sixth Assessment Report of the Intergovernmental Panel on Climate Change. Cambridge University Press. https://doi.org/10.1017/9781009157926.004

Institute for Transportation & Development Policy. (2023, February 22). *What is a low emission zone?* https://itdp.org/2023/02/22/what-is-a-low-emission-zone/

Kraft, M. E., & Furlong, S. R. (2024). *Public policy: Politics, analysis, and alternatives* (8th ed.). Washington, DC: CQ Press.

Leape, J. (2006). The London congestion charge. *The Journal of Economic Perspectives*, *20*(4), 157–176. https://doi.org/10.1257/jep.20.4.157

Lehe, L. J., & Devunuri, S. (2022). Large elasticity at introduction. *Research in Transportation Economics*, *95*, 101116. https://doi.org/10.1016/j.retrec.2021.101116

Mayor of London. (n.d.). *The Ultra Low Emission Zone (ULEZ) for London*. https://www.london.gov.uk/programmes-strategies/environment-and-climate-change/pollution-and-air-quality/ultra-low-emission-zone-ulez-london#:~:text=The%20ULEZ%20expansion,more%20polluting%20vehicles%20in%20London

Mayor of London. (2021). *London Low Emission Zone six-month report*. https://www.london.gov.uk/sites/default/files/lez_six_month_on_report-final.pdf

Mayor of London. (2022). *Expanded Ultra Low Emission Zone six-month report including Low Emission Zone one-year report*. https://www.london.gov.uk/sites/default/files/expanded_ultra_low_emission_zone_six_month_report.pdf

Noland, R. B., Quddus, M. A., & Ochieng, W. Y. (2008). The effect of the London congestion charge on road casualties: An intervention analysis. *Transportation (Dordrecht)*, *35*(1), 73–91. https://doi.org/10.1007/s11116-007-9133-9

OECD. (2022, November 7). *London's congestion charge and its low emission zones.* https://www.oecd.org/en/publications/2021/09/ipac-policies-in-practice_1a65968e/london-s-congestion-charge-and-its-low-emission-zones_1078722d.html

Tonne, C., Beevers, S., Armstrong, B., Kelly, F., & Wilkinson, P. (2008). Air pollution and mortality benefits of the London Congestion Charge: Spatial and socioeconomic inequalities. *Occupational and Environmental Medicine (London, England)*, 65(9), 620–627. https://doi.org/10.1136/oem.2007.036533

Transport for London. (n.d.). *Congestion charge.* https://tfl.gov.uk/modes/driving/congestion-charge

Transport for London. (n.d.). *Low emission zone.* https://tfl.gov.uk/modes/driving/low-emission-zone

Transport for London. (n.d.). *Your vehicle and LEZ.* https://tfl.gov.uk/modes/driving/low-emission-zone/your-vehicle-and-lez

Transport for London. (n.d.). *LEZ: Where and when.* https://tfl.gov.uk/modes/driving/low-emission-zone/about-the-lez?intcmp=40405

Transport for London. (n.d.). *Ultra low emission zone.* https://tfl.gov.uk/modes/driving/ultra-low-emission-zone?intcmp=26434

Transport for London. (n.d.). *Discounts and exemptions.* https://tfl.gov.uk/modes/driving/congestion-charge/discounts-and-exemptions

Transport for London. (n.d.). *Reimbursements of the congestion charge and ULEZ charge.* https://tfl.gov.uk/modes/driving/reimbursements-of-the-congestion-charge-and-ulez-charge#on-this-page-0

Transport for London. (n.d.). *The mayor's transport strategy.* https://tfl.gov.uk/corporate/about-tfl/the-mayors-transport-strategy

Transport for London, & Mayor of London. (2008). *Central London Congestion Charging: Impacts monitoring-sixth annual report*, July 2008. https://content.tfl.gov.uk/central-london-congestion-charging-impacts-monitoring-sixth-annual-report.pdf

Transport for London. (2020, June 16). *Temporary changes to the congestion charge to secure safe recovery* [Press release]. https://tfl.gov.uk/info-for/media/press-releases/2020/june/temporary-changes-to-the-congestion-charge-to-secure-safe-recovery

Transport for London. (2021). *Congestion charge zone.* https://lruc.content.tfl.gov.uk/congestion-charge-area-map.pdf

UK Parliament. (2002, November 1). *Air quality in the UK.* https://www.parliament.uk/globalassets/documents/post/pn188.pdf

University of London. (2003). *Air quality in London 2002: The tenth report of the London air quality network.* https://www.londonair.org.uk/london/reports/AirQualityInLondon2002.pdf

Veitch, E., & Rhodes, E. (2024). A cross-country comparative analysis of congestion pricing systems: Lessons for decarbonizing transportation. *Case Studies on Transport Policy*, *15*, 101128. https://doi.org/10.1016/j.cstp.2023.101128

Videos

What is London's Ultra Low Emission Zone? - BBC London https://www.youtube.com/watch?v=zHd0L6i8-uc

ULEZ - How To: Check, Pay, Challenge https://www.youtube.com/watch?v=a0rMp5_AAGQ

5

PARTICIPATORY BUDGETING

Abstract

This chapter provides a systematic examination of participatory budgeting, focusing on its theoretical foundations and fiscal implications. This chapter analyzes the implementation of participatory budgeting across institutional and geographic contexts, with particular attention to its adoption and evolution in the United States. It evaluates variations in funding commitments, and participant composition, including youth-led initiatives. This chapter evaluates participatory budgeting outcomes and identifies key administrative, political, and fiscal challenges.

Participatory budgeting

Participatory budgeting (PB) is a democratic approach to budgeting that enables residents to directly participate in budgetary decision-making and weigh in on how some of the resources can be allocated (Aziz & Shah, 2020). Instead of budgeting decisions being made solely by elected officials or administrators, PB invites community members to propose ideas, deliberate priorities, and vote on specific projects. The government then commits to funding and implementing the projects that receive the most public support.

The PB process is long (Aziz & Shah, 2020). First, government sets aside a defined amount of money, often for capital or neighborhood-level projects. The residents then participate in meetings and use online tools to share and discuss their ideas such as park improvements, street repairs, community programs, or public safety initiatives. Then focus groups and experts develop those ideas into proposals to ensure feasibility and cost accuracy. After several rounds of reviews,

DOI: 10.4324/9781003606833-6

residents finally vote on how the public budget will be distributed amongst the final proposals. Increasing engagement in these practices with advertisements and promotions is important for ensuring adequate participation and the inclusion of minorities and other more vulnerable groups (Aziz & Shah, 2020).

PB has been praised for being a democratic, transparent, equitable, educational, and efficient process of budget allocation (Baiocchi & Lerner, 2007). This process gives participants the essential knowledge, data, and procedures needed to appropriately partake in budgeting decisions. Engaged budgeting prioritizes transparency throughout the budgeting process and maximizes access for citizen participation, leading to increased satisfaction among citizens (Muthomi & Thurmaier, 2021). Hong (2015) notes, "Increasing the number of citizens participating in policy making may encourage 'the wisdom of the crowds.'" PB is the only form of civic engagement where citizens are spending real public dollars (Gilman, 2016).

Challenges to participatory budgeting

PB approach does not exist without flaws. The challenges to PB include the unclear goals, lack of participant motivations, and limiting structures (Pape & Lerner, 2016). Although PB is known to increase equity and citizen satisfaction with their government, several studies have found that there might not be enough empirical evidence to support these claims (Muthomi & Thurmaier, 2021).

PB originated in Porto Alegre, Brazil, in 1989 (Wampler, 2020), when the country was transitioning from military dictatorship to democracy. It was introduced by the newly elected Workers' Party (Partido dos Trabalhadores) to promote democracy and transparency. The increase in popularity in PB in Brazil was accompanied with a reduction in extreme poverty, better access to public services, greater spending on health services, and a reduction in child and infant mortality (Hagelskamp et al., 2018). The success of PB in Porto Alegre led to its rapid diffusion across Latin America in the 1990s, then to Europe, North America, Africa, and Asia in the 2000s. Over the last decade or so, PB has begun to spread in the United States, from large urban centers to smaller cities and towns (Hagelskamp et al., 2018).

In the United States, PB process is comparatively uncommon but gaining popularity. One of the first cases transpired in Chicago in 2009, where one of the city's aldermen, Joe Moore, pioneered the idea and facilitated allocation of about $1.3 million in PB efforts to one of the wards (Gilman, 2016). Since 2009 over $18 million of Chicago's budget has been allocated to fund 245 projects in the city, where about 13,000 residents in 12 communities participated in PB initiatives (PB Chicago). In 2011 the PB process was launched in four New York City (NYC) districts. With close to $35 million in annual spending, NYC PB has now become the largest PB process in the United States. Since then, the PB approach has spread to some other cities in the United States. Table 5.1 provides a summary of PB efforts in the United States.

TABLE 5.1 Participatory Budgeting in the United States

State	*City*	*Notes*	*Links*
AK	Anchorage	No PB in place. Anchorage utilizes a Balanced Budget process and allows for public comment twice throughout the process of adopting the budget. In 2025, Anchorage hosted a public workshop for residents that invited feedback to the budget plan.	https://www.muni.org/Departments/Assembly/Pages/FOCUS-Budget-and-Taxes.aspx
AK	Fairbanks	No PB process in place. In 2025, Fairbanks introduced the Balancing Act budget simulator, allowing the public to see how their priorities impact the budget and providing financial transparency.	https://files.aptuitivcdn.com/K9gxWNkmZ2-1856/docs/2025_city_capital_budget.pdf
AL	Birmingham	People's Budget Birmingham conducted community surveys to determine what the key goals/concerns were for residents.	https://peoplesbudgetbirmingham.org/wp-content/uploads/2020/09/pbb-survey-report-1.pdf
AL	Mobile	No PB process.	https://www.cityofmobile.org/uploads/file_library/com-fy2025-proposed-budget-document-(1).pdf
AL	Montgomery	No PB process.	
AR	Ft. Smith	No PB process.	https://www.fortsmithar.gov/government/departments/finance/purchasing/-folder-196#docan1738_2590_1056
AR	Little Rock	No PB process. Mayor said in 2019 that they are looking into adding a PB process in the future.	https://www.littlerock.gov/media/22909/reformattedfy25-budget-presentation.pdf https://www.arkansasonline.com/news/2019/sep/01/lr-s-2020-budget-needs-public-input-tim/?news-politics

(*Continued*)

TABLE 5.1 (Continued)

State	*City*	*Notes*	*Links*
AZ	Mesa	Mesa Public Schools has a PB process in place through five school districts. The districts have won $455,000 in student-developed school improvement projects over the span of the PB process.	https://www.arizonafuture.org/programs/education-programs/school-participatory-budgeting-in-arizona/
AZ	Phoenix	Phoenix Union High School District has a PB process. The 2019–2020 school year PB process allocated $55,000 to projects including water stations, cafeteria renovations, and a Digital Music Performance and Recording Club.	https://www.nationalcivicleague.org/promising-practices/phoenix-schools-implement-district-wide-participatory-budgeting-phoenix-az/
AZ	Tucson	The City of Tucson uses a program budget and allows for some public input in departments the offer direct services to the public. PB exists in Ward 1 under a program called Budget de la Gente.	https://city-tucson-az-cleardoc.cleargov.com/22311/855699/d https://budgetdelagente.tucsonaz.gov/
CA	Anaheim	No PB process in place. The city provides an online Balancing Act simulator that lets citizens submit their input.	https://data1-anaheim.opendata.arcgis.com
CA	Bakersfield	No PB process in place, but PB is used within Bakersfield's Transformative Climate Communities (TCC) grant program.	https://content.civicplus.com/api/assets/7fa32dcd-f986-47f2-93a4-149dd52219e0?cache=1800https://sgc.ca.gov/grant-programs/tcc/
CA	Fremont	No PB process in place.	https://www.fremont.gov/home/showpublisheddocument/18666
CA	Fresno	In 2017, Fresno was awarded $70 million for city improvements from the state, of which $37 million was allocated to projects in the Southwest neighborhoods for PB projects.	https://nextcity.org/urbanist-news/fresno-poorest-neighborhoods-city-plan-35-million-state-funds

CA	Huntington Beach	No PB process, but the city does have a Citizen Participation Advisory Board which helps make recommendations for the budget allocations.	https://cms3.revize.com/revize/huntingtonbeachca/Documents/Departments/Finance/Budget%20&%20Financial%20Reports/Budget%20Information/Adopted%20Budget%20FY%202025-26.pdf?t=202511251951550&t=202511251951550
CA	Long Beach	In 2014, Long Beach launched California's first fully developed PB process. The process consisted of community surveys, delegate meetings, neighborhood assemblies, and a vote. District 1 vote ($61,000), District 3 vote ($110,000), and District 9 vote ($295,000) for projects in the PB survey. In 2023, Long Beach started a PB program through Youth Power PB, allowing adolescents and young adults ages 13–26 to vote on how public funds should be spent.	https://publicagenda.org/wp-content/uploads/PublicSpendingByThePeople_PublicAgenda_2016.pdf https://www.longbeach.gov/press-releases/office-of-youth-development-announces-third-year-of-youth-power-pb-participatory-budgeting-long-beach/
CA	Los Angeles	In 2021, LA implemented the LA REPAIR PB program. The city will allocate $8.5 million across 9 neighborhoods highly impacted by COVID, high poverty rates, and pollution.	https://repair.lacity.gov/
CA	Modesto	No participatory budget process.	https://www.modestogov.com/ArchiveCenter/ViewFile/Item/4280
CA	Oakland	In 2017, Oakland allowed District 1 and 2 to begin a PB process. Projects are funded by the CDBG dollars. From 2017 to 2019, District 1 allocated a total of $227,308 for projects. In the same time frame, District 2 allocated $557,370 for PB projects.	https://pboakland.org/page/guidelines

(Continued)

TABLE 5.1 (Continued)

State	City	Notes	Links
CA	Riverside	No official PB process, but the city encourages public input through budget and council meetings. The city also used a priority-based budget process that reflects the needs of residents.	https://riversideca.gov/press/city-riverside-commences-two-year-budget-development-process-encourages-participation https://riversideca.gov/finance/budget.asp
CA	Sacramento	In 2021, Sacramento introduced a PB pilot program. The program allocated $1 million in Measure U funds for resident-proposed projects.	https://www.cityofsacramento.gov/city-manager/projects-and-programs/measureu/participatory-budgeting
CA	San Diego	No PB process.	https://www.sandiegocounty.gov/content/sdc/openbudget/en/budget-summary.html
CA	San Francisco	Started PB in one District (District 7) in 2013. Since 2017, the efforts have been expanded to Districts 8 and 9. The winning projects include traffic-calming, crime reduction efforts, and $250,000 to the Vision Zero project.	https://hoodline.com/2017/12/wisdom-of-the-crowd-residents-shape-neighborhoods-via-participatory-budgeting/ https://www.publicagenda.org/wp-content/uploads/2019/11/PublicSpendingByThePeople_PublicAgenda_2016.pdf https://www.participatorybudgeting.org/about-us/
CA	San Jose	Started as a small district-wide PB program in 2016. Since then, the city has expanded to a 5-neighborhood wide PB process. Funding comes from a $1 million grant that the city won, and projects are mostly neighborhood improvement projects such as better signage, and roads repairs.	https://sanjose.granicus.com/MetaViewer.php?meta_id=573358 https://nextcity.org/urbanist-news/san-jose-participatory-budgeting-spending-projects-decided

CA	Santa Ana	No PB process, but Santa Ana has created a Budget Priorities Survey for community input and participation. Citizens can also access the city's OpenBook portal to view budget data.	https://www.santa-ana.org/budget
CA	Stockton	No PB process.	https://www.stocktonca.gov/government/budget___financial_reports/index.php
CO	Aurora	No PB process, but citizen involvement is encouraged and possible through participation in the Citizens Advisory Budget Committee.	https://www.auroragov.org/city_hall/city_finances___budget/city_budget
CO	Colorado Springs	No PB process. However, the city website offers an online OpenBudget tool, creating more financial transparency.	https://coloradosprings.gov/document/2025-city-colorado-springs-budget-final.pdf https://coloradosprings.gov/budget/page/openbook-cos
CO	Denver	In 2021, Denver launched a PB process. The city allocated $1.7 million for neighborhood improvement projects. These projects have continued into 2024.	https://risetogetherdenver.org/hub-page/denverPB https://denvergov.org/Government/Agencies-Departments-Offices/Agencies-Departments-Offices-Directory/Department-of-Finance/Denver-Participatory-Budgeting
CT	Bridgeport	No PB process. However, local journalism has called for PB in Bridgeport and other cities in CT.	https://ctmirror.org/2023/03/20/ct-participatory-budgeting-change-democracy/
CT	Hartford	In 2015, the city partnered with an organization called Hartford Decide$, creating the first PB process in Connecticut. This partnership has led the community through several successful PB projects.	https://www.hartforddecides.org/about-us

(*Continued*)

TABLE 5.1 (Continued)

State	*City*	*Notes*	*Links*
CT	New Haven	In 2017, New Haven began a small approach to the PB process. The city's Neighborhood Public Improvement plan allocated $5,000 to traffic calming on one street (Olive Street). PB process in New Haven is planned to expand in the coming years.	https://www.newhavenindependent.org/index.php/article/calming_on_olive_street/
DC	Washington	No PB process in place, but testimonies are permitted.	https://dccouncil.gov/wp-content/uploads/2021/04/Instructions-for-Public-Participation-BUDGET-4.26.21-Final.pdf
DE	Dover	No PB process in place.	https://www.cityofdover.com/city-budget
DE	Wilmington	The city launched a citizen participation website in 2015 to try to engage more residents in the budgeting process. In 2025, the city implemented a PB process for residents of the 2nd District, allowing them to join the Steering Committee and submit ideas.	https://www.delawarepublic.org/politics-government/2015-04-03/wilmington-city-council-launches-citizen-participation-site https://www.wilmingtoncitycouncil.com/press-release-councilwoman-shane-darby-encourages-2nd-district-residents-to-submit-participatory-budget-ideas/
FL	Ft. Lauderdale	No official PB process, but the city offers an online Balancing Act simulation tool and a webpage explaining the ways that the public can engage with the budget process.	https://spotlightftl.com/community-engagement-in-the-budget-development-process https://fortlauderdale.abalancingact.com/fy2026
FL	Hialeah	No PB process.	https://www.hialeahfl.gov/217/Management-Budget

FL	Jacksonville	No established PB process, though there is an organization working with City Council to try to implement a PB process into the city charter.	http://apps2.coj.net/City_Council_Public_Notices_Repository/20191203%20Corresp%20New%20FL%20Majority%20Participating%20Budgeting%20Comm.pdf
FL	Miami	Miami has a Public Housing Citizen Participation program where citizens are surveyed and are able to propose projects for the city. Catalyst Miami also offers PB "Teach-Ins" and classes for the public to learn more about the PB process.	https://www.miamidade.gov/global/housing/citizen-participation.page https://www.catalystmiami.org/pb2025
FL	Orlando	No PB process.	
FL	St. Petersburg	No PB process, but the public has access to the city's interactive reporting tool on the website.	https://www.stpete.org/government/departments/finance/index.php
FL	Tallahassee	No PB process. However, the public is encouraged to contribute to meetings and participate and workshops during the budgeting process.	https://www.talgov.com/transparency/budget-fy26#s2.6
FL	Tampa	In 2021, citizens were encouraged to provide input for the use of funds from the American Rescue Plan. Residents could provide input through community meetings and surveys.	https://www.tampa.gov/document/american-rescue-plan-act-slfrf-2021-recovery-plan-performance-report-82531
GA	Atlanta	In 2020, Atlanta launched a PB pilot program. The program dedicated $1 million in funds for the downtown district to vote on transportation funding. After this pilot program, the city plans to expand the PB to other larger projects.	https://oidp.net/en/practice.php?id=1250
GA	Columbus	No PB process.	https://www.columbusga.gov/Portals/finance/financial-planning-resources/budgetbook-FY24.pdf?ver=x2KDMvyI4MZ9qK2anPRLiQ%3D%3D

(*Continued*)

TABLE 5.1 (Continued)

State	*City*	*Notes*	*Links*
IA	Cedar Rapids	No City-wide PB process. However, in 2020, the state of Iowa launched a five-year Citizen Participation Plan. This will allocate CDBG funds to community projects and will require resident feedback before voting. Cedar Rapids has also encouraged residents to fill out a survey providing feedback on the FY 2027 budget.	https://www.cedar-rapids.org/news_detail_T6_R2329.php https://opportunityiowa.gov/media/2450/download?inline https://cms8.revize.com/revize/cedarrapids/FY%202026%20Council%20Book%20-%20REVISED.pdf
IA	Des Moines	No City-wide PB process. However, in 2020, the state of Iowa launched a five-year Citizen Participation Plan. This will allocate CDBG funds to community projects and will require resident feedback before voting. As of 2026, the city is encouraging citizens to participate in the budgeting process and share priorities via online surveys and meeting attendance.	https://opportunityiowa.gov/media/2450/download?inline https://www.dsm.city/news_detail_T21_R417.php
ID	Boise	No PB process.	
ID	Nampa	No PB process.	https://www.cityofnampa.us/DocumentCenter/View/19993/APPROVED-BUDGET-BOOK-FY26-82525
IL	Aurora	The Block Grant Working Committee was established in 2020 as a part of the new Strategic Plan for the city. CDBG funds must be approved by the Block Grant Working Committee as well as City Council, encouraging more resident participation.	https://www.aurora.il.us/Government-and-Engagement/Boards-and-Commissions/Boards-Commissions-List/Block-Grant-Working-Committee

IL	Chicago	The City of Chicago initiated the PB process in 2013. In 2014–2015, the results for the PB were as follows: "22nd Ward, Alderman Ricardo Muñoz, April 2015 vote, US$924,950; 45th Ward, Alderman John Arena, April 2015 vote, US$1,030,000; 49th Ward, Alderman Joe Moore, April 2015 vote, US$992,000; Chicago Central Park TIF District, November 2014 vote, US$2,000,000."	https://www.publicagenda.org/wp-content/uploads/2019/11/PublicSpendingByThePeople_PublicAgenda_2016.pdf
IN	Ft. Wayne	No PB process.	https://www.cityoffortwayne.in.gov/ArchiveCenter/ViewFile/Item/216
IN	Gary	No PB process.	
IN	Indianapolis	No PB process.	
KS	Kansas City	Kansas City has many citizen participation tools included in their budgeting process. These engagement tools include citizen engagement with the budget process through surveys and interactions, meetings, the Balancing Act tool, and resident work sessions.	https://www.kcmo.gov/city-hall/departments/finance/office-of-management-and-budget-omb/public-process
KS	Topeka	No PB process.	https://budget.topeka.org/pages/about
KS	Wichita	No PB process. However, the city provided an online budget simulator for 2025.	https://www.wichita.gov/DocumentCenter/View/35247/00---2026-Adopted-Budget-PDF?bidId= https://www.wichita.gov/1828/2025-Budget-Simulator
KY	Lexington	No PB process, but the city does have a HUD-required citizen Participation Plan for the CDBG funds, as of 2016.	https://www.lexingtonky.gov/sites/default/files/2020-12/Citizens%20Participation%20Plan%20REVISED%204-2020%20Corona.pdf

(Continued)

TABLE 5.1 (Continued)

State	*City*	*Notes*	*Links*
KY	Louisville	Louisville's Metro Department of Public Health and Wellness founded a PB program called "Our Money, Our Voice" in 2018. The city has also launched a PB Steering Committee.	https://louisvilleky.gov/government/metro-council-district-21/participatory-budgeting-steering-committee https://louisvilleky.gov/news/neighborhood-residents-make-budgeting-decisions-two-metro-council-districts
LA	Baton Rouge	No PB process.	https://www.brla.gov/DocumentCenter/View/21316/2025-City-Parish-Annual-Operating-Budget-PDF
LA	New Orleans	In 2005, after Hurricane Katrina, the City of New Orleans used PB to decide what to do with relief funds. Since 2015, New Orleans' Citizen Participation Program has been allocated about $2 million annually for improvement projects.	https://participedia.net/case/5034
LA	Shreveport	No PB process.	https://www.shreveportla.gov/DocumentCenter/View/23241/10042023---2024-Annual-Operating-Budget
MA	Boston	City of Boston launched a PB process in 2014. The city allocates over $1 million of the capital budget annually to YLC. Anyone ages 12–22 who lives or attends schools in Boston can participate in a two-year process. In the first year, the projects are proposed and voted and in the second year implemented.	https://www.boston.gov/departments/youth-engagement-and-employment/youth-lead-change

MA	Springfield	Springfield does not have a PB process. The city's school district does, however, utilize evidence-based program budgeting with public input.	https://www.springfield-ma.gov/finance/fileadmin/budget/2022/FY22_Adopted_Budget_-_FINAL_Compressed.pdf https://sps.ss18.sharpschool.com/common/pages/GetFile.ashx?key=sFSQCt%2bh
MA	Worcester	Worcester does not utilize a PB process. However, in 2020, Worcester public schools began utilizing a participatory budget process, utilizing public input at a community forum hosted by Worcester Education Justice Alliance and other community-based organization. Funds through the Student Opportunity Act will support school projects for the fiscal year.	http://worcesteredjustice.org/wp-content/uploads/2020/03/Peoples-Budget-Forum-Report-Out.pdf https://www.worcesterma.gov/finance/budget-central
MD	Baltimore	No PB process. However, local journalism in Baltimore has called for more PB.	https://bbmr.baltimorecity.gov/budget-process https://marylandmatters.org/2021/04/14/opinion-we-need-participatory-budgeting-in-baltimore-city/
MD	Frederick	No PB process.	https://www.cityoffrederickmd.gov/194/Budget
ME	Lewiston	While Lewiston does not utilize a PB process for the city-wide budget, the city does have community participation in the budget process where CDBG projects are concerned. Since 2020, Lewiston has tasked the Citizen Advisory Committee with allocating the CDBG funds for specific wards in the city for community development projects.	https://www.lewistonmaine.gov/563/CDBG-Information
ME	Portland	While Portland does not currently utilize PB, it is on the table for council meetings in 2022.	http://www.portlandmaine.gov/ArchiveCenter/ViewFile/Item/1054

(*Continued*)

TABLE 5.1 (Continued)

State	*City*	*Notes*	*Links*
MI	Detroit	"In 2018, Detroit launched a pilot PB process with $250,000 in funds to spend on public infrastructure projects in the neighborhood surround Clark Park." Detroit plans to expand this process in the future to more disadvantaged areas in the city. In 2025, the City Council advocated for the implementation of a youth PB program and for $1 million to be allocated toward PB processes.	https://investdetroit.com/wp-content/uploads/2019/04/We-Decide-Detroit-Evaluation-Report.pdf https://detroitmi.gov/sites/detroitmi.localhost/files/2024-04/City%20Council%20Closing%20Resolution%20FY2025%20FINAL.pdf
MI	Flint	Flint does not use a PB process. In 2021, the city hired outside firms to decide how to spend the $94.7 million COVID relief package.	https://flintbeat.com/does-flint-need-a-compliance-firm-to-help-spend-covid-19-relief-funding/
MI	Grand Rapids	In the summer of 2021, Grand Rapids launched a pilot PB. The city allocated $2 million from the American Rescue Plan and allowed input from residents in every city ward as to how to spend the money. The city is repeating the process again for FY 2022 and the voting process is ongoing.	https://www.mlive.com/news/grand-rapids/2021/06/gr-residents-can-soon-decide-how-they-want-2-million-spent-in-their-neighborhoods.html https://www.grandrapidsmi.gov/Government/Programs-and-Initiatives/Participatory-Budgeting
MI	Warren	Warren does not utilize a PB process.	https://www.cityofwarren.org/wp-content/uploads/2025/04/Fiscal-2025-Council-Adopted-Budget.pdf

MN	Minneapolis	In 2017, Minneapolis launched a PB process. The city created a "Playbook" which helps city departments utilize a PB process for new projects and funding allocations. Since then, they have developed many PB-adjacent programs.	https://lims.minneapolismn.gov/Download/CommitteeReport/381/WM-12042017-CommitteeReport.pdf https://lims.minneapolismn.gov/Download/RCAV2/33954/Participatory%20Budgeting%20Overview%20and%20Introduction.pdf
MN	St. Paul	St. Paul has used a semi-PB process since 2014. The city allocates a portion of the Capital Improvement Budget's CDBG funds to community projects voted on with public input. The city also promotes public engagement with the budget process and has an Open Budget webpage that lets the public see how the budget is used.	https://academiccommons.columbia.edu/doi/10.7916/D89S1ZN7/download https://www.stpaul.gov/departments/financial-services/saint-pauls-budget https://information.stpaul.gov/pages/budget https://www.stpaul.gov/departments/mayors-office/city-budget-engagement
MO	Kansas City	Open Budget KC is an interactive tool for KC residents to understand the budget process and comment on their input. While Kansas City does not utilize an official public vote for their budget, they do rely on public comment.	https://www.kcmo.gov/city-hall/departments/finance/office-of-management-and-budget-omb/public-process
MO	St. Louis	St. Louis began a District-wide PB process in 2014. Ward 15 was awarded $97,000 for ward projects such as crime reduction and community parks. The process has since expanded to a city-wide effort in 2020, when a $4.7 million public health grant was awarded to the city. Residents voted on how to use the funds.	https://stlouiscountymo.gov/st-louis-county-departments/public-health/recast/project-reports/participatory-budgeting-toolkit/ https://www.publicagenda.org/wp-content/uploads/2019/11/PublicSpendingByThePeople_PublicAgenda_2016.pdf

(Continued)

TABLE 5.1 (Continued)

State	*City*	*Notes*	*Links*
MS	Gulfport	No PB process.	https://cms3.revize.com/revize/gulfportms/Documents/Departments/Finance/Audits%20&%20Budgets/FYE%202025%20Adopted%20Budget%20-%20Signed.pdf?t=202505081758330&t=202505081758330
MS	Jackson	In 2019, Jackson launched its first PB process. The Jackson People's Assembly helps facilitate the community outreach, survey, and voting process for the projects.	https://www.northsidesun.com/news-breaking-news/residents-invited-participate-jackson-budgeting-process#sthash.PqzrgEbT.dpbs
MT	Billings	No PB process.	https://www.billingsmt.gov/DocumentCenter/View/52831/FY-2025-Operating-Budget--5-Year-Capital-Improvement-Plan
MT	Missoula	No PB process.	https://www.engagemissoula.com/fy25budget
NC	Durham	Durham began a participatory budget process in 2016. The city allocated $2.4 million to the three wards, giving each ward $800,000 to spend for the fiscal year. The biggest winner of the 2019 PB process is the Durham Public School District, which received $405,000.	https://indyweek.com/news/durham/winners-of-durham-participatory-budget-2019/
NC	Greensboro	Greensboro adopted a PB process in 2014 for the 2015–2016 FY. Each of the city's five districts is allocated $100,000 in funds to spend on community-voted projects. In 2019, the city established a steering committee and a PB Commission to help with the PB process. The city is currently on its 4th PB cycle (1st cycle FY 2016–2017, 2nd cycle FY 2018–2019, 3rd cycle FY 2020–2021).	https://www.greensboro-nc.gov/departments/budget-evaluation/participatory-budgeting/about

NC	Raleigh	Raleigh includes a community survey in its budget process. This survey guides the City Council in budget decisions.	https://raleighnc.gov/grants-and-funding/current-city-budget
ND	Bismarck	No PB process.	https://www.bismarcknd.gov/DocumentCenter/View/49627/2025-Budget-?bidId=
ND	Fargo	No PB process.	https://fargond.gov/city-government/departments/finance/city-budget
NE	Lincoln	No PB process, beyond regular public hearings for the budget proposals.	https://www.lincoln.ne.gov/files/sharedassets/public/finance/budget/proposed-budget-calendar-22-24.pdf
NH	Manchester	No PB process.	https://www.manchesternh.gov/departments/finance/budget-info
NH	Nashua	In 2021, Nashua allocated $40,000 from their Tree Streets partnership to a PB project. Community members voted to spend all $40,000 on the Los Amigos ark Improvements project.	https://www.nashuanh.gov/1244/Tree-Streets-Neighborhood-Project
NM	Albuquerque	In 2019, Albuquerque spent $100,000 on a participatory budget for traffic improvements. The public voted on which traffic improvements they would like to see in their community. In 2023, PB Albuquerque was founded and has been creating equitable approaches to PB throughout the city.	https://www.cabq.gov/council/documents/final-martineztown-report.pdf https://www.pbabq.org/
NM	Las Cruces	No PB process, but residents are encouraged to provide their input at City Council sessions.	https://library.municode.com/nm/las_cruces/munidocs/munidocs?nodeId=776d423084cc7
NV	Las Vegas	No PB process.	https://files.lasvegasnevada.gov/finance/2025%20Fiscal%20Year/FY25%20Budget.pdf

(*Continued*)

TABLE 5.1 (Continued)

State	*City*	*Notes*	*Links*
NV	Reno	No PB process, other than public forums during budget meetings.	https://www.reno.gov/home/show publisheddocument/94474/638882733255870000
NY	Buffalo	In 2015, Buffalo's Masten District allocated $150,000 to 11 winning community projects. These projects included a farmers' market, community kitchen upgrades, road improvements, better trash infrastructure, a Healthy Cooking Campaign, community computer classes, street light replacements, and bus shelters. In 2017, the city allocated $10,000 to the Niagara district for improvement projects. Despite those efforts, the city cut the PB funding after the 2017–2018 FY.	https://www.cacwny.org/campaigns/participatory-budgeting/ http://www.pbbuffalo.org https://buffalonews.com/news/local/participatory-budgeting-cut-from-city-budget-continues-in-niagara-district/article_2ec32b74-ac8c-5905-838c-b4203812cad3.html
NY	New York	New York began the PB process in 2011. The process works through voter surveys and council and delegate facilitation. In 2019, the Council allocated $35 million to spend on PB projects. "PBNYC funds physical infrastructure projects in public spaces, cost at least $50,000 and have a lifespan of at least 5 years." In 2026, the Council Members are allotting $23 million in capital funding to the PB process.	https://council.nyc.gov/pb/ https://www.publicagenda.org/wp-content/uploads/2019/11/PublicSpendingByThePeople_PublicAgenda_2016.pdf
NY	Rochester	In 2019, the PB Rochester project allocated $200,000 to spend on capital projects to fight poverty and neighborhood improvement. The five winning projects included a city food garden, a tiny house projects, and Emergency Housing fund.	https://rmapiny.org/2022/08/24/participatory-budgeting-winners-announced/

NY	Syracuse	The CNYCF launched a PB project in 2022 for residents in Syracuse, also collaborating with other nonprofits and community organizations. The city also provides an online budget simulation tool with Balancing Act, promoting public engagement.	https://cnycf.org/about-us/publications-papers/2023-annual-report/participatory-budgeting-community-residents-make-their-own-funding-decisions/ https://www.syr.gov/Departments/Budget/Budget-Initiatives/Initiative-Balancing-Act
NY	Yonkers	In 2021, Yonkers City Council voted to establish a PB process. This process should be included in the next budget cycle.	https://www.yonkerstribune.com/2021/02/budget-finance-committee-meeting-monday-february-22-2021-500pm-est
OH	Akron	Akron does not have a PB process, but it does have a Citizen Participation Plan as a part of their five-year consolidated plan for the city's CDBG dollars. The city encourages public participation from low income and minority residents to decide what projects the CDBG funds should be put toward.	https://cms2.revize.com/revize/akronoh/Departments/Planning%20And%20Urban%20Development/Consolidated%20Plans/2024%20Action%20Plan%20Final.pdf
OH	Cincinnati	While Cincinnati does not have an official PB process, it does encourage public input for capital projects. Since 2018, the city has collected ideas for community projects in a survey on their website and listens to public input at city budget meetings. In the first year, the city collected over 110 suggested projects for the budget to focus on and implemented some in the next year's budget.	https://www.cincinnati-oh.gov/finance/budget/approved-fy-2020-2021-biennial-operating-budget/

(*Continued*)

TABLE 5.1 (Continued)

State	*City*	*Notes*	*Links*
OH	Cleveland	Cleveland does not have a PB process; however, there is a strong grassroots organization trying to get City Council to allocate $30.8 million in American Rescue Plan funds to a PB process.	https://www.cleveland.com/opinion/2022/03/give-clevelanders-a-voice-in-their-future-through-participatory-budgeting-molly-martin.html https://www.pbcle.com https://www.participatorybudgeting.org/resource/pbclecasestudy/
OH	Columbus	Columbus does not have a PB process, but a new Capital Improvement Budget was approved in 2025, and $9 million of the Capital Improvements program were planned to be allocated to PB.	https://abc6onyourside.com/news/local/columbus-city-council-approves-records-breaking-29-billion-capital-budget-mayor-andrew-ginther-crime-housing-safety-ohio
OH	Dayton	No PB process.	https://www.daytonohio.gov/DocumentCenter/View/15558/Budget-Overview-Presentation
OH	Toledo	No PB process. Kuorum worked with Toledo in 2017 on laying the groundwork for PB, but no formal process has been established.	https://stories.opengov.com/toledooh/16fc6c40-64f7-4ac2-86d5-426aaa751374/published/cYMVaqz7X?currentPageId=690233cbbbdd0b5efcd07218 https://www.kuorum.org/en/success-stories/a-participatory-budget-for-the-youth
OK	Oklahoma	No PB process. However, the Oklahoma Senate approved “an interactive budget website” that provides the public with a transparent view of the approved budget.	https://www.okc.gov/departments/finance/financial-and-budget-reports/budget-and-tax-reports/budget-book-breakdown https://oksenate.gov/press-releases/oklahoma-senate-launches-interactive-budget-website

OK	Tulsa	Tulsa does not have a PB process; however, it does have a Citizen Participation Plan which requires the city to allocate HUD funds for CDBG capital improvement projects under the direction of public input.	https://www.cityoftulsa.org/media/16959/citizen-participation-plan-revised_final-08-10-2021.pdf
OR	Eugene	No PB process.	https://city-eugene-or-cleardoc.cleargov.com/14058/473144/d
OR	Portland	Portland does not currently use PB; however, there are organizations with public support aiming to implement the PB process in the city.	https://www.pboregon.org/ https://www.pdxcityclub.org/wp-content/uploads/2025/05/2025-03-14-Participatory-Budgeting-final.pdf
OR	Salem	No PB process. However, Salem has ways for citizens to be involved in the budgeting process and attend committee meetings.	https://www.cityofsalem.net/government/budget-finance/annual-budget/get-involved-in-the-budget-process-1806
PA	Philadelphia	Philadelphia began a PB process in 2020. The city allocated $1 million to capital improvement projects.	https://www.phila.gov/programs/participatory-budgeting/
PA	Pittsburgh	Pittsburg does not have a PB process. However, the city's website also includes a page for budget engagement that the public can access.	https://engage.pittsburghpa.gov/city-pittsburgh-budget-engagements?_gl=1*xa43q5*_ga*MTQ5MzkwODU5My4xNzY4MjYxMTI2*_ga_6YKGFYBQNH*czE3NjgyNjExMjUkbzEkZzEkdDE3NjgyNjEzMDAkajYwJGwwJGgw
RI	Providence	No PB process. The State of Rhode Island's Department of Health, however, has launched a program that uses the PB process.	https://health.ri.gov/sites/g/files/xkgbur1006/files/publications/annualreports/participatory-budgeting-report-2024.pdf

(Continued)

TABLE 5.1 (Continued)

State	*City*	*Notes*	*Links*
RI	Warwick	The city of Warwick utilizes public input for their CDBG funds from HUD.	https://www.warwickri.gov/sites/g/files/vyhlif12206/f/uploads/draft_citizens_participation_plan_-_2025-2029.pdf
SC	Charleston	No PB process. There is public support for the PB process that is promoted by Charleston's ACLU.	https://www.aclusc.org/en/charleston-peoples-budget-coalition
SC	Columbia	No PB process. Columbia uses Zero-based budgeting.	https://budget.columbiasc.gov/ https://www.wltx.com/article/news/local/city-of-columbia-zero-based-budget-new-fiscal-year/101-9b14bc71-23fd-4077-87ce-c6927513089e
SD	Rapid City	No PB process. Rapid City utilizes the Priority-Based Budgeting process.	https://www.rcgov.org/index.php?option=com_docman&view=download&alias=31713-2025-mayor-s-proposed-budget&category_slug=finance-department&Itemid=149
SD	Sioux Falls	No PB process.	https://www.siouxfalls.gov/files/assets/public/v/1/city-government/budget/2025/fin24_006-2025-budgetbook_approved.pdf
TN	Chattanooga	No PB process. There is public support for a school district-wide and city-wide PB process as of 2020.	https://newschannel9.com/news/local/chattanooga-city-council-considers-participatory-budgeting-method-for-future-budgeting https://www.participatorybudgeting.org/people/ https://www.participatorybudgeting.org/people/
TN	Knoxville	No PB process; however, public support is gaining around implementing the process at a city-wide level.	https://www.knoxnews.com/story/opinion/2020/06/03/community-members-should-have-say-what-city-budget-funds/3126941001/

TN	Memphis	No PB process. A branch of Interface Studio LLC exists in the Memphis area and provides a Public Investment Guide for the City of Memphis that used PB.	https://interface-studio.com/projects/memphis-public-investment-guide/
TN	Nashville	As of 2021, "The Mayor's Office has allocated $2,000,000 in Capital Spending Plan funds (each year) to be distributed within the Bordeaux and North Nashville region. As of 2023, the city has expanded the Participatory Budgeting Cycle to be across Nashville and Davidson County."	https://www.nashville.gov/departments/mayor/participatory-budgeting
TX	Arlington	No PB process.	https://www.arlingtontx.gov/files/assets/city/v/6/finance/documents/budget-amp-business-plan/adopted-budget-documents/fy-2026-adopted-operating-budget-and-business-plan.pdf
TX	Austin	In 2018, Austin City Council recommended a PB process to be implemented. The city has since created a community engagement website called SpeakUp Austin, where citizens can have a say on the budgeting process.	http://www.austintexas.gov/edims/document.cfm?id=292640 https://speakupaustin.org/q3277
TX	Corpus Christi	No PB process.	https://www.corpuschristitx.gov/media/1d5phob4/adopted-budget-book-fy-2026-final-online.pdf
TX	Dallas	In 2019, Dallas Independent School District implemented a pilot PB process. "The Dallas ISD school board recently approved a district-wide pilot, allocating $60,000 to be divvied up in $20,000 increments to three winning projects nominated by high school students and judged by a council of their peers."	https://www.reformaustin.org/education/dallas-isd-tests-out-participatory-budgeting/ https://dallascityhall.com/departments/budget/financialtransparency/AnnualBudget/FY%202025-26%20Adopted%20Annual%20Operating%20and%20Capital%20Budget.pdf
TX	El Paso	No PB process.	https://www.elpasotexas.gov/assets/Documents/CoEP/OMB/FY25-Budget/FY25-Adopted-Budget-Book-new.pdf

(Continued)

TABLE 5.1 (Continued)

State	*City*	*Notes*	*Links*
TX	Ft. Worth	No PB process.	https://www.fortworthtexas.gov/files/assets/public/v/1/the-fwlab/documents/budget-documents/fy-2025-adopted-budget-book.pdf
TX	Garland	No PB process.	https://www.garlandtx.gov/DocumentCenter/View/22195/2025-26-Annual-Proposed-Operating-Budget-PDF
TX	Houston	No PB process. Houston does have a Citizen Participation Plan for allocating HUD CDBG dollars. Houston City Council also offers budget workshops for the public that allows residents to make comments/suggestions about the budget.	https://www.houstontx.gov/housing/plans-reports/cpp/2025/Citizen_Participation_Plan-2025-091725.pdf https://www.houstontx.gov/council/committees/fy2026budgetworkshops.html
TX	Lubbock	No PB process.	https://ci.lubbock.tx.us/storage/images/aSLt0pthDNHGMf3kPVsS61Lupl8HC6vN8kRDYK5Z.pdf
TX	San Antonio	Palo Alto College in San Antonio launched a Pilot PB program for San Antonio Alamo School District in 2013. In 2016, the program expanded to allocating $25,000 for student voted projects, and $25,000 for employee projects. In 2018, it expanded with San Antonio's District 9 and has since created multiple global partnerships.	https://www.alamo.edu/pac/about-pac/compliance/participatory-budgeting/ https://www.pbtx.org/
UT	Provo	No PB process.	https://www.provo.gov/DocumentCenter/View/1945/2025-Adopted-City-Budget?bidId=

VA	Chesapeake	No PB process.	https://www.cityofchesapeake.net/DocumentCenter/View/27964/FY-2025-to-2026-Adopted-Operating-Budget-PDF?bidId=
VA	Norfolk	No PB process. However, in 2023, Norfolk introduced an online simulation tool to create transparency and help engage residents with the budgeting process.	https://www.norfolk.gov/407/Budget-Strategic-Planning https://blog.polco.us/norfolk-budget-engagement
VA	Richmond	In 2021, Richmond approved a $15 million allocation to a PB process from funds from the city's capital improvement budget. Richmond has since developed a formal PB program through the PB Steering Commission.	https://www.rva.gov/office-city-clerk/news/city-councils-participatory-budgeting-steering-commission-applications-due https://www.rvapb.org/get-involved
VA	Virginia Beach	No PB process.	https://s3.us-east-1.amazonaws.com/virginia-beach-departments-docs/budget/Budget/Adopted/FY26/FY2025-26-Adopted-Operating-Budget.pdf
WA	Seattle	The PB process exists across multiple programs within the City of Seattle, including arts and culture, violence prevention, food equity, mental health, and public safety. The process was initiated for the BIPOC community following the 2020 protests for George Floyd, allowing members to have discretion over public safety spending. "In June 2021, the City of Seattle placed the development of a request for proposal (RFP) for the Participatory Budgeting process into the Seattle Office for Civil Rights (SOCR). SOCR will not be distributing the funds for participatory budgeting but will be developing the RFP that will contract the agency to run the participatory budgeting process."	https://www.seattle.gov/civilrights/participatory-budgeting

(Continued)

TABLE 5.1 (Continued)

State	*City*	*Notes*	*Links*
WA	Spokane	Spokane does not have a PB process, but it does have a Citizen Participation Plan, which engages and welcomes residents' budgeting input through a series of community meetings and forums during the executive preparation stage of the budget process.	https://static.spokanecity.org/documents/chhs/plans-reports/planning/draft-2024-citizen-participation-plan.pdf
WA	Tacoma	In 2018, the Tacoma-Pierce County Health Department began a PB process. The department allocated $100,000 to East and South Tacoma for community and neighborhood projects. The City of Tacoma formally adopted a PB process in 2024/2025, including youth-led and district-wide programs.	https://phnci.org/journal/introducing-participatory-budgeting-to-public-health-departments https://www.tpchd.org/Home/Components/Blog/Blog/21220/ https://tacoma.gov/government/departments/management-and-budget-office/participatory-budgeting/
WI	Madison	No PB process.	https://www.cityofmadison.com/finance/documents/budget/2025/Adopt2025-AdoptedBudgetBook.pdf
WI	Milwaukee	In 2025, the city set aside $600,000 for citizens to decide how the funding should be spent. The initiative was pushed by the African American Roundtable advocacy group.	https://www.jsonline.com/story/news/local/2025/04/01/milwaukee-participatory-budgeting-measure-advances-to-full-council/82647170007/
WV	Charleston	No PB process. There is public grassroots action to implement it in the city.	http://www.participatorybudgeting.org/wp-content/uploads/2016/06/PBP_AnnualReport_2016_small-1.pdf
WV	Huntington	No PB process. However, "citizen participation" is mentioned in the FY 2025 Annual Action Plan.	https://www.cityofhuntington.com/assets/pdf/Huntington_FY25-29_Five-Year_Consolidated_Plan_and_FY25_Annual_Action_Plan_-_DISPLAY_DRAFT.pdf

WY	Casper	Casper City Council wants to implement a “priority-based budget system” for FY 2026, where citizens can fill out a questionnaire and provide feedback. PB is not mentioned explicitly in the Adopted Budget plan, but participatory processes are mentioned in the Community Engagement section.	https://cms2.revize.com/revize/casperwy/Documents/Government/Finance/Current%20Budget%20Year/FY2026%20Adopted%20Budget.pdf?t=202509021219120&t=202509021219120 https://oilcity.news/community/city/2025/05/13/city-to-seek-input-on-priority-based-budgeting-plans/
WY	Cheyenne	No PB process.	https://www.cheyennecity.org/files/sharedassets/public/v/1/departments/city-treasurer/adopted-budgets/fy2025-adopted-budget.pdf

Interestingly, PB efforts in NYC, Boston, Cambridge, Vallejo, CA and Central Falls, RI were facilitated by the same prominent PB practitioner and educator, Pam Jennings. In many cities, including Detroit, MI, Seattle, WA, Boston, MA, and others, the PB process has been led by youth (Budget and Management Services Department, 2019, 2021; Department of Finance and Administrative Services, 2019; Office of the Chief Financial Officer, 2021; Seattle Department of Neighborhoods, 2015). In Boston, for example, PB started in 2014 when the city allocated close to one million dollars to the "Youth Lead the Change (YLC)" initiative, where residents of the city ages 12–22 could propose and vote for the capital budgeting projects (City of Boston, n.d.). Similarly, the first PB efforts in Seattle started in 2016 when the city allocated $700,000 to the "Youth Voice, Youth Choice" initiative. The age of participants was initially limited to 11–25-year-olds (Seattle Department of Neighborhoods, 2015). In 2019, Central Falls, RI, a small suburb of Providence, RI, allocated $10,000 of the city budget to its local high school to promote PB among students. This initiative expanded to the entire school district and increased to $100,000 after 2020, when COVID-19 pandemic stimulus funds became available. The school called this PB initiative "Voces Con Poder" (Voices with Power) (Guzman & Ermasova, 2023).

Since its inception, many locations have seen the expansion of PB. For example, in Seattle in 2017, the PB initiative was expanded from youth participation only to the entire community. The price tag also increased from $700,000 in 2016 to $2 million of the budget in 2017. The new PB initiative is called "Your Voice, Your Choice: Parks and Streets" (Seattle Department of Neighborhoods, 2015). In Central Falls, RI PB process expanded from $10,000 (of the city budget) allocated to its high school in 2019 to $100,000 (of COVID-19 stimulus funds) allocated to the entire school district in 2021, to $50,000 (of the city budget) allocated to the general public in 2022 (Deluca, 2022). At the same time, the take-up of PB budgeting efforts in some other places has declined. Vallejo, CA in the first round of funding in 2012 allocated $3.4 million to PB initiatives. The funding of PB efforts has been consistently declining in this city over time. In 2017–2018, only about $1 million was earmarked for PB projects (Guzman & Ermasova, 2023).

Conclusion

Participatory budgeting continues to expand as a democratic budgeting innovation that promotes civic engagement, transparency, and community input in public resource allocation despite persistent challenges related to its implementation and participation. The following case study is from New York City that currently runs the largest participatory budgeting initiative in the United States.

References

Aziz, H., & Shah, N. (2020). Participatory budgeting: Models and approaches. In *Pathways between social science and computational social science: theories, methods, and interpretations* (pp. 215–236). Cham: Springer International Publishing.

Baiocchi, G., & Lerner, J. (2007). Could participatory budgeting work in the United States? *The Good Society*, *16*(1), 8–13.

Budget and Management Services Department (2019). City of Raleigh, NC. Annual Budget FY beginning July 1, 2019. Online at: https://cityofraleigh0drupal.blob.core.usgovcloudapi.net/drupal-prod/COR11/FY2020AdoptedBudget.pdf

Budget and Management Services Department (2021). City of Durham, North Carolina Budget Fiscal Year 2019–20. Online at: https://durhamnc.gov/DocumentCenter/View/27412/FY20-Final-Budget

City of Boston (n.d.). Youth Lead the Change. Accessed on October 30, 2022 from https://www.boston.gov/departments/youth-engagement-and-employment/youth-lead-change

Deluca, Z., (July 6, 2022). Smart trash bins win Central Fall participatory budgeting vote. *The Valley Breeze*.

Department of Finance and Administrative Services (2019). City of Flint Five Year Financial Plan 2018–2022. Adopted Budget for FY18 and FY19. Online at: https://www.cityofflint.com/wp-content/uploads/FY18-19-Adopted-Budget-book-1.pdf

Gilman, H. R. (2016). *Democracy reinvented: Participatory budgeting and civic innovation in America*. Brookings Institution Press.

Guzman, T., & Ermasova, N. (2023). *Municipal fiscal stress, bankruptcies, and other financial emergencies*. Taylor & Francis.

Hagelskamp, C., Schleifer, D., Rinehart, C., & Silliman, R. (2018). Participatory budgeting: Could it diminish health disparities in the United States? *Journal of Urban Health*, *95*(5), 766–771. https://doi.org/10.1007/s11524-018-0249-3

Hong, S. (2015). Citizen participation in budgeting: A trade-off between knowledge and inclusiveness? *Public Administration Review*, *75*(4), 572–582.

Muthomi, F., & Thurmaier, K. (2021). Participatory transparency in Kenya: Toward an engaged budgeting model of local governance. *Public Administration Review*, *81*(3), 519–531. https://doi.org/10.1111/puar.13294

National Association of State Budget Officers. (2021). Budget Process in the States. Retrieved from https://www.nasbo.org/reports-data/budget-processes-in-the-states

Office of the Chief Financial Officer (2021). The City of Detroit. FY 2017–2020 Four Year Plan. Online at https://detroitmi.gov/departments/office-chief-financial-officer/ocfo-divisions/office-budget/detroit-budget-archives-information

Pape, M., & Lerner, J. (2016). Budgeting for equity: How can participatory budgeting advance equity in the United States? *Journal of Public Deliberation*, *12*(2). 1–15. https://doi.org/10.16997/jdd.261

Seattle Department of Neighborhoods (2015). *Youth voice, youth choice: 2015–2016 Rulebook. the Seattle Department of Neighborhoods*. Accessed on November 1, 2022

Wampler, B. (2020). Participatory budgeting: Core principles and key impacts. *Journal of Deliberative Democracy*, 8(2). 1–13. https://doi.org/10.16997/jdd.138

CASE STUDY 12

Participatory budgeting in New York City

Abstract

Participatory budgeting in New York City (PBNYC) is the largest and most sustained participatory budgeting experiment in the United States. It was launched in fiscal year 2013 by four City Council members. By 2024, PBNYC expanded to include 24 of 51 council districts and tens of millions of dollars in capital funding. The process allows residents to propose, deliberate, and vote on how a portion of their council member's discretionary capital funds are spent. While PBNYC has been praised for broadening participation among immigrants, youth, and other historically marginalized groups, it has also generated debate about whether it alters public spending priorities or reshapes how small-scale capital projects are pursued.

Topics

Participatory Budgeting; Local Government; Operating Budgeting; Capital Budgeting

Origins and institutional design of PBNYC

New York City (NYC), NY has 51 City Council districts representing neighborhoods across the five boroughs (Manhattan, Brooklyn, Queens, Bronx, and Staten Island). Each district elects one council member to the City Council (New York City Council, n.d.). Unlike city-wide budgeting systems, participatory budgeting in New York City PBNYC operates at the council-district level and focuses exclusively on capital funds controlled by individual council members rather than on operating budgets or city-wide revenues (New York City Council, n.d.). Each Council member is allocated a portion of the City's capital budget that they can spend on capital projects in their district. These funds are known as Council discretionary capital funds or member items.

PBNYC began during preparations for Fiscal Year 2013, when the following four City Council members voluntarily committed portions of their discretionary capital funds to a participatory budgeting (PB) initiative:

- Brad Lander, who represented Council District 39 in Brooklyn;
- Melissa Mark-Viverito, who represented Council District 8 in Manhattan and the Bronx;
- Eric Ulrich, who represented Council District 32 in Queens; and
- Jumaane D. Williams, who represented Council District 45 in Brooklyn (New York City Council, n.d.; Participatory Budgeting Project, 2012).

In that first cycle, about 6,000 people voted, selecting 27 projects totaling $5.6 million. The number of participating districts grew quickly in the early years of PB implementation as additional Council Members opted in, and both funding levels and participation rose steadily. Cycles 4–8 represent the program's peak years. During this period, PB expanded to more than half of the City Council, capital allocations exceeded $30–40 million annually, and voter participation surpassed 100,000 in multiple cycles. Cycle 6 (2016–2017) recorded 102,800 voters across 31 districts allocating over $40 million. In Cycle 8 (2018–2019), the Council reported more than 118,000 New Yorkers voting to allocate over $39 million across 32 Council Districts. During these years, the PB process started to include increasingly more immigrants and youth. There were also shifts in the types of projects funded, particularly toward schools, housing, and street safety. Participation and funding dipped after COVID-19 but still remains substantial. In 2022–2023, the Council reported over 60,000 voters, nearly $32 million in capital funding, and 29 participating districts. Most recently, the Council's FY 2026 PB cycle (announced May 30, 2025) reported more than 93,000 voters allocating $30 million across 24 Council Districts (Table 5.2).

The basic structure of PBNYC follows a recurring annual cycle. Residents of participating districts are invited to attend neighborhood assemblies where they identify local needs and generate project ideas. Volunteer "budget delegates," supported by city agency staff, then develop these ideas into feasible capital proposals. Residents vote on the final project list, and the projects receiving the most votes are included in the council member's capital budget submission. Participation is open to residents regardless of citizenship status, and many districts

TABLE 5.2 PBNYC in Numbers

Cycle	*Budget Year*	*Participating Council Districts*	*Capital Funds Allocated*	*Projects Funded*	*Voters/ Participants*
1	FY 2013	4	$5.6M	27	~6,000
2	FY 2014	8	~$9–10M	~50	~8,000
3	FY 2015	13	~$18–20M	~90	~15,000
4	FY 2016	24	$31.9M	122	51,362
5	FY 2017	28	$38.3M	132	67,690
6	FY 2018	31	>$40M	164	102,800
7	FY 2019	27	>$28.5M	124	>99,000
8	FY 2020	32	>$39M	168	118,308
9	FY 2021	~30	~$35M	~150	~105,000
10	FY 2022	~28	~$32–34M	~140	~80,000
11	FY 2023	29	~$32M	~130	>60,000
12	FY 2024	~26	~$31M	~120	~70,000
13	FY 2025	~25	~$30M	~120	~85,000
14	FY 2026	24	$30M	~130	>93,000

Source: Created by authors based on Urban Justice Center (2012, 2015) and New York City Council (2016, 2018, 2019, 2023, 2025).

allow youth as young as 11 or 12 to vote, lowering formal barriers to engagement compared to traditional electoral processes (Hayduk et al., 2017).

One of the most significant contributions of PBNYC has been its deliberate emphasis on inclusion. NYC is home to one of the largest immigrant populations in the world, yet many immigrants are excluded from formal political participation due to citizenship requirements. PB has partially mitigated this exclusion as noncitizens are allowed to participate in the PB process (Hayduk et al., 2017). Immigrant participation in PBNYC has been increasing steadily during the program's early years, reaching more than one-quarter of all PB voters citywide (New York City Council, n.d.). Districts that invested in multilingual outreach, partnerships with community-based organizations, and childcare and food assistance were more successful in engaging immigrant residents (Hayduk et al., 2017; Shybalkina, 2022).

PBNYC has been associated with broader civic engagement in general, not only among immigrants. Many participants reported little prior experience with civic engagement and increased knowledge of government processes and a greater sense of political efficacy after participating. These procedural benefits are often cited as central achievements of the program, even when its fiscal impact is debated (Hagelskamp et al., 2016).

A central question in evaluating PBNYC is whether PB changes how public resources are allocated. PB adoption is found to be associated with shifts in spending priorities toward schools, street and traffic improvements, and public housing, and away from areas such as parks and housing preservation (Hagelskamp et al., 2020). These findings suggest that when residents are directly involved, they prioritize investments tied to everyday infrastructure and basic services.

One of the issues with PBNYC specifically is that since funding comes from council members' discretionary capital allocations PBNYC process does not reallocate resources across districts. Instead, PB tends to produce a larger number of smaller projects, spreading funds more widely within districts rather than redirecting spending across council districts for larger city-wide capital projects (Calabrese et al., 2020).

These findings have fueled debate over whether PBNYC represents a transformative budgeting reform or a more limited participatory device. Some scholars argue that even modest reallocations and increased transparency constitute meaningful change in a centralized budgeting system. Others caution that PB risks becoming symbolic if the scale of funds remains small and elected officials retain ultimate control over budgetary authority (Calabrese et al., 2020; Shybalkina, 2022).

Another defining feature of PBNYC is the substantial variation in how it is implemented across council districts. While the City Council provides a general framework and support, participation levels, outreach strategies, and project types differ widely reflecting differences in council member commitment, the strength and commitment of community organizations, and local political dynamics (Hayduk et al., 2017; Shybalkina, 2022). Council members may adopt PB to signal progressive values, recover from governance scandals, or respond to demands for political renewal, while others opt out due to perceived costs or limited electoral benefits (Shybalkina, 2022). Districts with strong community organizations capable of mobilizing residents and supporting budget delegates were found to have more robust deliberation and participation. Where such capacity is lacking, PB may be dominated by organized interests or repeat participants, raising concerns about equity and representativeness.

Conclusion

PBNYC is the largest PB program in the United States. It has successfully expanded opportunities for civic participation, particularly among immigrants and residents traditionally excluded from formal political processes. PB enhances transparency and is found to shift spending priorities within but not between council districts. Its impacts depend heavily on political commitment, civil society capacity, and the scale of funds involved. The program reshaped how a limited portion of public resources is allocated in NYC and how residents engage with government.

Discussion questions

1 To what extent does PBNYC represent a transfer of decision-making power from elected officials to residents, and where does ultimate budgetary authority remain?
2 How does reliance on Council members' discretionary capital funds shape both the strengths and the limitations of PBNYC compared with PB models used in other cities or countries?
3 What factors help explain the substantial variation in participation rates, project types, and outreach strategies across NYC council districts?

References

Calabrese, T., Williams, D., & Gupta, A. (2020). Does participatory budgeting alter public spending? Evidence from New York City. *Administration & Society, 52*(9), 1382–1409. https://doi.org/10.1177/0095399720912548

Hagelskamp, C., Silliman, R., Godfrey, E. B., & Schleifer, D. (2020). Shifting priorities: Participatory budgeting in New York City is associated with increased investments in schools, streets and traffic improvements, and public housing. *New Political Science, 42*(2), 171–196. https://doi.org/10.1080/07393148.2020.1773689

Hayduk, R., Hackett, K., & Folla, D. T. (2017). Immigrant engagement in participatory budgeting in New York City. *New Political Science, 39*(1), 76–94. https://doi.org/10.1080/07393148.2017.1278855

New York City Council. (n.d.). *Participatory budgeting in New York City*. https://council.nyc.gov/pb/

New York City Council. (n.d.). *About PBNYC (Participatory Budgeting)*. https://council.nyc.gov/pb/

New York City Council. (n.d.). *Council members & districts*. https://council.nyc.gov/districts/

New York City Council. (2016, May 26). *Speaker Mark-Viverito and NYC Council announce results of 2015–2016 participatory budgeting cycle*. https://council.nyc.gov/press/2016/05/26/4/

New York City Council. (2018, June 7). *Speaker Corey Johnson, Council Member Carlos Menchaca and the New York City Council announce results of the 2017–2018 participatory budgeting cycle*. https://council.nyc.gov/press/2018/06/07/1616/

New York City Council. (2019, May 22). *Speaker Corey Johnson and the New York City Council announce results of 2018–2019 participatory budgeting*. https://council.nyc.gov/press/2019/05/22/1754/

New York City Council. (2023, May 31). *Speaker Adrienne Adams, New York City Council announce results of 2022–2023 participatory budgeting*. https://council.nyc.gov/press/2023/05/31/2413/

New York City Council. (2025, May 30). *Speaker Adams, New York City Council Members announce results of FY 2026 participatory budgeting*. https://council.nyc.gov/press/2025/05/30/2892/

Participatory Budgeting Project. (2012). *Participatory budgeting in New York City: Rulebook and pilot guide*. https://www.participatorybudgeting.org

Public Agenda. (2016). *Public spending by the people: Participatory budgeting in the United States and Canada.* https://www.publicagenda.org/wp-content/uploads/2019/11/PublicSpendingByThePeople_PublicAgenda_2016.pdf

Shybalkina, I. (2022). Toward a positive theory of public participation in government: Variations in New York City's participatory budgeting. *Public Administration, 100*(4), 841–858. https://doi.org/10.1111/padm.12754

Urban Justice Center, Community Development Project. (2012). *Participatory budgeting in New York City: The first year* (Executive summary). https://takerootjustice.org/wp-content/uploads/2019/06/pbreport_ES.pdf

Urban Justice Center, Community Development Project. (2015). *A people's budget: A research and evaluation report on participatory budgeting in New York City (Cycle 4: Key research findings).* https://takerootjustice.org/wp-content/uploads/2019/06/Report_PBNYC_cycle4findings_20151021.pdf

6

INTERNAL CONTROLS

Abstract

This chapter analyzes internal controls as a core element of public financial management, emphasizing their central role in the budget execution and audit phases of the public budget cycle. This chapter examines the practical application of internal controls in government, highlighting mechanisms such as segregation of duties, clear assignment of responsibility, timely recording of transactions, and independent verification of financial activities. It demonstrates consequences of internal control breakdowns, which include heightened risks of fraud, corruption, service disruption, and erosion of public trust. This chapter emphasizes the critical role of senior leadership in establishing a strong control environment, setting ethical standards, and ensuring consistent implementation and monitoring of control systems.

Definition of internal control

The typical budget cycle in a public entity begins with executive preparations, followed by legislative considerations, budget execution, and audit and evaluation. Internal controls discussed in this chapter are essential during the budget execution stage. Such controls safeguard public funds by keeping expenditures aligned with authorized purposes, approved limits, and in compliance with laws and policies. Internal controls are, however, also a major focus during the audit stage of the budget cycle. The U.S. Government Accountability Office's (GAO) Green Book requires auditors to evaluate internal controls as part of financial and performance audits (GAO, 2014).

DOI: 10.4324/9781003606833-7

Internal control refers to the system of processes, policies, and procedures implemented by organization to ensure the integrity of financial and accounting information, promote operational efficiency, safeguard assets, and ensure compliance with laws and regulations (COSO, 2013). Mikesell (2018) emphasizes that for government organizations, internal controls are not abstract concepts, but practical procedures designed to promote accountability and prevent misuse of public resources.

Internal controls not only ensure compliance with statutory and regulatory requirements but also help prevent and detect fraud, mismanagement, and errors. These actions reinforce public trust in government institutions. GAO (2014) emphasizes that effective internal controls enable managers to adapt to changing environments, mitigate operational risks, and ensure accurate and reliable financial reporting. In the public sector, internal controls provide assurance that taxpayer dollars are spent in line with legislative intent and that expenditures meet the "proper public purpose" requirement (Mikesell, 2018). Accurate and timely reporting supports informed decision-making and fosters public trust.

Basic steps in internal controls

Mikesell (2018) emphasized the following basic steps in internal controls:

- Availability of qualified personnel, and necessity of rotating duties;
- Segregation of responsibility between two or more qualified people (reduces the chances of error or fraud);
- Assigning clear responsibility (to make sure all aspects of work are done, and it is clear who is responsible for what in case of questionable activities);
- Separation of operations (purchasing, receiving, and such) and accounting (again reduces the chances of error and fraud);
- Controller proofs of transactions;
- And, quick, but prompt recording of events and transactions.

Internal controls extend beyond day-to-day accounting and operations to cover the broader financial and legal commitments of a public organization. They apply to the monitoring of contracts to ensure that vendors deliver goods and services as agreed, payments are supported and timely, and conflicts of interest are avoided. Internal controls apply to the oversight of debt instruments, such as bonds or loans, to monitor compliance with repayment schedules, interest obligations, and statutory debt limits. Internal controls apply to the monitoring of investments to make sure that they adhere to approved investment policies, to monitor portfolio performance, and to mitigate risks of loss or mismanagement. Finally, internal controls include oversight of legal obligations, such as grant conditions, regulatory requirements, and settlement agreements, to confirm that the government entity remains in good financial standing.

Despite their importance, internal controls frequently break down in public agencies, creating fertile ground for fraud and corruption. When a single individual is responsible for both recording and approving transactions, the lack of oversight increases the risk of misappropriation. Missed or delayed bank reconciliations open opportunities for theft, while absent or poorly maintained records erode transparency and compliance with laws and policies. What may begin as minor lapses in procedure can quickly evolve into more serious violations, including corrupt practices such as falsifying documents, concealing expenditures, or misappropriating funds for personal gain. Without continuous monitoring and review, small errors and inconsistencies accumulate, allowing misconduct to escalate.

In fact, internal control violations may result in wide-ranging negative outcomes for public organizations. First and foremost, they open the door to financial theft. But beyond the immediate monetary impact, they contribute to the erosion of public trust, as citizens lose confidence in government once financial mismanagement comes to light. Weak controls lead to operational disruptions, resulting in a decline in the quality of essential services delivered to the community.

Senior leadership is vital for internal controls because leaders set the tone at the top, shaping the organizational culture around accountability, ethics, and compliance. In the Committee of Sponsoring Organizations of the Treadway Commission (COSO) Internal Control – Integrated Framework, senior leadership is identified as the foundation of the entire control system through what is called the control environment (COSO, 2013). Leadership commitment influences whether internal controls are viewed as meaningful safeguards or bureaucratic hurdles. Strong leadership provides authority, resources, and oversight needed to design and maintain effective controls. It also holds managers and staff accountable for following them. When senior leaders actively review reports, question anomalies, and model ethical behavior, they reinforce a culture of integrity. Conversely, weak or disengaged leadership signals that control systems can be ignored, which may lead to fiscal mismanagement, fraud, and bribery.

Conclusions

Internal controls are the backbone of ethical and effective public financial management. These structures are essential to prevent fraud, ensure fiscal transparency, and uphold citizen trust. Weak controls undermine both financial integrity and governance legitimacy. Effective internal control relies on consistent application and improvement. Ethical leadership, clear policies, qualified personnel, and staff training build a foundation for good financial behavior. Assigning distinct roles and reconciling accounts monthly are simple yet powerful safeguards. Backup copies in off-site or digital systems protect against data loss and enable audits. Internal audit units and anonymous whistleblower systems (e.g., one can report any potential financial fraud in public entities in Ohio here: https://ohioauditor.gov/fraud/report-fraud.html#ReportFraud) help detect abuse early.

The following three case studies discuss various aspects of internal control violations. The first case is from Clark County, OH where a former county Fiscal Director spent hundreds of thousands of dollars from a county credit card on personal purchases, his home mortgage, and timeshare among other expenses. The second case is from Nelsonville, a small city in Ohio, where payroll clerk and income tax administrator was involved in the elaborate payroll and income tax return fraud schemes. The case of "Municipal fraud and whistleblowing in City of Dixon, IL" discusses the largest municipal fraud case in the U.S. history where Dixon's long-term comptroller and treasurer embezzled a staggering $53.7 million over twenty-one years.

Additional references to select federal and state internal control regulations

- U.S. Government Accountability Office (GAO). The Green Book: Basic steps in internal controls: https://www.gao.gov/greenbook
- Committee of Sponsoring Organizations of the Treadway Commission (COSO) guidance on internal control: https://www.coso.org/guidance-on-ic
- Indiana: https://www.in.gov/sboa/political-subdivisions/internal-control-standards/
- Kansas: https://covid.ks.gov/wp-content/uploads/2021/11/Internal-Controls-Job-Aid-for-State-and-Local-Governments-v.-10_28_01.pdf?utm
- New York: https://www.osc.ny.gov/files/local-government/publications/pdf/the-practice-of-internal-controls.pdf?utm and https://www.osc.ny.gov/files/local-government/publications/pdf/managements-responsibility-for-internal-controls.pdf?utm
- Ohio: https://ohioauditor.gov/ipa/UniformGuidance/2023/OMB_Part_6.pdf
- Washington: https://sao.wa.gov/bars-annual-filing/bars-cash-manual/accounting/accounting-principles-and-internal-control/internal-control?utm

References

Committee of Sponsoring Organizations of the Treadway Commission (COSO). (2013). *Internal control - Integrated framework.* COSO.

Government Accountability Office (GAO). (2014). *Standards for internal control in the federal government (Green Book)* (GAO-14–704G). GAO.

Mikesell, J. L. (2018). *Fiscal administration: Analysis and applications for the public sector* (10th ed.). Wadsworth.

CASE STUDY 13

The embezzlement of funds in Clark County, OH

Abstract

This case study examines the embezzlement of funds in Clark County, OH, by its former Director of Fiscal Services, Robert Vanderhorst. Mr. Vanderhorst used county funds to pay over $750,000 to credit card companies, over $100,000 each for a mortgage loan and a timeshare he owned, as well as to cover the costs of elite catering events, build a deck in his family home, and make multiple other personal payments. Vanderhost was sentenced to seven years in prison in 2022 and ordered to pay restitution of $1,873,979, among other charges. This case study offers students a practical framework for evaluating internal controls, financial oversight, and accountability mechanisms within public organizations.

Topics

Internal Control; Accountability; Transparency; Local Government; Embezzlement

Background

Clark County is a county in west central Ohio, with a population of 135,633 (Clark County, 2022), located west of the state's capital, Columbus, and just northeast of the city of Dayton, OH. This is the third smallest county in Ohio by area. The County includes two cities, eight villages, eleven townships, twelve school districts, two library districts, and one health district (Clark County, 2023). The largest city is Springfield, OH, with a population of 60,608 residents (CityDirectory.us, n.d.). The median household income in the County in 2022 was $59,431, and the per capita personal income was $30,098. The median age was 41.1 years (Clark County, 2022).

In October of 2021, an employee of the Clark County Auditor's Office was reviewing financial documentation in preparation for the upcoming external financial audit. One transaction caught his attention, as it was not accompanied by a corresponding invoice, had no vendor's information, no description of the work done, and no other supporting documentation. This transaction was a refund to R&M Company for $110,000 issued by Robert M. Vanderhorst, the Director of Fiscal Services at Clark County. The employee inquired about the transaction with Mr. Vanderhorst, who promised to look into it. Meanwhile, the employee further reviewed the vendor, the R&M Company, and found 17 additional warrants from June 2013 to December 2019. The 18 warrants totaled over $900,000. In November 2021, still awaiting a response from Mr. Vanderhorst, the employee informed Dan Driscoll, the Clark County Prosecutor, about his findings.

The Prosecutor obtained a copy of the canceled warrant for $110,000 and issued a subpoena to Wesbanco, the R&M's bank, to obtain account information and the company's statements for 2021. A quick investigation revealed that the savings account was opened on September 12, 2000, by none other than Robert M. Vanderhorst himself. The statements showed a balance of $14,701 on January 1, 2021, a warrant for $110,000 deposited on June 6, 2021, and multiple transfers from the R&M account to a checking account ending in 8256. On December 9, 2021, the Clark County Prosecutor contacted the Ohio Auditor of State West Region regarding a potential a bank account and fraudulent vendor scheme. The next day, on December 10, 2021, the Special Investigations Unit (SIU) of the Ohio Auditor of State opened a preliminary investigation.

Discovery of fraud and investigation

The SIU investigation uncovered multiple additional cash withdrawals from the R&M savings account over years, all of them made by Mr. Vanderhorst. The checking account ending in 8256 turned out to be Mr. Vanderhorst's personal checking account. In January 2022, SIU executed a search warrant for Mr. Vanderhorst's office and his personal residence. They located a receipt for $110,000 deposit, a stamp for R&M Company, and several statements for R&M bank account from 2009 to 2010. The account balance on April 1, 2009 was $53,420. The county also later located a hard copy of the detailed expense reports for R&M going back to 2005. On January 12, 2022, Robert Vanderhorst was fired from his job after the Clark County Auditor's office learned about the allegations. And on February 14, 2022, Mr. Vanderhorst received his first indictment for one count of theft related to $110,000 payment made to R&M Company.

Continuing SIU investigation uncovered 31 warrants for the amount of $1,860,613 issued by the County to R&M Company between 2005 and 2021.

Twenty-two of these warrants for the amount of $1,101,436 were confirmed to be deposited to R&M's bank account. During that time, a total of 45 cash withdrawals for the amount of $18,256 and 174 transfers for $740,950 were made from the R&M account to Mr. Vanderhorst's personal checking account. The review of personal bank statements and canceled checks revealed that between 8/10/2014 and 1/12/2022 $750,000 was paid to credit card companies, $145,000 in mortgage payments, $128,154 for timeshare through Wyndham Vacation Club and Club Windham Plus (according to County employee and documents obtained in search warrant these timeshare were used in Panama City Beach, and Orlando, FL, and potentially Gatlinburg, TN), almost $60,000 in car payments, $33,429 in cash withdrawals and cashed checks, $7,868 for elite catering events, $6,500 to a contractor to build a deck in Mr. Vanderhorst's personal residence, $5,965 for cruises, and for other purposes.

Prison – a timeshare without a view

Mr. Vanderhorst was re-indicted on April 25, 2022, for one count of theft in office and two counts of aggravated theft. Mr. Vanderhorst claimed that the embezzled funds were used to help pay mainly for a timeshare he owned, but also to provide financial support to his family and for charitable contributions. Robert Vanderhorst was sentenced to seven years in prison. He was obligated to pay a restitution of $1,873,979.39 which included theft amount and the cost of prosecution (Ohio Auditor of State, 2024, p. 21). The judge additionally forfeited Mr. Vanderhorst's 2019 Mazda, all money in R&M bank account, Mr. Vanderhorst's personal checking account, and retirement savings (Ohio Auditor of State, 2024, p. 18). The sentence also means that Mr. Vanderhorst will never be able to hold public office in Ohio (Bean, 2022), which probably will have a slight impact on the felon who was 64 years old when convicted.

It is interesting to mention that Mr. Vanderhorst worked for the Ohio Auditor of State before 1991. In March 1991, he was hired by the Clark County Auditor's Office team. In his 30-year tenure, he served different roles all the way to the Director of the County Fiscal services. Robert Vanderhorst retired in April 2018 and was rehired by the county. After spending 30 years in the County's Audit office, Mr. Vanderhorst was a trustworthy employee who was very familiar with the County's financial management system. Between 2013 and 2015, he was on a team that led a major system upgrade, which helped conceal his thefts even further (Bean, 2022). Following the conviction the Clark County Auditor John Federer said that "…It's been alleged that Bob Vanderhorst used the extensive knowledge, tenure, and trust gained over a thirty-year career in Clark County to steal money" … "A betrayal of the public trust on this magnitude is frustrating and difficult to digest, but I believe that our office responded well and that we have emerged with stronger operations than ever before" (Bean, 2022).

Discussion questions

1 What standards of internal control were violated?
2 How could the Clark Auditor's office emerge "with stronger operations than ever before"?
3 What practices should have been revised? How to reduce the possibility of fraud in the future?

References

Bean, S. (2022, September 16). Theft in office: Former Clark Co. Auditor's Office employee sentenced. *WDTN*. https://www.wdtn.com/news/crime/theft-in-office-former-clark-co-auditors-office-employee-sentenced/

CityDirectory.us (n.d.). Springfield, Ohio. https://www.citydirectory.us/city-springfield-ohio.html

Clark County, Ohio. (2022). *Clark County, Ohio annual report 2022*. Clark County. https://www.clarkcountyohio.gov/DocumentCenter/View/7288/Clark-County-Ohio-Annual-Report-2023?bidId=

Clark County, Ohio. (2023). *Clark County, Ohio Annual Comprehensive Financial Report 2022*. Ohio Auditor of State. https://ohioauditor.gov/Auditsearch/Reports/2023/Clark_County_2022_Clark_FINAL.pdf

Ohio Auditor of State. (2024). *Special Investigations Unit convictions in Ohio*. https://ohioauditor.gov/publications/docs/SIU_convictions_report.pdf

CASE STUDY 14

The internal control violations in the City of Nelsonville, OH

Abstract

This case discusses internal control violations and embezzlement of funds in the City of Nelsonville, OH by its former payroll clerk and the income tax administrator, Stephanie Wilson. In the city with a median household income of $38,458, Ms. Wilson managed to embezzle close to $300,000 in seven years in the elaborate payroll and income tax return fraud schemes before she was caught.

Topics

Internal Control; Accountability; Transparency; Local Government; Embezzlement

Background

Nelsonville is a small town in Athens County in Southeast Ohio with an area of only 4.98 square miles and a population of 5,392 (citydirectory.us).[1] The City of Nelsonville is 55 miles southeast of Columbus, the capital city of Ohio, and is near Hocking Hills State Park, one of the most picturesque places in Ohio, featuring breathtaking ledges, gorges, and waterfalls. Nelsonville does not have any large industries housed in the city. Its median household income is $38,458, and the cost of living is only $800 a month (CityDirectory.us, n.d.). There was a peculiar situation in 2021 when Nelsonville almost lost its status as a city. The 2020 U.S. Census counted 4,612 residents in Nelsonville. Under Ohio law, urban areas with fewer than 5,000 residents lose the status of a city and become villages. Nelsonville challenged the results of the Census and recounted the number of residents to 5,373 in 2021 (Doyle, 2021).

Two individuals in the center of the embezzlement story, Samantha Maikut and Michael McCollister spent several years "working" for the City of Nelsonville and getting paid out of the city coffers. The only twist is that these two were ghost employees who existed only on paper. The scheme came to light in January 2020 when Taylor Sappington, a young newly elected Nelsonville City Auditor, was spending the first month on the job familiarizing himself with his office operations. This familiarization included a review of some payroll records. To Mr. Sappington's surprise, he came across the names of employees on the city's payroll that he couldn't recognize. It should be noted that prior to assuming the auditor's position Mr. Sappington served four years as one of Nelsonville's nine city council members, and he was well acquainted with the city's personnel. The more in-depth Mr. Sappington investigated the payroll records, the more suspicious he became. After a month of reviews and deliberations, he decided to contact the Athens County Prosecutor about the matter.

Discovery of fraud and investigation

On February 5, 2020, the Prosecutor carried out a search warrant for the office of Nelsonville's payroll clerk and the income tax administrator, Ms. Stephanie Wilson. During the search, a desktop computer and numerous documents were seized from the office. Among the seized records, the search team found bank statements that showed that the payroll for the unknown employees was directly deposited into a bank account that belonged to Ms. Wilson. On the day of the search, Stephanie Wilson herself was vacationing in Las Vegas. The Prosecutor called Ms. Wilson in Vegas, and, surprisingly, she immediately confessed to a ghost employee payroll scheme during the call. On February 10, 2020, upon her return from the trip, Stephanie Wilson was indicted on felony charges of telecommunications fraud, tampering with records, and forgery (Ohio Auditor of State, 2022). The same day, the case was transferred to the SIU of the Ohio Auditor of State to conduct the forensic audit and continue the investigation. The theft in office charge was added on February 24, 2020, in a superseding indictment.

The SIU team researched Ms. Wilson's past prior to being employed by the city. Before Nelsonville, Stephanie Wilson worked at a local credit union. It was revealed that her contract with the Credit Union was terminated due to financial improprieties. At the union, she participated in a check kiting scheme.[2] Ms. Wilson was, however, not only allowed to resign from her job at the Credit Union without any criminal charges filed against her but this information was also never forwarded to her new employer. Having no knowledge about Ms. Wilson's prior misdemeanors, she was hired by the City of Nelsonville to process the city payroll and collect and record city income tax receipts.

As is usually the case, wrongdoers start out slow and ramp up as time goes on. Two fictitious employees discovered by Nelsonville's auditor were fabricated by Ms. Wilson earlier in her tenure with the city. Samantha Maikut's payroll account was created in 2012 and Michael McCollister's in 2016. SIU determined that Samantha and Michael's pay checks were deposited straight to Ms. Wilson's personal checking accounts she held jointly with her husband or sons. Over time, the amounts funneled through these ghost accounts steadily increased. In total, Stephanie Wilson embezzled $35,531 through Samantha's account and $78,150 through Michael's account for a total of $113,681 in fraudulent payments (Ohio Auditor of State, 2024, p. 21). $50,000 of this money was paid through Michael's account in 2019 alone, the last year Ms. Wilson was working for the city and prior to the allegations of financial misconduct.

Unfortunately, the embezzlement story doesn't end here. SIU discovered that in addition to running a ghost employee scheme, Ms. Wilson was also blatantly overpaying herself by adding additional wages to her own bi-weekly checks. In 2014, Stephanie received $2,392 more than her calculated salary. In 2015, $1,645.80 more. Stephanie's salary, approved by the city council, was $14.50/hour in 2016 – the first year when Ms. Wilson's approved salary was already noticeably different from what she was actually paid. She worked 1,931.5 hours that year. At $14.50/hour, she was to earn $28,006.75. That year, Stephanie Wilson overpaid herself $9,517.54. In her final full year (2019), her council-approved salary was $18.35/hour, for a total pay of $38,168. It was hard to determine how much exactly Ms. Wilson overcompensated herself during these years, as SIU was able to locate only 56 out of 211 timesheets for that period. However, the overpayment estimate totaled about $100,000, keeping in mind this is in a city with a median household income of $38,458 (CityDirectory.us, n.d.).

We should make a side note here to clarify that the hourly pay rates and salaries in Nelsonville are set up by the city council. Employees are supposed to have bi-weekly timesheets completed and signed by both the employee and a supervisor. After each pay period, a system generated a report that was supposed to be reviewed by the city auditor. That being said, the internal control process was in place, but SIU didn't find evidence that the process had been necessarily followed through.

Conviction

In December of 2020, Stephanie Wilson pleaded guilty to theft in the office, tampering with records, telecommunications fraud, and forgery charges and sentenced to 59 months in prison. Ms. Wilson began serving her time at Ohio Reformatory for women in May 2021 (Ohio Auditor of State, 2022). She was ordered to repay a total restitution of $241,839.31 (Ohio Auditor of State, 2024, p. 10), which included a repayment of the stolen funds and over $27,000 of the cost for the special audit. Samantha was additionally hit with about $20,000 worth of fines. In addition, Ms. Wilson's conviction of a "theft in office" means that she will not be able to be hired by any public entities in Ohio upon her release from prison.

The conviction was not the end of Stephanie Wilson's story. Before the sentencing in the initial case, in March 2021, the SIU identified a separate fraud scheme that Ms. Wilson did not disclose to the prosecutor when she confessed originally. If one recounts, Ms. Wilson was not only the payroll clerk but also the income tax administrator for Nelsonville. Wearing the hat of an income tax administrator, Ms. Wilson created a separate tax fraud scheme. SIU uncovered 13 income tax refund checks issued in the names of fictitious individuals and companies. Interestingly, one of the names that Ms. Wilson made up on bogus income tax refund applications was very similar to one of the names she used in her ghost employee scheme, and this is what caught the SIU's attention and led to a separate income tax fraud investigation. In this separate investigation, SIU scanned the City's check payments and identified a check, for example, payable to Richard Willison, which is very similar to Stephanie's husband Richard Wilson. After identifying the Richard Willison check, they requested the supporting documentation from the city and learned it was a bogus income tax refund payment. Given her position as an income tax administrator, Stephanie was able to manipulate the system in one case by using another person's social security number, in others by not providing supporting documentation for the income tax refund payments.

The income tax scheme netted Stephanie Wilson another $49,956.95. She was indicted for theft in office and engaging in a pattern of corrupt activity (Ohio Auditor of State, 2024, p. 21) and pled guilty on April 5, 2022. She was sentenced to four years in prison, but this sentence runs concurrently with her earlier sentence and to pay restitution of $49,956.95 as well. The total restitution in the case was $291,796.26.

Discussion questions

1 What are the red flags? What internal control standards do you think were violated in this case? SIU of the Ohio Auditor of State publishes a list of general "red flags," and red flags related to the use of credit cards, purchasing, payroll, and other areas: https://ohioauditor.gov/fraud/redflags.html
2 What actions would you suggest the City of Nelsonville take to improve its internal control practices to prevent future financial misconduct?

Notes

1 All information in the case, unless cited otherwise, comes from the presentation by Randy Turner, the director of the SIU, Ohio Auditor of State on April 14, 2022.
2 Check kiting is a fraudulent activity where check is intentionally written from an account with insufficient funds and deposited to a second account. The fraudster then withdraws money from the second account before the check bounces back, creating a free short-term loan. This process might be repeated.

References

CityDirectory.us. (n.d.). *Nelsonville, Ohio.* CityDirectory.us. https://www.citydirectory.us/city-nelsonville-ohio.html#school

Doyle, C. (October 12, 2021). "Nelsonville rejects census population loss, finds 700 more residents in recount to regain city status". The Columbus Dispatch.

Ohio Auditor of State. (2024). *Special Investigations Unit convictions in Ohio.* https://ohioauditor.gov/publications/docs/SIU_convictions_report.pdf

Ohio Auditor of State. (2022, April 8). *Former Nelsonville deputy auditor guilty on additional counts, ordered to repay another $40,000-plus*. https://ohioauditor.gov/news/pressreleases/Details/5911

CASE STUDY 15

Municipal fraud and whistleblowing in City of Dixon, IL

Abstract

This case presents an analysis of financial misconduct, whistleblowing, and the oversight system in Dixon, Illinois, a small town notorious for the largest municipal fraud case in U.S. history. Rita A. Crundwell, Dixon's comptroller and treasurer from 1983 to 2011, embezzled $53.7 million from the city between 1990 and 2011. She used the funds to maintain a luxurious lifestyle and establish one of the nation's leading quarter horse breeding empires, all while forcing staff cuts, slashing police budgets, and neglecting public infrastructure. Crundwell's ability to embezzle such a large amount of money over this extended period of time indicated the presence of significant vulnerabilities in the city of Dixon's financial management and oversight system. The Dixon case highlights the critical importance of internal controls, transparency, and oversight in public financial management.

Topics

Internal Control; Whistleblowing; Local Government; Transparency; Accountability; Public Finance

Background

Dixon, with a population of approximately 15,733, is located about 100 miles southwest of Chicago. In 2000, Dixon had a population of around 15,900 and a per capita income of $16,630 (City-Data.com, 2025). In 2000, the per capita income of the United States was $29,676 (Bureau of Economic Analysis, 2001).

The relative poverty of the community impacted the overall government capabilities, which led to limited oversight for financial operations in the city. All of the financial operations were consolidated into one person's role.

Rita Crundwell began working for Dixon's finance department in 1970 while still in high school. She was appointed comptroller/treasurer in 1983. When questions about the City of Dixon budget were raised, they were directed to Crundwell, the only person who fully understood the process. This level of jurisdiction allowed her to continuously hide her embezzlement and control the extent to which others understood the city's finances. Over time, Crundwell had expanded opportunities to continue this fraud, which included:

- Being the sole signatory for city checks.
- Receiving and sorting all city mail, even when on vacation
- Being solely responsible for withdrawals, deposits, maintenance of ledgers, and management of bank accounts.

The City of Dixon arranged for an external auditing firm to simultaneously manage the compilation of all its financial statements and complete annual audits. This additional consolidation of responsibilities removed the opportunity for effective oversight. With the firm handling both compiling and auditing processes, they essentially were responsible for the financial review of their own work, rendering them less effective.

Rita Crundwell began the fraud scheme on December 18, 1990, when she opened a secret bank account under the name "RSCDA – Reserve Sewer Capital Development Account," on behalf of the city but controlled solely by her. She maintained control of the city's mail to intercept bank statements and concealed fraudulent transactions through 159 falsified invoices that appeared to authorize state-funded infrastructure projects. Through false transfers and fabricated invoices, Crundwell systematically diverted municipal revenues into the RSCDA account. From the RSCDA account, she financed a lavish lifestyle, including luxury vehicles, jewelry, multiple homes, and a nationally recognized quarter horse breeding business, RC Quarter Horses, LLC. Between 1991 and 2012, Crundwell's thefts ranged from $181,000 in the first year to over $5.8 million in 2008, averaging more than $2.5 million annually.

U.S. Attorney's Office (2013) provided an example of Crundwell's fraud scheme. On September 8, 2009, Crundwell wrote checks for $150,000 and $200,000 drawn on two of the city's multiple bank accounts. She deposited both checks into Dixon's Capital Development Fund account and, later the same day, wrote a check for $350,000 payable to "Treasurer" and deposited that check into the secret RSCDA account. Crundwell created a fictitious invoice to support the payment of $350,000 to the State of Illinois that falsely indicated the payment was for a sewer project in Dixon that the state had completed. On September 8,

2009, Crundwell wrote a check drawn on the RSCDA account for $225,000, which she deposited into her personal RC Quarter Horses account. She used that money to cover a $225,000 check, dated September 1, 2009, drawn on the RC Quarter Horses account to purchase a quarter horse. The purchase check would not have cleared if Crundwell had not deposited $225,000, using city funds, into her horse account on September 8.

To conceal the fraud scheme, Rita Crundwell picked up the city's mail, including bank statements for the RSCDA account, to prevent other employees from learning about the secret account (Gravitas Free Documentaries, 2022). When Rita Crundwell was away, she asked a relative or other city employees to pick up the mail and separate any of her mail, including the statements for the RSCDA account, from the rest of the city's mail.

Discovery of fraud, whistleblowing, and investigation

Fraud scheme was finally discovered in 2011, when Crundwell took an extended unpaid vacation and an interim comptroller, Kathe Swanson, assumed her responsibilities. Upon reviewing the city's financial records, Swanson identified the suspicious RSCDA account and alerted the mayor, who notified federal authorities. In a small and closely connected community such as Dixon, Kathe Swanson was understandably reluctant to report suspicious behavior about a trusted longtime colleague. However, Mayor James Burke offered clear guidance and unwavering support. He ensured Swanson's protection throughout the investigation and cooperated discreetly with the FBI.

By affirming Swanson's concerns and responding swiftly yet confidentially, Mayor Burke prevented unnecessary public outcry and enabled the city to manage the emerging crisis with transparency and composure. According to Svara (2022), an ethical organizational culture empowers employees to speak out when they encounter misconduct. Although Swanson lacked formal whistleblower training, the respectful and supportive work environment in Dixon gave her the confidence to act, ultimately serving as a catalyst for accountability and reform.

In November 2012, Crundwell pleaded guilty to wire fraud and admitted to money laundering. U.S. District Judge Philip G. Reinhard emphasized that her actions constituted a "massive stealing of public money" and reflected a deeper betrayal of civic trust.

The court ordered restitution to the City of Dixon totaling $53,740,394. Following her arrest on April 17, 2012, Crundwell consented to the liquidation of assets obtained through her decades-long embezzlement scheme. The United States Marshals Service recovered more than $12.38 million through sales conducted both online and at live auctions. These sales included approximately 400 quarter horses, along with vehicles, trailers, a luxury motor home, jewelry, and personal property.

Crundwell was sentenced to 19 years (235 months) in federal prison in 2012. However, the Federal Bureau of Prisons released Crundwell in 2021 (Schroedter & Bradley, 2021). She had only served half her sentence.

Impacts and lessons

The City of Dixon lost a total of $53 million thanks to this 20-year fraud scheme, equating to $3,313.50 stolen per resident. The impact of this loss led to consistent cuts across public services, including police services, fire services, road maintenance, and others. Additionally, the city was forced to freeze wages, conduct layoffs, and refrain from hiring part-time staff during the summer seasons. To maintain its governing operations, the city had to consistently borrow funds to cover its expenses. Toward the end of the fraud scheme, the city was borrowing around the same amount that was being embezzled. The impact went beyond the financial losses. After the fraud was uncovered and exposed, public trust in the city government was also devastated. Judge Reinhard noted that the financial loss extended beyond monetary damage; it eroded public confidence in local governance and severely disrupted the city's ability to provide essential services.

The aftermath of Crundwell's conviction provided the City of Dixon with an opportunity to implement significant 21st-century governance and public administration reforms. Following the 2015 municipal elections, a new generation of city leaders, including a newly elected mayor and city council, initiated structural changes aimed at restoring accountability and public trust. Among the most consequential reforms was the appointment of a full-time city manager and the establishment of a comprehensive system of financial checks and balances to prevent future misuse of public funds. A 2023 Politico Magazine article documented Dixon's resurgence, crediting the city's recovery to the restoration of misappropriated assets and the adoption of prudent, transparent fiscal management practices that have since become a model for small-city governance reform (Gilsinan, 2023).

To prevent future incidents of fraud against the taxpayers of Dixon, the city must strengthen its internal controls and oversight mechanisms by ensuring that multiple employees are involved in all financial operations. No single individual should have exclusive authority over financial transactions. All disbursements, deposits, and reconciliations should require dual authorization and independent verification. Furthermore, the city should establish and enforce comprehensive financial management policies governing the procedures for deposits, withdrawals, bank account creation, and the review of checks and invoices. Regular and systematic invoice audits could have revealed the falsified documentation that facilitated Crundwell's fraudulent activities.

Equally important, the city should implement a formal whistleblowing system that allows employees to safely report any suspected misconduct. Whistleblowing remains one of the most effective mechanisms for detecting fraud. According to the Association of Certified Fraud Examiners (2024), 43% of frauds were detected by tips, which is more than 3× as many cases as the next most common method. While Dixon's previous reliance on external auditors proved inadequate, its primary safeguard moving forward should be the cultivation of a workplace culture where reporting unethical behavior is both possible and encouraged.

Dixon should adopt the following best practices for whistleblower protection and reporting:

- Establish clear administrative channels for raising and resolving concerns or disagreements.
- Provide anonymous reporting mechanisms, potentially through an independent third-party contractor.
- Offer regular staff training on how to recognize and report unethical conduct through proper channels.
- Implement and communicate strong anti-retaliation policies to ensure that whistleblowers are fully protected.

Conclusion

The Rita Crundwell fraud case illustrates how decades of complacency can lead well-intentioned officials to miss warning signs and overlook the real impact on their community. It also demonstrates how a workplace culture that values respect and privacy can empower employees, such as Kathe Swanson, to speak up when something seems wrong. Her willingness to come forward helped hold the City of Dixon accountable and ultimately put the community on a path toward recovery and a more stable future.

While it is impossible to completely prevent fraud, the institution of financial oversight policies, coupled with a strong whistleblowing culture, should provide significant support for fraud prevention. To prevent similar incidents of fraud and preserve public confidence, municipalities must cultivate an ethical and transparent organizational culture, adopt a council-manager form of government that separates political leadership from administrative oversight, and establish a robust system of checks and balances to ensure that no single individual or external consultant holds excessive control over financial operations.

Discussion questions

1. What factors contribute to significant vulnerabilities for fraud in the City of Dixon?
2. What structural and procedural weaknesses allowed fraud to continue undetected for more than 20 years?

3 What safeguards can be instituted to prevent significant vulnerabilities in the budget of the City of Dixon and financial losses?
4 What organizations or persons can be or should be the best "watchdog" in this situation?
5 How did whistleblowing prevent financial fraud in Dixon, IL? Explain.
6 In what ways did fraud and embezzlement influence the fiscal stability, operations, and public trust of the City of Dixon?
7 How could internal control mechanisms and segregation of duties have prevented this case?
8 In what ways did Crundwell's actions impact public trust in government institutions?
9 What reforms could municipalities implement to improve financial accountability and transparency?
10 Do you know of other examples like this situation in local governments in Illinois or other states?

Videos for class discussion

The Fifth Estate (2014). *Rita Crundwell - Fraud in Dixon Illinois : Small Town Shakedown - The Fifth Estate.* https://www.youtube.com/watch?v=WAYtaFxlw3M

Gravitas Free Documentaries. (2022, May 19). *All the queen's horses.* [Video]. Youtube. https://www.youtube.com/watch?v=RXSZhKEddxI

WCIA News (2021). *Rita Crundwell stole $54M then returned to the scene of the crime* https://www.youtube.com/watch?v=teUEFoFjUfIWCIA News.

References

Association of Certified Fraud Examiners (2024). Occupational Fraud 2024: A Report to the Nations. *ACFE.* https://www.acfe.com/-/media/files/acfe/pdfs/rttn/2024/2024-report-to-the-nations.pdf

Bureau of Economic Analysis. (2001, April 24). *State personal income & state per capita income:2000; State personal income: Fourth Quarter 2000.* U.S. Department of Commerce. https://www.bea.gov/news/2001/state-personal-income-state-capita-personal-income-2000-state-personal-income-fourth

City-Data.com (2025). *Dixon, Illinois (IL).* https://www.city-data.com/income/income-Dixon-Illinois.html

Gilsinan, K. (2023, May 12). She stole $54 million from her town. Then something unexpected happened. *Politico Magazine.* https://www.politico.com/news/magazine/2023/05/12/dixon-illinois-city-fraud-betrayal-00075869

Gravitas Free Documentaries. (2022, May 19). *All the queen's horses.* [Video]. Youtube. https://www.youtube.com/watch?v=RXSZhKEddxI

Schroedter, A., & Bradley, B. (2021, October 29). *Former Dixon comptroller Rita Crundwell stole $54 million then returned to the scene of the crime.* https://www.wcia.com/news/former-dixon-comptroller-rita-crundwell-stole-54-million-then-returned-to-the-scene-of-the-crime

Svara, J. H. (2022). *The ethics primer for public administrators in government and nonprofit organizations* (3rd ed.). Jones & Bartlett Learning.U.S. Attorney's Office. (2013). *Former Dixon Comptroller Rita Crundwell Sentenced To Nearly 20 Years In Federal Prison For $53.7 Million Theft From City*. U.S. Attorney's Office, Northern District of Illinois. https://www.justice.gov/usao-ndil/pr/former-dixon-comptroller-rita-crundwell-sentenced-nearly-20-years-federal-prison-537

Videos for class discussion

The Fifth Estate (2014). *Rita Crundwell - Fraud in Dixon Illinois : Small Town Shakedown - The Fifth Estate*. https://www.youtube.com/watch?v=WAYtaFxlw3M

Gravitas Free Documentaries. (2022, May 19). *All the queen's horses*. [Video]. Youtube. https://www.youtube.com/watch?v=RXSZhKEddxI

WCIA News (2021). *Rita Crundwell stole $54M then returned to the scene of the crime*. https://www.youtube.com/watch?v=teUEFoFjUflWCIA News.

7

CAPITAL BUDGETING

Abstract

This chapter examines capital budgeting as a core component of public financial management and provides the foundations of the capital budgeting framework and financial and risk management. It explains how local governments plan, evaluate, prioritize, and finance capital projects that support essential public services such as transportation, utilities, public facilities, and technology systems. This chapter highlights the importance of capital improvement planning in aligning infrastructure investments with fiscal capacity, community needs, and strategic objectives. It discusses the institutional and political dynamics that shape capital decisions, including the tension between technical assessments and the priorities of elected officials. This chapter also explores various financing approaches, including pay-as-you-go and pay-as-you-use funding, as well as the importance of sound debt management in maintaining fiscal health. This chapter highlights challenges such as limited resources, deferred maintenance, economic cycles, political pressures, and the growing demands created by aging infrastructure and environmental threats. This chapter concludes by highlighting the importance of transparent processes, public participation, and performance evaluation in improving capital budgeting outcomes.

Introduction

The availability and quality of services provided by public infrastructure (e.g., water systems, solid waste facilities, public transit and transportation systems, communication systems, and cultural and recreational facilities) are critical factors in enhancing economic growth. Public infrastructure is an essential

DOI: 10.4324/9781003606833-8

component of the U.S. economy. Businesses depend on a well-functioning and dependable infrastructure system to obtain supplies, manage inventories, and deliver goods and services to the market.

Capital budgeting includes preparing an inventory of capital assets owned by the government, evaluating the condition of those assets, estimating their cost of replacement, preparing a multiyear capital improvement plan (CIP), submitting the plan for legislative approval, and executing the plan. Capital budgeting can be analyzed as being partly political, partly economic, partly accounting, and partly administrative. As a political document, capital budgeting allocates the society's scarce investment resources among multiple conflicting, and competing interests of different state agencies. As an economic and fiscal document, capital budgeting is the primary instrument for evaluating capital improvement needs, stimulating economic growth and development, analyzing infrastructure conditions, and maintaining economic stability. As an accounting document, it provides a ceiling on government spending on capital projects. It also legally binds capital spending to remain within the funds allocated for this purpose. Finally, as a managerial and administrative document, capital budgeting specifies the ways and means by which public services are provided, and it establishes criteria by which they are monitored, measured, and evaluated (Ermasova, 2020; Ermasova & Mikesell, 2019).

Mikesell (2011) pointed out three differences between capital spending and spending for current operations:

> (1) capital assets decisions have future impact and thus merit extraordinary care;
> (2) capital assets usually have high price tags and their purchase may destabilize the finances of a government, and
> (3) capital asset purchases tend to occur at irregular intervals and may need special attention in regard to scheduling.
>
> *(p. 289)*

The coordination of capital and operating budgets is a crucial aspect of the capital budgeting process. The same set of programs' needs drives both capital and operating budget requests, and the two budgets affect each other. Projects and spending approved in the capital budget influence future operating budgets.

Capital budgeting at the federal level

The U.S. federal government does not have a separate capital budget. The President submits a comprchensive budget request to Congress in early February, outlining the Administration's policy and funding priorities, as well as the economic outlook for the upcoming fiscal year. This budget, which estimates spending, revenue, and borrowing levels, is compiled by the Office of Management and Budget (OMB) from input by the various federal agencies, with funding broken down into 20 budget function categories. The federal budget generally measures spending and revenues combined, including all the government's activities in one place. The budget makes no distinction between capital investments and operating expenses. Capital spending, social insurance outlays, and operating expenses are treated equally.

The U.S. federal budget presents the government's expenditures and revenues for each fiscal year. It serves many purposes: (1) enables policymakers to allocate resources to serve national objectives, (2) provides the basis for agencies' management of federal programs, (3) gives the Treasury needed information for its management of cash and the public debt, and (4) provides businesses and individuals with information to make an informed assessment about the government's spending and resources (Potter & Diamond, 1999).

The Capital Programming Guide A-11 is a U.S. government document issued by the OMB in the form of a written advisory that provides information related to the preparation of various budgets for Federal Government agencies (Office of Management and Budget, 2006). The Office of Management and Budget (2006) defines federal capital assets as "land, structures, equipment, intellectual property (e.g., software), and information technology (including IT service contracts) used by the Federal Government and having an estimated useful life of two years or more." The *Financial Report of the United States Government* provides financial statement information related to capital assets owned by the federal government (Congressional Budget Office, 2006, 2008, 2021; U.S. General Accounting Office, 1996, 1998, 2004). The President's Commission to Study Capital Budgeting (1999) distinguished between federal capital and national capital: federal capital refers to only those assets that belong to the federal government (like buildings or military aircrafts); national capital includes all government spending aimed at delivering long-term benefits to the nation.

In addition to defining and providing guidance for the management of capital assets, the *Capital Programming Guide* A-11 includes information on four phases of capital programming: Planning, Budgeting, Procurement, and Management-In-Use. It includes information about linking capital decisions to strategic goals and objectives, analyzing and ranking potential investments, and making informed decisions based on a project's full cost and risk (U.S. Government Accountability Office, 2004). The federal government provides budgetary data in two forms: budget authority and budget outlays. Budget authority includes all the funding that has been authorized in a given year and determines whether or not it is expected to be spent in that year. For example, the entire estimated expense for a new building might be appropriated by the budget authority in next year's budget, although the spending is expected to take place over several years. Budget outlays, the amount actually spent, or expected to be spent in a given year, are also reported in the budget. This "cash basis" reporting of outlays increases transparency and provides a better idea of the government's annual cash deficit or surplus.

Since capital projects are on budget and must be approved by the OMB, they are subject to benefit-cost assessment requirements, supporting long-term considerations. Total life-cycle costs and benefits, including the total budget authority required for the asset, are applied to all major capital projects (Office of Management and Budget, 1992). The benefits of a capital project accrue over the long term. A capital project should yield positive net benefits to society in order for it to be approved. An analysis of the investment risk includes how risks will be isolated, minimized, monitored, and controlled. The Chief Financial Officer evaluates and estimates the probability of achieving the proposed cost goals for major programs. Agencies and departments utilize a performance-based management system (e.g., earned value management) to estimate cost, schedule, and performance goals for the investment throughout the acquisition process. The discounted present value of a capital lease or lease-purchase over the life of the contract is also scored upfront, which helps guard against perverse incentives that result in inefficient decision-making (Office of Management and Budget, 2016b, 2016c).

Most federal agencies have established processes to review and select from competing project proposals, with a strong emphasis on linking them to strategic goals. However, the agencies have had limited success with using agency-wide asset inventory systems and data on asset conditions to identify performance gaps. According to the U.S. General Accounting Office (2004), "none of the agencies prepares an agency-wide long-term capital investment plan. Some have long-term capital planning documents that could serve as a base for developing a comprehensive agency-wide plan" (p. 4).

The Budgeting Phase begins with the agency's budget submission to OMB and ends with Congressional approval and OMB apportionment of funding. OMB is the integrator of specific capital project proposals into the larger budget process. OMB considers agency obligation rates, the overall budget request, and agency strategic plans during reviews of agency budget requests for capital acquisitions. Agencies collaborate with OMB to assess the impact of proposals on budget authority, collections, and outlays, considering economic and technical assumptions related to interest rates, housing prices, inflation rates, outlay rates, caseloads, and estimates for offsetting collections or receipts (Office of Management and Budget, 2016a).

If a federal agency requests funds to support capital facilities projects, including new construction, full or partial building renovation/modernization, or facility investments, the agency must provide supporting information. This includes documentation of compliance with federal capital policies, life-cycle cost analysis, a housing plan (indicating at a minimum the full-time equivalent to be housed and the types of facility space and square footage), and environmental/energy efficiency analysis (Office of Management and Budget, 2016a, p. 116).

The legislative budget process is driven by Congressional subcommittees that are appropriate by agency or department. Federal agency executives provide various Congressional committees with information related to their capital needs and the decision-making processes they use to assess those needs. The differences between full funding with regular appropriations in the budget year and full funding for a capital project (investment) over several years with regular appropriations for the first year and advance appropriations for subsequent years are following: (1) full funding with regular appropriations in the budget year leads to trade-offs within the budget year with spending for other capital assets and with spending for purposes other than capital assets; (2) full funding for a capital project (investment) over several years may bias trade-offs in the budget year in favor of the proposed asset because with advance appropriations the full cost of the asset is not included in the budget year (Office of Management and Budget, 2016c). The Office of Management and Budget (2016a) highlights the problems of large, temporary, year-to-year increases in budget authority (lumps or spikes) that may create a bias against the acquisition of justified capital assets. Agencies can mitigate this bias by segregating capital acquisitions into separate accounts. It would reduce spikes within an agency or bureau by providing roughly the same level of spending for acquisitions each year and help to identify and explain the source of spikes (Office of Management and Budget, 2016c).

The Management-In-Use Phase includes the execution of an operation and maintenance plan, a post-implementation review to evaluate the overall effectiveness of the agency's capital planning and acquisition process, and the execution of an asset disposal plan. Agencies and departments use performance-based management systems to provide contractor and government management visibility on the achievement of investment goals until the asset is accepted and operational. Performance-based management systems enable the early identification of problems, potential corrective actions, and adjustments to the original goals necessary to complete the investment (Office of Management and Budget, 2016c).

Congress enacted the Federal Acquisition Streamlining Act of 1994 to improve the federal acquisition process and the Clinger-Cohen Act in 1996 to improve the implementation and management of information technology investments. Federal agencies also employ a range of acquisition strategies to mitigate the risks of cost escalation and failure to meet schedule and performance goals. Thresholds are also established for acquisition cost, schedule, and performance goals, including return on investment. Contracts and pricing mechanisms are determined based on efficiency and their ability to incentivize contractors to allocate risk appropriately between the contractor and the government.

Federal capital investments

Federal capital investments include spending on goods and services that provide long-term benefits. As defined by the Congressional Budget Office (2006) and U.S. General Accounting Office (2004), federal investment consists of three broad categories of spending, which are listed in order of their combined outlays for defense and nondefense investments: major public physical capital investment (outlays for construction and rehabilitation, major equipment, and the purchase or sale of land and structures); conduct of research and development (outlays for activities that increase basic scientific knowledge or promote research and development); and conduct of education and training (activities to promote a more skilled and productive labor force, a category that consists mostly of financial assistance and loan subsidies for higher education). The federal budget records the full cost of commitments for federal investments when they are incurred, and it records the associated cash expenditures as outlays when they are disbursed (Congressional Budget Office, 2021). Table 7.1 provides the Total Investment Outlays for Major Public Physical Capital, Research and Development, and Education and Training from 1962 to 2024.

For example, in fiscal year 2022, direct federal spending on major public physical capital investment totaled $1,178.6 billion, with $259.2 billion allocated for defense and $919.3 billion for nondefense purposes (GovInfo, 2025).

Pros and cons of separate capital budgeting at the federal level

The idea of changing the process to have a distinct capital plan and budget has been discussed but is controversial. Proponents argue that a long-term federal government capital plan and budget would enhance financial management by estimating revenues and expenses associated with capital projects, determining the most effective financing method, and addressing intergenerational equity issues (Ermasova, 2020; Ermasova & Mikesell, 2019). The American Society of Civil Engineers (ASCE) supports the establishment of a federal multi-year capital budget for public works infrastructure construction and major rehabilitation, similar to those used by state and local governments. ASCE (2024) suggests that the current federal budget process does not differentiate between expenditures for current consumption and long-term infrastructure investment, and

> this causes major inefficiencies in the planning, design, and construction of long-term infrastructure investments. A federal capital budget could create mechanisms to help reduce the conflict between short-term and long-term needs. It also would help increase public awareness of the problems and needs facing this country's physical infrastructure and help Congress focus on programs devoted to long-term growth and productivity.
>
> *(p. 1)*

It may make more sense to borrow for capital projects with long useful lives that will benefit future generations, who can then repay the debt, rather than using current operating funds. A separate capital budget can enhance efficiency and equity by considering these long-term flows in budget and financing decisions.

TABLE 7.1 Total Investment Outlays for Major Public Physical Capital, Research and Development, and Education and Training from 1962 to 2024 ($billion)

	Total	*National Defense*	*Nondefense*	*Total in Billions of Constant (FY 2012) Dollars*	*National Defense*	*Nondefense*	*Total As Percentages of Total Outlays*	*National Defense*	*Nondefense*	*Total As Percentages of GDP*
1962	34,495	24,891	9,604	174.4	113.2	61.2	32.3	23.3	9.0	5.9
1963	38,425	26,571	11,854	192.0	118.3	73.7	34.5	23.9	10.6	6.2
1964	40,784	25,857	14,927	207.2	116.1	91.1	34.4	21.8	12.6	6.2
1965	38,062	21,327	16,735	196.9	96.0	100.9	32.2	18.0	14.2	5.4
1966	43,440	23,959	19,481	222.4	105.0	117.4	32.3	17.8	14.5	5.6
1967	51,135	29,455	21,680	256.9	125.6	131.4	32.5	18.7	13.8	6.1
1968	57,109	33,992	23,117	279.0	140.2	138.9	32.1	19.1	13.0	6.4
1969	57,565	34,565	23,000	268.6	136.5	132.1	31.3	18.8	12.5	5.9
1970	56,466	31,625	24,841	255.6	119.3	136.3	28.9	16.2	12.7	5.4
1971	56,724	28,823	27,901	246.9	103.6	143.3	27.0	13.7	13.3	5.1
1972	58,467	27,955	30,512	243.5	95.2	148.3	25.3	12.1	13.2	4.8
1973	59,158	26,794	32,364	236.8	87.0	149.9	24.1	10.9	13.2	4.4
1974	61,076	26,830	34,246	228.3	82.2	146.1	22.7	10.0	12.7	4.1
1975	69,407	28,421	40,986	237.2	79.5	157.7	20.9	8.6	12.3	4.3
1976	76,469	29,126	47,343	246.1	76.4	169.7	20.6	7.8	12.7	4.3
1977	82,789	32,499	50,290	248.0	79.0	169.0	20.2	7.9	12.3	4.1
1978	92,598	35,328	57,270	262.1	80.7	181.4	20.2	7.7	12.5	4.1
1979	105,873	40,874	64,999	275.6	85.6	190.0	21.0	8.1	12.9	4.1
1980	118,943	47,185	71,758	284.0	92.2	191.8	20.1	8.0	12.1	4.3
1981	132,141	56,079	76,061	283.7	100.1	183.6	19.5	8.3	11.2	4.2
1982	135,565	67,805	67,760	264.0	112.3	151.7	18.2	9.1	9.1	4.1

1983	146,848	81,568	65,280	268.5	127.3	141.2	18.2	10.1	8.1	4.2
1984	165,006	94,052	70,954	288.2	141.1	147.1	19.4	11.0	8.3	4.2
1985	186,631	108,394	78,236	317.0	160.2	156.7	19.7	11.5	8.3	4.4
1986	200,206	120,428	79,777	336.2	178.9	157.4	20.2	12.2	8.1	4.4
1987	204,295	126,749	77,546	335.6	188.2	147.4	20.3	12.6	7.7	4.3
1988	208,400	123,858	84,542	337.8	182.7	155.1	19.6	11.6	7.9	4.1
1989	220,895	131,033	89,862	348.8	188.1	160.7	19.3	11.5	7.9	4.0
1990	227,704	130,960	96,744	351.7	183.9	167.8	18.2	10.5	7.7	3.9
1991	231,246	127,319	103,926	347.7	173.5	174.2	17.5	9.6	7.8	3.8
1992	233,833	120,836	112,997	345.3	162.1	183.2	16.9	8.7	8.2	3.6
1993	236,715	116,636	120,078	343.4	153.3	190.1	16.8	8.3	8.5	3.5
1994	223,194	104,815	118,379	319.5	134.8	184.6	15.3	7.2	8.1	3.1
1995	233,180	97,583	135,597	327.8	123.1	204.7	15.4	6.4	8.9	3.1
1996	228,043	94,414	133,629	315.0	117.8	197.2	14.6	6.1	8.6	2.9
1997	228,756	92,587	136,169	313.1	115.1	198.0	14.3	5.8	8.5	2.7
1998	228,042	93,699	134,343	311.1	115.7	195.3	13.8	5.7	8.1	2.6
1999	239,874	94,162	145,712	322.0	114.9	207.1	14.1	5.5	8.6	2.5
2000	254,787	97,114	157,673	334.3	116.5	217.8	14.2	5.4	8.8	2.5
2001	284,950	105,193	179,757	367.3	124.7	242.7	15.3	5.6	9.6	2.7
2002	313,793	116,588	197,205	399.7	137.7	262.0	15.6	5.8	9.8	2.9
2003	346,329	132,044	214,285	433.0	154.1	279.0	16.0	6.1	9.9	3.1
2004	369,594	148,966	220,628	450.2	170.7	279.5	16.1	6.5	9.6	3.1
2005	393,596	160,131	233,465	461.4	179.2	282.2	15.9	6.5	9.4	3.1
2006	430,400	170,318	260,082	487.7	186.1	301.6	16.2	6.4	9.8	3.2
2007	429,813	184,905	244,908	469.9	198.0	271.9	15.8	6.8	9.0	3.0
2008	459,716	205,912	253,804	488.6	216.2	272.4	15.4	6.9	8.5	3.1
2009	482,246	222,650	259,596	505.5	231.6	273.9	13.7	6.3	7.4	3.3
2010	562,205	228,412	333,793	585.6	236.2	349.5	16.3	6.6	9.7	3.8

(*Continued*)

TABLE 7.1 (Continued)

	Total	*National Defense*	*Nondefense*	*Total in Billions of Constant (FY 2012) Dollars*	*National Defense*	*Nondefense*	*Total As Percentages of Total Outlays*	*National Defense*	*Nondefense*	*Total As Percentages of GDP*
2011	537,905	221,235	316,670	548.4	224.3	324.1	14.9	6.1	8.8	3.5
2012	503,313	213,198	290,115	503.3	213.2	290.1	14.3	6.0	8.2	3.1
2013	464,917	198,019	266,898	458.6	196.3	262.3	13.5	5.7	7.7	2.8
2014	464,296	187,643	276,653	449.5	183.2	266.4	13.2	5.4	7.9	2.7
2015	489,156	179,628	309,528	469.3	174.3	295.1	13.2	4.9	8.4	2.7
2016	480,805	181,212	299,593	459.4	175.4	284.0	12.5	4.7	7.8	2.6
2017	528,091	185,321	342,770	497.9	178.7	319.2	13.3	4.7	8.6	2.7
2018	485,419	195,121	290,298	448.5	185.7	262.8	11.8	4.7	7.1	2.4
2019	556,174	218,972	337,202	502.8	205.5	297.2	12.5	4.9	7.6	2.6
2020	710,185	246,641	463,544	630.5	229.2	401.3	10.8	3.8	7.1	3.4
2021	790,780	261,844	528,936	680.5	237.6	442.9	11.6	3.8	7.8	3.5
2022	1,178,630	259,289	919,341	950.4	223.1	727.3	18.8	4.1	14.7	4.7
2023	836,202	280,021	556,181	645.3	229.4	415.9	13.1	4.4	8.7	3.2
2024	855,167	325,768	529,399	643.9	260.4	383.5	12.4	4.7	7.7	3.1

Source: Table created by authors based on GovInfo (2025).

The Congressional Budget Office (CBO, 2021) argues that adopting an accrual approach with a separate capital budget would spread the cost of investments over the period when potential benefits accrued, rather than appearing in full when the spending occurred (as is the current cash-based approach). Based on this approach, the budget would record costs for physical capital as the assets lost value over time. CBO (2021) suggests that this approach would "eliminate some of the spikes in programs' budgets from up-front funding of new capital investments and facilitate comparisons of competing programs' costs and benefits" (p. 2). Capital budgets can also help smooth out tax rates over time in governments where projects are large enough to significantly influence tax rates through debt financing and making careful decisions about project timing. In addition, capital projects typically have a long life; the use of separate capital budgets is said to increase the review of these projects, which can reduce expensive errors and can also help in the need to "balance spending with the resources available within political, economic, and legal tax and debt limits" (Mikesell, 2011, p. 245).

Other proponents of a separate capital budget suggest that it would alter the incentive structure, allowing Congress to favor investment over consumption and enabling more informed choices through improved information. Gershberg and Benning (1999) suggest that Congress could utilize a capital budget as a budget enforcement tool to limit federal borrowing to the amounts necessary to finance capital investments while balancing the operating budget. The U.S. General Accounting Office (1996) suggested that insufficient attention was given to the balance between long-term and short-term needs in the federal budget format. Gershberg and Benning (1999) suggest that a capital budget could also be a useful counter-cyclical economy policy tool to speed up capital spending in times of economic downturns.

However, there is opposition to the concept of a separate capital budget. The President's Commission on Budget Concepts (1967) and the President's Commission to Study Capital Budgeting (1999) note that there are technical challenges to making this change, and they fear that it would lead to reduced transparency, increased borrowing, and inefficient allocation of spending. The increased borrowing might occur because a wide range of federal activities could be broadly construed as "investments," including human capital, which could lead to incentives to increase the capital budget and, therefore, debt financing. There is also an argument that a separate capital budget is not necessary at the federal level because of its size; in smaller governments, the lumpiness of large capital projects may influence tax rates, but that is not the case with the federal government where "smoothing" is not required for this purpose (Mikesell, 2011). CBO (2021) notes that

> an accrual approach with a separate capital budget could lessen lawmakers' control over budgetary resources, increase complexity, and diminish transparency.

> It would also make the federal budget process more prone to manipulation by federal agencies and policymakers that might adopt a broad definition of capital investment or understate depreciation costs.
>
> *(p. 2)*

Capital budgeting at the state and local levels

Capital budgeting at the state and local government levels is a crucial function of public financial management, playing a critical role in shaping the physical, economic, and social infrastructure of communities. State and local governments engage in capital budgeting to maintain and expand public infrastructure, respond to population growth, stimulate economic development, and ensure the health and safety of residents.

Various state agencies are involved in the development process, including the Governor's Office, Legislative Budget Board, Higher Education Coordinating Boards, Facilities Commission, and other agencies (Ermasova, 2012). Based on the input from these organizations, Central Budget Office (CBO) develops program guidelines, instructions, and a formal application process for submitting capital project requests based on the legislative mandate. From a budgetary and capital planning standpoint, several state agencies collaborate to varying degrees in coordinating the budgetary and capital reporting and approval processes. The CBO coordinates the submission of capital projects, develops a report, and determines the effect of the additional capital requests on the state's budget and debt capacity. The completed plan is then forwarded to the Legislature. The Legislature makes the final decision on which projects will be funded. The CBO develops the Capital Projects Database, a statewide, web-based, secure application used to capture agency capital project information.

States define the types of expenditures allowed in capital budgets to include such items as construction, improvements, land acquisition, site improvements, major renovations, and equipment. Definitions of what constitutes a capital outlay range from the fairly standard (e.g., the useful design life of a building as 20 years in Hawaii, 40 years in Oregon, 50 years in Delaware; outlays greater than $50,000 in West Virginia or $1,000,000 in South Carolina for a project that provides benefits beyond the immediate year) to some that are normally considered operating outlays (e.g., Alabama defines a capital outlay as any item with a life span of more than one year).

In some states (e.g., Montana and New Jersey), maintenance has been shifted from the state Capital Budget to the departments' budgets since the beginning of the Great Recession. Other states (Alabama, Indiana, Maryland, Massachusetts, South Dakota, Utah, and New York) have developed a system to rate maintenance projects as part of the effort to preserve facilities. Many states place additional emphasis on the planning and execution of preventive maintenance

(Alabama, Indiana, Massachusetts, Nebraska, New York, Oregon, Tennessee, and Virginia).

Financing strategies constitute a critical element of capital budgeting. Local governments rely on a mix of pay-as-you-go financing, *pay-as-you-use* financing, and grants. *Pay-as-you-go* financing uses current revenues for capital expenditures and is often applied to smaller projects or technology upgrades. Pay-as-you-use financing (borrowing, commonly through bonds) is used for larger investments with long service lives. The rationale for borrowing is based on intergenerational equity, whereby future taxpayers who benefit from infrastructure also contribute to its cost.

State government pay-as-you-go sources include: (1) annual, general-purpose revenues that are applied to capital projects and acquisitions; (2) general fund taxes; (3) special fund taxes; (4) annual revenues that are earmarked (either by state law or local policy) for capital projects and acquisitions; (5) cash; (6) operating fund balances that are not needed to support operations; (7) capital reserves; (8) equipment or vehicle replacement revolving funds, or infrastructure and facility rehabilitation revolving funds; (9) special assessments, capital recovery charges, and impact fees; (10) federal grants; (11) cooperative arrangements with other state governments; and (12) public sector-private sector partnerships or privatization (Ermasova, 2012).

The following pay-as-you-use resources are typically available for agencies to draw upon to finance capital projects at the state level: (1) use of treasury loans; (2) revenue bonds; (3) general obligations; (4) bond anticipation notes; (5) interfund borrowing; (6) revenue notes; and (7) tax-exempt commercial papers (Ermasova, 2012).

At the local level, capital budgeting typically operates as part of a broader CIP. The CIP is a multi-year planning document that identifies infrastructure needs, estimates costs, prioritizes projects, and outlines funding strategies. Most local governments adopt a five- to six-year planning horizon, with the first year representing the formal capital budget and subsequent years serving as forecasts and priorities for future investment. The plan is updated annually to reflect changes in economic conditions, political leadership, inflation, population growth, and regulatory requirements.

One of the defining features of capital budgeting at the local level is the tension between professional planning and political discretion. Administrators and financial officers evaluate capital needs based on technical assessments, asset condition reports, and service delivery standards. Elected officials, however, often prioritize projects based on visibility, constituent demand, and political considerations. While this dynamic can lead to conflict, it also ensures that investment decisions reflect both professional judgment and democratic accountability. Effective capital budgeting systems balance these forces through formal criteria, public participation, and structured evaluation processes.

Project identification is the first stage in the capital budgeting process. Departments submit proposals for capital projects based on asset deterioration, service expansion, legal mandates, or economic development objectives. Common triggers include outdated infrastructure, safety concerns, technological change, and community demands. Engineering studies, facility inspections, and infrastructure audits frequently inform this stage. Local governments are increasingly relying on asset management systems to track the condition and replacement cycles of key facilities, such as water systems, bridges, and public buildings.

Once needs are identified, capital projects are evaluated using financial, operational, and strategic criteria. Financial feasibility involves analyzing total project cost, future maintenance obligations, and potential debt service requirements. Operational feasibility examines whether the government has the capacity to staff, maintain, and operate the facility after construction. Strategic alignment ensures that projects support community goals, land-use plans, and economic development strategies. Many local governments use scoring systems that assign weights to factors such as urgency, legal requirements, economic impact, and community benefit. The major stages in the capital budgeting process are shown in Figure 7.1.

Prioritization is one of the most challenging aspects of capital budgeting. Because available resources rarely meet all capital demands, state and local governments must rank projects, make trade-offs, and sometimes privatize government assets. Deferred maintenance often competes with new construction, and politically popular projects may crowd out less visible infrastructure investments. Inadequate prioritization leads to infrastructure decay and escalating repair costs. To mitigate these risks, best practices encourage objective criteria, long-term planning, and independent review by finance departments or citizen advisory boards.

Public participation is increasingly recognized as a vital component of capital budgeting at the local level. Community engagement enhances transparency, improves trust, and helps align investment decisions with the needs of citizens. Public hearings, surveys, and participatory budgeting programs allow residents to express preferences and evaluate priorities. While community input may slow

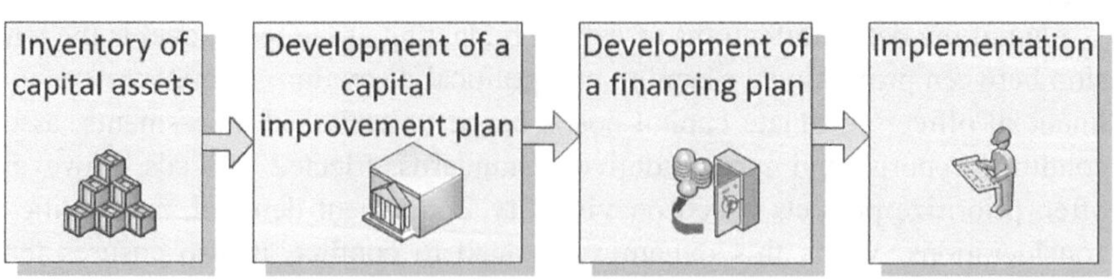

FIGURE 7.1 Steps in the capital budgeting process

Source: Created by authors

decision-making, it strengthens the legitimacy of capital plans and reduces conflict during implementation.

Implementation and monitoring form the final stages of capital budgeting. Once projects are approved, governments must oversee contracting, construction, and expenditure control. Cost overruns, delays, and contractor disputes are common risks. Effective oversight requires coordination between finance departments, public works agencies, and external auditors. Regular reporting and performance monitoring ensure that projects remain within budget and serve their intended purposes. Post-project reviews assess whether outcomes match original expectations and identify weaknesses in planning, financing, or execution.

In recent years, state and local capital budgeting has been shaped by new challenges, including aging infrastructure and the impacts of climate change. Flood control, water system modernization, and energy-efficient facilities now compete with traditional infrastructure needs. Equity-oriented capital budgeting seeks to address historical disinvestment in underserved communities by integrating social justice considerations into capital project selection.

Conclusions

The federal government does not maintain a separate, distinct budget for capital projects. Rather, it prepares and executes budgets for both capital and operating expenditures in a unified budget. The budget process does not focus on investment spending apart from other types of spending that support current consumption. As a result, investment spending is less visible and explicit than it could be, and investment projects often have a mismatch between when costs are incurred and when benefits are realized. Careful financial planning and efficient management of budget delivery are essential. Both planning and management work well only if the budget information systems are comprehensive, timely, accurate, and reliable, and all the departments involved cooperate closely.

Capital budgeting is also affected by economic conditions. During economic downturns, revenues decline, debt becomes more expensive, and projects may be delayed or canceled. However, recessions can also create opportunities for lower construction costs and external assistance. Strategic governments utilize capital planning to stabilize local economies by investing in infrastructure during periods of economic stress. Conversely, economic recovery often encourages expanded capital programs, which must be managed carefully to avoid overextension.

Capital budgeting at the state and local levels is a multidimensional process that requires technical expertise, political negotiation, financial discipline, and public accountability. It is not merely a financial document but a statement of community priorities and future direction. State and local governments that maintain updated CIPs are better equipped to anticipate future needs, allocate resources strategically, and manage risk effectively. Multi-year planning allows for smoother expenditure patterns and prevents the crisis-driven approach to infrastructure investment that leads to deferred maintenance, reactive spending, and fiscal stress. In contrast, jurisdictions that treat capital budgeting as an annual exercise often struggle with unexpected costs, project delays, and inefficient allocation of funds. When conducted effectively, capital budgeting promotes economic growth, enhances infrastructure resilience, and improves the quality of life.

In this chapter, the first case study, "Critical needs of capital investments in the infrastructure at the federal level in the United States," examines the capital budgeting and the need for capital investments in the infrastructure at the federal level in the United States. This case study describes the current condition and critical needs for capital investments in federal infrastructure in the United States, using the 2025 Report Card for America's Infrastructure and evaluations from the ASCE Committee on America's Infrastructure. During the budget simulation game, students should decide on ranking priorities and allocate $1.2 trillion across different sectors of the United States' infrastructure system. The findings of this case study have important implications for public administration practitioners and scholars interested in understanding capital budgeting.

The second case study, "Financing Challenges in the U.S. Surface Transportation System," examines the financing of the United States' surface transportation system. It reviews the fiscal sustainability of the Highway Trust Fund and its funding issues.

References

ASCE (2024). Policy statement 453 - Federal capital budgeting. Adopted by the Board of Direction on July 18, 2024. https://www.asce.org/advocacy/policy-statements/ps453---federal-capital-budgeting

Congressional Budget Office (2006). Comparing budget and accounting measures of the federal government's fiscal condition. December 2006. Washington: Congressional Budget Office.

Congressional Budget Office (2008). Capital budgeting. May 2008. Washington: Congressional Budget Office. https://www.cbo.gov/sites/default/files/110th-congress-2007-2008/reports/05-08-capital.pdf

Congressional Budget Office (2021). Budgeting for ffederal investment. Washington: Congressional Budget Office. https://www.cbo.gov/publication/57142

Ermasova, N. (2012). *Capital budgeting at the state level: An empirical analysis from the economic downturn through the present*, PhD Dissertation, Bloomington, IN: SPEA, IU Publishing house.

Ermasova, N. (2020). The 35 years of public capital budgeting: A review and future research agenda. *Public Finance and Management*, *19*(4), 297–326.

Ermasova, N., & Mikesell, J. (2019). Public capital budgeting and management: The concept and its application in three important federations. *Public Finance and Management*, *19*(3), 175–199.

Gershberg, A., & Benning, J. (1999). Federal capital investment and the balanced budget amendment: the pros and cons of a federal capital budget. Research paper. The Nelson A. Rockefeller Institute of Government.

GovInfo (2025). Budget FY 2024 - Table 9.1 - Total investment outlays for major public physical capital, *Research and Development, and Education and Training: 1962–2024*. https://www.govinfo.gov/app/details/BUDGET-2024-TAB/BUDGET-2024-TAB-10-1

Making, GAO/AIMD-99-32. December 1998. Washington, DC: U.S. General Accounting Office.

Mikesell, J. (2011). *Fiscal administration.* Eights Edition. Cengage Learning.

Office of Management and Budget (1992). Circular A–94: Guidelines and discount rates for benefit-cost analysis of federal programs.

Office of Management and Budget (2006). Circular A-11, Part 7. https://georgewbush-whitehouse.archives.gov/omb/circulars/a11/current_year/s300.pdf

Office of Management and Budget (2016a). Capital programming guide, V 3.0, Supplement to office of management budget circular A-11: Planning, budgeting, and acquisition of capital assets. Washington: Office of Management and Budget. https://obamawhitehouse.archives.gov/sites/default/files/omb/assets/a11_current_year/a11_2016.pdf

Office of Management and Budget (2016b). Appendix A - scorekeeping guidelines (OMB Circular A-11).

Office of Management and Budget (2016c). Appendix J - principles in budgeting for capital asset acquisitions. (OMB Circular A-11). Retrieved from https://obamawhitehouse.archives.gov/sites/default/files/omb/assets/a11_current_year/app_j.pdf

Potter, B., & Diamond, J. (1999). Guidelines for public expenditure management. IMF. Retrieved from https://www.imf.org/external/pubs/ft/expend/guide5.htm

President's Commission on Budget Concepts (1967). Report of the president's commission on budget concepts. Washington: U.S. Government Printing Office.

President's Commission to Study Capital Budgeting (1999). Report of the president's commission to study capital budgeting. February 1999. Washington. Retrieved from https://clintonwhitehouse3.archives.gov/pcscb/report.html

U.S. General Accounting Office (1996). Testimony 7/11/96, GAO/T-AIMD-96-129. Washington: U.S. General Accounting Office.

U.S. General Accounting Office (1998). Executive guide: Leading practices in capital decision-

U.S. General Accounting Office (2004). Agency implementation of capital planning principles is mixed. GAO-04-138. Washington: U.S. General Accounting Office.

CASE STUDY 16

Critical needs of capital investments at the federal level in the United States

Abstract

This case study describes the current condition and critical needs of capital investments in the infrastructure at the federal level in the United States, using the 2025 Report Card for America's Infrastructure and evaluations from the American Society of Civil Engineers (ASCE) Committee on America's Infrastructure. It illustrates the persistent challenges of aging and underfunded systems across sectors such as Aviation, Dams, Roads, Schools, and Wastewater, which have received grades of D+ in ASCE's Report Card for America's Infrastructure. This case study highlights the need for capital investments and a strategic plan to modernize the nation's infrastructure. With the passage of the $1.2 trillion Bipartisan Infrastructure Law in 2021, federal agencies face the urgent task of ranking priorities and determining how to allocate these capital funds. In this case study, students should decide on ranking priorities and how to allocate $1.2 trillion in different sectors of the infrastructure system across the United States.

Topics

Capital Budgeting; Federal Government; Capital Investments; Capital Infrastructure

Background

The condition of capital infrastructure in the United States has become a central concern in public finance and public budgeting due to decades of underinvestment, deferred maintenance, and growing demands placed on aging systems. Inadequate capital investment has resulted in increased safety risks, service disruptions, traffic delays, economic inefficiencies, and reduced resilience to natural hazards. Aging transportation networks, deteriorating water and wastewater systems, unreliable energy infrastructure, and insufficient broadband access impose significant costs on households, businesses, and governments.

Capital investments in the United States are typically directed toward major infrastructure categories such as transportation, water resources, energy, schools, public buildings, and communications systems. Federal, state, and local governments share responsibility for financing these investments, with the federal government playing a particularly important role in addressing large-scale, nationally significant infrastructure needs.

Grades to the nation's infrastructure

The American Society of Civil Engineers (ASCE) represents more than 160,000 members of the civil engineering profession in 177 countries (ASCE, 2024). Founded in 1852, ASCE is the nation's oldest national civil engineering society. For 25 years, the ASCE has been releasing its quadrennial Report Card for America's Infrastructure, a comprehensive evaluation of the nation's 17 major infrastructure categories through its Report Card for America's Infrastructure (ASCE, 2025a). This assessment employs a standardized grading system, ranging from A to F, to evaluate the current state and future public infrastructure needs. The report not only assigns grades but also provides strategic recommendations for improvement.

The Report Card is developed by the ASCE Committee on America's Infrastructure. With decades of expertise in various infrastructure sectors, these professionals collaborate with ASCE Infrastructure Initiatives staff to prepare the assessment. The grading process involves a thorough review of relevant data and reports, consultations with technical and industry experts, and an evaluation of infrastructure performance based on the following criteria: (1) capacity to which the infrastructure meets current and projected future demands; (2) condition of the infrastructure; (3) funding allocated by federal, state, and local governments in relation to the estimated funding needs; (4) the projected costs required for infrastructure improvements and the likelihood that future funding will address these needs; (5) the ability of infrastructure owners to effectively manage and maintain systems while ensuring compliance with regulatory standards; (6) the potential risks posed by infrastructure deficiencies and the possible consequences of failure; (7) the infrastructure system's capacity to withstand and recover from multi-hazard threats while minimizing adverse effects on public safety, economic stability, and national security; and (8) the implementation of

TABLE 7.2 The Grades of Capital Infrastructure in the United States (2001–2025)

Subject	*2001*	*2005*	*2009*	*2013*	*2017*	*2021*	*2025*
Aviation	*D*	D+	D	D	D	D+	D+
Bridges	*C*	*C*	C	C+	C+	C	C
Dams	D	D	D	D	D	D	D+
Drinking water	*D*	D-	D-	D	D	C-	C-
Energy (national power grid)	*D+*	D	D+	D+	D+	C-	D+
Hazardous waste	*D+*	*D*	D	D	D+	D+	C
Navigable waterways	*D+*	D-	D-	D-	D	D+	C-
Public parks and recreation	–	*C-*	C-	C-	D+	D+	C-
Rail	–	*C-*	C-	C+	B	B	B-
Roads	*D+*	*D*	D-	D	D	D	D+
Schools	*D-*	*D*	D	D	D+	D+	D+
Solid waste	*C+*	C+	C+	C+	C+	C+	C+
Transit	*C-*	*D+*	D	D	D-	D-	D
Wastewater	*D*	D-	D-	D	D	D+	D+

Source: Created by authors based on Report Cards for America's Infrastructure (ASCE American society of civil engineers (2001, 2005, 2009, 2013, 2017, 2021, 2025).

Each category was evaluated on the basis of condition and performance, capacity vs. need, and funding vs. need: **A** = Exceptional 90–100%; **B** = Good 80–89%; **C** = Mediocre 70–79%; **D** = Poor 51–69%; **F** = Failing 50% or lower.

advanced techniques, materials, technologies, and delivery methods to enhance infrastructure performance (ASCE, 2025a).

By systematically applying these criteria, the Report Card provides a grading of the state of the nation's infrastructure and the necessary steps for improvement. Table 7.2 provides the United States' capital infrastructure grades from 2001 to 2025.

The 2025 Report Card for America's Infrastructure, released by ASCE, assigns an overall grade of C to the nation's infrastructure (ASCE, 2025b). The 2025 grades range from Grade B for ports to Grade D for stormwater and transit. Aviation, Dams, Roads, Schools, and Wastewater were rated D+ (Poor condition); Bridges and Hazardous Waste were rated C; Solid Waste and Broadband were rated C+ (Mediocre condition) (Table 7.1). For the first time since 1998, no Report Card categories were rated D-. Table 7.1 shows that the United States has made some incremental progress toward restoring its infrastructure. For the first time in 25 years, the infrastructure's overall grade is in the C range.

Federal funding and cumulative investment needs

The Bipartisan Infrastructure Law (BIL) signed on November 15, 2021 directs \$1.2 trillion of federal funds toward transportation, energy, and climate infrastructure projects (U.S. Treasury, 2025). The longer critical investments to improve the nation's infrastructure's operability, safety, and resilience are withheld, the greater the future cost and risk of failure (ASCE, 2025a).

Based on the 2025 Report Card for America's Infrastructure, ASCE estimates investment needs a total of \$9.1 trillion for all 18 Report Card categories to reach a state of good repair (ASCE, 2025b). Table 7.3 demonstrates cumulative investment needs by infrastructure category.

Budget simulation on capital budgeting and investments

Reducing federal investment levels will escalate the costs and risks of an aging infrastructure system. Infrastructure investments must be made with consideration of a project's full life cycle, including the impact of more frequent extreme weather. Public safety and efficient use of public dollars are advanced by building projects that withstand increasingly severe weather events and natural and man-made hazards. To realize the benefits of recent infrastructure investments, the nation should advance forward-thinking policies and innovations necessary to build systems today that will provide clean drinking water, ensure safer transportation systems, and produce reliable electricity and broadband over the next 100 years.

For the simulation exercise students should be divided into groups of 3 or 4. As it is seen from Table 7.3, ASCE estimates \$9.1 trillion total needs for capital

TABLE 7.3 Cumulative Investment Needs by Infrastructure Category (\$ Billions)

Infrastructure System	*Needs*
Aviation	\$310
Bridges	\$538
Broadband	\$61
Dams	\$185
Drinking water	\$670
Energy	\$1,886
Hazardous and solid waste	\$162
Inland waterways and ports	\$45
Levees	\$97
Public parks	\$106
Rail	\$145
Roads	\$2,233
Schools	\$1,100
Transit	\$618
Wastewater + stormwater	\$983
TOTAL	**\$9,139**

investments in the infrastructure at the federal level in the United States. Yet, the BIL provides only $1.2 trillion in funding. Each group will act as a budget review team tasked with evaluating and proposing capital investments in the 15 infrastructure categories totaling $1.2 trillion. Instructors can provide bonus incentives for ideas that would increase the lowest-grade categories with Grades D and D+. Every group of students should present their findings and priorities. Students are encouraged to visit ASCE website for details about infrastructure needs: https://infrastructurereportcard.org/.

Questions for discussion after budget simulation

1. What role should the federal government play in providing guidance and funding to address public capital infrastructure needs?
2. How should ASCE Grades influence decisions about capital investments?
3. How do we balance limited resources and public needs of capital investments?
4. What guiding principles did your team use to allocate capital funds?
5. Did you prioritize based on ASCE Grades, investment need, or political feasibility?
6. How did the funding constraint of $1.2 trillion shape your priorities?
7. What trade-offs did you make when underfunding or defunding some sectors?
8. If the budget was unlimited, how would your decisions change?
9. Should certain sectors be funded more by state/local or private actors?
10. How did your team make decisions? Was it consensus, majority vote, or leadership-led?

References

ASCE (2024). *About ASCE.* https://www.asce.org/about-asce

ASCE (2025a). *Trends we can see from the US infrastructure grade* https://infrastructurereportcard.org/infrastructure-categories/

ASCE (2025b). *A comprehensive assessment of America's infrastructure 2025.* https://infrastructurereportcard.org/

U.S. Treasury (2025). Infrastructure investment in the united states. *Press Release.* November 15, 2023. https://home.treasury.gov/news/featured-stories/infrastructure-investment-in-the-united-states

Videos

1. The $1.2 Trillion Plan to Rebuild America: https://www.youtube.com/watch?v=uyQjnW5ZQp8
2. The Value of the ASCE Report Card: https://www.youtube.com/watch?v=BY6ayB0xTIQ
3. America's Vital Infrastructure is on the Verge of Collapse: https://www.youtube.com/watch?v=WLFBoASIQ0s

CASE STUDY 17

Financing challenges in the U.S. surface transportation system

Abstract

This case study examines the financing challenges facing the United States' surface transportation system, with a particular emphasis on the fiscal sustainability of the Highway Trust Fund (HTF). Federal investment in highways and mass transit has historically relied on a user-pay financing model, primarily supported by motor fuel and truck-related excise taxes. However, revenues from these sources have failed to keep pace with growing infrastructure needs. Most notably, the federal gasoline tax has lost nearly half of its real value since it was last increased in 1993, contributing to a widening gap between revenues and expenditures. The HTF's deficits reflect fundamental weaknesses in a revenue system that has failed to evolve alongside changes in vehicle efficiency, travel behavior, and infrastructure costs. Drawing on data and analysis from the Federal Highway Administration, the Congressional Research Service, the Congressional Budget Office, and independent policy research organizations, this case study demonstrates the magnitude and persistence of this funding shortfall and examines its implications for intergovernmental finance and capital budgeting. Alternative financing strategies designed to address the declining productivity of fuel tax revenues are examined, with a particular focus on vehicle-miles-traveled fees as a potential long-term solution.

Topics

Capital Budgeting; Highway Trust Fund; Transportation System; Vehicle miles traveled (VMT) taxes

Background

The United States' surface transportation system (including highways, public transit, maritime ports, and rail infrastructure) forms the backbone of national mobility and economic activity. Every day, millions of people commute to work, and supply chains depend on a functioning network of roads, bridges, and transit systems. However, the U.S. surface transportation system that supports this activity is aging, deteriorating, and increasingly unable to meet modern demands. The Report Card for America's Infrastructure, released by the American Society of Civil Engineers, assigns an overall grade of C to the nation's infrastructure (ASCE, 2025). In the 2025 report, roads were rated D+ (poor condition), while bridges were rated C (mediocre condition) (ASCE, 2025).

An essential contributor to the deterioration of the surface transportation system is the persistent inadequacy and instability of its funding structure. The surface transportation sector is primarily funded through a mix of federal, state, and local revenues, but the most significant source (federal fuel taxes) has not kept pace with long-term needs.

The Highway Trust Fund

Since 1956, the Federal Highway Trust Fund (HTF) has been the primary mechanism for financing federal highway and transit expenditures. HTF is a federal accounting mechanism that primarily receives revenue from transportation-related excise taxes, providing a dedicated source of funding for surface transportation (Congress.gov, 2025). HTF consists of two accounts, the Highway Account and the Mass Transit Account, both established in FY 1983. The highway account, which has been financed primarily through federal fuel taxes and other transportation-related excise taxes, provides funding mainly for the federal-aid highway program, highway and vehicle safety programs, and highway research (Congress.gov, 2025; U.S. Department of Transportation, 2026). The Mass Transit Account provides funding for capital infrastructure needs and is financed mostly by the funds set aside for commuting costs by employees.

Approximately 85% of the highway account's annual revenue, which is the focus of this case study, is derived from motor fuel taxes. These taxes include federal gasoline tax of 18.3 cents per gallon, federal diesel tax of 24.3 cents per gallon, and truck-related taxes (tire taxes, heavy vehicle use fees, etc.). The highway account receives an allocation equivalent to 15.44 cents of the gasoline tax and 21.44 cents of the diesel tax, while the mass transit account receives 2.86 cents of the gasoline tax and 2.86 cents of the diesel tax.

The federal gasoline tax was first introduced on June 6, 1932, at 1 cent per gallon. The tax was increased to 3 cents per gallon in 1956 when HTF was established, 4 cents per gallon in 1959, 9 cents per gallon in 1982, 14 cents per gallon in 1990, and 18.30 cents per gallon in 1993.

Several taxes that support HTF are subject to scheduled expiration or rate reductions. Taxes imposed on tires and on truck and trailer sales are scheduled to expire at the end of FY 2028, while taxes on heavy vehicle use are set to expire at the end of FY 2029. Three fuel-related taxes, the gasoline tax, the diesel tax, and the methanol tax, are scheduled to be reduced at the end of FY 2028. Under current law, the gasoline and diesel tax rates would decline to 4.30 cents per gallon at that time.

However, even at its current rate, the federal gasoline tax has not been raised since 1993. From that year, inflation has eroded nearly half of its real purchasing power. Since its inception in 1932, the gasoline tax has served as a quasi-price for road usage. But, as vehicle fuel efficiency has improved, and the adoption of electric vehicles has increased, the per-mile revenue growth of fuel tax receipts has declined. From 1972 to 2022, the average fuel economy across all vehicles increased by more than 50% (Muresianu et al., 2024). Yet, Figure 7.1 demonstrates that miles per gallon traveled by passenger cars and heavy-duty vehicles have increased by more than 75% since 1977.

To account for growth in fuel efficiency and inability to collect fuel tax revenues from electric vehicles, on May 22, 2025, the House passed H.R. 1, reconciliation legislation that would, among other things, created tiered annual registration fees for vehicles: $250 for EVs, $100 for hybrid vehicles, and no fee for other vehicles (e.g., internal combustion engine vehicles). These fees would increase on an annual basis to account for inflation (Congress.gov, 2025).

When adjusted for inflation, the purchasing power of highway account revenue varied considerably over time. Real revenue was the highest from the mid-1990s to the mid-2000s, reaching its peak in fiscal year 2007. By FY 2023, the purchasing power of highway account revenue had fallen to its lowest level since FY 1984 (Congress.gov, 2025).

Expenditures from the highway account increased steadily in nominal dollars, beginning in FY 1983. When adjusted for inflation, spending patterns fluctuated, reflecting alternating periods of higher and lower outlays. Through FY 2000, revenues from the highway account were generally sufficient to meet or slightly exceed annual expenditures, and the account remained fiscally balanced. Beginning in FY 2001, a persistent structural imbalance emerged, as annual expenditures consistently exceeded revenues. From FY 2001 onward, the gap between revenues and expenditures widened, with annual shortfalls ranging from $430 million in FY 2006 to $16 billion in FY 2016, measured in 2023-adjusted dollars (Congress.gov, 2025). These sustained deficits raised concerns about the long-term fiscal sustainability of the highway account (Figure 7.2).

In FY 2024, the HTF spent $26.7 billion more than it collected in net highway user taxes, meaning a significant portion of its outlays (about 38.5 cents of every dollar spent) came not from user fees but from the general fund (Davis, 2024). The fund received roughly $42.5 billion in net user-tax receipts (from gasoline, diesel, truck and trailer sales, heavy vehicle use, and tire taxes), with

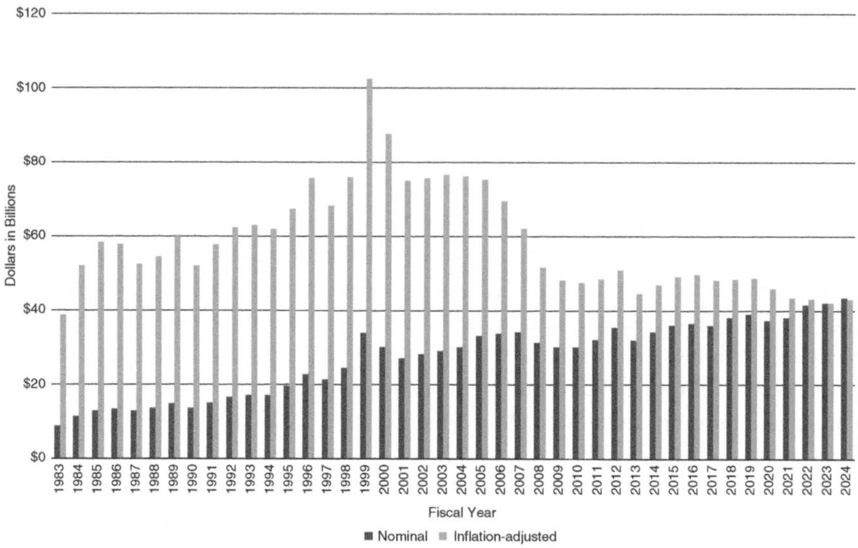

FIGURE 7.2 Highway account revenue, FY 1983-FY 2024, in nominal and FY 2023 inflation—adjusted dollars

Source: Congress.gov (2025)

net gas tax receipts alone at about $25.2 billion, up 7.5% from the prior year. Diesel net receipts were around $9.5 billion, while taxes on new truck and trailer sales dropped to about $6.1 billion, a 15.6% decline from the previous year (Figure 7.2). In FY 2024, the Highway Account's $19.5 billion real deficit amounted to 35 cents of every Highway Account dollar spent (Davis, 2024).

To address these growing shortfalls, Congress increasingly relied on transfers from the U.S. Treasury's General Fund. In 2015, under the Fixing America's Surface Transportation Act, Congress transferred $51.9 billion to the highway account (Congress.gov, 2025).

Enacted in 2021, the Infrastructure Investment and Jobs Act (IIJA; P.L. 117–58) authorized an additional $90 billion transfer to the highway account and significantly expanded federal investment in surface transportation. Obligations authorized under the IIJA resulted in notable increases in highway account expenditures in FY 2023 and FY 2024, as the legislation established several new highway programs.

Since 1973, state and local governments have had authority to shift some of their highway formula funding to mass transit projects, and vice versa. When state and local governments do this, the amount of money spent is then transferred as cash between the Federal Highway Account and the Mass Transit Account. In 2024, the transfer was $1.46 billion in cash transferred from the Highway Account to the Mass Transit Account, matching an identical amount of outlays made by the Federal Transit Administration that originated as highway funds (Davis, 2024). The Mass Transit Account recorded a deficit of $7.2 billion, indicating that approximately 52.8 cents of every dollar expended from the trust fund was effectively financed through transfers from the U.S. Treasury's General Fund rather than through dedicated trust fund revenues.

Based on current trends, the Congressional Budget Office (CBO) projects that by FY 2028, the highway account will not have sufficient funds to meet federal obligations to states and local governments for authorized transportation projects, thereby renewing policy debates regarding the long-term financing and sustainability of the HTF (Congress.gov, 2025). In early 2023, the Congressional Budget Office projected that HTF expenditures would exceed revenues beginning in 2028. A cumulative shortfall of approximately $208 billion is expected through 2032.

Alternative financing options

There are several potential funding options to avoid HTF deficit that are discussed below

Increasing and indexing the federal fuel tax

The first option is to raise the gasoline tax and index it to inflation. Increasing and indexing fuel taxes could restore some lost purchasing power but may prove insufficient over the long term as electric vehicles become more prevalent. However, political resistance to this option has been strong.

Vehicle-miles-traveled fees

Vehicle miles traveled (VMT) taxes, mileage-based user fees, or road usage charges are charges assessed on drivers for each mile traveled on public roadways. These charges may be differentiated based on vehicle characteristics, such as weight per axle, as well as contextual factors including the time, location, or congestion level associated with travel. Unlike fuel taxes, which rely on gasoline consumption as an indirect measure of roadway use, VMT taxes directly measure actual road usage and impose charges accordingly. When appropriately calibrated, a VMT-based system has the potential to more closely align roadway revenues with infrastructure expenditures and to insulate transportation funding from the effects of increasing fuel efficiency, technological change, and evolving consumer travel preferences.

VMT taxes are still in the early stages of policy development in the United States. At present, no federal VMT framework exists, and no state has fully replaced its motor fuel tax with a VMT-based revenue system. Currently, four states operate active opt-in VMT programs for passenger vehicles, and five states have implemented VMT programs targeting heavy commercial vehicles. Oregon, for example, operates programs for both categories.

VMT designs can be categorized into two systems: low-tech solutions based on manual submissions of odometer readings, and higher-tech solutions based on global positioning system (GPS) tracking of vehicle usage (Macumber-Rosin & Hoffer, 2024). Of the four states with active programs, Oregon and Virginia offer both GPS and non-GPS reporting options, Utah utilizes GPS only, and Hawaii is set to use odometer readings during regular registration renewal inspections. The primary challenge to GPS tracking is privacy concerns. Many Americans would be understandably hesitant to support a system that provided a government agency with detailed, GPS-specific tracking of their vehicle's movements.

Sixteen states have launched pilot programs to assess the administrative, technological, and equity implications of implementing VMT. Existing VMT programs for heavy vehicles are mandatory, whereas passenger vehicle programs are voluntary and typically allow participants to offset gasoline taxes, vehicle registration fees, or other charges. Hawaii represents a notable exception, as it has announced plans to make its VMT program mandatory, applying first to electric vehicles in 2028 and subsequently to all passenger vehicles in 2033.

Tolling and congestion pricing

Expanding tolling authority or implementing congestion pricing in metropolitan areas can generate revenue while managing demand.

General fund transfers

Continuing the practice of supplementing HTF with general revenues is possible but raises questions about fiscal sustainability.

Conclusions

The nation's transportation system is facing a long-term, structural funding issue. Fuel-tax revenues continue to decline while infrastructure needs to grow, making the HTF unsustainable under existing policies. This case study highlights the increasing reliance on transfers from the federal general fund to sustain surface transportation programs, raising important questions regarding fiscal sustainability, transparency, equity, and the continued viability of the user-pay principle.

Options such as indexing the gas tax to inflation, implementing VMT fees, expanding tolling, introducing congestion pricing, or adopting other innovative funding tools must be evaluated to stabilize the funding. The long-term planning must reflect technological changes. The continued rise of electric vehicles and improved fuel efficiency make it essential to move beyond traditional fuel-based revenue models. Hybrid approaches that combine reformed fuel taxes, targeted VMT charges, and greater state-level experimentation may therefore represent the most realistic path forward.

Discussion questions

1 What features of the Highway Trust Fund's revenue structure make it vulnerable to long-term fiscal imbalance, and why are these weaknesses considered structural rather than temporary?
2 In what ways do rising vehicle fuel efficiency and the growth of electric vehicles challenge the traditional user-pay model of transportation finance?
3 What are the advantages and disadvantages of increasing and indexing fuel taxes to inflation compared to introducing new revenue instruments?
4 How do vehicle miles traveled (VMT) taxes differ from fuel taxes in terms of economic efficiency and alignment with actual road usage?
5 How might privacy concerns influence public acceptance of mileage-based user fees, and what design features could mitigate these concerns?
6 In what ways could VMT taxes improve or worsen equity outcomes for rural residents, low-income households, and commercial vehicle operators?
7 Should the federal government continue to play a central role in surface transportation finance, or should greater responsibility be devolved to states and local governments?

References

ASCE (2025). *A comprehensive assessment of America's infrastructure 2025.* https://infrastructurereportcard.org/

Congress.gov (2025). *The highway trust fund's highway account.* https://www.congress.gov/crs-product/R48472

Davis, J. (2024). Highway trust fund ran $26.7 billion user-pay deficit in FY 2024. *ENO Center for Transportation.* https://enotrans.org/article/highway-trust-fund-ran-26-7-billion-user-pay-deficit-in-fy-2024/

Macumber-Rosin, J., & Hoffer, A. (2024, May 9). Vehicle miles traveled taxes rollout across states. *Tax Foundation.* https://taxfoundation.org/blog/state-vmt-vehicle-miles-traveled-taxes/.

Muresianu, A., Hoffer, A., Macumber-Rosin, J., & Durante, A. (2024, August 7). Expanding user fees for transportation: Roads and beyond. *Tax Foundation.* https://taxfoundation.org/wp-content/uploads/2024/08/Expanding-User-Fees-for-Transportation-Roads-and-Beyond.pdf

U.S. Department of Transportation (2026). *Highway trust fund balance - FY 2025.* https://highways.dot.gov/media/74106

8

COST-BENEFIT ANALYSIS

Abstract

This chapter introduces benefit-cost analysis (BCA) as an analytical framework for evaluating the financial and economic viability of public capital projects. It explains how BCA systematically compares the discounted stream of societal benefits and costs over a project's life cycle to determine whether a project generates positive net present value and enhances overall economic efficiency. The chapter highlights the strengths and limitations of monetizing market and non-market impacts, emphasizing the challenges associated with valuing public goods, externalities, and long-term social outcomes. This chapter also explains fiscal impact analysis (FIA), and the major steps involved in conducting both BCA and FIA.

Introduction

In this chapter, we continue the discussion of capital budgeting by introducing an important analytical tool for assessing the financial viability of capital projects before they are included in a capital improvement plan. This assessment instrument is called benefit-cost analysis (BCA).

BCA is a method of organizing information about a project under consideration that compares societal benefits over the lifetime of the project with the societal costs.

A project is desirable if it produces a positive net present value (PV) (NPV), meaning that aggregate social benefits exceed aggregate social costs (Boardman et al., 2018; Mikesell, 2015). BCA is designed to help policymakers rank

DOI: 10.4324/9781003606833-9

alternatives by explicitly identifying, quantifying, and comparing gains and sacrifices across society, rather than focusing on any single stakeholder or institution (Harvard SEAS, 2022). This reduces the likelihood that important impacts are ignored in favor of more visible or politically salient considerations. A key advantage of BCA is its focus on economic efficiency. By translating diverse impacts into a common monetary metric and discounting them to PV, BCA enables direct comparison across projects, sectors, and time horizons.

Monetizing every potential benefit and cost, even those not reflected in market prices, is a big advantage of BCA as this analysis helps prevent systematic underinvestment in socially valuable projects whose benefits might otherwise be overlooked. But it is also a major drawback as many impacts are inherently difficult to value in monetary terms because they involve non-market goods, uncertain outcomes, ethical considerations, or long-term effects that are not easily observed. Attempts to monetize such impacts often rely on strong assumptions, imperfect data, or indirect valuation methods, which can introduce uncertainty and controversy into the analysis. This limitation, combined with numerous assumptions made about future behavior, prices, impacts, growth, and valuation, further undermines BCA accuracy.

Additionally, BCA is explicitly designed to pursue one primary objective: determining whether a project generates positive net societal benefits, as measured in monetary terms. However, as famous quote says, “Not everything that can be counted counts, and not everything that counts can be counted” (the quote is often attributed to Albert Einstein), some projects may not be financially viable, but if the goal is reducing mortality, improving public safety, strengthening democratic institutions, or protecting freedom of speech, they may be only partially captured, or not captured at all, by monetary valuation. Projects aimed primarily at achieving these goals may fail a benefit-cost assessment despite reflecting widely held social values or constitutional priorities. In such cases, BCA alone may provide incomplete guidance, and decision-makers may need to rely on complementary analytical tools, ethical considerations, or political judgment to determine whether a project should be pursued.

Fiscal impact analysis (FIA) is a closely related yet conceptually distinct tool used to evaluate public capital infrastructure projects. Both BCA and FIA seek to inform public decision-making by systematically organizing information on expected benefits and costs over the lifetime of the project. BCA, however, asks whether a project generates net gains to society, while FIA focuses narrowly on the implications of a project for government. FIA is a special form of BCA conducted from the government rather than societal perspective. Instead of asking whether a project improves overall economic welfare, FIA asks whether a project strengthens or weakens government fiscal position. As such, FIA focuses on government revenues and expenditures, including capital construction costs, maintenance obligations, tax revenues, and cost savings to public services. FIA provides critical insight into fiscal sustainability and budgetary feasibility but may understate broader economic benefits.

Major steps in benefit-cost analysis and fiscal impact analysis

Any BCA and FIA should follow the following major steps (Boardman et al., 2018):

1 Specify the set of alternative projects
   The first step in BCA is to define the set of project alternatives to be evaluated. This typically includes the proposed project and at least one baseline alternative, commonly referred to as the status quo or no-action alternative, which assumes no change in current government policy.
2 Decide whose benefits and costs count
   This step involves determining standing, or from which perspective benefits and costs should be counted. In a societal BCA, standing is typically broad and includes all members of society, regardless of where benefits or costs occur or who experiences them. Alternatively, BCA can be done from the perspective of a certain state or a jurisdiction, or only government (FIA), or a private sector. Clear specification of standing is essential, as it directly affects which impacts are included and how results are interpreted.
3 Catalogue the impacts (inputs and outputs) quantitatively over the life of the project and select measurement indicators
   Once standing is defined, analysts identify all relevant inputs and outputs generated by the project over its expected life span. Inputs or costs can be direct capital expenditures and operating costs, but also indirect ones such as unintended consequences caused by pollution and other negative externalities. Benefits may include time savings, health improvements, higher income and better employment opportunities, better living conditions, environmental outcomes, and others. Comprehensive cataloging helps ensure that important effects are not omitted.
   The correct identification of benefits, costs, and economic transfers is one of the most significant challenges of BCA. Many impacts that appear to be benefits may simply be transfers that redistribute benefits across groups rather than generate net social gains. For example, from a societal perspective, sales revenues represent transfers from consumers to producers (costs to consumers and benefits to producers) rather than net benefits to society. Similarly, wages and salaries constitute transfers from producers to employees (costs to employers and benefits to employees). Employment created by a capital project may be counted as a social benefit only if the jobs represent genuinely new positions rather than the relocation of labor from other projects

or regions. The distinction among benefits, costs, and transfers also differs depending on the analytical perspective adopted. In a societal BCA, taxes are treated as transfers from taxpayers (costs to taxpayers) to the government (benefits to the government) and therefore do not affect net social welfare. In FIA, however, tax revenues are explicitly counted as benefits to government budgets. Conversely, tax credits are treated as transfers from government to eligible taxpayers in societal BCA, while in FIA, they are counted as costs to the public sector (Guzman, 2018). These differing treatments underscore why BCA and FIA can produce divergent conclusions for the same capital project.

4 Predict the impacts quantitatively over the life of the project

Each impact must be linked to a measurable indicator, such as hours saved, fires prevented, acres preserved, or lives protected.

5 Monetize all impacts

The next step in the BCA process is to attach dollar value to all benefits and costs. While some benefits and costs are easy to quantify as they have a defined unit of measurement, and subsequently monetize, valuing other benefits and costs might be challenging as they lack observable market prices. Such difficult to monetize impacts can be the value of the lives saved, improved public health, better environmental quality or preserved historic and cultural resources, among others. Over decades, economists have developed numerous non-market valuation techniques to address these challenges. For example, death benefit in life insurance can serve as a proxy for monetizing a value of human life. Some of the other popular methods are:

- Contingent valuation (CV) relies on surveys that ask respondents directly about their willingness to pay for a specified benefit or their willingness to accept compensation for a specified cost. CV has been widely used to value environmental amenities, mortality risk reductions, and historic preservation, though it is subject to concerns about strategic responses.
- Travel cost methods infer the value of recreational sites or amenities from the time and money people spend traveling to them. By observing how visitation rates vary with travel costs, analysts can estimate demand curves and consumer surplus associated with non-market goods such as parks, historic sites, or scenic highways.
- Hedonic pricing models estimate the implicit prices of non-market attributes by examining how they are capitalized into market transactions, most commonly property values or wages. For transportation projects, hedonic models are often used to estimate how proximity to highways affects residential and commercial property values, capturing both positive accessibility effects and negative externalities such as noise or pollution.
- Benefit transfer approach involves adapting valuation estimates from previous studies to a new context when primary data collection is infeasible.

Benefit transfer approach requires careful attention to differences in population, geography, and project characteristics to avoid misapplication of results.

6 Discount benefits and costs to obtain PVs

The concepts of PV and future value (FV) are really important in BCA, as BCA looks into a period of time in future. An analyst should understand that a dollar received or paid at different points in time does not have the same economic value. These formulas provide the mathematical foundation for discounting and compounding streams of benefits and costs in capital budgeting.

As was mentioned before, capital projects are very expensive and it is typical to borrow funds to finance their construction. Any loan consists of two components, the principal or the amount borrowed, and the interest. FV measures the total amount that will be owed or paid at a future point in time when interest is applied to a PV – the principal. Under simple annual compounding, the FV of a loan is estimated using the following formula:

$FV_t = PV \times (1 + r)^t$,

where

PV is the present value, or the original amount borrowed, also called principal,

r is the interest rate, also called compound rate in FV estimates, and

t is the number of periods in future; for a 15-year loan t is 15.

This formula illustrates that the longer the repayment period and the higher the interest rate, the greater the FV of the obligation.

In the context of capital budgeting, understanding FV is particularly important for assessing the true long-term cost of debt-financed projects. While borrowing allows governments to smooth costs over time and align payments with the flow of benefits, FV calculations make explicit how interest payments can substantially increase total expenditures relative to the original construction cost. For this reason, FV is often used in fiscal analysis to project debt service obligations and evaluate the affordability of capital investments.

BCA, however, relies on a concept of PV. The PV converts money received or paid in the future into its equivalent value today, using a discount rate r. So, all the benefits and costs estimated over the life of a project in step 4 and monetized in step 5 should be discounted to their PV. PV is calculated by a simple transformation of a FV formula:

$PV = FV_t/(1 + r)^t$

the interest rate, r, in the PV formula, is called a discount rate.

In BCA, discount rates convert future streams of benefits and costs into PVs, allowing meaningful comparison across time. Common approaches to approximating an appropriate discount rate include using long-term government bond yields, estimated social rates of time preference, or guidance issued by federal governments. The choice of discount rates and time horizon affects the valuation of long-lived capital projects. The higher the discount rate, the lower is PV of future flows. And the more distant in the future the flow is received, the lower the PV.

7 Compute NPV of each alternative

A central feature of BCA is the use of quantitative decision metrics that summarize the net economic value of a project after accounting for the timing of benefits and costs. The three most commonly used indicators are NPV, the benefit-cost ratio (BCR), and the internal rate of return (IRR). Each metric answers a slightly different question, and together they provide a robust basis for evaluating public investment projects.

NPV is defined as the PV of total benefits minus the PV of total costs: NPV = PV(B) − PV(C). A project is considered acceptable if NPV is positive, meaning that total societal benefits exceed total societal costs. When evaluating multiple mutually exclusive alternatives, standard economic guidance recommends selecting the option with the highest NPV, as it yields the greatest net gain to society.

The BCR expresses the relative efficiency of a project by dividing the PV of benefits by the PV of costs: BCR = PV(B)/PV(C). A project is considered acceptable if BCR exceeds one, indicating that every dollar of cost generates more than one dollar of benefit. BCR is especially useful when comparing projects of different scales. However, BCR should be interpreted carefully, as a project with a very high BCR but small scale may produce fewer total benefits than a larger project with a lower BCR, if BCR is still higher than 1.

The IRR generated by the project is the discount rate at which the PV of benefits equals the PV of costs (i.e., the rate at which NPV equals zero). A project is economically desirable if its IRR exceeds the chosen social discount rate.

8 Perform sensitivity analysis

Sensitivity analysis addresses uncertainty surrounding key assumptions. Rather than relying on a single set of point estimates, sensitivity analysis examines how NPV, BCR, and IRR change when underlying parameters are varied. Key variables commonly altered in sensitivity analysis include different discount rates as well as varying assumptions about costs and benefit estimates, and treatment of transfer payments. Scenario analysis may also be employed to explore optimistic, baseline, and pessimistic scenarios. A project whose NPV remains positive and whose BCR remains above one across a wide range of plausible assumptions is generally considered robust.

Sensitivity analysis does not eliminate uncertainty, but it clarifies which assumptions matter most and where analytical results are most vulnerable.

9 Make a recommendation

Conclusion

This chapter has demonstrated the central role of BCA in evaluating public capital investment decisions. BCA provides a systematic and transparent framework for evaluating and ranking public capital projects by comparing the PV of societal benefits and costs, while FIA complements this approach by assessing affordability and long-term budgetary implications for government. The use of PV, NPV, BCRs, and internal rates of return provides a basis for comparing capital projects that differ in scale, timing, and sectoral focus.

This chapter emphasized that BCA depends on key assumptions about the identification of benefits, costs, and transfers, as well as the choice of discount rates. These assumptions can substantially influence conclusions about the desirability of capital projects and must be made explicit to ensure transparency. While BCA addresses whether a project improves overall economic well-being, FIA focuses on whether a project is affordable and sustainable from the public sector's budgetary perspective.

In this chapter, the first case study, "Benefit–Cost Analysis: Route 30, Ohio," engages students in applying benefit-cost and fiscal impact analyses to assess the proposed expansion of U.S. Route 30 (RT-30) in Stark, Carroll, and Columbiana counties in eastern Ohio. Approximately 35 miles of RT-30 currently operate as a largely unimproved two-lane roadway, and the proposed project would upgrade this segment to a four-lane freeway.

The second case study, "Revenue Today, Costs Tomorrow: A Public Finance Perspective on the Chicago Skyway 99-year lease," explores the fiscal, political, and ethical implications of the City of Chicago's decision to privatize the Skyway for $1.83 billion in 2005, the first long-term lease of an existing toll road in the United States.

References

Boardman, A. E., Greenberg, D. H., Vining, A. R., & Weimer, D. L. (2018). *Cost–benefit analysis: Concepts and practice* (5th ed.). Cambridge University Press.

Guzman, T. (2018). Cost-benefit and fiscal impact analysis of Ohio Historic Preservation Tax Credit (OHPTC). *Journal of Benefit-Cost Analysis*, *9*(2), 342–373.

Harvard University School of Engineering and Applied Sciences. (2022). Introduction to cost–benefit analysis. https://read.seas.harvard.edu/cs161/2022/lectures/IntroToCBA.pdf

Mikesell, J. L. (2015). *Fiscal administration: Analysis and applications for the public sector* (9th ed.). Cengage Learning.

Center for Economic Development. (2018). Fiscal impact analysis of the RT-30 expansion. Maxine Goodman Levin College of Urban Affairs, Cleveland State University.

CASE STUDY 18

Benefit-cost analysis RT-30 Ohio

Abstract

This case study invites students to evaluate the proposed expansion of U.S. Route 30 (RT-30) in eastern Ohio using benefit-cost analysis and fiscal impact analysis frameworks. Approximately 35 miles of RT-30 between Canton, OH, and State Route 11 near Lisbon, OH, remain largely unimproved, operating as a two-lane roadway with at-grade intersections across Stark, Carroll, and Columbiana counties. The proposed expansion would upgrade this segment to four-lane freeway.

Topics

Benefit-Cost Analysis; Fiscal Impact Analysis; Local Government; Budgeting; Public Finance

Background

U.S. Route 30 (RT-30) is a major east-west highway running roughly 246 miles across northern Ohio, forming part of the historic Lincoln Highway corridor that links the Indiana state line to the Ohio River at East Liverpool, OH (about 40 miles west of Pittsburgh, PA). Today, most of RT-30 is a four-lane divided highway or freeway with speed limits of 65 mph. However, about 35 miles of RT-30, or the distance between Canton, OH, and State Route 11, is a two-lane road passing directly through communities such as East Canton, Minerva, and Lisbon. This stretch has long been viewed as inconsistent with the rest of the improved corridor (Pieper, 2025). At-grade intersections, driveways, rail

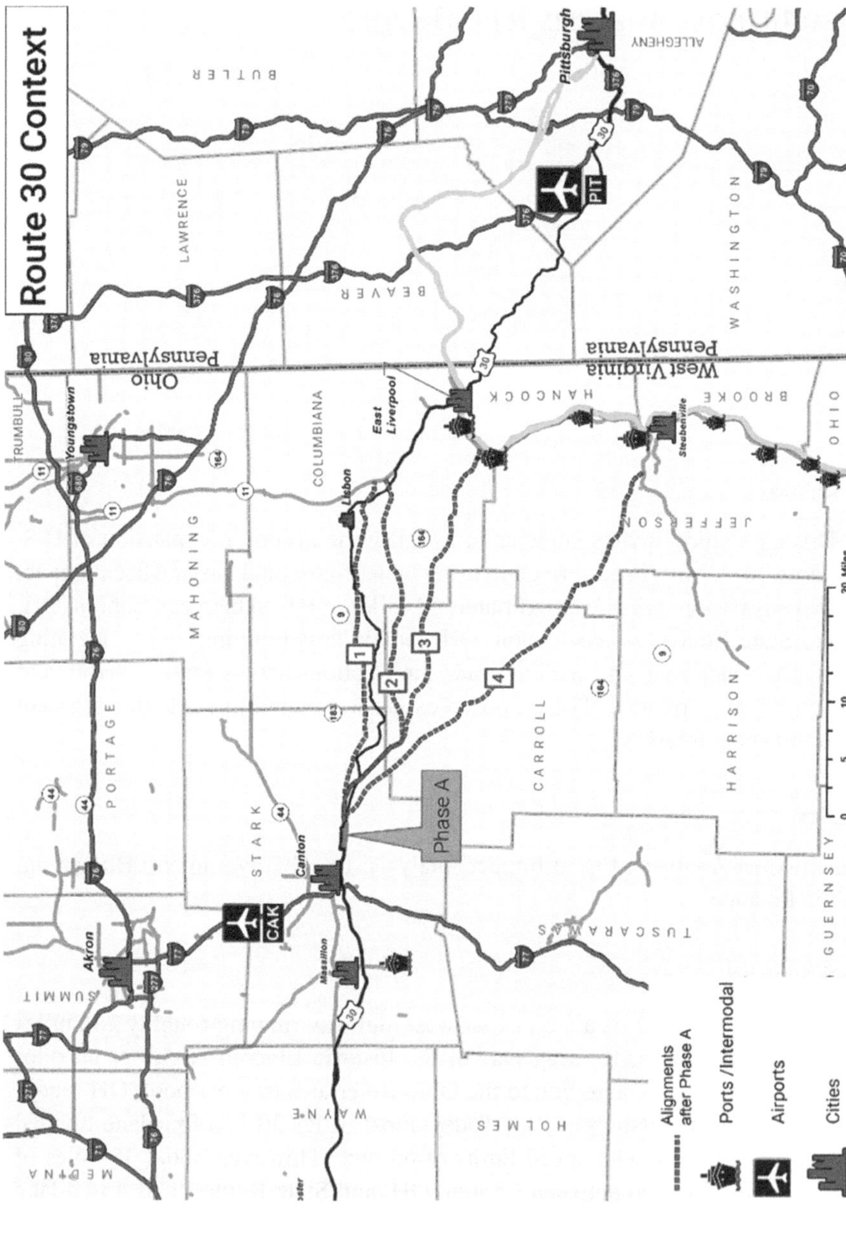

FIGURE 8.1 Map of RT-30 expansion project

Source: CED, 2018. Used with permission.

crossings, and mixed local and through traffic characterize this part of the highway (see Figure 8.1), along with speed limits of 55 mph on non-freeway segments, and 35–50 mph in urban segments.

Benefit-cost analysis and a fiscal impact analysis of RT-30 expansion project

Your consulting team was selected to develop a benefit-cost analysis (BCA) and a fiscal impact analysis (FIA) of the RT-30 expansion project that would upgrade the mentioned 35 miles of roadway between Trump Avenue in Canton (the avenue is named after George J. Trump, a 19th-century sawmill owner, not President Donald J. Trump) and State Route 11 near Lisbon. Figure 8.1 shows the existing RT-30 road marked with a black solid line and four road construction alternatives marked with blue dotted lines. The 3-mile bypass on the map, marked Phase A, is already developed.

The construction project also seeks to close a longstanding gap in east-west connectivity across Stark, Carroll, and Columbiana counties, where the absence of a continuous four-lane throughway has limited freight mobility, hampered regional competitiveness, and curbed economic development linked to shale production, manufacturing, and logistics. The project, among other goals, seeks to reduce travel times and avert about 629 crashes a year. The travel time from Canton's airport to Pittsburgh's airport, for example, is estimated to be reduced from what is currently 96 minutes to 79, 81, 89, and 84 minutes, respectively, under Alignments 1–4 (RSG, 2015) (Figure 8.1).

The RT-30 corridor passes through a part of eastern Ohio located at the intersection of the Midwest and Appalachian energy and manufacturing economies. Extending from near the Indiana border to the Pennsylvania state line, and connecting directly toward Pittsburgh, RT-30 links the Midwest's interstate freight networks and the tri-state (Ohio, Indiana, and Pennsylvania) energy sector. Despite this strategic positioning, the portion of RT-30 that passes through Stark, Carroll, and Columbiana counties is currently not developed and lacks a high-capacity transportation capability. The RT-30 expansion is designed to address this regional infrastructure deficit.

Stark, Carroll, and Columbiana counties form a largely rural-to-small-metro region in eastern Ohio, characterized by aging demographics and modest household incomes relative to state and national averages. Overall, 374,853 people resided in Stark, 101,877 in Columbiana, and 26,721 in Carroll in 2020 (U.S. Census Bureau, 2021). Stark County, at the western end of the RT-30 expansion corridor, is the area's population and employment center. It houses the Pro Football Hall of Fame Village, the Akron-Canton Regional Airport, and established manufacturing clusters. Moving eastward, Carroll County is located at the core of the Marcellus-Utica shale development region. Of the three counties, Carroll County has by far the largest oil and gas reserves. The shale oil production was over 2.1 million barrels in Carroll County, compared to 24,000 barrels in Columbiana and 694 barrels in Stark Counties in 2021. Shale gas production was over 79 million mcf in Carroll County, compared to 32.8 million mcf in Columbiana and 83 thousand mcf in Stark Counties in 2021 (ODNR, 2021). Carroll County is also projected to experience the largest job gains of as high as 65 thousand jobs, and the highest population growth of as high as 39 thousand residents under high-growth conditions, which is higher than Stark and Columbiana counties combined (RSG 2015). Columbiana County, located at the eastern end of the proposed RT-30 expansion project, is bounded by Pennsylvania on the east and Ohio River on the south.

Collectively, Stark, Carroll, and Columbiana counties form an emerging economic corridor whose growth depends heavily on improved freight mobility, energy-sector logistics, and access to the Pittsburgh metropolitan economy. The RT-30 expansion would provide regional opportunity to connect the Midwest's manufacturing base with Appalachian energy assets and national rail and river shipping networks.

Conclusions

This case study demonstrates the value and limitations of BCA and FIA as tools for evaluating large-scale transportation infrastructure investments. The proposed expansion of U.S. RT-30 in eastern Ohio highlights how economic efficiency, budgetary feasibility, and regional development objectives do not always align neatly within a single analytical framework. BCA demonstrates that the project offers clear potential benefits, including improved safety, reduced travel times, increased economic development, and enhanced freight mobility. Collectively, Stark, Carroll, and Columbiana counties form an emerging economic corridor whose growth depends heavily on improved freight mobility, energy-sector logistics, and access to the Pittsburgh metropolitan economy. The RT-30 expansion would provide a regional opportunity to connect the Midwest's manufacturing base with Appalachian energy assets and national rail and river shipping networks. However, these benefits must be carefully weighed against substantial construction, maintenance, and environmental costs over a long-term horizon.

A central lesson of the case is the importance of distinguishing between economic benefits to society and fiscal impacts on public budgets. BCA captures broader social gains (e.g., reducing travel times and crash reductions) that may justify a project from a welfare economics perspective, even when direct fiscal returns to governments are limited or negative. FIA focuses on revenues, expenditures, and budgetary sustainability, which may lead to more cautious conclusions about financial viability. The RT-30 case illustrates how reliance on a single framework can lead to incomplete or misleading policy conclusions.

Discussion questions

1 Identify the RT-30 project alternatives and describe the status quo. Refer to Figure 8.1 for guidance and discuss any additional alternatives not shown in the figure or described in the case narrative.
2 Identify the primary beneficiaries of the RT-30 expansion project and explain how they benefit.
3 Identify the groups that may bear costs or losses from the RT-30 expansion project and explain how these negative impacts occur.
4 Contrast the benefits identified under fiscal impact analysis with those identified under benefit-cost analysis.
5 Contrast the costs identified under fiscal impact analysis with those identified under benefit-cost analysis.
6 Identify which of the discussed benefits and costs should be classified as transfers and explain why.
7 Which benefits and costs might be more difficult to quantify and monetize? Explain why.
8 Which strategies/approaches can be used to quantify and monetize such benefits and costs?
9 Identify the types of data required to conduct benefit-cost analysis and fiscal impact analysis for the RT-30 expansion.
10 One of the proper ways to estimate potential effect of highway expansion in three Ohio counties is to study interstate highway expansion in other comparable counties in the United States. Which characteristics should you look for to select a list of such comparable counties?
11 Select an appropriate discount rate for evaluating the RT-30 expansion project and justify your choice.
12 Under what conditions would you pursue the project? Discuss net present value (NPV), benefit-cost ratio (BCR), Internal Rate of Return (IRR), and any other indicators that might be important to assess the viability of such project?
13 Which factors should be accounted for in the sensitivity analysis?
14 The 2018 study by the Center for Economic Development at Cleveland State University conducted an economic and fiscal impact analysis of the RT-30 expansion that concluded that the project is not financially viable. Explain why this might be the case.
15 Discuss under which conditions the project could be financially viable.

References

Center for Economic Development (CED). (2018). *The economic impact of RTIP on U.S. Route 30 in Carroll, Columbiana, and Stark Counties.* Maxine Goodman Levin College of Urban Affairs, Cleveland State University.

Ohio Department of Natural Resources (ODNR), Division of Oil and Gas Resources Management. (2021). 2021 Ohio oil & gas annual report [PDF]. https://dam.assets.ohio.gov/image/upload/ohiodnr.gov/documents/oil-gas/resources/2021-O_G-Annual.pdf

Pieper, B. (2025, March 11). After state study snub, Ohio county pursues private partnership for highway expansion project. *GovMarketNews*. Retrieved from https://govmarketnews.com/after-state-study-snub-ohio-county-pursues-private-partnership-for-highway-expansion-project/

RSG. (2015). *US 30 feasibility study* (Prepared for the Columbiana County Transportation Improvement District)

U.S. Census Bureau. (2021). *2020 decennial census.*

CASE STUDY 19

Revenue today, costs tomorrow: a public finance perspective on the Chicago Skyway 99-year lease

Abstract

This case study examines the 99-year lease of the Chicago Skyway, a 7.8-mile toll bridge spanning the Chicago River and connecting Chicago and Indiana. It explores the fiscal, political, and ethical implications of the City of Chicago's decision to privatize the Skyway for $1.83 billion in 2005, the first long-term lease of an existing toll road in the United States. When evaluated using a 3% discount rate, the Chicago Skyway's terminal value of $1.83 billion at the end of a 99-year lease is reduced to approximately $98 million in present-value terms, illustrating the significant impact of discounting over extended time horizons. The long-term lease of the Chicago Skyway provides a valuable illustration of the implications of discounting for the valuation of an upfront payment. Using toll rate data from 2005 to 2025, the case demonstrates how privatization shifted financial risk to private investors but led to sharp toll increases and declining traffic volumes. This case study offers recommendations for monetizing public assets and mitigating negative consequences.

Topics

Local Government; Accountability; Privatization; Public Finance; Economics; Toll Roads; Public-Private Partnership

Background

Built by the City of Chicago in 1958, the Chicago Skyway Toll Bridge (also known as the "Skyway") is a 7.8-mile-long toll road that connects the Indiana

Toll Road to the Dan Ryan Expressway on Chicago's South Side. The main feature of the Skyway is a 1/2-mile-long steel truss bridge, known as the "High Bridge." The bridge itself spans the Calumet River and Calumet Harbor, a major harbor for industrial ships. Its main span extends 650 feet long and provides 125 feet of vertical clearance.

The Chicago Skyway was operated and maintained by the City of Chicago until January 2005, when Skyway Concession Company (SCC), LLC, assumed its operations under a 99-year operating lease. The Skyway was leased for 99 years for $1.83 billion. The lease agreement between Skyway and the City of Chicago was the first privatization of an existing toll road in the United States (U.S. Department of Transportation, n.d.). In February 2016, Skyway was purchased by three Canadian Pension Funds: OMERS Infrastructure, CPP Investment Board, and Ontario Teachers' Pension Plan (OTPP).

In June 2016, the remaining 89-year lease on the toll road was re-sold to another private company for $2.8 billion (Chicago SunTimes, 2022). Atlas Arteria Group, a worldwide toll road operator based in Australia, acquired 66.67% interest in the Skyway in December 2022, with OTPP retaining the remaining 33.33%.

Financial structure of a lease

In January 2005, the City of Chicago entered into a 99-year operating lease with the SCC. The agreement provided the city with an upfront payment of $1.83 billion, enabling it to retire existing Skyway debt, pay down other municipal obligations, and create several reserve and investment funds. The City of Chicago benefited immediately from the upfront payment, which funded:

- Debt retirement: $463 million (Skyway debt)
- Long-term debt reduction: $134 million
- Short-term debt elimination: $258 million
- Reserves: $500 million (long-term) and $375 million (mid-term)
- Community investment fund: $100 million

These actions provided the City of Chicago with fiscal flexibility and a strong liquidity position in 2005. The project's financing package consisted of private equity, bank loans, capital accretion bonds, and subordinated debt, while funding was provided exclusively through user-paid tolls. To finance the lease payment, SCC issued two bond series totaling $1.4 billion.

However, long time horizons (99 years) and discounting substantially reduce the present value (PV) of the upfront payment. Under a lease agreement valued $1.83 billion, Chicago exchanged future control and revenue streams for an upfront lump-sum payment. When evaluated using a 3% discount rate, the PV of the Chicago Skyway, valued at $1.83 billion at the conclusion of a 99-year lease, is substantially reduced. The discounted value of the Chicago Skyway at the end of the lease period is approximately $98 million in PV terms.

This example highlights the critical role of discount rates and time horizons in the economic assessment of long-term public-private partnership (PPP) agreements, as well as the long-term opportunity costs associated with asset monetization.

Negative consequences

Chicago Skyway Tolls increased by 80% for passenger cars and over 200% for large trucks between 2005 and 2015 (U.S. Department of Transportation, n.d.). The traffic declined from 48,422 vehicles daily in 2005 to 41,249 in 2013 (a 17% drop). However, toll revenues rose from $50.4 million to $80.7 million during the same period. Table 8.1 provides information about Chicago Skyway Bridge Tolls from 2005 to 2025.

Between 2005 and 2025, passenger car tolls (two axles) increased from $2.50 to $7.80, a 312% rise, while truck tolls rose by over 530%. The sharpest increases occurred for vehicles with four or more axles. The table illustrates the uneven burden placed on heavy vehicles, likely reflecting revenue optimization under private management. Users faced higher tolls, leading to negative public perceptions of privatization. The sharp toll increases raised equity concerns and questions about the balance between public benefit and private return.

TABLE 8.1 Chicago Skyway Bridge Tolls from 2005 to 2025

Axles	*2005*	*2008*	*2011*	*2013*	*2015*	*2025 Peak Hour Toll*	*2025 Off-Peak Hour Toll*	*Percentage Increase from 2005 to 2025 (Peak Hour Toll)*
2	$2.50	$3.00	$3.50	$4.00	$4.50	$7.80	$7.80	312
3	$5.10	$7.60	$10.10	$12.60	$15.20	$27.20	$19.50	533
4	$6.80	$10.10	$13.50	$16.80	$20.20	$36.30	$25.90	533
5	$8.40	$12.60	$16.80	$21.00	$25.20	$45.40	$32.40	540
6	$10.10	$15.20	$20.20	$25.20	$30.30	$54.40	$38.90	538
7	$11.80	$17.70	$23.60	$29.40	$35.50	$63.50	$45.40	538

Source: Authors' calculations from U.S. Department of Transportation (n.d.) and Chicago Skyway (n.d.).

Conclusion

The Chicago Skyway Bridge privatization remains a landmark case in U.S. infrastructure finance and public asset management. It underscores the political complexity and fiscal trade-offs inherent in monetizing public assets to address immediate budgetary pressures. The $1.83 billion upfront payment provided the City of Chicago with short-term fiscal relief, debt reduction, and liquidity. However, critics argued that the city exchanged long-term revenue for short-term gain, sacrificing future financial flexibility and intergenerational equity.

While privatization transferred operational and maintenance risks to private investors, it also imposed substantial toll increases, over 300% for passenger cars and more than 500% for heavy trucks between 2005 and 2025. It is raising concerns about affordability, equity, and public accountability. The long-term nature of the 99-year lease underscores the challenges of ensuring fiscal sustainability, effective regulatory oversight, and transparent governance across multiple generations.

The Chicago Skyway case illustrates that long-term leases can provide immediate fiscal benefits and mitigate government exposure to operational risk. However, they also expose municipalities to potential pitfalls if contracts lack clear performance benchmarks, equitable toll policies, or adaptive renegotiation clauses. Effective asset monetization requires a balance among accountability, intergenerational equity, and social welfare.

The key lessons from this case study include the following:

1. Municipalities should conduct long-term cost-benefit analyses before converting public assets into one-time revenue.
2. Comprehensive risk assessment.
3. Regular performance audits and transparent reporting mechanisms can help safeguard public interest and maintain accountability.

Recommendations for future infrastructure privatizations:

4. More restrictive toll escalation caps to protect users from excessive toll increases.
5. Enhanced transparency and performance reporting mechanisms to ensure accountability and ongoing evaluation of private operator performance.
6. Profit-sharing or revenue reversion clauses to allow the public sector to share in financial gains when toll revenues exceed projections.
7. Periodic contract review provisions to enable mid-term adjustments reflecting economic, technological, and social changes.

Discussion questions

1 What fiscal challenges or policy goals might have motivated the City of Chicago to lease the Skyway Bridge for 99 years? Was this primarily a financial necessity or a strategic innovation?
2 Did the $1.83 billion upfront payment justify the loss of long-term toll revenue for nearly a century? How should public administrators evaluate such intergenerational trade-offs?
3 What does the decline in traffic despite rising toll revenues suggest about price elasticity and the financial sustainability of the privatization model?
4 What governance or oversight mechanisms could have improved transparency and accountability over the 99-year term?
5 What lessons from the Skyway case should inform future long-term lease agreements or public-private partnerships in transportation infrastructure?
6 Based on the Skyway experience, under what fiscal and political conditions should municipalities consider asset monetization as a viable public finance strategy?
7 What policy safeguards, such as toll escalation limits, profit-sharing, or reversion clauses, could make future public-private partnerships more equitable and sustainable?
8 Based on this case, under what conditions should local governments consider privatizing or leasing public assets as a fiscal management tool?

References

Chicago Skyway (n.d.) Skyway Concession Company, LLC. https://www.chicagoskyway.org/the-skyway/#about-the-skyway

Chicago Skyway sold — again — generating windfall for beleaguered taxpayers. *Chicago Sun-Times*, September 13, 2022. https://chicago.suntimes.com/city-hall/2022/9/13/23351264/chicago-skyway-sold-pension-plans-australian-toll-road-daley-99-year-lease

U.S. Department of Transportation (n.d.). Infrastructure case study: Chicago skyway bridge. https://www.fhwa.dot.gov/ipd/pdfs/value_capture/case_studies/chicago_skyway_bridge.pdf

9

DEBT MANAGEMENT

Abstract

This chapter explores debt management as a central component of public finance. This chapter provides definitions of debt, debt management, long-term obligations, and credit ratings. It demonstrates different debt management strategies for issuing, structuring, and repaying government debt to ensure fiscal stability. Effective debt management requires transparency, sound financial forecasting, adherence to legal limits, and maintaining creditworthiness. Debt management can minimize borrowing costs, mitigate fiscal risk, and enhance a government's ability to respond to emergencies or economic shocks.

Introduction

Government debt is a critical element in public finance, encompassing the borrowing practices of national, state (regional), and local governments. Debt includes long-term credit obligation of the government and its agencies and interest-bearing short-term (i.e., repayable within one year) credit obligations (Mikesell & Ross, 2024). Government debt refers to the cumulative amount of funds a government has borrowed that remain unpaid. It differs from a deficit, which is the shortfall between annual revenues and expenditures. Public debt includes revenue bonds, general-obligation bonds, also called full-faith-and-credit bonds, other types of bonds, notes, and interest-bearing warrants. Debt does not include non-interest-bearing short-term obligations, interfund liabilities, advances, contingent loans from other governments, and individuals' claims to benefits from employee retirement funds.

DOI: 10.4324/9781003606833-10

Municipal bonds represent a promise of the *issuer* (state, locality, or other issuer) to repay to lenders/investors an amount of money borrowed – *principal*, along with *interest* according to a fixed schedule.

Debt management serves as a strategic tool for financing infrastructure, managing economic fluctuations, and responding to crises. Debt management involves determining the amounts, maturities, terms, and conditions, as well as the schedule of offerings for federal debt securities, and raising new cash to finance government operations. The objective of debt management is to raise the money necessary for the government operations at the least cost to the taxpayer.

By strategically planning and monitoring debt issuance and repayment, governments can ensure fiscal sustainability, maintain liquidity, and protect creditworthiness. Proper debt management enables public entities to finance essential infrastructure, services, and development initiatives without overburdening future budgets or taxpayers.

Approaches to public debt financing

Two primary approaches to public finance define how governments conceptualize and use debt: pay-as-you-go and pay-as-you-use. The *pay-as-you-go approach* implies that governments fund projects with current revenues, avoiding interest costs, issuance fees, and future debt burden. However, this approach can constrain the government's ability to undertake large or urgent projects because available funds are limited to current revenue streams. Consequently, major infrastructure projects may need to be postponed or scaled down. Pay-as-you-go is most suitable for smaller, routine capital purchases or in periods of fiscal stability when surpluses or designated capital funds are available.

The *pay-as-you-use approach* relies on debt financing, distributing the cost across generations that will benefit from the investment. Revenue bonds exemplify this strategy, as they are repaid through revenues generated by the financed project, such as tolls or utility fees. It is grounded in the intergenerational equity principle: those who benefit from public investment should contribute to its financing over time. This method enables governments to undertake large-scale or time-sensitive projects without depleting current resources. Nevertheless, excessive reliance on borrowing can lead to higher debt service burdens and reduced budget flexibility, especially during economic downturns.

In practice, most governments employ a balanced approach, combining both pay-as-you-go and pay-as-you-use methods. Smaller capital expenditures are financed on a pay-as-you-go basis, while major long-term investments, such as bridges, water systems, or public facilities, are financed through borrowing. Effective debt management and capital budgeting require careful assessment of fiscal capacity, debt limits, and the timing of benefits to ensure a sustainable mix of these two strategies. Many scholars examine whether intergenerational debt transfer is ethically or economically appropriate. Some scholars argue it unjustly burdens future taxpayers; others suggest that as long as future generations inherit valuable public infrastructure and services, the burden is justified.

Methods of debt management

Governments use several complementary methods to manage their debt portfolios effectively. These include debt structuring and maturity management, refinancing and refunding, sinking funds, debt service restructuring, and debt limits.

Debt *matures* when the issuer makes the last payment of principal and interest on debt. Debt structuring and maturity management involve designing the composition and maturity profile of outstanding debt to balance cost and risk. A mix of short-term and long-term debt instruments allows flexibility in response to changing market conditions. Short-term debt provides liquidity and flexibility but exposes the government to refinancing risk. Long-term debt locks in interest rates and reduces refinancing risk but may carry higher interest costs.

Refinancing and refunding method of debt management refers to the issuance of new debt to repay maturing obligations. Refunding replaces higher-cost debt with lower-cost instruments when market conditions allow, thereby reducing interest expenditures. This approach requires careful timing to avoid increasing the overall debt burden or extending maturities excessively.

A *sinking fund* is a reserve account established to accumulate resources for repaying principal on long-term debt. Regular contributions to this fund help governments avoid large repayment spikes and demonstrate fiscal responsibility to investors and credit rating agencies. Although this method improves predictability, it requires disciplined budgeting and consistent allocations over time. Sinking funds, which had originally been established to retire war debts, were reintroduced to ensure that specific revenues were earmarked exclusively for debt repayment. The creation of such dedicated funds was intended to prevent the diversion of resources into general government expenditures and to strengthen the government's creditworthiness and borrowing capacity. Over time, as public debt levels expanded, it became evident that repayment was less often financed from the revenue generated by the projects funded through borrowing and increasingly dependent on new borrowing. As a result, several countries (the United Kingdom, etc.) gradually abandoned the traditional use of sinking funds. Another factor contributing to the decline of sinking funds was their inflexibility. Legal or statutory provisions often restricted how the funds could be invested, compelling governments to borrow externally even while maintaining substantial cash balances in these accounts. Although many governments still retain sinking funds in principle, their practical function has diminished.

Debt restructuring is an effective method for managing debt. When fiscal pressures arise, governments may restructure debt service schedules by negotiating changes to repayment terms, extending maturities, or converting variable-rate obligations into fixed-rate instruments. Debt restructuring should aim to restore fiscal sustainability while maintaining creditor confidence. In extreme cases, it may involve debt swaps or consolidation under new terms.

Statutory debt limits serve as institutional mechanisms to prevent excessive borrowing. These limits may be expressed as a percentage of gross domestic product (GDP), total revenues, or expenditure. Adherence to such rules reinforces fiscal discipline and helps preserve intergenerational equity. The debt ceiling may limit the total amount of debt issued, debt outstanding, or debt service. On the federal level, debt ceiling was established during World War I through the enactment of the Second Liberty Bond Act of 1917. Its purpose was to provide Congress with a mechanism for oversight of federal borrowing while granting the Treasury more flexibility in managing debt issuance.

Most advanced economies rely on rules-based frameworks rather than numerical caps to ensure debt sustainability. European countries emphasize fiscal discipline through structural balance rules, and nations like Japan and Canada focus on long-term debt sustainability rather than short-term limits. The United States and Denmark enforce an absolute numerical ceiling rather than a percentage of GDP. Many economists and policy experts have advocated for reform or repeal of the debt ceiling, suggesting alternative mechanisms such as automatic adjustments tied to the approved federal budget, or fiscal rules based on debt-to-GDP ratios.

Modern public debt management adopts an integrated framework that coordinates borrowing decisions with fiscal policy, monetary policy, and capital budgeting. Effective coordination ensures that borrowing supports long-term investment priorities.

National debt: comparative overview and global trends

National debt refers to the total amount of money that a government owes to creditors, both domestic and foreign. It represents the accumulation of annual budget deficits over time, offset by any budget surpluses. Table 9.1 presents debt-to-GDP ratios for the top ten countries with the highest amount of national debt in 2025.

Japan, Italy, and France have the highest national debt-to-GDP ratios (Table 9.1). High national debt-to-GDP ratios are not inherently problematic if borrowing supports productive investments that enhance future economic growth. Countries that adhere to clear fiscal rules, maintain credible macroeconomic frameworks, and engage in prudent borrowing, such as Germany and Canada, tend to have lower borrowing costs and higher investor confidence.

TABLE 9.1 The Top Ten Countries with the Highest Amount of National Debt in 2025 ($mln)

	National debt	*GDP*	*National debt to GDP ratio, %*	*Main causes of national debt accumulation*
USA	38,175,492	31,565,648	96,68	Military spending, tax cuts, COVID-19 pandemic spending
China	16,487,586	18,954,023	87.03	Infrastructure expansion
Japan	12,447,766	4,221,686	294.99	Aging population, social security costs
UK	4,288,297	3,721,515	115.28	COVID-19 pandemic spending, energy subsidies
France	4,128,964	3,292,707	125.46	Welfare spending, low growth
Italy	4,009,271	2,464,552	162.75	Low growth, high interest burden
India	3,782,541	4,034,044	93.81	Subsidies, infrastructure spending
Germany	3,642,682	4,885,538	74.59	Welfare spending, low growth
Canada	2,750,046	2,296,514	119.81	COVID-19 pandemic spending
Brazil	2,241,681	2,334,478	96.07	Pension liabilities, slow growth

Source: Created by the authors based on USDebtClock (November 20, 2025).

However, excessive debt can constrain fiscal flexibility, increase vulnerability to interest rate shocks, and crowd out private investment. Sustainable debt management, therefore, depends on maintaining a balance between borrowing for growth and preserving fiscal discipline.

The United States has maintained a national debt since the Revolutionary War. Major increases in national debt have followed military conflicts (e.g., the Civil War and World War II, the wars in Iraq and Afghanistan), the 2008 financial crisis, and the COVID-19 pandemic. The debt-to-GDP ratio exceeded 100% in 2013. On November 10, 2025, the national debt per citizen in the United States was $111,041 (USDebtClock, 2025). The Federal Reserve is the largest single holder of U.S. debt. Foreign holders include countries like China, Japan, and the United Kingdom.

The role of credit ratings

Credit ratings are the third party's judgment about borrower's (issuer's) ability to pay debt in full and on time (Guzman & Clark, 2025). Credit ratings significantly influence municipality's borrowing costs. Rating agencies such as Moody's, Standard & Poor's (S&P), and Fitch assess government creditworthiness using a combination of weighted metrics. These typically include the municipality's fiscal discipline and budgeting practices, the strength and

TABLE 9.2 Comparison of Credit Rating Scales by Moody's, S&P, and Fitch

Category	*Moody's*	*S&P*	*Fitch*
Highest quality	Aaa	AAA	AAA
High quality	Aa1, Aa2, Aa3	AA+, AA, AA-	AA+, AA, AA-
Upper-medium quality	A1, A2, A3	A+, A, A-	A+, A, A-
Medium grade (investment grade)	Baa1, Baa2, Baa3	BBB+, BBB, BBB-	BBB+, BBB, BBB-
Speculative (non-investment)	Ba1, Ba2, Ba3	BB+, BB, BB-	BB+, BB, BB-
Highly speculative	B1, B2, B3	B+, B, B-	B+, B, B-
Substantial risk	Caa1, Caa2, Caa3	CCC+, CCC, CCC-	CCC+, CCC, CCC-
Extremely speculative	Ca	CC	CC
Default	C	C/D	C/D

diversity of its local economy, demographic trends, political stability, and the overall capacity and effectiveness of its management team. The resulting credit rating directly influences the interest rates a municipality must pay when issuing debt, making strong financial management essential for maintaining affordable access to capital.

Table 9.2 provides a comparison of credit rating scales by Moody's, S&P, and Fitch.

Default on debt

Several countries have experienced defaults on their international debt obligations in recent decades, illustrating the risks and consequences of sovereign borrowing. Notable cases include Russia (2022), which faced economic sanctions and a sharp decline in foreign exchange reserves; Sri Lanka (2022), triggered by a severe balance-of-payments crisis and fiscal mismanagement; Argentina (2020), reflecting chronic debt restructuring challenges and economic instability; Venezuela (2017), driven by hyperinflation, collapsing oil revenues, and political instability; and Greece (2012 and 2015), amid the Eurozone sovereign debt crisis.

Sovereign defaults typically arise from a combination of factors, including currency crises, where sudden devaluations make foreign debt repayment more costly, poor fiscal governance, such as unsustainable budget deficits or overreliance on debt financing, and external economic shocks, including commodity price collapses or global recessions.

While the United States has never defaulted on its federal debt, it has faced situations that brought it close to default during political deadlocks over the debt ceiling, highlighting that even highly rated sovereigns are vulnerable to institutional and political risks. Defaults can severely impact a country's access to international capital markets, increase borrowing costs, and erode investor confidence, often necessitating years of economic adjustment and debt restructuring.

Conclusions

Debt, when managed effectively, is a powerful tool for public investment and economic development. Effective debt management relies on transparent budgeting and reporting practices, careful selection of debt instruments and repayment structures, and the involvement of skilled financial intermediaries and legal experts. It also requires continuous monitoring of key economic indicators, such as the debt-to-GDP ratio, and a commitment to fostering public understanding and informed discussion about debt policy. In a financial environment shaped by global economic shifts and domestic political pressures, responsible debt management remains crucial to maintaining public trust and ensuring fiscal stability.

Effective debt administration must navigate several key challenges. Administrators must ensure compliance with complex regulations governing debt issuance, disclosure requirements, and tax status. Another critical concern is debt sustainability, or maintaining debt at levels that align with the government's long-term revenue capacity. Political pressures can further complicate decision-making when elected officials favor short-term benefits over long-term fiscal stability. Finally, public perception often presents difficulties; misunderstandings about government debt, particularly when it is compared to personal credit card debt, can make informed policy discussions more difficult.

In this chapter, the first case study, "Mozambique: Lessons from "the hidden debt scandal"," focuses on the greatest corruption scandal in the history of Mozambique. It explores how undisclosed sovereign guarantees enabled state-owned enterprises to accumulate over $2 billion in debt without parliamentary approval. This case examines the negative consequences of hidden debt, including fiscal and economic crises, suspensions of International Monetary Fund support, downgrades by credit rating agencies, political conflict, high inflation, and increased poverty.

The second case study, "The recovery of Illinois credit ratings – an institutional and fiscal analysis," examines the historical trajectory of Illinois' credit ratings from 1973 to 2025. This case study identifies the economic, managerial, and political factors influencing its downgrade period and evaluates the policy shifts that led to subsequent improvements in the credit ratings.

References

Guzman, T., & Clark, B. Y. (2025). Estimating the negative credit impacts of police-involved fatalities. *Public Finance Review*, *53*(1), 3–28.

Mikesell, J. L., & Ross, J. M. (2024). *Fiscal administration: Analysis and applications for the public sector* (12th ed.). Cengage Learning.

USDebtClock (2025, November 20).World Debt. https://www.usdebtclock.org/world-debt-clock.html

CASE STUDY 20

Mozambique: lessons from "the hidden debt scandal"

Abstract

This case focuses on the largest corruption scandal in Mozambique history, commonly known as "the hidden debts scandal." It explores how undisclosed sovereign guarantees enabled state-owned enterprises to accumulate over $2 billion in debt without parliamentary approval. This case examines the negative consequences of hidden debt, including fiscal and economic crises, suspensions of IMF support, downgrades by credit rating agencies, political conflict, high inflation, and increased poverty. The case highlights key failures in public financial management, the role of international financial institutions, and subsequent reform efforts by the Government of Mozambique and its development partners, including the World Bank. This case study examines the governance failures associated with Mozambique's "hidden debts scandal" and analyzes the principal lessons derived from the crisis. It further explores the key public budgeting reforms implemented in response, with particular attention to institutional transparency, fiscal oversight, and debt management practices. This case offers critical insights for policymakers, practitioners, and students of public administration on the risks posed by opaque fiscal practices and the importance of public budgeting and debt management.

Topics

Public Budgeting; Public Financial Management; Corruption; World Bank; Fiscal Risk; Mozambique; Governance Reform; Debt Management

Background

For over two decades following its 1992 civil war, Mozambique was celebrated as a model of post-conflict recovery and economic growth. Between 1993 and 2013, Mozambique became one of the fastest-growing economies in sub-Saharan Africa, with increasing incomes and living standards. Political and macroeconomic stability provided the foundation for robust growth led by a rebounding agricultural sector and significant donor support. For the two decades following the end of the civil war in 1992, GDP expanded at an average annual rate of almost 8%, making Mozambique one of the world's 10 fastest-growing economies. The expansion boosted incomes and living standards, with GDP per capita growing at an annual average of 4.8% and poverty rate declining from 60.3% in 2002–2003 to 48.4% in 2014–2015. This success was facilitated by political and macroeconomic stability, which provided the foundation for a rebounding agricultural sector and significant foreign direct investment. During this period, Mozambique received massive donor support, for which the country gained a reputation of being a "rising star" or a "donor darling." From 2008 to 2021, the World Bank Group committed "$5.7 billion from the International Development Association and $1.3 billion from the International Finance Corporation" (World Bank, 2023, p. 13). The country benefited from significant budget aid, with most of the associated prior actions focused on reforms in public administration, the financial sector, and energy and extractives. The World Bank and other international institutions played a pivotal role in sustaining this growth trajectory through development programs, budget support, and capacity-building initiatives.

The 2016 hidden debt crisis in Mozambique

In 2016, the revelation of hidden government debt triggered a severe financial crisis, exposing weaknesses in governance, transparency, and public financial management (PFM). The crisis originated from the undisclosed borrowing of over $2 billion by three state-owned enterprises (SOEs), ProIndicus, EMATUM (Mozambique Tuna Company), and MAM (Mozambique Asset Management). In 2013 and 2014, the Credit Suisse and VTB banks loaned "622 million dollars to ProIndicus, 535 million to MAM, and helped place 850 million dollars of bonds on the international market for EMATUM" (Cortez et al., 2021, p. 24). With the help of these and other banks, EMATUM securitized the loans, slicing them into smaller chunks and issuing them as unlisted securities with a sovereign guarantee (World Bank, 2023).

The acquisition of these loans was facilitated by state guarantees provided by the Mozambican government under President Armando Guebuza. These guarantees, authorized by then Finance Minister Manuel Chang, covered the full loan amounts. However, they were in violation of national legal frameworks, exceeding the ceilings on loan guarantees established by the 2013 and 2014 budgetary legislation (Fauvet, 2024). The total amount in loans contracted by the Mozambican government was initially $2,007 million, accounting for 21.5% of Mozambique's foreign debt of $9,682 million and 15% of the country's total public sector debt in 2018. This $2 billion loan to Mozambique was equivalent to nearly 12% of the country's GDP at the time.

The loan however was kept hidden. None of the borrowed money was used to benefit Mozambican people (Cortez et al., 2021). According to Gebregziabher and Pijuan Sala (2022), financing was arranged by three major banks, Credit Suisse, VTB of Russia, and BNP Paribas. The borrowing was supposedly intended to support maritime security, tuna fishing operations, and related infrastructure. Significant concerns later emerged regarding the lack of transparency, inadequate due diligence, inflated procurement contracts, and allegations of corruption involving Mozambican officials and foreign actors. An audit of the three companies in 2017, by the auditing company Kroll found hundreds of millions of dollars unaccounted for, and large portions of the money appear to have been misused through bribes, kickbacks, and inflated contracts involving Mozambican officials and bankers. Substantial sums paid out were likely diverted into private accounts or spent on corrupt deals instead of public goods, and auditors could not trace roughly $500 million of the funds. Tens of millions have been linked to illegal transfers out of Mozambique to international accounts.

Investigations revealed that the three SOEs responsible for the loans were unable to service their debts and subsequently declared bankruptcy, thereby transferring the full liability to the Mozambican government (Fauvet, 2024). Consequently, what were initially concealed loan commitments effectively became undisclosed sovereign debts.

In 2016, large previously unreported external borrowing came to light while the government was negotiating a restructuring deal for a different highly controversial loan taken in 2013 to finance the Mozambique Tuna Company (EMATUM). The undisclosed non-concessional borrowing, equivalent to 10% of GDP ($1.4 billion), was contracted by the government between 2009 and 2014 through guarantees to state-controlled companies and direct borrowing from bilateral lenders (Gebregziabher & Pijuan Sala, 2022). These loans breached the International Monetary Fund (IMF) program in place at the time and the International Development Association's non-concessional borrowing policy, resulting in the outright suspension of budget support by both institutions and other development partners (Gebregziabher & Pijuan Sala, 2022). The IMF formally accused the Mozambican government of misrepresenting the actual scale of its foreign debt obligations, leading to the suspension of its financial assistance program in April 2016 (Fauvet, 2024).

In January 2018, the Mozambican attorney general's office opened a case at an administrative tribunal to establish "financial responsibility" for the loans (Williams, 2018). According to the indictment issued by the New York District Court (2018), $174.4 million was paid in bribes to members of the Mozambican government and to others involved in the fraud (Cortez et al., 2021, p. 25). Evidence suggests that bribes were deliberately concealed within official financial transactions, including bank fees and payments to contractors. These illicit payments were embedded in 15% of the total costs labeled as "bank service fees." This structure indicates that the financial arrangements were not incidental but rather purposefully designed to defraud the Mozambican state. The scheme benefited a small group of individuals operating with clear criminal intent, highlighting severe weaknesses in oversight, accountability, and financial governance.

The negative consequences of Mozambique's "hidden debt scandal"

The negative consequences of Mozambique's hidden debt crisis have been significant. Mozambique is scheduled to pay "nearly $4 billion more in direct costs" (Cortez et al., 2021, p. 6). Although the initial sum received as a loan by the companies EMATUM, ProIndicus, and MAM was $2 billion, "the direct costs and the damage that this fraud has inflicted on the Mozambican economy have already exceeded $11 billion," which is approximately equivalent to the country's entire GDP in 2016 (Cortez et al., 2021, p. 9).

In 2016, real public expenditures were cut to less than half of what they were in 2014. That reduction in public expenditures decreased spending on social welfare. Comparing the three-year average of 2016–2018 to the three previous years, spending on health and education fell by $1.7 billion (Cortez et al., 2021). Because of the "hidden debt scandal," at least 1.9 million people had fallen below the consumption-based poverty line by 2019 (Fauvet, 2024). From 2016 to 2019, the currency depreciated drastically, inflation increased, and average annual growth decreased from 7.7% between 2000 and 2016 to 3.3% between 2016 and 2019 (Gebregziabher & Pijuan Sala, 2022). In 2016, the rate of inflation reached its maximum level over the previous ten years. "Average inflation reached 19.85%, and year-end inflation was 25.27%" (Cortez et al., 2021, p. 40).

When the hidden debt was accounted for, Mozambique's external public and publicly guaranteed debt increased from 61% of GDP in 2016 to 104% in 2018. The debt/GDP ratio increased from 42.9% in 2013 to 79% in 2019 (Cortez et al., 2021, p. 36). With a precipitous increase in debt service, Mozambique defaulted on its debt in 2016, further complicating efforts to stabilize the economy and restore international confidence (World Bank, 2023, 2024). "Hidden debt scandal" contributed to the downgrades by the ratings agencies, when it became obvious that Mozambique would likely not manage to repay its foreign debt.

This downgrade led to worse conditions for Mozambique on the international capital markets. In 2016, 14 international donors that had previously provided aid through direct budget support halted all further disbursements. This suspension of foreign aid resulted in an immediate fiscal shortfall of approximately $831 million in 2016 compared to 2015 levels, cascading negative effects on the country's fiscal stability and development prospects in subsequent years (Fauvet, 2024; Maldonado et al., 2023). The official aid decreased from 17.5% of GDP in 2015 to 12.4% of GDP in 2018.

According to World Bank (2023), "resource management, accountability, and access to basic services by poor people were deteriorating, and decentralization had stalled" (p.vii). The corrosive impact of corruption and ineffective public institutions has diminished trust in the state and had "negative implications for the quality of most public services" (World Bank, 2023. p. 10). The corruption, the difficulties of managing the situation created by the hidden debt contributed "to less democracy and worse governance" (Cortez et al., 2021, p. 20). In FY 18, Mozambique was formally classified as a fragile country.

This "hidden debt scandal" highlighted shortcomings in governance, transparency, and PFM systems. The Economist and its Economist Intelligence Unit (EIU) classify 167 countries in terms of democracy, using a continual scale ranging from full democracy to flawed democracy, to a hybrid regime, and to an authoritarian regime. The EIU publishes the annual Democracy Index, which assesses the state of democracy using five key dimensions: electoral process and pluralism, functioning of government, political participation, democratic political culture, and civil liberties. According to the Democracy Index, Mozambique ranked 120th in 2019. Notably, 2018 marked the first year Mozambique was classified as an "authoritarian regime" (The Economist, 2020).

Turning a crisis into an opportunity for public budgeting reform

The "hidden debt crisis" in Mozambique revealed critical structural weaknesses in public budgeting and financial management. This crisis highlighted inadequate legislative oversight, deficient debt management systems, and a lack of transparency and accountability in the operations of SOEs. Furthermore, the crisis illustrated the substantial risks posed by non-concessional borrowing by SOEs underwritten by sovereign guarantees, particularly in governance environments characterized by institutional fragility and limited checks and balances.

Before the scandal, the World Bank's approach to addressing these challenges relied heavily on technical and institutional capacity building with insufficient attention to the underlying political economy and associated corruption risks. Fiscal risks were largely addressed through reforms and capacity support to produce and publish Medium Term Debt Strategies and debt and fiscal reports. The lack of attention to such systemic shortcomings was the result of inadequate internal coordination and prioritization in World Bank support for public financial and debt management. While the World Bank provided significant support for some aspects of debt management (e.g., preparation of debt management strategies), with belated attention to other aspects such as debt reporting and recording, cost and risk analysis, and debt processes and procedures. Moreover, for most of the evaluation period, support for debt management was not systematically accompanied by efforts to improve public investment management.

The "hidden debt crisis" created conditions for comprehensive reforms in public budgeting. Since 2016, World Bank support to Mozambique has focused on improving PFM (central government), public debt management, decentralization, and transparency. The Government of Mozambique enacted a series of reforms to address weaknesses in PFM. In 2017, new regulations were introduced to improve the control and oversight of public debt and government guarantees. A subsequent 2018 law enhanced the governance framework for SOEs, establishing clearer accountability and stricter approval processes for SOE borrowing. The government resumed the publication of comprehensive debt reports in 2019, which now include liabilities incurred by SOEs, thereby promoting greater fiscal transparency (Gebregziabher & Pijuan Sala, 2022).

Since 2019, Mozambique has initiated the development of fiscal risk statements. These statements serve to identify and manage fiscal risks, particularly those associated with contingent liabilities from SOEs. In addition, a credit risk assessment framework was adopted to evaluate guarantees and on-lending to public enterprises (Gebregziabher & Pijuan Sala, 2022). Applying these methodologies, the authorities have completed credit risk assessments for seven key SOEs, establishing a systematic approach to monitoring and mitigating fiscal exposure.

In 2020, the government adopted a regulatory framework for public investment management, requiring all public investment projects to undergo pre-appraisal for their socioeconomic returns and resilience to disasters. With World Bank support, the authorities have taken a series of critical policy and institutional measures, such as the development of appraisal methodologies, capacity building for public officials, and the implementation of digital tools to improve the quality and consistency of investment evaluations (World Bank, 2023).

SOEs were also integrated into the National Budget System. These reform efforts were consolidated with the adoption of a revised PFM Law in 2020 (Gebregziabher & Pijuan Sala, 2022). For the first time, the law brought SOEs and decentralized public bodies under the formal budget framework, representing a significant advancement in the comprehensiveness and transparency of the fiscal system.

Finally, the Government of Mozambique is working on improving debt recording and consolidation. Despite progress in publishing debt reports covering central government and SOEs, challenges persist in consolidating and centralizing debt information. Central government debt remains dispersed across multiple platforms, and SOE debt is not yet systematically recorded by the Ministry of Finance (Gebregziabher & Pijuan Sala, 2022). The government focuses on migrating to the Commonwealth Secretariat's Debt Recording and Management System to facilitate unified and comprehensive debt management across the public sector.

Conclusions

Four factors created the "hidden debt crisis": a power of elites, access to abundant non-concessional finance associated with the discovery of large gas deposits, insufficient regulatory and managerial oversight of SOEs, and ineffective public budgeting and debt management.

The disclosure of Mozambique's hidden debts caused multiple negative consequences, significantly affecting the country's economy, financial situation, social policy, and governance:

- The IMF suspended its financial program with Mozambique;
- The cooperation partners suspended all budget and programmatic support;
- Private investors drastically reduced the flow of funds to Mozambique;
- The rating agencies reduced the classification of Mozambique from "CC with negative prospects" to "selective default."

These developments generated a macroeconomic shock that disrupted Mozambique's growth trajectory. The economy experienced a sharp deceleration, reversing prior gains in economic expansion, macroeconomic stability, and international financial credibility.

In the aftermath of the crisis, the Mozambican government faced significant pressure – both domestically and internationally – to pursue reforms aimed at enhancing fiscal transparency, improving debt reporting, strengthening oversight mechanisms, and addressing corruption. The implementation of reforms at the subnational level showed improvement, particularly through the use of Program-for-Results financing mechanisms, which incentivized performance and accountability. These initiatives contributed to measurable improvements in municipal revenue collection, demonstrating the potential for localized reforms even in the absence of a comprehensive decentralization strategy. While some progress has been made in institutional reform and accountability measures, the full recovery of public trust and macroeconomic stability remains an ongoing challenge.

Discussion questions

1. What factors contributed to Mozambique's economic success between 1992 and 2015?
2. What public budgeting failures allowed the "hidden debt crisis to unfold"?

3 What institutional weaknesses allowed the hidden debt crisis in Mozambique to occur?
4 How have the post-crisis reforms addressed (or failed to address) these vulnerabilities?
5 How does the integration of state-owned enterprises (SOEs) into the national public financial management system enhance fiscal transparency and accountability?
6 What challenges remain in implementing effective SOE oversight?
7 To what extent can crises serve as catalysts for structural public sector reforms in fragile states?
8 What factors determine whether such reforms are sustained in the long term?
9 How can fiscal risk statements and credit risk assessments be improved in developing countries?
10 What are the limitations of these tools in practice?
11 What lessons can be drawn for similar debt management challenges?

Case memorandum assignment

Imagine you have been hired as a policy advisor to the World Bank's country team working on Mozambique. Your task is to write a professional policy memo that analyzes the World Bank's engagement in Mozambique from 2008 to 2025. The World Bank is reassessing its strategy following the "hidden debt crisis," public budgeting reforms from 2016 to 2025, and their long-term implications. The goal is to help the World Bank design better public budgeting programs moving forward, particularly in countries facing governance challenges and political risks.

Your policy memo should address the following sections:

1 Analyze the World Bank's engagement before and after the hidden debt crisis.
2 If you were advising the World Bank today, how would you design a program that addresses different aspects of PFM in Mozambique to prevent "hidden debt"?

Propose two or three recommendations for how the World Bank should approach its work to improve public budgeting in Mozambique in the future. Offer concrete ideas for how the World Bank could improve its financial management, transparency, and accountability to ensure more effective program implementation.

References

Cortez, E., Orre, A., Fael, B., Nhamirre, B., Banze, C., Mapisse, I., Harnack, K., & Reite, T. (2021). Costs and consequences of the hidden debt scandal of Mozambique. Maputo, Bergen: Centro de Integridade Pública (CIP), Moçambique, and

Chr. Michelsen Institute, Norway. https://www.cmi.no/publications/7841-costs-and-consequences-of-the-hidden-debt-scandal-of-mozambique

Fauvet, P. (2024, May 16). *Mozambique: Hidden debts ruin anti-poverty strategy – AIM report*. Club of Mozambique. https://clubofmozambique.com/news/mozambique-hidden-debts-ruin-anti-poverty-strategy-aim-report-260472/

Maldonado, E., Iarossi, G., & Chelsky, J. (2023, March 20). *The world bank group in Mozambique: Lessons from a success story gone awry*. Independent Evaluation Group, World Bank Group. https://ieg.worldbankgroup.org/blog/world-bank-group-mozambique-lessons-success-story-gone-awry

Gebregziabher, F. H., & Pijuan Sala, A. (2022, April 19). *Mozambique's "hidden debts": Turning a crisis into an opportunity for reform*. World Bank Blogs. https://blogs.worldbank.org/en/africacan/mozambiques-hidden-debts-turning-crisis-opportunity-reform

Kroll. (2017). Independent audit related to loans contracted by ProIndicus S.A., EMATUM S.A., and Mozambique Asset Management S.A. Report prepared for the Office of the Public Prosecutor of the Republic of Mozambique.

The Economist (2020). *Global democracy has another bad year*. https://www.economist.com/graphic-detail/2020/01/22/global-democracy-has-another-bad-year

US Indictment (2018). Indictment against Jean Boustani, Manuel Chang, Andrew Pearse, Surjan Singh and Detelina Subeva. At United States District Court, Eastern District of New York, December 19.

Williams, A. (2018). *The Mozambique hidden loans case: An opportunity for donors to demonstrate anticorruption commitment*. Maputo, Bergen: Centro de Integridade Pública (CIP). https://www.u4.no/publications/the-mozambique-hidden-loans-case-an-opportunity-for-donors-to-demonstrate-anti-corruption-commitment.pdf

World Bank. (2023). *The World Bank Group in Mozambique, fiscal years 2008–21: Country program evaluation*. Independent Evaluation Group. https://ieg.worldbankgroup.org/evaluations/world-bank-group-mozambique-fiscal-years-2008-21

World Bank. (2024). *Mozambique*. https://www.worldbank.org/en/country/mozambique

CASE STUDY 21

The recovery of Illinois credit ratings – an institutional and fiscal analysis

Abstract

This case study evaluates historical trends in Illinois' credit ratings from 1973 to 2025. From October 2015 to May 2022, the State of Illinois maintained one of the lowest credit ratings among the 50 U.S. states. In 2020, Illinois had BBB- (Fitch and [Standard & Poor's] S&P Global Inc. credit ratings) and Baa3 (Moody's rating). Illinois received nine credit upgrades from 2021 to 2025. In June 2021, Illinois received its first credit rating upgrade from Baa3 to Baa2 (Moody's rating). By 2023, S&P Global Inc. had upgraded Illinois to A- and Moody's to A3. This case study examines the historical trajectory of Illinois' credit ratings, identifies the economic, managerial, and political determinants that influenced its downgrade period, and evaluates the policy shifts that led to subsequent improvements in its credit rating.

Background

It is not very typical for a municipality and especially for the state to receive a lot of rating updates, as state credit ratings typically remain unchanged for years. Yet, this is not the case in Illinois. A review of Illinois' bond rating history reveals a long-term deterioration from AAA/Aaa in the late 1970s to the lowest investment-grade ratings, BBB- by 2017, and gradual improvements in its credit ratings between 2020 and 2025 (Illinois State Comptroller, 2020, 2025). Table 9.3 provides the dynamics of Illinois' Credit Ratings from 1973 to 2025.

The lowest investment-grade rating was assigned to the state in June 2017, when Standard & Poor's (S&P) Global Inc. decreased its grade on the state's

TABLE 9.3 Illinois' Credit Ratings from 1973 to 2025

Date of Rating Action	*Fitch Rating*	*Fitch Up/ Down*	*S&P Global Rating*	*S&P Up/ Down*	*Moody's Rating*	*Moody's Up/Down*
2023 November	A-	Up				
2023 March					A3	Up
2023 February			A-	Up		
2022 May	BBB+	Up 2	BBB+	Up		
2022 April					Baa1	Up
2021 July			BBB	Up		
2021 June					Baa2	Up
2020 April	BBB-	Down				
2017 June			BBB-	Down	Baa3	Down
2017 February	BBB	Down				
2016 September			BBB	Down		
2016 June			BBB+	Down	Baa2	Down
2015 October	BBB+	Down			Baa1	Down
2013 June	A-	Down			A3	Down
2013 January			A-	Down		
2012 August			A	Down		
2012 January					A2	Down
2010 June	A	Down			A1	Down
2010 April					Aa3 (recalibration)	Up 2
2010 March	A-/A+ (recalibration)	Down/Up				
2009 December			A+	Down	A2	Down
2009 July	A	Down				
2009 April					A1	Down
2009 March			AA-	Down		
2008 December			AA-	Down		
2003 May			AA	Down	Aa3	Down
2000 June	AA+	Up				
1998 June					Aa2	Up
1997 July	AA	Up				
1997 February					Aa3	Up
1996 September	AA	Initial				

(*Continued*)

TABLE 9.3 (Continued)

Date of Rating Action	*Fitch Rating*	*Fitch Up/ Down*	*S&P Global Rating*	*S&P Up/ Down*	*Moody's Rating*	*Moody's Up/Down*
1995 February					A1	Down
1992 August	AA-	Down			Aa	Down
1991 Aug/Sep	AA	Down			Aa1	Down
1983 March	AA+	Down				
1979 February	AAA	Initial				
1973					Aaa	Initial

Source: Illinois State Comptroller (2025).

general-obligation bonds one level to BBB-minus. Moody's Corp. also dropped its Illinois rating to Baa3, one notch above junk. Fitch Ratings has rated Illinois BBB, two notches above junk (Gillers, 2017).

Between 2021 and 2025, Illinois received a total of nine credit rating upgrades (State of Illinois, 2025). In June 2021, Illinois achieved its first upgrade when Moody's raised its rating from Baa3 to Baa2. By 2023, Illinois's credit standing had further improved, with S&P Global Inc. upgrading the state's rating to A- and Moody's elevating it to A3.

Causes of the downgrade of Illinois' credit rating

So, what happened to the state? Why are credit rating agencies so unsure about Illinois creditworthiness and keep revising their ratings and credit outlooks? The causes of this issue are multifaceted and rooted in years of public corruption, demographic changes, unfunded pension obligations, and fiscal instability.

Outstanding debt obligations and pension liabilities

In 2017, Illinois had \$26 billion outstanding general obligation bonds. The state's budget deficit was more than \$5 billion (Gillers, 2017). The problems were aggravated by substantial debt obligations that significantly constrain the resources available for the state's operational needs.

The state's pension liabilities reached \$251 billion in the previous year. S&P Global reported that the combined costs of retirement and health benefits, along with debt service payments, now account for approximately 29% of the state's general fund expenditures (Gillers, 2017). Illinois' unfunded pension obligations grew by 11.6 points relative to personal income from fiscal 2007 to fiscal 2019 (Biernacka-Lievestro & Fleming, 2022). Measuring liabilities as a percentage of personal income reflects their size relative to the state's economic resources. Unfunded retirement liabilities mean that states have set aside less than is needed to cover the expected full costs of benefits earned by their employees. The aggregate funded ratio across all five state pension systems declined from 52.4% in FY 1994 to just 44.9% in FY 2023. By 2023, the state's unfunded pension liability was over $142 billion, the largest of any U.S. state, and represented over 20% of the state's GDP (Center for Tax and Budget Accountability, 2024). The aggregate 44.9% funded ratio of Illinois' state-level pension systems is below the 78.1% national average of all funded ratios for all public pension systems across the United States (Center for Tax and Budget Accountability, 2024).

Budget deficit

In the 1970s, Illinois used to be a relatively low-expenditure, low-revenue state. From the late 1980s, Illinois has spent more than it has collected in revenues. Illinois's spending averaged 115.9% of its revenues compared with 105.7% for the typical U.S. state from FY 1994 to FY 2010 (Walstrum, 2016). The accumulation of pension liabilities has become a major source of Illinois's fiscal problems. Illinois also spent 1.3 percentage points more on general debt interest than the average state (Walstrum, 2016). Illinois had not had a balanced budget since 2001 (Illinois Policy, 2016) (Table 9.4).

TABLE 9.4 General Fund Annual Balance, in Millions of Dollars

Fiscal Year	*General Fund Annual Balance*
2001	300
2002	−1,220
2003	−1,094
2004	−410
2005	−474
2006	−291
2007	−135
2008	−834
2009	−3,673
2010	−6,094
2011	−4,507
2012	−4,984
2013	−3,988
2014	−3,931
2015	−2,900

Source: Illinois Policy (2016).

In January 2011, with the intent to address Illinois' structural deficit and an unpaid bill backlog, the personal income tax rate increased from 3% to 5%, and the corporate income tax rate increased from 4.8% to 7%. However, the enacted rate changes were temporary, with rates decreases scheduled for 2015. By the time Gov. Bruce Rauner took office on January 12, 2015, the individual and corporate income tax rates had dropped, creating a $6.2 billion pressure point in the fiscal year 2016 budget. In 2016, Illinois had a $5.5 billion operating deficit, $7.7 billion in unpaid bills, and an estimated $111 billion in unfunded pension liabilities (Walstrum, 2016).

Inefficiency of the budgeting process

During the 736-day period from 2015 to 2017, Illinois operated without a full-year budget, the longest standstill of its kind in the state's history. The state used continuing resolutions to make payments to some court orders, consent decrees, and ongoing statutory appropriations. However, the deadlock between then-Governor Bruce Rauner and the Democratic-controlled legislature led to the accumulation of unpaid bills, delays in vendor payments, and penalties reaching $900 million in interest alone (Office of the Illinois Comptroller, 2026). By the end of fiscal year 2017, Illinois' backlog of bills reached an estimated $14.71 billion, a threefold increase from the end of fiscal year 2015 (Office of the Illinois Comptroller, 2026). The state is obligated to pay interest on past-due bills. This interest is either 9% or 12% annually, depending on the associated bill type. So, for every $1 billion in late bills, Illinois pays between $90 million and $120 million in interest per year, depending on the type of bill (Commission on Government Forecasting and Accountability, 2024). During the budget impasse, Illinois' general obligation bond rating was downgraded a combined eight times by Moody's Investors Service, Fitch Ratings, and S&P Global Ratings (Illinois State Comptroller, 2026).

Public corruption

Illinois' fiscal challenges were exacerbated by decades of public corruption that eroded public trust and financial accountability. Since 1976, Illinois has recorded more than 2,100 federal public corruption convictions, the third highest among U.S. states, behind only New York and California (McKinney, 2023; U.S. Department of Justice, 2021).

Former governors George Ryan and Rod Blagojevich both served prison time for corruption charges. Rod Blagojevich was attempting to "sell" Barack Obama's vacated Senate seat in 2008. At the municipal level, Cook County and Chicago have faced multiple corruption scandals involving zoning kickbacks, ghost payrolling, and mismanagement of public funds. This culture of corruption indirectly impacted credit ratings by undermining investor confidence, delaying reforms, and increasing borrowing costs due to perceived governance risks.

TABLE 9.5 The Population in Illinois from 2000 to 2020

Year	*Population*
2000	12,419,293
2001	12,482,301
2002	12,600,620
2003	12,419,293
2004	12,589,773
2005	12,763,371
2006	12,831,970
2007	12,852,548
2008	12,901,550
2009	12,910,409
2010	12,830,632
2011	12,869,360
2012	12,875,280
2013	12,890,552
2014	12,880,580
2015	12,859,995
2016	12,801,539
2017	12,802,023
2018	12,724,685
2019	12,667,017
2020	12,812,508

Source: Created by authors based on U.S. Census (n.d.)

Declining population

Another reason for rating downgrades has been the declining population. Table 9.5 demonstrates the positive population dynamics in Illinois from 2000 to 2015 and the shrinking population from 2016 to 2020.

High tax rates were the main reason why Illinoisans considered leaving the state. Around 61% of Illinoisans thought about moving out of state in 2019, and the No. 1 reason was taxes (NPR Illinois, 2019). In 2016, the Paul Simon Public Policy Institute (2016) found 47% of Illinoisans wanted to leave the state, with 27% of respondents citing taxes as the motive for departing.

Stabilization and recovery measures

A bipartisan override of Governor Rauner's veto in July 2017 allowed passing a permanent income tax increase from 3.75% to 4.95% for individuals and passing a full-year budget. Governor J.B. Pritzker, elected in 2018, doubled down on stabilization efforts by paying down the bill backlog, expanding infrastructure investment, and seeking long-term revenue sources.

Federal aid, particularly through the American Rescue Plan Act, provided Illinois with $8.1 billion in relief, allowing the state to eliminate short-term borrowing and bolster rainy day reserves. Illinois has distributed more than $2 billion in COVID-19 recovery funds and American Rescue Plan resources to support small businesses and local governments throughout the state. These efforts prioritized assistance to disproportionately impacted communities and industries most affected by the pandemic (Urban Institute, 2025).

In 2024, Illinois allocated more than $1.9 billion to its Rainy-Day Fund to strengthen its fiscal resilience against potential economic downturns (State of Illinois, 2025).

The state has recently experienced significant growth in tax revenues from adult-use cannabis sales. Under the state's adult-use cannabis legislation, 25% of the tax revenue generated is allocated to support communities that face economic distress, high rates of violence, or have been disproportionately affected by drug-related criminalization.

Illinois contributed an additional $500 million beyond certified requirements to its pension system, a move projected to save taxpayers approximately $1.8 billion over the long term (State of Illinois, 2025).

Table 9.6 demonstrates Illinois' Fiscal Progress from 2019 to 2024.

Base General Funds revenue totaled $50.7 billion in FY 2023, reflecting a $373 million increase, or 0.7% growth compared to FY 2022 (Commission on Government Forecasting and Accountability, 2024). Most of this increase was driven by a nearly $1.2 billion rise in transfers from the Income Tax Refund Fund, resulting from above-average income tax receipts in the prior fiscal year. Additional growth came from increases in corporate income tax, interest on state funds and investments, and sales tax revenues. General Funds' expenditures were $50.8 billion in FY 2023.

Illinois enacted the bipartisan Rebuild Illinois plan with a $45 billion capital investment initiative focused on infrastructure and economic development. Additionally, Illinois announced nearly $1 billion in planned or ongoing

TABLE 9.6 Illinois' Fiscal Progress from 2019 to 2024

	2019	*2024*
Overdue bill backlog	$8 billion	Eliminated
Rainy day fund	$60,000	$1.9 billion
Gross domestic product	$881 billion	$1.024 trillion
Pension funded ratio	40.30%	43.80%

Source: Created by authors based on the State of Illinois (2025).

TABLE 9.7 The Population in Illinois from 2021 to 2024

Year	*Population*	*Changes (Increase/Decline)) (%)*
2021	12,700,641	0.77 decline from 2020
2022	12,621,821	0.62 decline from 2021
2023	12,642,259	0.16 increase from 2022
2024	12,710,158	0.54 increase from 2023

Source: Created by authors based on U.S. Census (n.d.).

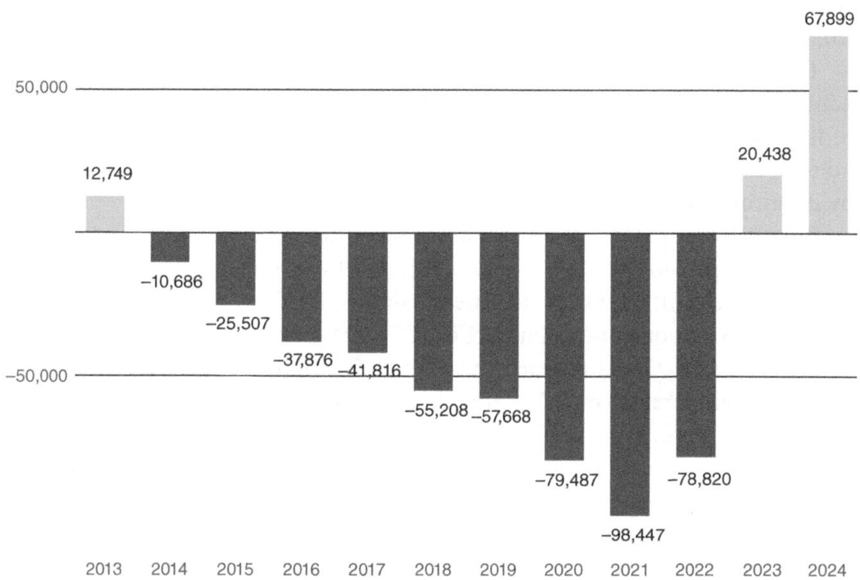

FIGURE 9.1 Illinois' population from 2013 to 2024

Source: Created by authors based on U.S. Census (n.d.)

investments in state facilities that provide continuous care for some of Illinois's most vulnerable populations (State of Illinois, 2025).

Illinois' population grew by 20,438 residents in 2023 and by 67,899 residents in 2024 (U.S. Census, 2025) (Table 9.7). In 2025, Illinois' population stands at approximately 12,516,863, continuing a slight decline from 12.64 million in 2023 (McAllister, 2025).

Examining historical data, Illinois's population increased only in three out of the 12 years between 2013 and 2024 (Figure 9.1).

The state continues to see a natural increase in population as births outpace deaths, but by an increasingly narrow margin, adding only 11,012 residents during the year. International migration added 112,955 new residents, ten times more than what the state received in 2021 and nearly five times what the state gained on average from 2010 to 2020 (Hill, 2024).

Reversing the trend: credit rating improvements

By 2023, all three major credit rating agencies had restored Illinois' GO bonds to the "A" category. S&P Global Ratings announced an upgrade to A- in November 2023, its third upgrade of Illinois' GO bonds since July 2021. This marked the first time since May 2016 that Illinois held an A- rating from S&P. Fitch Ratings issued a two-notch upgrade in May 2022, bringing the state's rating to BBB+, and followed with another increase to A- in February 2023. This was the first upgrade for Fitch since June 2000. Moody's Investors Service raised Illinois' rating from Baa3 to Baa1 in June 2021, and then to A3 in April 2022, citing improvements in budgetary performance and long-term liability management.

Conclusions

The main reasons for Illinois's credit downgrades were years of persistent structural budget deficits, unfunded pension liabilities and retiree health benefits, inefficiencies in the budgeting process, public corruption, and a declining population base.

In 2024, Illinois went from $17 billion in unpaid bills and a credit rating one notch above junk status to a fiscally responsible state. By 2024, Illinois had generated $1 trillion in Gross State Product (GSP) and experienced 18 consecutive months of job growth, with historic business creation.

Although Illinois has not fully resolved all its financial challenges over the past four years, the state has made significant progress in strengthening its fiscal position. This includes the planned reduction of more than $10 billion in outstanding debt between fiscal years 2022 and 2024, alongside investments exceeding $1.9 billion in the state's Rainy-Day Fund. The fiscal year 2025 budget proposal builds on these achievements by continuing to prioritize debt reduction and investments aimed at securing the state's long-term financial stability.

However, Illinois' fiscal future is still at risk due to enormous pension liabilities that remain structurally underfunded, ongoing debt service obligations that crowd out education and social service spending, and a shrinking population, which reduces the state's tax base. While the state has stabilized its financial trajectory, its recovery has been complicated by persistent structural imbalances and deep-seated political dysfunction.

Discussion questions

1 What fiscal, political, and institutional factors contributed to Illinois' sustained credit rating downgrades from 2009 to 2020?

2 How does long-term corruption affect a state's credit rating?
3 How did the state's management of pension liabilities influence credit ratings?
4 Could Illinois have avoided the near-junk credit rating (BBB-) status if it had enacted budgeting and fiscal reforms earlier?
5 How does federal aid affect Illinois' fiscal outlook and credit rating?
6 Should credit rating agencies incorporate federal aid into long-term credit ratings?
7 What budgeting and fiscal reforms were most instrumental in enabling Illinois to regain an "A" credit rating classification?
8 What is your perspective on the stability of Illinois' recent credit rating upgrades?
9 How does Illinois' credit rating experience inform the relationship between fiscal policy, credit ratings, and borrowing costs for other U.S. states?

References

Biernacka-Lievestro, J., & Fleming, J. (2022). *States' unfunded pension liabilities persist as major long-term challenge.* PEW. https://www.pew.org/en/research-and-analysis/articles/2022/07/07/states-unfunded-pension-liabilities-persist-as-major-long-term-challenge

Center for Tax and Budget Accountability. (2024) Understanding – and resolving Illinois' Pension Funding Challengeshttps://www.ctbaonline.org/reports/understanding-%E2%80%93-and-resolving-illinois%E2%80%99-pension-funding-challenges-volume-ii

Commission on Government Forecasting and Accountability (2024). *Three-year budget forecast FY 2025 – FY 2027.* https://cgfa.ilga.gov/Upload/3YearBudgetFY2025-2027.pdf

Gillers, H. (2017, June 2). S&P downgrade brings Illinois debt one step closer to junk: Illinois may become the first U.S. state to be given a junk rating. *The Wall Street Journal.* https://www.wsj.com/articles/s-p-downgrade-brings-illinois-debt-one-step-closer-to-junk-1496350098.

Hill, B. (2024, December 19). Illinois population grows in 2024 despite 56K residents leaving for other states. *Illinois Policy.* https://www.illinoispolicy.org/illinois-population-grows-in-2024-despite-56k-residents-leaving-for-other-states/

Illinois Policy (2016). *The-history-of-illinois-fiscal-crisis* https://www.illinoispolicy.org/reports/the-history-of-illinois-fiscal-crisis/

Illinois State Comptroller (2017). *Consequences of Illinois' 2015–2017 budget impasse and fiscal outlook.* https://illinoiscomptroller.gov/__media/sites/comptroller/Consequences%20of%2020152017%20Budget%20Impasse2.pdf

Illinois State Comptroller (2020). *Illinois' bond debt.* https://illinoiscomptroller.gov/financial-reports-data/data-sets-portals/illinois-bond-debt.

Illinois State Comptroller (2025). *Illinois' bond debt.* https://illinoiscomptroller.gov/financial-reports-data/data-sets-portals/illinois-bond-debt.

McAllister, R. (2025, August, 28). *Illinois population in 2025 – analyzing the latest data. North American Community Hub Statistics.* https://nchstats.com/illinois-population/

McKinney, D. (2023, December 1). How does corruption impact democracy? Take a look at Illinois. *Northern Public Radio*, https://www.northernpublicradio.org/illinois/2023-12-01/how-does-corruption-impact-democracy-take-a-look-at-illinois.

NPR Illinois. (2019). *Survey: Voters diverge On Gov, economy.* https://www.nprillinois.org/statehouse/2019-10-07/survey-voters-diverge-on-gov-economy#stream/0

Office of the Illinois Comptroller. (2026). *Accounts Payable Statement.* https://illinoiscomptroller.gov/financial-reports-data/data-sets-portals/accounts-payable-statement

Paul Simon Public Policy Institute (2016). *Illinois voters ask: Should I stay or should I go?* https://paulsimoninstitute.siu.edu/_common/documents/opinion-polling/simon-institute-poll/2016/oct-10-psppi-simon-poll-illinois-voters-should-i-stay.pdf

State of Illinois (2025). *Illinois state budget. Fiscal year 2024.* https://budget.illinois.gov/content/dam/soi/en/web/budget/documents/budget-book/fy2024-budget-book/Fiscal-Year-2024-Operating-Budget.pdf

Urban Institute (2025). *Illinois.* https://www.urban.org/policy-centers/cross-center-initiatives/state-and-local-finance-initiative/projects/state-fiscal-briefs/illinois

U.S. Census (n.d.). *Population and housing unit estimates datasets.* https://www.census.gov/programs-surveys/popest/data/data-sets.html

U.S. Department of Justice (2021). *Report to congress on the activities and operations of the public integrity section for 2021.* https://www.justice.gov/criminal/media/1256431/dl?inline.

Walstrum, T. (2016). The Illinois Budget Crisis in Context: A History of Poor Fiscal Performance. Chicago Fed Letter, No. 365, 2016. Federal Reserve Bank of Chicago. https://www.chicagofed.org/publications/chicago-fed-letter/2016/36

10

BUDGETING DURING FISCAL EMERGENCY AND BANKRUPTCY

Abstract

This chapter examines the municipal fiscal health conditions (fiscal health, fiscal stress, financial emergency, and Chapter 9 bankruptcy) and explains Chapter 9 of the U.S. Bankruptcy Code, its historical origins, legal constraints, and authorization across states. It highlights why municipal bankruptcy represents a distinct governance challenge compared to corporate or individual insolvency. Based on the HEI theoretical model by Guzman and Ermasova, this chapter presents a framework of municipal responses to fiscal stress: hazardous, emergency, and innovative strategies. This chapter illustrates how governments initially rely on fragmented, often ineffective measures, then escalate to extreme budget cuts during fiscal crises, and finally adopt more strategic, transparent, and forward-looking financial practices.

Introduction

When municipalities generate sufficient revenues to cover their ongoing expenditures, meet debt and other obligations, and provide adequate services to their residents, they are considered fiscally healthy. With any deviations from this state, municipalities are deemed fiscally stressed. Guzman and Ermasova (2023) distinguish between the following definitions of fiscal stress (see Figure 10.1).

Fiscal Health is "the ability of government to meet its financial and service obligations" (Hendrick, 2004).

DOI: 10.4324/9781003606833-11

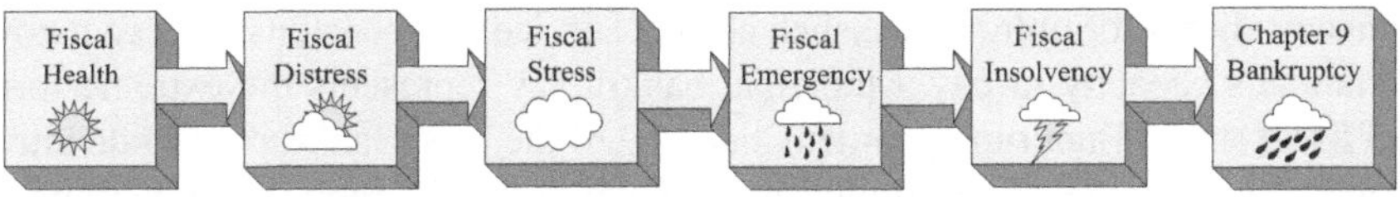

FIGURE 10.1 Definition of fiscal stress

Source: Guzman & Ermasova, 2023

Fiscal Distress is a relatively mild fiscal disturbance when a municipality cannot pay its bills by the due date, meet its payroll, balance its budget, or carry out essential public services for a certain period of time.

Fiscal Stress is a fiscal situation, when a gap between projected revenues and expenditures is "short-term, in the case of transitory economic shocks, or long-term, in the case of structural budget imbalance" (CBO, 2010, p. 2).

Financial Emergency, Insolvency, or Crisis is a fiscal situation when municipality is

1 unable to meet principal and/or interest payments on any of its debt obligations;
2 unable to pay for any other financial obligations to employees, retirees, suppliers, banks, and other government agencies which are not represented by certificate of indebtedness; and
3 unable to provide services for its residents' needs.

Chapter 9 bankruptcy is the worst and terminal state in the fiscal crisis.

Chapter 9 bankruptcy of the U.S. Bankruptcy Code was created in 1937, during the Great Depression, specifically for municipal governments and their subdivisions.

Unlike corporate bankruptcy (Chapter 11), or individual bankruptcy (Chapter 7), Chapter 9 is tailored for governments because municipalities cannot simply liquidate assets and dissolve; they must remain operational to deliver essential services like policing, sanitation, and schools.

Bankruptcy proceedings allow struggling governments to restructure their debt, providing protection from creditors by creating a plan between the municipality and its creditors to resolve the outstanding debt. Only 12 states unconditionally authorize bankruptcies. A total of 23 states do not allow municipalities to apply for Chapter 9 bankruptcy, and 15 states offer only conditional authorization (Moldogaziev et al., 2017).

Municipalities experiencing fiscal emergency or bankruptcy face profound challenges that force a rethinking of traditional budgeting processes. A fiscal emergency typically occurs when revenues sharply decline, costs rise uncontrollably, or obligations, such as debt service and pensions, exceed a government's capacity to pay. Municipal bankruptcy represents the extreme form of fiscal stress. Bankruptcy under Chapter 9 of the U.S. Bankruptcy Code introduces additional legal constraints and judicial oversight, requiring governments to balance financial recovery with statutory obligations. In both situations, budgeting is no longer a routine exercise in resource allocation but a critical tool for economic stabilization and ultimate survival.

Main steps in budgeting during a fiscal emergency and bankruptcy

The first and most important step in budgeting under fiscal stress is understanding the roots of fiscal problems. Effective fiscal stress management begins with identifying the causes of structural budget deficits, declining tax bases, and the inability to meet fixed obligations (Guzman & Ermasova, 2025). Without this clarity, emergency measures risk treating symptoms rather than causes. The assessment phase, therefore, informs the difficult decisions about which services to cut, which obligations to restructure, and what long-term reforms are necessary.

The causes of fiscal crisis can range from economic, political, demographic, and to even environmental. Detroit, MI, bankruptcy is considered the largest municipal bankruptcy in U.S. history, with $18.6 billion in debt when the city applied for Chapter 9 bankruptcy protection on July 18, 2013. For Detroit, the bankruptcy was a result of the years of lower demand for American cars, failure to properly fund city pension funds, racial tensions and white flight, and corruption. Corruption, including bribery, cheating on sewer repair contracts and their financing and other indictments, were at the core of the fiscal downfall of Jefferson County, Alabama that filed for bankruptcy on November 9, 2011, with $4.3 billion in debt. A small city of Fairfield, Alabama, a suburb of Birmingham, applied for bankruptcy on May 19, 2020, when two major employers, U.S. Steel's Fairfield Works, closed portions of their facility in 2015, and Walmart Supercenter closed in 2016. New Orleans, LA credit rating was downgraded to junk in Fall 2005 following historical flooding and destruction of the city by Hurricane Katrina and subsequent levees' failure. In 1978, Cleveland was the first city to default on bond payments since the Great Depression. Between 1980 and 1987, the city spent about 7.5 years in a state of fiscal emergency. The downfall of the city was attributed to deindustrialization and inability to timely raise city income tax (from 1% to 1.5%).

Legal and institutional frameworks shape the options available to municipalities in bankruptcy. To qualify for Chapter 9 bankruptcy protection, a city must demonstrate insolvency, show it has negotiated with creditors in good faith, and comply with state laws that authorize filing. These requirements ensure that bankruptcy is a last resort rather than a shortcut, and they impose a framework within which the budget must operate (McDonald et al., 2020). Debt restructuring often becomes central during the Chapter 9 bankruptcy process. Municipalities renegotiate principal and interest payments, extend maturities, or revisit labor and pension contracts. All these actions directly affect the expenditure side of budgets.

Once insolvency is declared or emergency measures are in place, governments must prioritize essential services. Budgeting under these circumstances often means reducing or suspending nonessential programs, renegotiating contracts, freezing capital projects, and cutting personnel costs. Some governments implement across-the-board reductions to signal fairness, while others make targeted cuts to preserve high-priority services. Research suggests that proportional cuts can promote efficiency by forcing agencies to function with fewer resources, but when slack has already been eliminated, further reductions may undermine organizational performance and erode capacity (Ermasova & Guzman, 2023; Guzman & Ermasova, 2023, 2025).

Transparency and credibility are also central to budgeting during fiscal crises. Residents, creditors, unions, and other stakeholders must be assured that sacrifices are necessary and that recovery is possible. Stakeholder engagement, particularly in negotiating debt adjustments or redefining service levels, can help legitimize unpopular budgetary choices. Without transparency, governments risk deepening distrust and provoking resistance to necessary reforms.

Budgeting under stress must also look beyond immediate survival. Long-term planning is critical for preventing repeated cycles of fiscal emergency. Exit strategies often include rebuilding reserves, restoring financial flexibility, and rebalancing revenues and expenditures to achieve structural balance. Even during bankruptcy, municipalities should still pursue capital projects, prioritizing infrastructure essential to economic recovery and deferring less urgent capital constructions.

Taxonomy of financial and budgeting practices during fiscal emergency and bankruptcy

The causes of fiscal stress and the process of exiting it have been well documented by Guzman and Ermasova (2023, 2025) and are shown in Figure 10.2. Although it takes years if not decades for the conditions causing fiscal stress to develop, municipalities start paying more serious attention to it and begin to introduce fiscal stress relief actions much later, when they realize that their fiscal situation worsens and they can no longer effectively balance their budgets or even pay their debts.

During the initial stage of fiscal emergency, Hazardous strategy, municipalities attempt to cut random expenditures, raise tax revenues, usually unsuccessfully

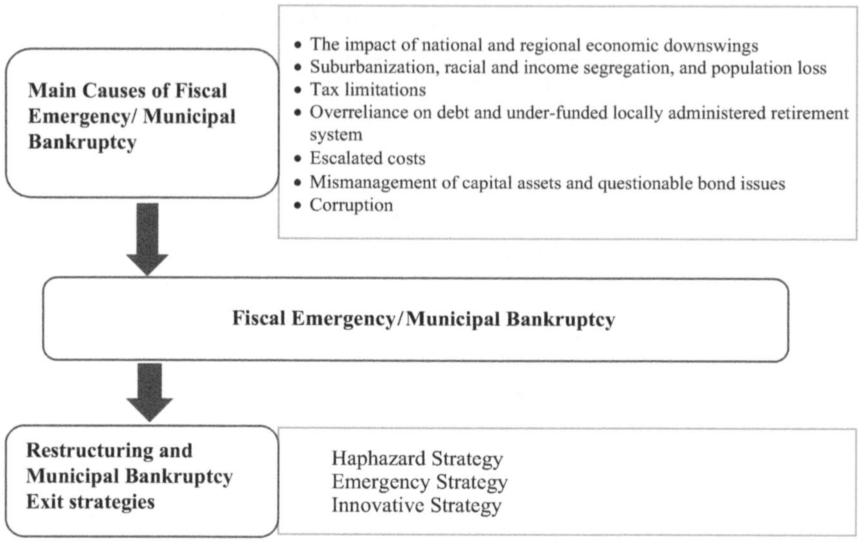

FIGURE 10.2 Taxonomy of financial and budgeting practices during fiscal emergency and bankruptcy

Source: Guzman and Ermasova (2025, p. 7)

due to state tax limitations, and renegotiate debt and other contractual obligations with their creditors (Guzman & Ermasova, 2023, 2025). Unfortunately, in this initial stage, the actions are quite disorganized, sometimes rushed and unthoughtful, and usually unsuccessful. Municipalities often do not engage in any innovative or transforming budgetary practices and continue to use old budgeting and administrative approaches that caused the financial problems in the first place.

In the second stage, Emergency strategy, municipalities often face an unexpected, and often disruptive external event that significantly alters an organization's operating environment and worsens situation even more. On a national or international scale, such relatively recent events were the Great Recession of 2007–2009, and Covid pandemic. On a local scale, such event can be a natural or a man-made disaster, or a departure of a major employer, for example. While such events affect all government entities, they hit those with underlying fiscal issues much harder, and municipalities find themselves in a fiscal-emergency or bankruptcy situation. During bankruptcy or fiscal emergency, municipalities resort to extreme budget cuts. This strategy cannot be a long-term solution though as municipalities need to deliver basic public services, particularly those related to safety, social insurance, and economic development. This stage is additionally characterized by positive changes in decision-making and budgeting, such as cost-saving public-private partnerships or collaborations between various departments or agencies.

The third stage, Innovative strategy, embraces the municipality's organizational, budgeting, and fiscal actions. During this stage, while still enduring a long and challenging path to recovery, municipalities no longer experience the pressures of bankruptcy and fiscal emergency. At this stage, municipalities develop new financial management, budgeting, and administrative principles. In this third stage, the studied municipalities establish new guiding budgeting principles to direct their budget decisions, maintain minimum reserves, create strategic five-year investment plans, and establish longer-term, often five-year financial forecasts. They rely on more conservative revenue estimates and adopt standard accounting practices. Collectively, such innovations lead to higher transparency and accountability in government operations. In this stage, municipalities also heavily invest in economic development, rebranding, initiating marketing campaigns to attract and retain younger residents, businesses, and hosting various big events. Resource scarcity can spur new approaches to capital planning to maximize public value with limited resources (Ermasova & Guzman, 2023).

In general, budgeting during a fiscal emergency and bankruptcy requires balancing immediate austerity with long-term sustainability. Governments must begin with an accurate diagnosis, operate within legal constraints, prioritize essential services, restructure debt, maintain transparency, and plan for recovery. While the process is filled with painful trade-offs, careful and thoughtful budgeting can stabilize operations, restore credibility, and ultimately return municipalities to fiscal health.

The following two case studies are from Milwaukee, WI, and the city of East Cleveland, OH. Milwaukee experienced its worst fiscal crisis in 177 years of history in 2022, with a budget deficit exceeding $200 million annually. The second case is from a small city in Ohio that many have probably never even heard of, East Cleveland, OH, which has been in a state of fiscal emergency for the longest in U.S. history.

References

Congressional Budget Office (2010). *Fiscal stress faced by local governments*. https://www.cbo.gov/sites/default/files/111th-congress-2009-2010/reports/12-09-municipalitiesbrief.pdf

Ermasova, N., & Guzman, T. (2023). Capital budgeting during municipal bankruptcy: Cases of Jefferson County, AL; Central Falls, RI; and Vallejo, CA. *State and Local Government Review*, *55*(4), 303–321.

Guzman, T., & Ermasova, N. (2023). *Municipal fiscal stress, bankruptcies, and other financial emergencies*. Routledge.

Guzman, T., & Ermasova, N. (2025). Causes and exit strategies from municipal fiscal stress and bankruptcy: A taxonomy. *Journal of Urban Affairs*, 1–30. https://doi.org/10.1080/07352166.2025.2548829

Hendrick, R. (2004). Assessing and measuring the fiscal heath of local governments: Focus on Chicago suburban municipalities. *Urban Affairs Review*, *40*(1), 78–114.

McDonald, H. M., Lawall, F. J., & Marsh, G. (2020). A Primer on Municipal Bankruptcy. *Pratt's Journal of Bankruptcy Law*, *16*, 371.

Moldogaziev, T. T., Kioko, S. N., & Hildreth, W. B. (2017). Impact of bankruptcy eligibility requirements and statutory liens on borrowing costs. *Public Budgeting & Finance*, *37*(4), 47–73.

CASE STUDY 22

Fiscal crisis and recovery in the City of Milwaukee, WI

Abstract

This case presents an analysis of fiscal crisis and recovery in the City of Milwaukee. It provides an analysis of the primary reasons for financial challenges, including rising pension obligations, declining state-shared revenues, and state-imposed limitations on local taxation. It examines the various approaches the City of Milwaukee employed to improve its financial position between 2023 and 2024. This case describes the collaborative recovery process and highlights the policy tools and strategic decisions that helped Milwaukee avoid bankruptcy and restore financial stability. This collaborative process resulted in a comprehensive, multi-year recovery strategy that incorporated innovative reforms in budgeting, diversified the city's revenue base, and strategic restructuring of pension and employee benefit systems.

Topics

Revenue Generation; Fiscal Stress; Local Government; Recovery; Fiscal Policy; Public Finance

Background

The City of Milwaukee is the largest municipality in Wisconsin and serves as the economic and cultural hub of the state's southeastern region. Like many major American cities, the City of Milwaukee experienced population decline for several decades. The historic peak of population (741,324) was in 1960 (City of Milwaukee, 2025). In 2000, the city's population had fallen to 596,974, a 19%

FIGURE 10.3 The Milwaukee art museum

Source: Photo provided by the authors

decline from 1960 levels. In 2025, Milwaukee's population was 560,124 (World Population Review, 2025). Milwaukee has experienced high levels of poverty in recent two decades. Since 2002, the city's poverty rate has remained above 20%, reflecting enduring socioeconomic challenges. In 2006, the poverty rate reached a peak of 26.2%, placing Milwaukee eighth in poverty level among U.S. cities with populations exceeding 250,000. Employment in Milwaukee varies significantly by ethnicity. In 2000, African Americans had the highest unemployment rate of any race at over 16%. Hispanics and American Indians both had rates around 12% and Asians and Whites had the lowest rates with 10% and 5%, respectively (City of Milwaukee, 2025).

Milwaukee has undergone decades of economic restructuring, contributing to population decline and a loss of its traditional tax base. Milwaukee transitioned toward a more diversified economy, in which the service sector, particularly healthcare, finance, insurance, and professional services, plays an increasingly central role.

Despite this diversification, manufacturing remains an important component of the local economy, with ongoing production of medical equipment, mining machinery, engines, electronics, and related goods, alongside continued activity in shipping and brewing-related industries. Milwaukee faces significant service demands related to aging infrastructure, public safety needs, and socioeconomic disparities among neighborhoods. These fiscal challenges have placed increasing pressure on the city's operating budget and pension obligations.

Fiscal crisis in Milwaukee, WI

The city's fiscal capacity has been constrained by state-imposed limits on property tax growth and a longstanding prohibition on local sales taxation. The State-Shared Revenue (SSR) system is a longstanding state program that redistributes state-collected revenues generated by sales, income, and excise taxes and sends them to local units of government to provide services. Over the past several decades, this revenue stream from the State of Wisconsin has either decreased or remained stagnant, with no adjustments for inflationary or cost-of-living increases.

In 2022, the City of Milwaukee faced one of the most serious fiscal crises in its 177-year history. A structural budget deficit was projected to exceed $200 million annually. Emergency federal relief funds provided during the COVID-19 pandemic offered temporary fiscal support; however, these resources were set to expire in 2025, heightening concerns about the city's long-term financial stability. In response, Milwaukee undertook a coordinated and methodical fiscal planning process. This effort was facilitated through a partnership involving the Mayor's Office, the City Council, the Greater Milwaukee Committee (GMC), and external fiscal strategy consultants from EY-Parthenon.

Recovery strategies

Milwaukee's recovery strategies align with the recommendations of Taxonomy of financial and budgeting practices during fiscal emergency and bankruptcy by Guzman and Ermasova (2023, 2025) and Ermasova and Guzman (2024). During the first stage, the Hazardous strategy, Milwaukee employed cutback practices and attempted to raise tax revenues (usually unsuccessfully due to state tax limitations). During the emergency strategy stage, Milwaukee implemented extreme budget cuts, attempted to raise tax rates or introduce new charges and fees, and continued to rely on traditional budgetary, financial, and administrative practices. This stage is also characterized by the initiation of positive changes in decision-making and budgeting, such as cost-saving public-private partnerships or collaborations between various departments or agencies.

The third stage, Innovative strategy, embraces Milwaukee's organizational, budgeting, and fiscal actions. During this innovative strategy stage, Milwaukee used budget reforms, cost-saving initiatives, and investments in economic development. Milwaukee established new guiding budgeting principles to direct its budget decisions, started maintaining minimum reserves, created strategic six-year investment plans, established more conservative revenue estimates, and improved transparency. A coordinated fiscal planning process was facilitated through a partnership among the Mayor's Office, the City Council, the GMC, and external fiscal strategy consultants. The City of Milwaukee partnered with advisors from EY-Parthenon to conduct a comprehensive financial review and develop potential recovery strategies. The team was composed of professionals with expertise in public sector finance, fiscal restructuring, policy analysis, taxation, pension planning, and data analytics. Members also had practical knowledge in areas such as real-estate transactions, renewable energy, waste management, and public health. Several team members had direct experience managing municipal budgets and were familiar with best practices used in other cities facing similar financial challenges. In collaboration with city officials, the team conducted a diagnostic review of the 50 most costly municipal services to identify opportunities for cost savings and revenue enhancement. The goal was to develop recommendations in three core areas: improving service delivery, strengthening financial planning, and building capacity for long-term innovation.

Team reviewed core service costs, evaluated pension structures, fee systems, and city-owned assets. Workshops and performance analysis tools were introduced to encourage employee-driven improvements and support ongoing efficiency initiatives. Benchmarking against peer cities confirmed that Milwaukee's fiscal challenges stemmed primarily from insufficient revenue, rather than excessive spending.

Revenue generating

In 2000, the City received $236.2 million in SSR, but in 2023, it received only $219.2 million. This $17 million decrease in nominal dollars equates to a $199 million decrease in real dollars after adjusting for the inflation that occurred in the intervening decades.

In 2024, the City received a 10% increase, or $21.9 million, over previously frozen SSR levels. In future years, the City's SSR distributions are expected to increase in alignment with increases in total statewide collections. The State Department of Revenue (DOR) has informed the City that in 2025, this increase will be 2.3%, or $5.55 million, above 2024 levels.

Milwaukee developed updated fines and forfeiture schedules and strengthened collection practices. For example, more than half of the projected $6 million transfer from the Transportation Fund is expected to come from new parking ticket and collection strategies.

Drawing on practices in other medium-sized and large cities, the EY team suggested new ways to generate revenue from city assets. These included selling advertising rights on trash containers, benches, and bus shelters, as well as exploring opportunities to generate income from parking assets, water systems, and even streetlighting.

The Wisconsin Legislature granted Milwaukee new authority to adjust its local tax structure, enabling the city to generate approximately $180 million annually in new revenue. After decades of being the largest city in the United States without either a local sales or income tax, the City of Milwaukee began collecting a 2% local sales tax on January 1, 2024 (City of Milwaukee, 2024). The City Comptroller estimated that this sales tax would be $192.9 million in 2025.

Service improvements

In the area of service improvement, the EY team identified 41 recommendations estimated to generate about $140 million in savings over ten years (EY Parthenon, 2025). The recommendations involved a wide range of city services, including fire, health, police, public works, neighborhood services, and the public library. Recommendations included consolidating certain services with Milwaukee County (such as greenhouses and tree nurseries), outsourcing tasks like leaf collection and street sweeping to external contractors to increase efficiency, and introducing new incentive systems to lower fleet maintenance costs. The team highlighted how technology could be used to streamline functions such as street and garbage maintenance.

The team identified several financial planning strategies. The project proposed alternative uses for several city-owned buildings and facilities. For example, it suggested selling the aging fleet and recycling facilities located on valuable riverfront property and constructing more modern facilities elsewhere (EY Parthenon, 2025). This approach could generate a one-time revenue boost from the sale, increase long-term tax revenues from new development on the site, and reduce operating costs with more efficient facilities. The team identified three centrally located government office buildings that could be consolidated into two. The third building could then be redeveloped into rental housing or private office space, creating an ongoing revenue source for the city.

The team recommended consolidating the maintenance and operations staff for the city's 20 staffed drawbridges, revising the service model for public health clinics to improve services while reducing expenses, modifying overtime policies, and implementing a 10% cost-recovery fee for special events such as parades (EY Parthenon, 2025).

With more than $200 million in projected new revenue, city leaders were in a position to consider where to invest, rather than where to cut. Total capital spending in the proposed 2024 budget is $344.9 million, an 18.4% increase from the $291.4 million approved in 2023. Of this amount, $193.8 million represents city-funded capital improvements (those not supported by grants or other external sources), which is $29.7 million (18.2%) higher than the current year (City of Milwaukee, 2023).

The proposed 2025 capital budget includes several major new items, such as:

- $40 million project to replace police and fire radios;
- $8.6 million toward the $28 million total cost of replacing the City's outdated ERP system, which supports human resources and financial management;
- $17 million for completion of the port cruise dock terminal.

During strategic reforms, a municipal Innovation Director position was created. A new performance accountability system was designed to ensure efficiency improvements. These organizational changes helped establish a culture of continuous improvement throughout the city's departments.

Conclusions

Milwaukee's case shows that the city's fiscal crisis was driven more by long-term revenue constraints than by excessive spending. State laws limited the city's ability to raise revenue, while SSR remained stagnant for decades. This created a structural imbalance that could not be solved through budget cuts alone.

Milwaukee's experience demonstrates that structural fiscal challenges require comprehensive solutions rather than short-term cuts. In addition to outlining specific revenue and cost-reduction strategies, the project identified priority areas and estimated both the potential savings and the time frame in which those savings could be realized. It highlights the value of cross-sector collaboration, data-driven analysis, employee engagement, and revenue diversification.

The innovative approach serves as a model for other municipalities seeking to achieve fiscal stability and sustain essential public services through strategic budgeting and administrative reforms.

Discussion questions

1 Was Milwaukee's fiscal crisis primarily a revenue problem, a spending problem, or both?
2 How did political and legal constraints shape the city's available choices?
3 Which stakeholder group (state government, city leaders, EY consulting team, frontline employees) was most influential during decision-making?
4 Which elements of the reform plan do you find most appropriate, and which do you consider problematic? Provide justification for your position.
5 What are the potential benefits and risks of monetizing city-owned assets or expanding user fees? Under what conditions might these strategies be appropriate or risky?

6 In what ways does Milwaukee's case demonstrate the importance of long-term financial planning and capacity-building within city government?
7 How does this case illustrate the value of intergovernmental cooperation in fiscal recovery?

References

City of Milwaukee (2023). Budget brief 2024 proposed City of Milwaukee Budget.

City of Milwaukee (2024). Proposed plan and executive budget summary.

City of Milwaukee (2025). Demographics and data. https://city.milwaukee.gov/ImageLibrary/Groups/cityDCD/planning/plans/Citywide/plan/Data.pdf

Ermasova, N., & Guzman, T. (2024). Approaches to solutions of municipal fiscal distress: A descriptive case of Matteson, Illinois. *Illinois Municipal Policy Journal, 9*(11), 1–22.

EY Parthenon (2025). How an American city tackled a major budget gap. https://www.ey.com/en_gl/insights/strategy-transactions/how-an-american-city-tackled-a-major-budget-gap

Guzman, T., & Ermasova, N. (2023). Municipal fiscal stress, bankruptcies, and other financial emergencies. Routledge.

Guzman, T., & Ermasova, N. (2025). Causes and exit strategies from municipal fiscal stress and bankruptcy: A taxonomy. *Journal of Urban Affairs*. https://doi.org/10.1080/07352166.2025.2548829

World Population Review. (2025). Milwaukee.https://worldpopulationreview.com/us-cities/wisconsin/milwaukee

CASE STUDY 23

Fiscal emergency in East Cleveland

Abstract

The city of East Cleveland, Ohio, has spent nearly 30 of the last 37 years under state-declared fiscal emergency. This case study explores how structural economic decline, institutional failure, administrative turnover, and corruption undermined the city's ability to achieve financial recovery despite decades of state oversight. East Cleveland's experience illustrates how fiscal-emergency frameworks can falter when local governments lack the political stability and administrative capacity necessary to implement recovery plans.

Topics

Fiscal Emergency; Fiscal Oversight; Budget Techniques; Corruption; Governance Failure; White Flight

Background

The city of East Cleveland, Ohio, has been in fiscal emergency perhaps the longest in U.S. history. Once regarded as a model inner-ring suburb with strong schools, stable neighborhoods, easily accessible public transportation, and robust municipal services, the city has now become synonymous with poverty, corruption, failing infrastructure, and overall fiscal decline. It first entered a state-declared fiscal emergency in 1988, exited briefly in 2006, and re-entered fiscal emergency in 2012, where it remains today (Ohio Auditor of State, 2024). Despite repeated state oversight, multiple recovery plans, and decades of state fiscal monitoring, East Cleveland has been unable to regain financial stability.

In the early 20th century, East Cleveland, a three-square-mile inner-ring suburb of the city of Cleveland, OH, embodied the aspirations of many American suburbs. The city expanded rapidly in the 1910s, 1920s, and 1930s as middle-class residents moved into newly built neighborhoods near Cleveland's streetcar lines. General Electric's Nela Park, the nation's first planned industrial park, became a major employer, while Huron Hospital served as another economic anchor (Case Western Reserve University, 2020; Guzman, 2026). The world's first billionaire and the founder of the Standard Oil Company, John D. Rockefeller, owned a summer estate in East Cleveland at the dawn of the 20th century. His son John D. Rockefeller Jr. built 81 Norman-style homes in the city in the 1930s (Cleveland Historical, n.d.). The population peaked at roughly 40,000 by 1950.

By the 1960s, however, East Cleveland began to experience rapid racial and socioeconomic transitions. Black residents started moving into the city seeking better living and work opportunities, while the white population began to leave, responding to racial integration and fearing falling home prices. The segregation and white flight were further accelerated by realtors who engaged in blockbusting and steering practices[1] to encourage more real-estate sales (Keating, 1994). East Cleveland's racial composition changed from 2% Black in 1960 to 94% Black in 1990. As middle-income households departed, the tax base weakened, home values declined, and poverty increased. At the same time, the aging housing stock required more intensive maintenance than the city could afford. According to Keating (1994), the absence of strong community organizations and a failure by city leadership to confront discriminatory real-estate practices further intensified the city's deepening instability.

FIGURE 10.4 Nela Park in East Cleveland

Source: Photo by Alex Philip

East Cleveland's first fiscal emergency and crisis

These socioeconomic downfalls culminated in East Cleveland's first fiscal emergency in 1988 after the Ohio Auditor of State found that the city carried severe general-fund deficits, negative fund balances, and serious accounting failures (Ohio Auditor of State, 2002). A state-appointed Financial Planning and Supervision Commission attempted to guide the city's recovery, but its efforts were repeatedly hindered by political turnover, administrative weakness, and limited coordination among departments (Guzman, 2026). Audit reports documented persistent internal control failures, unrealistic revenue projections, and the absence of long-term financial planning. Although the city managed to exit fiscal emergency in 2006 after balancing its budget for two consecutive years, the recovery was weak, built on borrowing to finance city's current operations.

The Great Recession quickly exposed the fragility of East Cleveland's fiscal position. Income and property tax revenues, two major sources of the city's own revenues, declined by 13.5% and 54.4%, respectively, between 2008 and 2013 (Guzman, 2026). Population loss accelerated, with only 13,792 residents remaining by 2020. Poverty rose to more than 44% (U.S. Census Bureau, 2020). These demographic and fiscal pressures, the accumulation of nearly $6 million in debt obligations and a structural budget deficit, combined with the city's failure to file financial reports on time, led to the reinstatement of a fiscal emergency in 2012 (Ohio Auditor of State, 2022).

Governance instability and fiscal crisis in East Cleveland

Governance instability played a central role in prolonging the city's fiscal emergency. East Cleveland has experienced a succession of political scandals and administrative failures that have consistently undermined recovery efforts. Mayor Emmanuel Onunwor, who held office from 1998 to 2004, was convicted on 22 federal counts of racketeering, bribery, mail fraud, and tax evasion in 2005 (U.S. Department of Justice, 2005). His departure was followed by years of political dysfunction, including the loss of reelection by Mayor Eric Brewer in 2009 due to his provocative photos resurfacing online, recall of Mayor Gary Norton in 2016, and the suspension and eventual conviction of Mayor Brandon King in 2025 on multiple charges including theft in office and filing false disclosures (Carey, 2025). In the first half of 2025 alone, the city cycled through three different mayors, reflecting profound instability in executive leadership (Guzman, 2026; St. Clair, 2025).

Administrative capacity eroded alongside political stability even further. East Cleveland's finance department frequently lacked a permanent director, and state officials repeatedly described the city's financial records as "inauditable" due to missing documentation, errors in bookkeeping, and a failure to reconcile accounts (Castele, 2019; Ohio Auditor of State, 2022). These deficiencies prevented the city from producing reliable budgets or complying with state recovery requirements (Guzman, 2026). In the mid-1980s, three city commissioners, the municipal judge, and the finance director were convicted of bribery and misappropriation of funds. East Cleveland Director of Community Development was convicted of various misdemeanors in 2004, and the City's Chief of Staff was convicted in 2025 (Guzman, 2026). Between 2018 and 2022, 16 current or former police officers were indicted on charges of assault, dereliction of duty, and theft in office in the city whose entire police department had 20 active police officers in 2023 (Haidet et al., 2023). The last three police chiefs resigned or were removed from the office for misconduct and tax fraud. The city owes tens of millions of dollars in police misconduct settlements (Guzman, 2026).

As revenues contracted and governance capacity declined, East Cleveland increasingly relied on budget cuts (Guzman, 2026). Over time, this has led to the deterioration of infrastructure and city services. Reports described potholes left unfilled for months if not years, chronic water-system leakage, and widespread blight as vacant lots and abandoned homes multiplied (Castele, 2015; Guzman, 2026). Public-safety response times slowed as the number of fires in abandoned structures increased (Zook, 2009). Crime rates rose well above state averages, with East Cleveland's violent crime rate more than five times higher than that in Ohio overall (NeighborhoodScout, n.d.). In the absence of sustainable revenue sources, the city turned to punitive strategies such as aggressive traffic-camera enforcement and one-time revenues such as the sale of land to Arco Recycling. The latter decision resulted in one of the largest illegal construction dumps in Ohio history and required a $9 million cleanup funded largely by state taxpayers (Castele, 2019; Guzman, 2026).

Other distressed municipalities in the United States (such as Jefferson County, AL; Detroit, MI; or Pittsburgh, PA) have often responded to fiscal stress by pursuing intergovernmental collaboration, service sharing, or consolidation (Kim & Warner 2016; Guzman & Ermasova, 2023, 2025). East Cleveland's attempts at regional collaboration, including discussions of merging with the City of Cleveland in 2016, or the 2009 attempt to regionalize its fire and emergency services, stalled because of concerns about the city's liabilities, corruption scandals, and administrative instability (Guzman, 2026). The departure of the city's major employers, including Huron Hospital in 2011 and General Electric in 2022, further weakened the city's ability to attract investment or form partnerships.

By 2025, after repeated failures to implement viable recovery plans, the Ohio Auditor of State announced that the office would seek a court-ordered receivership to assume control of the city's finances (Ohio Auditor of State, 2025). This unprecedented step for Ohio signaled that East Cleveland's challenges were not merely financial but institutional. A receiver would have powers that local officials lacked, including the authority to renegotiate labor contracts, restructure debt, reorganize municipal operations, and impose fiscal controls independent of local politics.

Conclusions

East Cleveland's prolonged distress illustrates the limitations of state fiscal-emergency frameworks when local governance capacity collapses. The city's experience demonstrates how structural decline, corruption, administrative turnover, and extensive and prolonged budget cuts can combine to erode a municipality's ability to deliver services, maintain infrastructure, and plan for the future. It also raises questions about what obligations states have in supporting deeply distressed municipalities and what tools might be necessary to ensure both financial stability and democratic accountability. Ultimately, the case highlights that fiscal emergencies are not solely technical problems but institutional ones, and that recovery may require not only financial reforms but also comprehensive organizational overhaul.

Discussion questions

1 To what extent was East Cleveland's fiscal emergency the result of structural forces such as demographic transition, economic decline, and the loss of major employers, and to what extent was it shaped by internal governance failures, including corruption and weak administrative capacity?
2 How effective can a fiscal-emergency framework be in circumstances where a municipality lacks the institutional capacity or political stability to implement recovery plans? Should states revise their oversight models in response to cases like East Cleveland?
3 What are the long-term consequences of prolonged austerity for municipal service delivery, public trust, and economic recovery, and how might austerity itself contribute to a downward spiral in distressed cities?
4 Should the state pursue receivership, consolidation, or regional service sharing as tools for addressing extreme municipal distress, and what implications would such interventions have?

Note

1 Blockbusting is the practice where real-estate agents deliberately fueled racial anxieties by suggesting that Black families were moving into a neighborhood to pressure white homeowners to sell quickly, usually at below-market price.
Steering is the practice where real-estate agents directed buyers toward or away from specific neighborhoods based on race.

References

Carey, T. (2025, February 21). East Cleveland mayor, chief of staff Michael Smedley indicted in alleged bribery scheme involving fake "royals." *WKYC*. https://www.wkyc.com/article/news/local/cuyahoga-county/east-cleveland-mayor-chief-of-staff-michael-smedley-indicted-alleged-bribery-scheme-charges-fake-royals/95-4b8a0ffe-84c1-407d-b7c8-c3e204d816b9

Case Western Reserve University. (2020). East Cleveland. *Encyclopedia of Cleveland History*. https://ech.case.edu/cgi/article.pl?id=EC

Castele, N. (2015, March 26). East Cleveland shaves its barebones services down to slivers. *Ideastream Public Media.*

Castele, N. (2019, April 22). Trash piled up in East Cleveland for years. Why was it so hard to clean up? *Ideastream Public Media.* https://indepth.ideastream.org/east-cleveland-dump/

Cleveland Historical. (n.d.). Forest Hill Park. Cleveland State University. https://clevelandhistorical.org/items/show/83

Guzman, T. (2026). Theory and practice of decision-making in state and local governments during fiscal stress: The case of East Cleveland. *Public Finance and Management*, 25(1–2), 41–53.

Guzman, T., & Ermasova, N. (2023). *Municipal fiscal stress, bankruptcies, and other financial emergencies.* Routledge.

Guzman, T., & Ermasova, N. (2025). Causes and exit strategies from municipal fiscal stress and bankruptcy: A taxonomy. *Journal of Urban Affairs*. https://doi.org/10.1080/07352166.2025.2548829

Haidet, R., Meyer, A., Fischer, N., & DeNatale, D. (2023, March 8). 11 current and former East Cleveland police officers indicted on criminal charges. *WKYC*. https://www.wkyc.com/article/news/crime/east-cleveland-police-officers-indicted-criminal-charges-cuyahoga-county-prosecutor-michael-omalley/95-296e3073-adf2-4b6e-a19f-4329765f06de

Keating, D. W. (1994). *The suburban racial dilemma: Housing and neighborhoods.* Temple University Press.

Kim, Y., & Warner, M. (2016). Pragmatic municipalism: Local government adaptation in an era of austerity. *Urban Affairs Review, 52*(1), 163–195.

NeighborhoodScout. (n.d.). Crime rates for East Cleveland, OH. https://www.neighborhoodscout.com/oh/east-cleveland/crime

Ohio Auditor of State. (2002). *City of East Cleveland performance audit.* https://ohioauditor.gov/auditsearch/Reports/2002/city_of_east_cleveland_02_performance-cuyahoga.pdf

Ohio Auditor of State. (2022). *City of East Cleveland: Findings for recovery and material weaknesses.*

Ohio Auditor of State. (2025, September 29). Auditor Faber to request emergency receivership for the City of East Cleveland. https://ohioauditor.gov/news/pressreleases/Details/7704

St. Clair, J. (2025, February 28). Sandra Morgan appointed interim mayor of East Cleveland. *Ideastream Public Media.* https://www.ideastream.org/government-politics/2025-02-28/sandra-morgan-appointed-interim-mayor-of-east-cleveland

U.S. Census Bureau. (2020). East Cleveland city, Ohio. https://data.census.gov

U.S. Department of Justice. (2005, August 19). Former East Cleveland Mayor Emmanuel Onunwor sentenced to 9 years in prison. https://www.justice.gov/archive/usao/ohm/

Zook, D. (2009). *Reducing the risks of abandoned buildings in East Cleveland,* Ohio. FEMA. https://apps.usfa.fema.gov/pdf/efop/efo44006.pdf

11

ECONOMIC INCENTIVES, ECONOMIC DEVELOPMENT, AND THEIR REVENUE IMPACT IN LOCAL GOVERNMENTS

Abstract

This chapter analyzes the economic incentives used by local governments in the United States. It examines local economic development and its importance for communities, businesses, tax revenues, and sustainable growth. This chapter examines various incentive mechanisms, including tax abatements, tax increment financing, sales tax sharing agreements, enterprise zones, low-interest loan programs, infrastructure grants, investment and job credits, and loan guarantees.

Introduction

The purpose of economic development is to build and stimulate a municipality's potential, to provide for a better economic future, and to improve the quality of life of residents (Kisman & Tasar, 2014). It is important to establish connections between the intentions of local governments to develop a municipality with the creation of favorable conditions for business activity (Walzer, 2009). Main economic development instruments may include local tax incentives, facilitation of networks between investors and business support institutions, collaboration with research and development entities, and improvements to the technical and social infrastructure. Economic development depends on the availability and quality of investment-ready land, efficient administrative services, a supportive local business climate, and the development of a skilled workforce through access to education and training. Economic incentives aim to encourage business location and expansion, stimulate redevelopment of underutilized areas, and promote job creation.

DOI: 10.4324/9781003606833-12

Economic incentives for local economic development

Economic incentives are designed to attract, retain, and expand business activity within a community by reducing the costs of private investment or by improving the overall business environment. According to Peters and Fisher (2004), economic incentives serve as tools for municipalities to compete for investment, employment, and tax base growth in an increasingly globalized and competitive marketplace.

Local governments provide a variety of financial incentives for economic development, such as tax abatements, tax increment financing (TIF), sales tax sharing agreements, enterprise zones, low-interest loans, grants for infrastructure improvements, credits for investment or job creation, and loan guarantees, among others.

Tax abatement is a local agreement between a taxpayer and a taxing unit that exempts a business from property taxation for five to ten years, based on local legislature.

TIF laws permit local governments to designate TIF districts for the redevelopment of areas that meet the "blight" criteria and provide tax incentives to businesses for locating in impoverished neighborhoods. When local government creates a TIF district, the property tax revenues from the TIF district are divided into two streams: (1) the first stream is secured to the original property values or "base value" before the redevelopment takes place; property taxes collected on this "based value" continue to go to the city, county, school district, and other taxing bodies as before TIF district was created: (2) the second stream contains the increases in property tax revenues that were resulting from the redevelopment, the "tax increment" (Talanker et al., 2003). This second stream of incremental revenues subsidizes the redevelopment in the TIF district and/or is dedicated to paying off bonds that are issued to finance their development projects. TIF funds can pay for land acquisition through eminent domain, for building new infrastructure such as streets and facilities, and for site preparation and construction. Some local governments have used TIF to clean up contaminated "brownfield" areas. Improvement in the infrastructure will increase the value of land and make the area more attractive for development. When development takes place, it will likely raise the assessed value of the property and bring more "tax increment." A TIF will only become successful if it generates growth in property value and thus must generate revenue streams for the territory within itself. TIF essentially relies on the appreciation of land value in its territory; the increase of property value within a TIF accounts for the "increment" money available to use for paying debt service or generating funds to pay for economic development projects.

A sales tax sharing agreement, also known as a rebate sharing agreement, is an arrangement made by a local government (municipality or county) to share or rebate any portion of retailers' occupation taxes generated by retail sales.

By sharing a portion of the sales tax revenue, local governments can encourage business retention, expansion, and new investment, while businesses are incentivized to reinvest the rebated funds into local economic activities, such as facility improvements, infrastructure development, or job creation initiatives.

Enterprise Zones offer businesses a combination of tax incentives, financial assistance, and regulatory flexibility designed to attract investment and stimulate job creation. Many municipalities have incorporated Enterprise Zones as a central component of their long-term economic development strategies. Empirical evidence indicates that these zones can effectively stimulate local economic activity, promote regional collaboration, and enhance the overall business climate. Main benefits of Enterprise Zones include property tax abatements for qualifying businesses to reduce operating costs, sales tax exemptions on building materials for construction and renovation projects, investment tax credits, infrastructure improvements that modernize key commercial areas and enhance their appeal to new and existing enterprises. Many municipalities participate in multi-jurisdictional Enterprise Zones that serve as regional economic development partnerships. Within such zones, fiscal incentives are strategically employed to attract and retain businesses by improving financial feasibility and reducing barriers to investment.

Local governments can stimulate economic development by offering *low-interest loans* to support business creation, expansion, and retention. These financing opportunities are often made possible through partnerships with federal and state programs that provide capital for local initiatives. One example is the U.S. Department of Agriculture's (USDA) Intermediary Relending Program, which provides 1% low-interest loans to local lenders or "intermediaries" that re-lend to businesses to improve economic conditions and create jobs in rural communities (USDA, 2025). Similarly, the U.S. Economic Development Administration supports local lending through its Revolving Loan Fund program, which supplies capital to eligible local entities for the purpose of assisting businesses seeking to start up or expand operations. Some studies indicate that credits for jobs can generate employment at reasonable costs. Positive effects have been documented for customized job training programs (Hollenbeck, 2008; Holzer et al., 1993).

Grants for infrastructure improvements are government funds intended for municipal projects that aim to upgrade or expand communities through land or infrastructure improvements. One example of these grants is the ST.A.R. Business Grant Program of the Village of Mundelein, IL. The ST.A.R. Business Grant Program is intended to help businesses overcome hardships and needs that they could not otherwise undertake without financial assistance. Businesses may apply by submitting a proposal for a project that addresses the specific hardship or needs of that business (Village of Mundelein, 2025). Examples of project grants include several major categories: (1) economic development grants to provide financial assistance for initiatives that support community improvement, business expansion, or local revitalization; (2) Community Development Block Grants (CDBG) to fund projects related to housing, infrastructure, and urban renewal, often with a focus on benefiting low- and moderate-income populations; (3) green infrastructure and environmental protection grants to support projects that address environmental concerns such as land, air, water, or energy conservation, while encouraging sustainable and environmentally responsible development; and (4) surface transportation program grants to assist local governments with the maintenance, repair, and improvement of roadways that are part of the federal highway system.

Local governments in the United States can encourage economic development through various *investment tax credits*, including the federal Opportunity Zones program, which incentivizes investment in distressed areas through tax benefits on capital gains. Opportunity Zones are an economic development tool that allows people to invest in distressed areas in the United States. Their purpose is to spur economic growth and job creation in low-income communities while providing tax benefits to investors. One example is the Kankakee Riverfront Opportunity Zone in Kankakee (Economic Alliance of Kankakee County, 2025). Some municipalities offer free or discounted building permits and inspection fees based on local authority policies in Opportunity Zones.

Local governments use loan guarantees to stimulate economic development by using *federal programs* like the U.S. Department of Housing and Urban Development Section 108 Loan Guarantee Program and the USDA loan guarantee programs. The Section 108 Loan Guarantee Program provides CDBG recipients with the ability to leverage their annual grant allocation to access low-cost, flexible financing for economic development, housing, public facility, and infrastructure projects (HUD Exchange, 2025). The Section 108 Loan Guarantee Program (Section 108) provides communities with a source of low-cost, long-term financing for economic and community development projects to create an avenue for municipalities to undertake larger, more costly projects, where they may have limited resources to invest in upfront.

Local governments may also provide non-financial economic incentives through streamlining permit issuance processes, technical assistance, and workforce development partnerships. These incentives reduce barriers to investment and enhance local competitiveness. Many non-tax incentives, such as a city using general funds to build a road to a new plant, are hidden (Peters & Fisher, 2004).

Challenges of economic incentives

The use of economic incentives requires careful design and evaluation. Mattera et al. (2014) argued that many incentives subsidize low-wage jobs and go to large, profitable companies. Targeted economic incentives are often described as "picking winners," but this approach can lead to supporting suboptimal businesses due to political lobbying or limited knowledge of which investments yield the highest returns. Favoring less productive firms may distort investment and hinder economic growth, while political factors can encourage businesses to focus more on lobbying than on productive activities (Bartik, 2017).

Overreliance on incentives may lead to fiscal stress, particularly when benefits, such as job creation or increased tax revenues, fail to materialize. Competition among municipalities can result in a "race to the bottom," in which local governments offer increasingly generous subsidies to attract businesses, often with limited regional or long-term benefits (Bartik, 2017). According to Peters and Fisher (2004), states and cities have created a system of taxes and incentives that offers little clear motivation for firms to invest in areas with higher unemployment, and it is likely that investment returns would have favored the least distressed locations.

Economic incentives differ substantially across states. In many instances, states offer more generous economic incentives than neighboring states, even when their economic conditions are comparable and business tax burdens are similar or lower (Bartik, 2017). These variations appear to be shaped more by a state's political culture and historical practices than by its economic or fiscal circumstances. For example, in North Carolina, South Carolina, and Georgia, larger incentives are offered to businesses locating in lower-income rural counties than in the larger and wealthier cities of Charlotte, Columbia, and Atlanta. For state and local incentive competition to yield net benefits at the national level, the gains to communities attracting jobs must outweigh the losses to communities that would otherwise have received them (Peters & Fisher, 2004). This outcome is more likely when economic incentives are directed toward low-income populations, who benefit more from job growth than residents of low-unemployment or middle-income areas.

However, persisting with conventional incentive-based economic development policies risks creating a perpetual cycle of tax cuts and subsidies, which ultimately deprives governments of fiscal resources needed to provide essential services and increases the regressivity of state and local tax systems.

Conclusions

Targeted economic development tools align public fiscal policy with private investment to stimulate commercial activity, enhance the local tax base, and promote sustained community growth. Reducing unemployment or poverty provides an additional rationale for economic incentives.

Economic incentives serve as catalysts for business investment, leading to job creation and the stimulation of local demand for goods and services. This process generates multiplier effects that contribute to sustained economic growth within the community. The second rationale for providing economic incentives is their potential to expand the local revenue base. As economic activity improves, municipal revenues from taxes and fees typically increase, enabling local governments to enhance public service provision or reduce tax rates while maintaining fiscal stability.

Economic incentives can stimulate business investment by creating new jobs, industrial diversification, and increasing local demand for goods and services. This growth expands public revenues, enabling either enhanced public services or reduced tax rates. Economic incentives can serve as a catalyst for local economic transformation, particularly when aligned with broader development goals such as workforce enhancement, innovation, environmental sustainability, and community revitalization.

The following four case studies discuss various economic incentives, their impact and limitations. The case of South Holland, IL examines the city's longstanding blue laws. The case of Cleveland, OH explores the largest TIF district in U.S. history. The case of Matteson, IL is a simulation game in which students assume the roles of the village's board of trustees' members, department chairs, and residents and are invited to introduce various revenue generation and cost saving options to improve the village's fiscal position. The case of Bradley, IL similarly discusses various economic development tools and revenue-side budgeting strategies the village used to improve its fiscal situation

References

Bartik, T. J. (2017). A new panel database on business incentives for economic development offered by state and local governments in the United States. Prepared for the Pew Charitable Trusts. W.E. Upjohn Institute for Employment Research. https://research.upjohn.org/reports/225

Economic Alliance of Kankakee County (2025). News & Events. Retrieved from https://kankakeecountyed.org/about-us/news-and-updates/

Hollenbeck, K. (2008). Is there a role for public support of incumbent worker on-the-job training? Upjohn Institute Working Paper No. 08–138. W.E. Upjohn Institute for Employment Research.

Holzer, H. J., Block, R. N., Cheatham, M., & Knott, J. H. (1993). Are training subsidies for firms effective? The Michigan experience. *Industrial and Labor Relations Review*, *46*(4), 625–636.

HUD Exchange (2025). Section 108 Loan Guarantee Program. https://www.hudexchange.info/programs/section-108/

Kisman, Z. A., & Tasar, I. (2014). The key element of local development. *Procedia Economics and Finanse*, *15*, 1689–1696.

Mattera, P., Tarczynska, K., & LeRoy, G. (2014). *Tax breaks and inequality enriching billionaires and low-road employers in the name of economic development*. Good Jobs First.

Peters, A. H., & Fisher, P. S. (2004). The failures of economic development incentives. *Journal of the American Planning Association, 70*(1), 27–37.

Talanker, A., Davis, K. & LeRoy, G. (2003). Straying from good intentions: How States are weakening enterprise zone and tax increment financing programs. *Good job first.* https://www.goodjobsfirst.org/sites/default/files/docs/pdf/straying.pdf

USDA (2025). Rural development business programs. https://www.rd.usda.gov/programs-services/business-programs/intermediary-relending-program

Village of Mundelein (2025). STAR business grant pilot program. https://www.mundelein.org/165/STAR-Business-Grant-Pilot-Program

Walzer, N., (ed.) (2009). *Entrepreneurship and local economic development.* Lexington Books, United Kingdom.

CASE STUDY 24

Economic development incentives and limitations and their impacts on revenues: Case of South Holland, IL

Abstract

This case presents an analysis of changes to Blue Laws (Sunday-closing laws, Sunday statutes) in the United States. It provides a history of Blue Laws in South Holland, IL. Between 2009 and 2015, the Village of South Holland's Blue Law evolved from a strict retail closure policy into a modern ordinance focusing on residential peace and selective professional activity. This change reflects the Village's balance between honoring its historic Sunday traditions and responding to the economic and social needs of the community. This Case shows how Blue Laws impact economic development based on local government in Illinois (South Holland). The intent of this Case study is to conduct an empirical evaluation of the impact of limitations (Blue Laws) and incentives on economic development in South Holland, IL.

Topics

Revenue Generation; Limitations on Revenue Generation; Blue Laws; Economic Development; Local Government; Fiscal Policy

Introduction

The historical development of South Holland distinguishes itself from the broader transformation of Chicago's southern suburbs over the past century. Originally established in 1847 by Dutch settlers along the Calumet River, the community initially known as "De Laage Prairie" ("Low Prairie") evolved into what is now the Village of South Holland. Incorporated in 1894 with an estimated population of 1,000 residents, South Holland experienced significant demographic growth in the post-World War II era. The population increased from approximately 3,000 in 1950 to nearly 10,000 by 1960, fueled by the postwar baby boom and the village's reputation as a small, family-oriented community. Many families from Chicago neighborhoods such as Englewood, Riverdale, and Roseland were drawn to South Holland for its strong religious foundations and perception of safety and stability. As migration intensified, developers capitalized on the village's expansive farmland and open spaces, converting them into residential subdivisions. The construction of Interstates 57 and 94 further enhanced connectivity to employment opportunities in downtown Chicago, accelerating South Holland's transition from an agrarian settlement to a suburban community.

Despite suburbanization, South Holland's residents preserved the religious ethos established by the Dutch founders. Currently, the village contains 33 churches and over 30 parks within its seven square miles, a density that led to the formal adoption of the slogan "A Community of Churches" in 1976. This religious character shaped local policy, including the enactment of stringent Blue Laws prohibiting business operations on Sundays. Zoning ordinances further reinforced the community's preference for single-family residences by restricting the construction of multifamily housing. Since the 1980s, South Holland's population has stabilized at roughly 22,000 residents, with notable demographic shifts. African Americans now comprise approximately 78% of the village's population, reflecting broader suburban migration trends in the Chicago metropolitan area. Today, South Holland continues to define its civic identity through the guiding principles encapsulated in its official motto: "Faith, Family, and Future."

The Blue Laws ordinance was adopted in South Holland in 1959. Having this ordinance in place prevents the mayor from allowing major restaurants and businesses that serve alcohol in the village. Due to the restrictions of the Blue Laws, it has impeded the village's possible revenue-generating sources. Moreover, the ordinance cuts into what could have brought in major revenue and possibly made South Holland a desired venue of choice for people dining out and other adult activities where alcohol is served.

History of Blue Laws

The term Blue Laws (Sunday-closing laws, Sunday statutes) commonly refers to the prohibition of a variety of activities on Sundays, ranging from liquor sales to hunting to car-buying. Many blue laws are county and city ordinances, though some are statewide statutes. Blue laws are unique because they impose criminal sanctions on what is generally regarded as legitimate commercial enterprise, merely because such commerce occurs on a particular day of the week. Because they are used to restrict activities on Sundays, Blue Laws in the United States are also known as Sunday laws. Most have been enacted at local or state levels, and most were intended to protect Sunday as a day of rest and religious worship. "Despite their connection with the Christian Sabbath, the Supreme Court of the United States has many times ruled them constitutional, though some have been overturned by the courts" (Holzwarth 2020, p. 1). Therefore, the laws are generally presumed to be a valid exercise of power.

Litigation over Sunday laws was common throughout the 19th century and the first half of the 20th century. By 1961, in the state of Maryland, blue laws made illegal "all labour, business, and other commercial activities on Sunday." There were some exceptions: the state law allowed the sale of "foodstuffs, automobile and boating accessories, flowers, toilet goods, hospital supplies, and souvenirs." In 1961, the U.S. Supreme Court issued four opinions that rejected challenges to Sunday laws in Maryland, Pennsylvania, and Massachusetts on the basis of the equal-protection clause of the 14th Amendment and the religious-liberty clauses of the First Amendment. In 1961, the United States Supreme Court finding that "they bear no relationship to the establishment of religion as those words are used in the Constitution" (Holzwarth, 2020, p. 3). Since 1961, legal actions at the state level have eliminated blue laws in many states. Most remaining blue laws regulate alcohol sales, but the number of states with such laws is declining. In 2022, 28 states had some kind of alcohol sales restrictions on Sundays (World Population Review, 2022).

Blue Laws in the Village of South Holland, IL

Blue Laws were adopted in the Village of South Holland, IL, where strong religious roots were fashioned after the Dutch Reformed traditions. The purpose of the Blue Laws was to preserve one day of rest. Because Sunday is typically a Christian's day of rest many of the Blue Laws were originally created explicitly to accommodate Sunday worship services. This ordinance prohibits the sale of most goods and services on Sunday except for a few necessities such as medicine, gasoline, and emergency repairs. South Holland's ordinance was modeled after a similar law in Evanston, IL after their original ordinance was struck down by the state supreme court in 1965. Because South Holland is a community of family, faith, and future, bringing alcohol into the community conflicts with their values. It is believed that businesses that sell/serve alcohol may bring a whole array of unsavory issues to the village.

In 1989, South Holland's advisory referendum was upheld by the Illinois Appellate Court, and to this day, the Blue Laws remain in effect. The Blue Laws' reform in South Holland is a bit unique. Rather than adopting a blanket ordinance to permit business operations on Sundays, the Village made a series of targeted amendments over time. The first major amendment came in 2009, allowing retail food and automotive-related businesses to open on Sundays (Village of South

TABLE 11.1 Detailed Timeline of Changes in Blue Laws in South Holland, IL from 2009 to 2015

Year	*Ordinance No.*	*Key Provisions/Amendments*
2009	2009–22	Amended Sunday closing rules. Allowed retail food and automotive stores to operate on Sundays if at least 25% of monthly sales were from food, drugs, fuel, or auto-related goods. Opening is restricted to after 11:00 a.m. Restaurants, gas stations, and pharmacies are exempt. Businesses must submit six months of receipts to qualify and re-certify annually.
2014	2014–1	Reaffirmed and clarified the 2009 ordinance without major change. Reiterated the 25% qualifying sales rule, annual verification requirement, and exclusion of auto body shops.
2014	2014–24	Repealed the Sunday business closure law. Replaced it with a ban on construction, demolition, and commercial landscaping in residential zones on Sundays. Focused on preserving neighborhood tranquility.
2015	2015–17	Further revised Section 9-3. Maintained construction restrictions but allowed realtors to show properties and host open houses 2:00–5:00 p.m. on Sundays. Effective July 1, 2015.

Source: Created by authors.

Holland, 2009). This primarily affected key commercial operations such as quick service restaurants, grocery stores, prescription drug stores, gas stations, and oil change shops. Beginning on November 22, 2009, retail businesses where sales of food, drugs, medicine, vehicle fuel, automotive parts, automotive accessories, automobile car washes, automobile repair garages, automobile oil change facilities and automobile tire repair and sales facilities account for 25% of the businesses' monthly sales total shall be allowed to operate and sell merchandise on Sunday.

In June 2014, a follow-up amendment clarified that auto body shops would not be included in the repeal of Sunday operating restrictions. The most recent revision in July 2015 prohibited contractors from performing work in residential areas on Sundays, effectively restricting construction activity within the community on that day. Currently, the primary business categories still restricted from Sunday operations are contractors and industrial businesses. Table 11.1 summarizes the evolution of the Village of South Holland's "Blue Law" ordinances, which governed Sunday business and activity restrictions from 2009 through 2015.

Between 2009 and 2015, the Village of South Holland's Blue Law evolved from a strict retail closure policy into a modern ordinance focusing on selective professional activity (Hudson, 2009). This change reflects the Village's balance between honoring its historic Sunday traditions and responding to contemporary economic and social needs.

South Holland issued the first liquor license in October 2023 and a second license in early 2025. The Village Board is still very selective in approving liquor licenses in an effort to maintain the community's values of being faith-rooted, family-focused, while adapting to the changing landscape by being future-oriented.

Impact of Blue Laws in South Holland on economic development

While the reasoning behind Blue Laws is clear, such legislative constraints in South Holland have prevented the village from generating thousands of dollars in additional revenue that could be used for its schools, parks, public infrastructure, and public services. The Village of South Holland maintained that its Sunday closing ordinances and prohibitions on alcohol sales did not pose significant inconveniences to residents. The community has been quite supportive of the conservative approach to liquor licensing and Sunday closings. Nevertheless, certain restrictions, such as the ban on the sale of alcoholic beverages, orange juice, and soda by hotels and restaurants, appeared arbitrary and inconsistent. For instance, while residents could purchase a gallon of milk, they were prohibited from buying a carton of juice; similarly, gasoline sales were permitted, yet the purchase of a can of soda at a gas station was not. These inconsistencies highlight the complex and restrictive nature of South Holland's Blue Laws, which ultimately constrained the village's economic potential.

In 2019, South Holland tried to enter a joint venture with The Wyndham Hotel chain to build a multiple complex venue that would have a movie theater, five on-site restaurants that serve alcohol, and eventually a sports center at a cost of $60 million. However, given the constraints South Holland's blue laws present, the developer would only move forward with the project if the restaurants were allowed to serve alcohol. The project required an amendment to the zoning ordinance to permit alcohol service within the Town Center. Rather than revisiting the entire blue law, the village adopted a special tax increment financing (TIF) arrangement to allow the project to proceed despite decades-old restrictions.

Economic development incentives in South Holland, IL

Economic development is programs, policies, and activities that seek to improve the economic well-being and quality of life for a community by creating and retaining jobs and providing a stable tax base. Since 2012, the Village of South

Holland has implemented a series of economic development initiatives designed to attract investment, redevelop vacant properties, and strengthen the local tax base (Village of South Holland, 2018). With support from the Chicago Metropolitan Agency for Planning (CMAP) Local Technical Assistance program, South Holland developed a comprehensive plan in 2018.

South Holland uses a combination of financial and non-financial incentives to promote economic growth. These tools include creation of TIF districts, enterprise zones (EZs), Façade Improvement Grant Program, Landscape Improvement Grant, Cook County property tax incentives, and infrastructure improvement partnerships (Village of South Holland, 2025). Each incentive program is tied to measurable performance criteria such as job creation, property redevelopment, or increased sales tax revenue.

South Holland established TIF districts that allow assistance with TIF-eligible costs, including infrastructure and site conditions. In South Holland, TIF districts are used strategically to promote sustainable redevelopment and support both new and expanding businesses. Village-owned properties within these areas may qualify for additional local incentives, aimed at ensuring long-term occupancy, economic vitality, and alignment with the community's development goals.

Since 2017, the Calumet Region EZ has stimulated economic growth and neighborhood revitalization in key opportunity areas in Calumet City, Dolton, Lansing, Riverdale, South Holland, Thornton, and unincorporated Cook County. The Calumet Region EZ provides a sales tax exemption on construction materials, in addition to other tax incentives depending on use and the number of jobs created. Key benefits offered by the EZ program include: a sales tax exemption on building materials for eligible projects, contingent upon possession of a valid Illinois Department of Revenue building materials sales tax exemption certificate; a 50% abatement of the municipal portion of real estate taxes on the incremental tax value generated by the project for a period of five years (with projects located within a TIF district or already receiving other property tax abatements being ineligible); and a 50% reduction in local building permit fees, with all other fees and inspections subject to local ordinance requirements. Projects eligible for EZ incentives encompass commercial, industrial, and residential developments consisting of 12 or more units under a single ownership structure. The tax incentives provided through EZs can amount to millions of dollars annually over the designated program period. Such fiscal support can substantially enhance the feasibility of business startups and expansions, particularly those that require significant capital investment, thereby facilitating economic revitalization within the designated zones.

Recognizing the significant role that building aesthetics and property investment play in the visual and economic vitality of commercial districts, the Village of South Holland established the Façade Improvement Grant Program to encourage private-sector investment in exterior building enhancements. This program provides financial rebates covering between 35% and 50% of eligible project costs, up to a maximum of $50,000. Projects that employ local contractors may qualify for additional incentives. This economic incentive aims to promote visual cohesion, commercial revitalization, and increased property values throughout the village's business areas.

The Landscape Improvement Grant Program complements the Façade Improvement Grant Program by encouraging outdoor enhancements to commercial properties. The program aims to increase the physical attractiveness, environmental quality, and marketability of South Holland's commercial corridors. Eligible landscape renovation and beautification projects may receive financial rebates between 35% and 50% of total costs, up to a maximum of $10,000. As with the façade program, higher incentive levels are available for projects that utilize local contractors.

The Village of South Holland does not directly administer the Cook County Property Tax Incentives but it supports applicants through the required local application process. To promote industrial and commercial growth, Cook County offers a series of property tax reclassification incentives that reduce the tax burden for qualifying developments or redevelopments. These programs are designed to attract new industry, encourage reinvestment, and stimulate job creation. Class 6b Incentive applies to industrial properties that have been substantially rehabilitated or reoccupied after abandonment. Qualifying properties are assessed at 16% of market value for the first ten years, 23% in the eleventh year, and 30% in the twelfth year before returning to the standard 36% assessment rate in the thirteenth year. Class 8 Incentive is applicable to both commercial and industrial properties. This classification supports new development, substantial rehabilitation, or reoccupation of abandoned facilities. The Class 8 Property Tax Incentive in Cook County provides a 12-year reduction in the property assessment rate for eligible commercial and industrial properties in areas with significant economic depression, lowering real estate tax liabilities for businesses in targeted zones. Eligible properties are assessed at 10% of market value for the first ten years, 15% in the eleventh year, and 20% in the twelfth year. Qualifying properties can see their assessment reduced from the standard rate to the 25% commercial and industrial rate for up to 12 years. South Holland provides incentives in the Class 8 property tax incentive area, where property is assessed at 10% of its value (instead of 25% for hotel, retail, and office) to reduce the property tax burden in areas with severe economic stagnation. Both Class 6B and Class 8 Incentives can be renewed in the tenth year of the incentive. There is currently no limit on how many renewals a property can receive, but the Village does have the choice to determine if they will support a property's renewal. While the Village does not administer these incentives, the County does require a resolution of support from the municipality to approve these incentives.

Interested businesses and developers are encouraged to explore available opportunities, both Village-owned and privately held properties, to contribute to South Holland's continued growth and to participate in shaping a thriving, sustainable future for the community.

Conclusions

When the Blue Laws ordinance was adopted in South Holland in 1959, it restricted the operation of major restaurants and businesses that serve alcohol within the village. By limiting these commercial activities, the ordinance constrained potential revenue-generating sources and reduced opportunities to attract visitors for dining and entertainment. These restrictions had implications not only for local business growth but also for the village's broader economic development, as they limit the diversification of the commercial sector and constrain the potential for hospitality and entertainment-based revenue streams. The Village Board has acknowledged these challenges, which have led to progressive changes in how the Village of South Holland approaches Economic Development within the hospitality sector. Since 2024, the Village of South Holland has made it easier for restaurants to do business in town year-round. The Village of South Holland has become more open to liquor licensing for restaurants and has issued the first couple of licenses. The Village of South Holland adopted a strategic approach to issuing these types of licenses.

South Holland has demonstrated a proactive approach to economic development through a range of programs and incentives designed to support business investment, enhance commercial districts, and promote sustainable growth. Initiatives such as façade and landscape improvement grants, engagement with Cook County property tax incentives, and the strategic use of TIF districts have facilitated private investment and revitalization in key commercial areas. These efforts have contributed to maintaining South Holland's appeal as a family-oriented, stable, and attractive community while also fostering opportunities for local businesses to expand and thrive. South Holland's economic development strategy has leveraged grants, tax incentives, and redevelopment tools to sustain growth, enhance the village's commercial corridors, and support the long-term vitality of the community.

Discussion questions

1 When were Blue Laws created in the United States? What was the main goal of Blue Laws?
2 How do South Holland's Blue Laws illustrate the tension between maintaining community values and promoting economic development?
3 What lessons can public administrators draw when balancing cultural norms with fiscal goals?
4 Evaluate the effectiveness of South Holland's economic development programs (e.g., Landscape Improvement Grant Program, the Façade Improvement Grant Program, TIF districts, and Cook County property tax incentives). How can local government measure success and ensure equitable outcomes?

5 What policy trade-offs are involved in restricting certain commercial activities, such as alcohol sales, while offering incentives for business growth? How should public administrators assess and prioritize these trade-offs?
6 Considering South Holland's suburban context and demographic trends, how might local policymakers design strategies that attract new investment without undermining the village's historical identity and community character?
7 What are the alternative ways to generate new revenues in the Village?

References

Holzwarth, L. (2020). The random history of blue laws in the United States. Retrieved from https://historycollection.com/the-random-history-of-blue-laws-in-the-united-states/

Hudson, D. (2009). Blue laws. Retrieved online October 13, 2022 from https://www.freedomforuminstitute.org/first-amendment-center/topics/freedom-of-religion/free-exercise-clause-overview/blue-laws/

Village of South Holland (2009). Ordinance No. 2009–22. An Ordinance of the Village Of South Holland Amending Chapter 9, "Licenses and Business Regulations" in the Village of South Holland.

Village of South Holland (2018). Comprehensive plan. https://cms5.revize.com/revize/southholland/Departments/business_residential%20services/economic%20development/VSH-ComprehensivePlan2018.pdf

Village of South Holland (2025). Available Incentives. Department of Community Development. https://southholland.org/department/community-development/economic-development/available-incentives/

World Population Review (2022). Blue Law by State 2022. https://worldpopulationreview.com/state-rankings/blue-laws-by-state

Further readings

Holzwarth, L. (2020). *The random history of blue laws in the United States*. Retrieved from https://historycollection.com/the-random-history-of-blue-laws-in-the-united-states/

The Shepherdstown Chronicle (2017). *The old blue laws of Maryland*. Retrieved from https://www.shepherdstownchronicle.com/opinions/guest-columns/2017/02/10/the-old-blue-laws-of-maryland/

Video

https://www.khou.com/article/news/americas-blue-laws-once-involved-a-lot-more-than-just-alcohol-sales/285-7e2f11ca-18ee-4ebd-b6fc-0271287f0915

CASE STUDY 25

Case study of a mega Shore-to-Core-to-Shore TIF District in Cleveland, OH

Abstract

While typical tax increment financings (TIFs) last 24 years and usually cover a single project that is located on no more than a block or two of a street, in 2024, the City of Cleveland approved a 42-year citywide TIF district, called Shore-to-Core-to-Shore TIF (SCS TIF). This ambitious redevelopment plan seeks to connect Cleveland's lakefront, downtown, and riverfront through multimodal transportation, public space improvements, and mixed-use development. The initiative is projected to generate between $3.3 and $7.5 billion in incremental tax revenue over 42 years. In addition to the SCS TIF, Cleveland extended five TIF districts in 2024 for a period of 30 years. In 2027, Cleveland will create a 45-year Bedrock Project TIF. This case study examines the use of citywide nested TIFs as an innovative local economic development tool, exploring both its potential benefits and its risks. Students are asked to assess whether Cleveland's strategy serves as a model for urban redevelopment or constitutes a high-risk investment in long-term economic growth.

Topics

Local Government; TIFs; Public Finance; Economic Development; Capital Investments

Background

Since 2022, the City of Cleveland and its partners have surveyed more than 5,000 people to develop a plan for redeveloping the lakefront area through the

Shore-to-Core-to-Shore (SCS) initiative. Based on this survey, the Coast Master Plan was created as the guiding vision for Cleveland's lakefront transformation (City of Cleveland, 2025).

It provided the foundation for a more connected, inclusive, and vibrant lakefront area (City of Cleveland, n.d.). The plan advances a policy vision centered on sustainable infrastructure financing, inclusive economic development, and environmental stewardship along Lake Erie. This plan includes three focus areas: Lakefront Shore by creation of the North Coast Connector, Downtown, and Riverfront Shore.

The first component of the initiative is the North Coast Connector, a proposed land bridge that would link Cleveland's civic center to the Lake Erie front. This project aims to eliminate longstanding physical and socioeconomic barriers created by the railroad tracks and the Shoreway. It will enhance public access, improve connectivity, and generate new land value for future development. As part of this transformation, State Route 2 is planned to be transformed from a limited-access freeway into a safer, lower-speed urban boulevard, integrating multimodal transport facilities and creating a more efficient urban circulation system. The project's design incorporates a multimodal transportation hub that connects Amtrak, light rail, and local transit modes. This infrastructure investment is expected to produce long-term fiscal benefits through enhanced property values, reduced congestion, and increased tax revenue generation.

For the second part is the Downtown Core Investment Program, planned investments include roadway resurfacing, pedestrian safety enhancements, streetscape modernization, and the construction of improved public transit waiting areas. A central component of this strategy is the implementation of a separated bicycle network designed to accommodate riders of all ages and abilities, thereby promoting modal equity and reducing automobile dependency.

The third part is the Cuyahoga Riverfront Redevelopment Project. It constitutes a multi-year comprehensive plan designed to revitalize the river corridor through coordinated public and private investment. The initiative has been adopted and refined through a partnership between the City of Cleveland and Bedrock Real Estate, a private development firm serving as the lead partner in implementing the project's public infrastructure and land use improvements. The Riverfront area, situated directly behind Tower City, a Bedrock-owned property that serves as Cleveland's primary light rail and multimodal transit hub, has historically been inaccessible to pedestrians and cyclists, thereby limiting its economic and social potential.

The Cuyahoga Riverfront Master Development Plan represents a significant capital investment in urban revitalization, integrating approximately 12 acres of dedicated green space, enhanced multimodal transportation infrastructure, 2,000 residential units, and 1.4 million square feet of new office, retail, and

FIGURE 11.1 Lakefront and downtown Cleveland.

Source: Photo provided by the authors.

entertainment development. In total, the project encompasses 35 acres of currently inaccessible riverfront property, strategically positioned to connect the Tower City Center with the broader downtown core through new pedestrian and bicycle linkages.

The plan's design reflects an innovative public-private partnership (PPP) model, wherein public investment in infrastructure and environmental remediation leverages substantial private capital to achieve broader economic development goals. The resulting 3.5 million square feet of new mixed-use development with 12 acres of public parks and approximately 3,000 linear feet of continuous riverfront boardwalk. It is projected to generate long-term fiscal benefits through increased property values, enhanced tax revenues, and sustained commercial activity. The proposed tax increment financing (TIF) district in Cleveland would enable the city to issue debt to fund public infrastructure improvements (streets, utilities, sidewalks, etc.) that support and enhance private development. This includes projects like Cleveland Cavaliers owner Dan Gilbert's $3.5 billion plan to redevelop the Terminal Tower complex and the Cuyahoga Riverfront, which is expected to leverage an additional $400 to $500 million in public subsidies to complement private investment (Astolfi, 2024). The City of Cleveland and the

North Coast Waterfront Development Corporation aim to align redevelopment expenditure with its broader capital improvement and TIF strategies.

The SCS initiative and TIFs

A TIF district is a tool that local governments use to encourage private economic development by providing upfront financing incentives. TIF districts enable the city to redirect a portion of property tax revenues to cover project-related costs. When a TIF district is created, the existing property tax base is "frozen," and any increases in property tax revenues resulting from higher property values (the tax increments) are reinvested in the district. Municipalities often issue bonds to fund these projects, with future tax increments used to repay the debt over the life of the TIF.

To qualify for a TIF, a project usually must meet several criteria. First, it must be in a blighted area or an area at risk of blight. Second, the developer must demonstrate that the project would not be feasible without TIF financing. Third, the project should provide tangible benefits not only to the developer but also to the surrounding community. TIFs are designed to operate over a long-term horizon, typically from 20 to 23 years. During this period, property tax increments help finance the project, and once the TIF expires, the additional tax revenues are allocated to the general fund to support broader public services. From a broader perspective, TIF projects are part of the larger urban system where economic, social, political, and environmental factors in the district and surrounding area are interconnected (Bowen & Guzman, 2024). Changes within a TIF district can influence the wider urban system, creating ripple effects that impact the city's overall development, fiscal health, and community outcomes.

In 2024, Mayor Justin Bibb's administration introduced the SCS TIF District (SCS TIFs) (Ordinance No. 38–2024). The City of Cleveland has committed approximately $400 million from the SCS TIF district revenues to finance a series of public infrastructure improvements along the Cuyahoga Riverfront, including transportation facilities, green space development, and environmental remediation (Cleveland Department of Economic Development, 2023). Under the terms of the agreement, the project-level TIF will capture incremental property tax revenues generated from the construction and renovation of new buildings within the designated development area. The SCS TIF district will remain in effect for 42 years, until 2075, ensuring a sustained funding stream for long-term capital investments. The SCS TIF is structured to support the riverfront over multiple phases. From 2024 to 2056, 40% of TIF revenues will be allocated exclusively to the riverfront, subject to the City's cap designated for public infrastructure. From 2056 to 2075, the allocation increases to as much as 90% of TIF revenues for the riverfront, again subject to the City's cap for public infrastructure (Cleveland City Council, 2025). If, at the beginning of 2056, the

TABLE 11.2 SCS TIF District and TIF Extensions

Eligible TIF	*Original End Year*	*New End Year*
Lower Euclid	2033	2063
Steelyard	2037	2067
VA Hospital	2038	2068
Westin	2042	2072
Hilton	2045	2075

Source: Created by authors based on Cleveland City Council (2025).

City of Cleveland has not fully met its obligations to fund public improvements for the Riverfront project, it may allocate up to 90% of the SCS TIF district toward the Riverfront until the city's portion of public improvements is fully satisfied (Cleveland City Council, 2025).

The SCS TIF district is also a non-school TIF, which means the Cleveland Metropolitan School District will continue to receive the amount of property tax payments that would have been payable to the school district if there were no TIF in place. Same with Cleveland Public Library and Cleveland Metroparks that are not part of the SCS TIF and will continue to receive property tax revenues unaffected by the TIF. TIF will dedicate 35% of "excess funds" to neighborhood investments (Cleveland City Council, 2025).

In November 2023, Ordinance No. 1299–2023 authorized the extension of five existing TIF districts (Westin, Hilton, Steelyard, VA, and Lower Euclid) for an additional 30 years (Table 11.2). These five TIF extensions (Westin, VA, Steelyard, Lower Euclid, and Hilton) are incorporated into the SCS TIF District.

In addition to the SCS TIF district, Cleveland entered into a project-specific TIF agreement with Bedrock Real Estate to advance the Cuyahoga Riverfront Master Development Plan (Ordinance No. 746–2024). The Bedrock TIF is a 45-year, non-school TIF that will run from 2027 through 2071 and will operate within the boundaries of the broader downtown TIF district (Kraynak, 2025). As part of the project agreement, Bedrock TIF will contribute a total of $25 million to designated project milestones to support neighborhood and community development. Of this amount, $15 million will be directed to a neighborhood investment fund, with the first $5 million provided at the time of the initial bond issuance, supported by the SCS TIF. Additional contributions include $1 million for city resident programs, $1 million for mentorship and training initiatives, $3 million for workforce development efforts, and $5 million invested in the Minority Business Credit Fund (Cleveland City Council, 2025).

As part of the project, the Community Benefits Agreement (CBA) commits $25 million to City of Cleveland priorities, including neighborhood funds, which are distributed as the project reaches key milestones. The CBA also includes additional commitments, such as reserving 20% of residential units as affordable housing and requiring 40% participation by minority-owned, female-owned, and certified small businesses, among other obligations (Cleveland City Council, 2025).

Benefits and risks of citywide TIFs

The seven TIF districts illustrate a layered financing structure designed to maximize the capture of incremental tax revenues in Cleveland over the next 45 years. This approach offers potential benefits, such as attracting private investment, funding major infrastructure improvements, and promoting long-term neighborhood revitalization. However, it also carries possible risks, including fiscal overreliance on future tax increments, unequal distribution of benefits across communities, and uncertainty about whether projected revenues will materialize over time. This model demonstrates how nested TIF structures can be strategically deployed to align local revenue generation with targeted economic development objectives, while leveraging private investment through PPPs. Proponents of the SCS initiative argue that the TIF provides a sustainable, locally controlled funding mechanism to catalyze development and attract private and federal investment.

This complex, nested citywide TIF structure necessitates robust fiscal oversight to manage potential risks, including revenue overlap, interdistrict dependency, and the equitable allocation of tax benefits (Kraynak, 2025). One of the most significant and often unanticipated risks associated with large-scale TIF districts arises when property assessors assign inflated valuations that do not accurately reflect the true market value of real estate following project completion. Such overvaluation can lead to artificially high property tax bills, placing additional financial burdens on property owners. This outcome is particularly concerning for small businesses, homeowners, and low-income residents who may struggle to absorb the increased costs (Bowen & Guzman, 2024).

Perceptions of inequity in the assessment process can further erode public trust. If residents believe that assessments are being manipulated to favor developers or specific stakeholders at the expense of the broader community, confidence in both the fairness of the TIF mechanism and the integrity of local government institutions may be undermined (Bowen & Guzman, 2024).

Large-scale TIF districts often encompass areas with varying economic conditions. While some subareas may indeed be blighted and in need of redevelopment, others may already be relatively prosperous. When an entire district is designated as a TIF area, profit-driven developers may naturally prioritize investments in commercially advantageous subareas rather than those most in need of revitalization, thereby limiting the intended equity and community development benefits of the TIF. According to Bowen and Guzman (2024), when a TIF district encompasses a very large portion of a city and extends over several decades, the number of affected residents, businesses, and stakeholders grows substantially.

The interactions among these actors multiply, and the amount of information required to understand the district's economic, social, and fiscal dynamics expands exponentially. As a result, the overall system becomes increasingly complex. This expanded scale, heightened complexity, and less clearly defined scope of TIFs projects, combined with long planning horizons, virtually ensure a greater number of unanticipated outcomes and increase the potential for political manipulation or mismanagement.

These large, multifaceted, nested, and long-lasting TIF districts are inherently more difficult to plan, manage, and evaluate effectively. Human cognitive capacity to process and anticipate complex, interdependent events is not scale-independent. As the number of variables and relationships within a system grows and becomes less clearly defined, decision-makers face increasing difficulty in predicting outcomes, identifying feedback loops, and maintaining effective oversight eventually reaching a point where the system's complexity exceeds the limits of human understanding and administrative control (Bowen & Guzman, 2024).

Successful TIFs

Many municipalities have effectively employed TIF districts as instruments for promoting economic development while ensuring community benefits. TIFs have been applied successfully to a wide range of concentrated, well-defined development projects, including shopping centers, historic building restorations, office complexes, sports arenas, museums, big-box retail stores, upscale housing and commercial developments, infrastructure upgrades, streetscape improvements, environmental remediation, site preparation, and even recreational facilities such as water parks. The number of successful outcomes demonstrates that establishing TIF districts for relatively small-scale, clearly scoped projects can, in many cases, be an effective and beneficial economic development strategy.

In Chicago, Illinois, the LaSalle Central TIF district facilitated the revitalization of a major financial corridor, attracting over $1 billion in private investment and allocating resources to transit and infrastructure improvements (Chicago Department of Planning and Development, 2021). Similarly, Cincinnati, Ohio, utilized TIF financing to support the redevelopment of the Over-the-Rhine neighborhood, transforming a historically disinvested area into a vibrant mixed-use community while preserving affordable housing (City of Cincinnati Economic Development, 2020). The district generated $2 million in 2017, and proceeds climbed every year since, leaping to over $7.5 million in 2023. From a base property value in 2002 of $278 million, values in that district had grown to over $441 million by 2018 (Astolfi, 2024).

In Columbus, Ohio, TIF resources were utilized to develop commercial and residential properties in the Arena District, generating a sustainable revenue stream that continues to support public services (Columbus Department of Development, 2019). Austin, Texas, introduced a TIF reform initiative that enabled retroactive policy adjustments, promoting equitable tax distribution and strengthening environmental safeguards (Austin Economic Development, 2022). These cases demonstrate that, under appropriate oversight, TIF districts can serve as an effective mechanism for stimulating both economic growth and community development.

Conclusions

Cleveland's SCS initiative represents an ambitious effort to combine infrastructure renewal, PPPs, and TIF as mechanisms for long-term urban revitalization. The city's layered TIF structure demonstrates how strategic financing tools can be leveraged to stimulate private investment and fund essential public improvements when traditional revenue sources are constrained. TIFs can offer cities valuable opportunities to reinvest in neighborhoods, enhance infrastructure, and foster equitable economic growth. However, these benefits depend on careful fiscal management, realistic revenue projections, and consistent oversight. Public engagement and transparency are crucial for maintaining the legitimacy of large-scale financing strategies and ensuring meaningful community participation and trust.

The risks associated with large-scale, nested long-duration TIFs districts are considerably higher than those linked to smaller, more precisely defined, and shorter-term projects, where the system's behavior is easier to monitor and comprehend. Critics raise concerns about delayed benefits to neighborhoods, loss of property tax revenue for public services, and the risk of uneven development. Cleveland's approach illustrates both the potential and the challenges of using TIFs to balance economic development objectives with fiscal responsibility and social equity.

Discussion questions

1 What are the economic and fiscal benefits of using a citywide TIF district to finance public infrastructure projects like Shore-to-Core-to-Shore?
2 How does Cleveland's TIF differ from traditional, project-specific TIFs used in other cities?
3 How might Cleveland ensure that TIF-generated revenue benefits both downtown and neighborhoods equitably?
4 Does this complex nested structure with 7 TIFs create benefits or burdens for future taxpayers in Cleveland and neighborhood communities?

5 What potential fiscal and social risks arise from tying public investment to future property tax increases?
6 In what ways could TIF revenues crowd out funding for essential public services (e.g., libraries, parks, or public safety)?
7 If you were advising the Cleveland City Council, what modifications or safeguards would you recommend to improve the TIF's design?
8 Considering both the potential benefits and drawbacks, do you believe the nested TIFs structure, which includes Shore-to-Core-to-Shore TIFs and Bed Rock TIFs, are sound public finance strategy for Cleveland?

References

Astolfi, C. (2024, February 18). What's a TIF, anyway? The mechanics of Cleveland's big development tool – and why the neighborhoods will have to wait for their share. *Cleveland.com.* https://www.cleveland.com/metro/2024/02/how-tif-districts-work-and-why-clevelands-plan-is-different.html

Austin Economic Development. (2022). TIF reform initiative in Austin, Texas: Ensuring equitable tax distribution and stronger environmental protections. *Austin Economic Development.* https://www.austintexas.gov/department/economic-development

Bowen, B., & Guzman, T. (March 5, 2024). The promises and risks of large-scale TIF districts. *The Urban Lens Newsletter.* https://theurbanlens.substack.com/p/the-promises-and-risks-of-large-scale.

Chicago Department of Planning and Development. (2021). LaSalle Central TIF District: Revitalizing the financial district of Chicago. *Chicago Department of Planning and Development.* https://www.chicago.gov/city/en/depts/dcd/supp/chi/pro/bus/LaSalleTIF.html

City of Cincinnati Economic Development. (2020). Over-the-Rhine TIF district redevelopment: A successful model for mixed-use communities. *City of Cincinnati Economic Development.* https://www.cincinnati-oh.gov/economic-development/over-the-rhine-tif/

City of Cleveland (n.d.). Shore-to-Core-to-Shore. https://www.clevelandohio.gov/city-hall/office-mayor/mayors-initiatives/shore-core-shore.

City of Cleveland (2025). Shore-to-Core-to-Shore. https://www.clevelandohio.gov/city-hall/office-mayor/mayors-initiatives/shore-core-shore

Cleveland Department of Economic Development. (2023). Shore-to-Core-to-Shore TIF District: A transformative economic opportunity for Cleveland. *Cleveland Department of Economic Development.* https://www.cleveland-oh.gov/eco-dev/tif-programs

Columbus Department of Development. (2019). Arena District TIF: Economic growth and public service benefits. *Columbus Department of Development.* https://www.columbus.gov/development/arena-district-tif

Cleveland City Council. (2025, February 10). Public hearings. City of Cleveland City Council: Finance, Diversity, Equity & Inclusion Committee. [Video] [YouTube]. https://www.youtube.com/live/F9lKSpia4t0?t=4024s

Kraynak, M. (2025, May 31).WTF is a TIF? And why are they used for development projects across Greater Cleveland? *Signal Cleveland.* https://signalcleveland.org/what-is-a-tif-and-why-are-they-used-for-development-projects-across-greater-cleveland/

CASE STUDY 26

Case study and simulation game. Economic incentives and budget revenue diversification in the Village of Matteson, IL

Abstract

This budget simulation game is based on the fiscal and operational challenges the Village of Matteson, IL, faced and examines approaches it used to improve its financial position between 2009 and 2024. In this simulation exercise, students are assigned the roles of the village's board of trustees' members, department chairs, and residents and participate in the village's board of trustees meeting simulation. This case study replicates budget hearing process and invites students to discuss such cost saving and revenue-generating options as "stretching the budget," creating business district and tax increment financings, implementing new taxes including municipal hotel tax, installing traffic-light cameras on heavy traffic roads, collecting higher service charges and permit fees, improving budgeting practices, achieving Home Rule status, and providing financial incentives to businesses to support economic development.

Topics

Revenue Generation; Fiscal Stress; Local Government; Recovery; Fiscal Policy; Public Finance

Background

The Village of Matteson is a medium-sized village in a rapidly growing region in the midwestern United States. Matteson was a non-home rule municipality that could only exercise powers for which authority was provided by state law till 2022. The Village of Matteson operates under a mayor-village administrator form of government where the elected mayor presides over a six-member Board of Trustees (BoT). The mayor and BoT determine the compensation of all village officers and employees, levy taxes, appropriate funds, borrow money and make all decisions relating to the village's finances and general affairs. The mayor is also the chief executive officer of the village and possesses the power to veto ordinances, resolutions, and any expenditure. The mayor is the chief political officer. The mayor and council appoint the village administrator, and his/her duties are included in local ordinances. The village administrator serves as the chief administrative officer and is responsible for daily operations. The mayor, village clerk, and trustees are elected at-large to four-year terms.

The 1970s brought about a decade of incredible growth and development. When Lincoln Mall opened its doors in 1973, Matteson became a major regional retail center with such main anchor stores as Carson Pirie Scott, Montgomery Ward, Wieboult's, and JCPenney. Thanks to the higher tax revenues generated from the new retail development, the Matteson Public Library was able to relocate to a larger building, the Parks and Recreation department was reorganized, and public works added two new garage facilities. Matteson was a thriving community in the 1990s. The median household income in the village ($73,729) was substantially higher than in other similar-sized cities in the Midwest. As Matteson moved into the 21st century, it continued to prosper, support its successful businesses and residents, and celebrate its diversity. From 1990 to 2000, the village issued over 2,000 building permits for the construction of single-family homes.

In 2000, Montgomery Ward went bankrupt, and JCPenney closed its store in Lincoln Mall due to its own financial struggles. After losing two out of four anchors, Lincoln Mall traffic declined. The Great Recession, from 2008 to 2009, also negatively impacted the finances of both the Lincoln Mall and the Village of Matteson. Many stores began to vacate in 2008–2010. Sears that moved into Wieboult's space in the 1990s began a store-closing sale on May 11, 2012. An investor, Mehran Kohansieh purchased the Lincoln Mall at a tax auction in 2012 for $150,000, assuming $9 million in accumulated fines and unpaid taxes. A court-ordered receiver, Collateral Trustee, was appointed in August 2013 to collect unpaid taxes and fees. However, Mehran Kohansieh made only a total of $150,000 in payments since 2013. In total, the Village of Matteson lost more than $10 million in unpaid taxes and fees (Ermasova & Guzman, 2024). Matteson had to provide safety and basic maintenance to the abandoned site and had to pay to demolish the Mall. On November 11, 2014, Cook County Judge Thomas Condon ordered that the mall be closed permanently as of January 7, 2015.

The closure of Lincoln Mall and several big chain stores affected many people in the village, resulting in fewer jobs, increased property tax rates, and

TABLE 11.3 Revenues and Expenditures in Matteson, IL from 2013 to 2014 (in current dollars)

	2013	*2014*
Revenues		
Sales taxes	4,914,671	4,997,379
Property taxes	4,322,459	5,685,385
Other taxes	4,327,721	4,070,339
Charges for services	2,256,859	2,491,234
Intergovernmental transfers	191,984	219,654
Recreation programs	1,311,428	1,213,695
Interest	10,839	1,992
Fines, forfeitures, and penalties	395,786	431,371
Miscellaneous	138,535	179,734
Total revenues	18,249,321	20,093,126
Expenditures		
General government	4,229,472	3,885,580
Public safety	11,729,563	12,141,204
Public works	1,478,214	937,212
Parks and recreations	2,015,549	2,046,473
Capita	467,095	64,145
Total expenditures	22,121,831	21,052,993
Budget surplus (or deficit)	(3,872,510)	(959,867)

Source: Created by the authors from the Village of Matteson, IL CAFRs (Village of Matteson, 2013, 2014, 2015a, 2015b, 2016, 2017).

reduced funds for programs. In 2013, the Village of Matteson's expenditures totaled $22.1 million, while total revenues were $18.2 million, leading to a deficit of $3.8 million that year (Table 11.3).

Village BoT Meeting Simulation

Roles

Mayor
Village Administrator
Village Treasurer
Chief of Police
Economic Development Director
Village residents
Village Board of Trustees members

The mayor met with the Village Administrator, Treasurer, and Police Chief to discuss various proposals for addressing a budget shortfall. After these meetings, the mayor presented several proposals to the BoT, where elected officials must decide the following (with advice from the administrator and staff):

- What expenditures could be cut?
- Should these reductions be across-the-board or targeted cuts?
- Which services should be provided, and which ones should be reduced or eliminated?
- If services are reduced or eliminated what will the effects be?
- What departments can sustain the biggest cuts with the least effect on quality of life for residents?
- What are the options for increasing revenues and what is the feasibility for each?
- What are the arguments against the revenue options (like equity concerns)?

Matteson's residents are unusually active in local politics and are very vocal in BoT meetings. Over 100 residents came to the BoT budget meeting to hear the proposals by the mayor. The board did not make any decisions at the meeting. Instead, they asked the administrator to develop recommendations with associated benefits and costs, both direct and indirect.

Village board members were facing a $5 million deficit for the next fiscal year (in addition to the $3.8 million shortfall in FY2013), and they now had to decide how to handle the fiscal emergency in view of the political and public pressure. They feared for Matteson's future, realizing this decision was extremely important to the village and the citizens. Board members shared these concerns with the mayor and administrator and asked that they present the council with a proposal that addresses all those considerations.

The Proposals

Due to the dramatic revenue drop that has led to fiscal stress for the village, village leadership needs to reduce expenditures while avoiding service disruptions, especially those related to public safety and health.

PROPOSAL 1: Budget cuts.

- Eliminate vacancies.
- Reduce the spending on infrastructure projects.
- "Stretch the budget" to get through the fiscal year.
- Cut 13 police officers (40% of the police force) and eight firefighters (30% of the fire department).

PROPOSAL 2: Install Red-light cameras

PROPOSAL 3: Increase Property Taxes, Service Charges, and Introduce New Taxes

- Levy a 1% tax on gross receipts for prepared food sold at retail.
- Introduce occupation taxes, service occupation taxes, and hotel occupation taxes.
- Increase property tax rate from 0.819% to 1.891%.

PROPOSAL 4: Provide economic and financial incentives to businesses.

- Establish District No. 3, which includes the Lincoln Mall and surrounding property to help fund the development and commercial improvement of certain designated areas through an additional 1% sales tax levy.
- Establish a Tax Increment Financing (TIF) district.

PROPOSAL 5: Improve the budgeting process.

- Rank capital projects and investments.
- Improve transparency of the budgeting process.
- Establish long-term planning.
- Develop formal mechanisms to set aside funds for preserving existing facilities and increase collaboration between departments.

Simulation Schedule

PART 1: Background information about the case

Background information can be used for decision-making. This should be presented to the full set of stakeholders for consideration and input.

PART 2: Deliberations by the Village Administrator, Mayor, Treasurer, Chief of Police, Economic Development Director, and village residents

In a role-play, each student will prepare proposals for the BoT. The players will have an opportunity to share support or opposition for each of the proposals. Each player will know what role he or she plays and what incentive he or she is proposing, supporting, and opposing. However, each player will NOT be aware of other players' positions on each proposal. The goal of this section is to develop an actual proposal that will be presented.

PART 3: Proposal to the Board of Trustees

Each player will present its proposal to the Board. The Board will be able to ask any stakeholders for clarification and vote to approve the proposal (in whole or in part) or reject it.

PART 4: Reflection and discussion

Follow-up reflections

Content-related questions

1 What negative and positive long-term implications of fiscal stress do you see for the community in the Village of Matteson?
2 What are some examples of extreme budget cuts you have heard from other municipalities? Do these examples provide any useful suggestions for Matteson? (ex. privatization, contracting out)
3 Given the $3.8 million budget gap, what services do you propose should be cut during fiscal stress? Would different stakeholders choose different priorities?
4 How do you propose more revenues could be generated in Matteson?
5 What were some of the reasons for voting for and against raising property taxes and other taxes during fiscal stress?
6 What additional economic incentives could the Village of Matteson implement during fiscal stress?
7 What are the benefits and risks of using TIF? How can the risks be minimized?
8 What additional information do you wish you had to be able to make more informed decisions?
9 Do you feel like the Board made the right decision?

Experience-related reflections

1 Do you feel like the Board made the right decision?
2 What was the most interesting thing about going through this case study?
3 What was challenging about going through this case study?

The Proposal Descriptions

PROPOSAL 1: Budget Cuts

Eliminate vacancies.

Reduce spending on infrastructure projects.

"Stretch the budget" to get through the fiscal year.

Cut 13 police officers (40% of the police force) and eight firefighters (30% of the fire department).

Village Administrator suggested reducing the spending on infrastructure projects and "stretching the budget" to get through the fiscal year and also proposed eliminating vacancies and cutting staff to get through the fiscal year. At the core of this proposal was a substantial reduction in the public safety workforce, the largest expenditure in the village budget. The Village Administrator proposed cutting the public safety workforce most significantly, with possible layoffs of 13 police officers (about 40% of the police force) and eight firefighters (around 30% of the fire department). The Village Administrator reasoned that public safety expenses accounted for 49% of total expenses, so substantial cuts were needed in those departments. Village Administrator proposed cutting work hours for remaining hourly, non-uniform employees and institute hiring freezes in many job classifications.

With the removal of these officers, the village would save on salaries, benefits, and any future pensions that would result from the retirement of these public servants. To compensate for the decrease in law enforcement officers, the Village Administrator proposed hiring private security firms to handle routine security at events and creating volunteer auxiliary services. In addition to personnel cuts, Village Administrator proposed deferring infrastructure spending, reducing parks and road maintenance, and postponing spending for economic development incentives. The total savings would be approximately $3.2 million.

PROPOSAL 2: Install Red-light Cameras

This proposal recommends the installation of red-light cameras at high-traffic intersections and an increase in fees and penalties for red-light violations in the municipality. The goal is to enhance public safety, reduce traffic accidents, and generate a new stream of revenue to support community infrastructure and public safety initiatives. Each red-light camera ticket in the Midwest costs drivers an average of $100.

The Police Chief prepared a proposal about the installation of two red-light cameras on main roads in Matteson. It was estimated that two red-light cameras could bring around $1.5 million per year in new revenues. Automated red-light camera project includes fixed costs (the costs of the equipment and installation) and variable costs (the cost associated with the back-office ticket processes). Overall, the cost of implementing an automated red-light enforcement system depends on the geometry of the intersection and the number of lanes/approaches monitored. The project costs include the cost of the camera (approximately $50,000), in-pavement inductive loop detectors ($5,000 per leg), and costs associated with camera housings, poles, flash slaves, and wiring ($8,000). The City of Jackson, Michigan, spent $67,000 on fixed costs per intersection for a system that included one camera, housing, loop, pole, and installation (Sisiopiku et al., 2002). The variable costs are around $8,500 per month (Citrus Height Sentinel, 2017). However, these costs are unique to each jurisdiction's ticketing process and procedures, as well as the agreement between the jurisdiction and contractor processing the violations. Operational costs are fees charged by the camera vendor and can be charged as a flat monthly fee or per citation issued.

PROPOSAL 3: Increase Property Taxes, Service Charges, and Introduce New Taxes

Levy a tax of 1% on gross receipts for prepared food sold at retail

Introduce occupation taxes, service occupation taxes, and hotel occupation taxes.

Increase property tax rate from 0.819% to 1.891%.

The Treasurer proposed implementing new fees and taxes. Raising the property tax rate from 0.819% to 1.891% would generate sufficient revenue to cover the deficit and put the village in good fiscal standing for the future without cutting services. The proposed new property tax rate would still be lower than the county's average of 2.09%.

The Treasurer also suggested levying a 1% tax on gross receipts for prepared food sold at retail establishments and proposed levying a municipal hotel tax of 6% on the gross rental receipts (not including taxes or other non-room rental charges added to the hotel or motel bill) for each hotel or motel room rented for every 24-hour period. Based on forecast, the proposal would bring around $2.5 million in additional revenues to the budget.

PROPOSAL 4: Provide economic and financial incentives for businesses

Establish a Business District, which includes the Lincoln Mall and surrounding property, to help fund the development and commercial improvement of certain designated areas through an additional 1% sales tax levy.

Establish TIFs district.

The Director of Economic Development wanted to ensure that economic development remained a top priority. The Director of Economic Development highlighted the village's main economic development goals: strengthening and diversifying the village's tax base, increasing employment opportunities, attracting new businesses while retaining current businesses, and promoting a positive business and community environment.

The director suggested the village implements new property tax incentives for Industrial Development (up to 50% reduction in manufacturing, warehouse, or distribution centers total property tax bill for two years), and Commercial Development (up to 50% reduction in property taxes for two years). These financial incentives could help attract new businesses that should contribute significantly to general fund revenues. If Matteson could attract Sam's Club E-Commerce Distribution Center or Amazon distribution center, it would bring large sales tax revenues (a minimum of $2 million in tax revenue annually). In addition, either facility would create approximately 1,000 full-time jobs.

The director also suggested creating a TIF district at the former Lincoln Mall site for 20 years and recommended repurposing the site into a mixed-use development combining retail, residential, and other commercial uses. The director argued that the TIF will positively affect the municipality's development by attracting new commercial and residential development while renovating an abandoned commercial site. With these options considered, this initiative may solve the village's financial issues, and while it would take some time and require some upfront investment from the village, it would provide a long-term sustainable solution to the fiscal problems the village was currently facing. All the land associated with the retailers of the Lincoln Mall and related parking areas would be included in this TIF district. The total area encompassed within this redevelopment would be approximately 125 acres. Once redeveloped, the village could collect all the taxes on the increment of increase in the assessed value of the property.

The treasurer supported the proposal and suggested the creation of a business district to help fund the development and commercial improvement of certain designated areas, which would be made possible through an additional 1% sales tax levy. The additional sales taxes would be deposited into separate funds, and this revenue would be used to incentivize business attraction and expansion efforts in the village. The treasurer also forecasts that the fourth proposal would bring around $3.5 million in additional revenue to the budget after two years from the creation of a business district.

PROPOSAL 5: Improve the budgeting process

Rank capital projects and investments.

Improve transparency of the budgeting process.

Establish long-term planning.

Develop formal mechanisms to set aside funds for preserving existing facilities.

Increase collaboration between departments.

To address ongoing fiscal challenges, the village treasurer proposed a strategic, long-term approach to managing capital expenditures and improving the overall budgeting process, including capital budgeting. This proposal emphasizes the need for better planning, prioritization, and preservation of existing assets to ensure financial sustainability without increasing the burden on residents.

The treasurer recommended that the village implements a formal system for ranking and prioritizing capital projects in Matteson. A critical first step would be to conduct a comprehensive inventory of all equipment, buildings, and facilities. This would allow the village to assess the current condition of capital assets and determine which projects are most urgent, particularly in relation to safety and economic development.

Recognizing the constraints of limited capital funding, especially during periods of fiscal stress, the treasurer stressed the importance of evaluating the trade-offs between competing projects. The goal is to focus on spending where it is most needed and to avoid costly deferred maintenance in the future.

To guide decision-making, the treasurer proposed that capital investments be ranked based on the following criteria:

Compliance with safety, health, regulatory, security, environmental, or accreditation requirements.

Upgrading or replacing major mechanical systems and utility infrastructure.

Renovating or maintaining existing facilities.

Constructing, expanding, or acquiring facilities to meet essential program needs.

Improving energy efficiency and reducing long-term operating costs.

Additionally, the treasurer advised prioritizing repairs, renovations, and capital renewal over new construction. During times of financial strain, this approach would help the village direct resources only to the most essential projects, maximizing the value of every dollar spent.

To further improve fiscal stewardship, the proposal calls for increased transparency in the budgeting process, the establishment of long-term capital planning, and the development of formal mechanisms to set aside funds for facility preservation. It also encourages greater collaboration between departments to align budget priorities and improve resource allocation.

The treasurer estimated that implementing Proposal 5 could result in capital expense savings of approximately $1.5 million while also strengthening the village's financial planning and infrastructure management practices.

Village Board Meeting Simulation Roles

Mayor

No suggested proposals are being brought forward directly.

It is one of the leading roles as the chief political officer. The mayor will be up for reelection soon. The mayor should bring his/her arguments and responses as he/she listens to proposals and hears from various stakeholders.

Proposals this role is in support of:

PROPOSAL 2: Install red-light cameras.

PROPOSAL 4: Provide economic and financial incentives to businesses.

PROPOSAL 5: Improve the budgeting process.

Proposals in opposition to:

PROPOSAL 2: Budget cuts

The mayor was also skeptical about this proposal. The mayor suggested that this strategy cannot be a long-term solution because it undermines residents' quality of life.

PROPOSAL 3: Increase property taxes, service charges, and introduce new taxes.

Village Administrator

Suggested proposal:

PROPOSAL 1. Budget cuts

The Village Administrator came to Matteson with the goal of solving fiscal problems without burdening the residents with higher taxes and fees. The administrator proposed cutting staffing to get through the fiscal year. The Village Administrator proposed cutting the public safety workforce most significantly, with possible layoffs of 13 police officers (about 40% of the police force) and eight firefighters (about 30% of the fire department).

Proposals in support of:

PROPOSAL 3: Increase property taxes, service charges, and introduce new taxes.

PROPOSAL 4: Provide economic and financial incentives to businesses.

PROPOSAL 5: Improve the budgeting process.

Proposals in opposition to:

PROPOSAL 2: Install red-light cameras.

Support for Village Administrator Role:

The administrator had only a few days to develop a reasonable solution to the deficit issue. As the administrator saw it, there are the following options (or combinations of options):

- Implement the budget cuts initially recommended by the village administrator. This decision may lead to increased response times for fire and police, and to potential increases in the crime rate. It will solve the budget deficit for the current year.
- Increase the property tax rate, impose a hotel/motel tax, and a sales tax of 1% of gross receipts for prepared food sold at retail.
- Implement the red-light camera program. Even though they would likely face an extremely unhappy citizen and it potentially will not generate enough revenue. Also, it will not solve the current budget year deficit.
- Implement a TIF district to renovate the former shopping mall and create a business district. TIF is a local economic development policy that allows municipalities to designate an area for redevelopment and use the expected increase in property taxes there to pay for initial and ongoing redevelopment expenditures. TIF programs have a positive influence on economic activity in their municipalities and offer a range of development incentives, beginning with an infrastructure that powers businesses and creates opportunities for struggling communities, serving as the building block of redevelopment and the path to increasing economic development. The village prioritizes economic development by proposing new development incentives and a new business improvement district. Again, this does not offer short-term release. This option would take several years to generate revenue.

- Place a ranking of prioritization on capital projects and focus most spending on preventive maintenance rather than construction of new facilities. The consequences of not performing regular maintenance and repairs could include increased safety hazards, poor service to the public, higher future costs, and inefficient operations. Decision-making should shift from reactive to proactive as asset management programs develop. The Village of Matteson could develop comprehensive, multi-year plans that indicate which facilities need maintenance, renovations, and replacement (Village of Matteson, 2018a; 2018b; 2019; 2020a; 2020b;2021a;2021b; 2023).

Treasurer

Suggested proposal:

PROPOSAL 3: Increase property taxes, service charges, and introduce new taxes.

PROPOSAL 5: Improve the budgeting process.

Proposals in support of:

PROPOSAL 2: Install red-light cameras.

PROPOSAL 4: Provide economic and financial incentives to businesses.

Proposals in opposition to:

PROPOSAL 1. Budget cuts

Police Chief

Suggested proposal:

PROPOSAL 2: Red-light camera program

The Police Chief prepared a proposal about the installation of two red-light cameras on main roads in Matteson. The Police Chief estimated that two red-light cameras can bring around $1.5 million of additional revenue to the budget.

Proposals in support to:

PROPOSAL 3: Increase property taxes, service charges, and introduce new taxes.

PROPOSAL 4: Provide economic and financial incentives to businesses.

PROPOSAL 5: Improve the budgeting process.

Proposals in opposition to:

PROPOSAL 1. Budget cuts

Director of Economic Development

Suggested proposal:

PROPOSAL 4: Providing economic and financial incentives to businesses.

The Director of Economic Development wants to ensure that economic development remains a top priority. The Economic Development Director highlighted the village's main economic development goals: strengthening and diversifying the village's tax base, increasing employment opportunities, attracting new businesses while retaining current businesses, and promoting a positive business and community environment.

Proposals in support to:

PROPOSAL 5: Improve the budgeting process.

Proposals in opposition to:

PROPOSAL 1. Budget cuts

The Economic Development Director was skeptical about this proposal and suggests that this strategy cannot be a long-term solution, as it undermines residents' quality of life.

PROPOSAL 2: Install red-light cameras.

The Director of Economic Development opposed this proposal because red-light cameras are a headache for drivers and people from neighboring villages would use other roads and go shopping in other villages to avoid red-light cameras in Matteson, which could negatively affect sales tax revenues.

PROPOSAL 3: Increase property taxes, service charges, and introduce new taxes.

The Director of Economic Development opposed this proposal because higher taxes and service charges might drive current residents and businesses away from Matteson, especially as surrounding communities offer lower tax burdens. The Director argued that this could weaken the village's competitive position, discourage new investment, and ultimately shrink the tax base.

While Proposal 3 could provide short-term fiscal relief, its potential impact on economic development and population retention raises important concerns about its long-term sustainability and social equity implications.

Village Residents

Suggested proposals:

Residents suggest to reduce expenditures by closing community centers, reducing police department staffing, selling city-owned utilities, selling the municipal community center, and decreasing salaries and benefits to village employees.

Part of your role is to interrupt and engage during presentations to better understand why residents' proposals are not being considered.

Proposals in support of:

PROPOSAL 2: Budget cuts.

PROPOSAL 4: Provide economic and financial incentives to businesses.

PROPOSAL 5: Improve the budgeting process.

Proposals in opposition of:

PROPOSAL 2: Install red-light cameras.

PROPOSAL 3: Increase property taxes, service charges, and introduce new taxes.

References

Citrus Height Sentinel. (2017, July 30). *How much money do red light cameras actually make?* https://citrusheightssentinel.com/2017/07/30/much-money-red-light-cameras-actually-make/

Ermasova, N., & Guzman, T. (2024). Approaches to Solutions of municipal fiscal distress: A descriptive case of Matteson, Illinois. *Illinois Municipal Policy Journal, 9*(11), 1–22.

Sisiopiku, V. P., Thigpen, S., & Sullivan, A. (2002, January). Assessment of red light running camera enforcement technologies. Paper presented at the 81st Annual Meeting of the Transportation Research Board, Washington, DC. https://www.itskrs.its.dot.gov/2003-sc00011

Village of Matteson. (2013). AFR 2012–2013 Village of Matteson, IL. https://www.villageofmatteson.org/document_center/finance/annual%20finance%20reports/AFR12-13.pdf

Village of Matteson. (2014). AFR 2013–2014 Village of Matteson, IL. https://www.villageofmatteson.org/document_center/finance/annual%20finance%20reports/AFR13-14.pdf

Village of Matteson. (2015a). AFR 2014–2015 Village of Matteson, IL. https://www.villageofmatteson.org/document_center/finance/annual%20finance%20reports/AFR13-14.pdf

Village of Matteson. (2015b). Annual municipal budget. https://www.villageofmatteson.org/document_center/finance/annual%20budget%20reports/Fiscal%20Year%2014-15%20Budget.pdf

Village of Matteson. (2018a). CAFR 2017 Village of Matteson, IL. https://www.villageofmatteson.org/document_center/finance/annual%20finance%20reports/AFR16-17.pdf

Village of Matteson. (2018b). Official Statement. General Obligation Debt Certificate, Series 2018. https://www.munios.com/munios-archive.ashx?e=H4X07

Village of Matteson. (2019). CAFR 2018 Village of Matteson, IL. https://www.villageofmatteson.org/document_center/finance/annual%20finance%20reports/AFR18-19.pdf

Village of Matteson. (2020a). CAFR 2019–2020 Village of Matteson, IL. https://www.villageofmatteson.org/document_center/finance/annual%20finance%20reports/CAFR19-20.pdf

Village of Matteson. (2020b). Messages from the Village President and COVID-19 Resources for Residents and Businesses in 2020. https://www.villageofmatteson.org/news_detail_T10_R108.php

Village of Matteson. (2021a). Village of Matteson Proposed Budget for the Year beginning May 1, 2020 and ending April 30, 2021. https://www.villageofmatteson.org/departments/finance_department/annual_reports.php#outer-1858
Village of Matteson. (2021b). COVID-19 Updates and Info. https://www.villageofmatteson.org/community/covid-19_updates_and_information.php
Village of Matteson. (2022). Annual Comprehensive Financial Report for the Year Ended April 30, 2021. Village of Matteson, IL. https://www.villageofmatteson.org/departments/finance_department/annual_reports.php#outer-1858
Village of Matteson. (2023). Annual Budget May 1, 2024 to April 30, 2025. Village of Matteson, IL. https://www.villageofmatteson.org/departments/finance_department/annual_reports.php#outer-1858

CASE STUDY 27

Economic development and revenue impact: Case of Village of Bradley, IL

Abstract

This case presents an analysis of economic development and its impact on revenues in the Village of Bradley, IL. It explores how the Village of Bradley, Illinois, used economic development tools and revenue-side budgeting strategies to improve its fiscal health between 2013 and 2025. This case illustrates how local governments can recover from fiscal stress, diversify their revenue base, and enhance long-term sustainability through economic development and strategic planning. The intent of this case study is to conduct an empirical evaluation of the impact of economic development on revenues in the Village of Bradley, IL.

Topics

Revenue Generation; Economic Development; Local Government; Fiscal Policy; Public Finance

Background

Bradley sits in the scenic Kankakee River Valley of Illinois and is part of a larger urban area that includes the City of Kankakee and the Villages of Manteno and Bourbonnais in Kankakee County. The Village of Bradley's motto is "Proud of Our Past, Focused on Our Future." Its name was changed from North Kankakee to Bradley in 1895 after the David Bradley Manufacturing Company agreed to move its operations to the growing industrialized area. Since its establishment in the late 1800s, Bradley has grown in manufacturing, shopping, and population.

Bradley is now home to 80% of the county's retail and commercial businesses. The nearness of the Kankakee River and Illinois Central Railroad played large roles in the development of Bradley and its surrounding area. The Village has a current population of approximately 15,695 people (U.S. Census, 2024). The median household income in Bradley was $67,400 in 2024.

Financial situation

From 2012 to 2016, the Village of Bradley, Illinois, faced a period of fiscal stress. On April 30, 2013, the Village reported a budget deficit of $504 thousand (Village of Bradley, 2014). As a response to fiscal stress, the Village of Bradley implemented budget cuts and reduced the capital spending across all departments in the FY 2015–2016 budget (Village of Bradley, 2016, p. MD&A5). However, the Village's financial position continued to decline. The government-wide fund had a deficit of $570,358 in FY2015 and $1,881,764 in FY2016 (Village of Bradley, 2016).

Since 2016, the Village's leadership has initiated a budgeting and financial reform plan aimed at collecting more revenues and providing economic incentives to restore long-term fiscal stability. Bradley significantly increased its sewer rates, implemented a capital maintenance and replacement fee, and introduced a 5% hotel tax.

Recognizing that the Village of Bradley is primarily a sales tax-driven community that relies heavily on its retail corridor to fund operations, the Village Board sought additional revenue diversification measures. In 2020, the Board proposed and successfully passed a 1% non-home rule sales tax referendum (Village of Bradley, 2021). This sales tax, largely supported by external consumers from Bradley's commercial corridor, allowed the Village to maintain essential services without increasing the burden on residents.

As part of the referendum's trade-off, the Village also launched a property tax rebate program designed to return a portion of collected revenues directly to local taxpayers. Beginning in 2023, the Village began rebating up to 100% (a minimum of $2,000,000) of its portion of property taxes to residents and businesses, effectively reducing the overall property tax burden. To support tourism and hospitality-related development, the Hotel Tax Fund was established in FY 2020, imposing a 5% tax on overnight stays. This hotel tax generates approximately $600,000 annually.

Economic development

Economic development incentives

From FY2021 to FY2025, the Village of Bradley's budget incorporated a series of strategic infrastructure investments, including significant improvements to Village-owned roads, storm sewer systems, park and recreation facilities, sewer rehabilitation, and the replacement of an aging fleet of municipal vehicles. These enhancements were designed not only to improve the quality of life for residents but also to support long-term economic development by increasing the Village's capacity to attract new businesses and enhance public safety and accessibility.

The Village of Bradley uses such economic development incentives as tax incentives through the Kankakee River Valley Enterprise Zone, property tax abatement, free or discounted building permits, investment tax credit, utility tax exemptions, and tax increment financings (TIFs). The Illinois Enterprise stimulates business investment and encourages job creation in designated areas by offering targeted tax incentives. The Village of Bradley is part of the Kankakee River Valley Enterprise Zone, one of two Enterprise Zones in Kankakee County. New construction projects in Bradley are eligible for property tax abatements in participating taxing districts, structured as follows:

- Year 1: 100%
- Year 2: 80%
- Year 3: 60%
- Year 4: 40%
- Year 5: 20%

The Village of Bradley offers free building permits. Building materials eligible for enterprise zone sales tax exemptions include items permanently affixed to real property, such as lumber, mortar, glued-down carpets, and wallpaper (Village of Bradley, 2025). Businesses in Bradley can receive a 0.5% credit against state income tax for investments in "qualified property" placed in service within the enterprise zone. "Qualified property" includes tangible assets like buildings, structural components, material tanks, elevators, and major computer installations. Businesses can obtain a sales tax exemption on machinery and equipment, provided they secure state certification and meet qualifying criteria. Companies in Bradley may qualify for a 5% exemption on state taxes for gas, electricity, and certain telecommunications, pending state certification and meeting specific criteria (Village of Bradley, 2025).

As part of its ongoing economic development efforts, the Village of Bradley initiated the creation of a TIF district in 2023 to support the redevelopment of approximately 27 acres of village-owned land located southeast and north of the mall area, extending to St. George Road. This TIF district facilitates opportunities for economic development and infrastructure investment, including the planned construction of an aquatic water park, a minimum of eight baseball and softball fields designed for league play, and a state-of-the-art indoor turf facility encompassing at least 70,000 square feet. Furthermore, an adjacent 75,000-square-foot area is designated for future development to include a conference center, brewery, entertainment venues, and outdoor festival grounds.

Economic development projects

Perry farm park

In 2022, Bradley started annexing Perry Farm Park, allowing the Village to expand the park's amenities. Perry Farm Park serves as home to the Exploration Station, a children's museum, and the Park District Administrative Offices within the historic Perry Farmhouse. Perry Farm Park has been enriching the lives of the community through recreation, education, and preservation across 170 acres of lush farmland nestled in Bradley, Illinois. This historic farmstead has been offering recreational opportunities for outdoor enthusiasts and families to explore fields, trails, and riverside caves. However, changes were needed to ensure this park is sustainable. The economic development plan was designed to revamp the park, with an initial investment budget of $4 million. These enhancements include a brewery, horseback riding, accessibility to the Kankakee River, a community performance stage, improved paved trails, open recreational fields, playground equipment, shelters, picnic areas, farm animals, Native American caves, fruit tree orchards, and flower gardens.

Bradley sports complex

In 2023, Bradley started developing a unique facility, the Bradley Sports Complex, in central Kankakee County. The 126-acre land purchase was designated for baseball-softball complexes. These land purchases provide Bradley with development opportunities and allow for stimulating growth and an increased economic future. The $50 million baseball-softball complex started hosting games in May 2025. The Bradley Sports Complex is a tournament-quality, destination ballpark complex that is positioned to host from 9 to 16 large baseball tournaments per year (approximately 100 teams per tournament), and from 7 to 13 softball tournaments per year (approximately 70 teams per tournament). S&P Global (2025) noted that Bradley Sports Complex is estimated to have 500,000 attendees annually and has 100 teams reserved per weekend from April to October. The amusement area includes baseball fields, a golfing area, hotels, shopping, and restaurants. The $50-million Bradley Sports Complex is expected to be a cornerstone for new development within Bradley. It is projected to have an annual economic impact between $33 million and $35 million.

Indoor water park

In 2025, Bradley planned construction of 90,000 square feet of an indoor water park. Indoor water parks will bring families and friends together and attract people to the community. This water park was proposed to have a variety of water entertainment options, including a lazy river, wave pool, 4-lane mat racer slides, speed slides, drop slides, a children's pool, a zero-depth pool, an 8,000-square-foot adult pool, multi-person raft rides, a surf machine, and a 7,000-square-foot outdoor pool with a floating obstacle course. The project's design should be completed in a year, and construction should start within two years. The proposed multi-acred site will be owned by the Village. The remainder of the land would be marketed to hotels, restaurants, or retail shops. The site is strategically located less than ¼ of a mile from U.S. Route 50 and approximately 1 mile from the Interstate I-57 interchange. Olivet Nazarene University, St. Mary's & Riverside Hospitals, with multiple retail shops and restaurants, are located nearby.

The proposed Bradley Indoor Waterpark is projected to generate significant economic benefits for the community. The preliminary construction cost is expected to be approximately $90 million. Bradley plans to use government-backed bonds to finance this project. In its first year of operation, the water park complex is projected to generate $20 million in profit, with $15 million derived from park admissions alone. In ten years, the total profit is projected to be around $94 million. Revenue-related taxes are anticipated to cover the initial construction cost. In addition to its fiscal contributions, the water park is expected to create approximately 200 new jobs in Bradley. This project aims to promote overnight tourism and strengthen the Village's position as a regional economic destination.

Conclusions

This case study analyzes Bradley's fiscal and economic changes from 2013 to 2025. After facing a deficit $0.5 million in 2013, the Village had surpluses of $5.4 million in 2021, $7.4 million in 2022, $6.2 million in 2023, and $3.4 million in 2024. The Village of Bradley demonstrates how strategic financial management and targeted economic development initiatives can revitalize a community and strengthen its fiscal foundation. The Village successfully attracted private investment and stimulated commercial revitalization through the coordinated use of grants, tax incentives, and strategic planning. Effective fiscal management and economic development policies contributed to measurable financial improvements.

On March 19, 2025, S&P Global Ratings upgraded the Village of Bradley's long-term general obligation bond rating from AA- to AA, citing continued enhancement of fiscal management, economic performance, and financial stability (S&P Global, 2025). These improvements underscore the impact of deliberate policy choices and investments in economic development.

Bradley's fiscal recovery was achieved through a combination of initiatives, including participation in the Kankakee River Valley Enterprise Zone, the implementation of a 1% business district sales tax, a 5% municipal hotel tax, and new sewer fees. The Village also enhanced its strategic planning and budgeting practices, established the Bradley Economic Development Corporation, and prioritized major projects such as Perry Farm Park and the Bradley Sports Complex.

Understanding how economic development supports the community and what decisions need to be made may be helpful for other municipalities in similar conditions. It is imperative that localities diversify their economic incentives, tax base, and tax structure and, over time, adapt to changing economic and demographic conditions. This case study demonstrates that economic development incentives can be one of the tools that contribute to revenue generation and diversification.

Discussion questions

1. What fiscal management and economic development strategies were most effective in helping the Village of Bradley transition from fiscal stress (2013–2018) to fiscal health (2019–2025)?
2. What are the advantages and risks of relying on sales taxes as a primary revenue source?
3. Why is revenue diversification important for local governments, and how did Bradley's introduction of a 1% business district sales tax, 5% hotel tax, and new sewer fees support this goal?
4. How can municipalities ensure that economic development projects lead to sustainable fiscal health?
5. What fiscal or economic risks might threaten the sustainability of Bradley's current growth?
6. How could the Village mitigate the risks of investments in an Indoor Water Park?
7. If you were a financial advisor to the Village, what additional revenue diversification strategies would you recommend?
8. Considering Bradley's suburban context and demographic trends, how might local policymakers design strategies that attract new investment without undermining the village's historical identity and community character?
9. Which elements of Bradley's approach could be realistically replicated by other local governments facing fiscal stress? Which strategies might not be transferable?

10 How likely do you think the water park project is to succeed in promoting economic development in the Village of Bradley?

11 How can the Village of Bradley measure whether the water park project successfully stimulated local economic growth (e.g., through job creation, business expansion, and tax revenue generation)? What specific indicators or data sources should be used?

References

S&P Global. (2025, March 19). *Bradley, IL GO debt rating raised to 'AA' on multi-year surpluses, robust reserves.* https://disclosure.spglobal.com/ratings/en/regulatory/article/-/view/type/HTML/id/3340000

Village of Bradley. (2014). *Annual financial report for the fiscal year ended April 30, 2013.* https://bradleyil.org/transparency-portal/

Village of Bradley. (2016). *Annual financial report for the fiscal year ended April 30, 2015.* https://bradleyil.org/transparency-portal/

Village of Bradley. (2021). *Annual financial report for the fiscal year ended April 30, 2020.* https://bradleyil.org/transparency-portal/

Village of Bradley. (2025). *Annual financial report for the fiscal year ended April 30, 2024.* https://bradleyil.org/transparency-portal/

U.S. Census (2024). Quick Facts Bradley village, Illinois. https://www.census.gov/quickfacts/fact/table/bradleyvillageillinois/BZA010223

CONCLUSIONS

As the public finance and budgeting field has become more complex and data-driven, traditional lecture-based instruction alone is increasingly insufficient to prepare students for the realities of public sector decision-making. Case-based learning offers a much-needed complement to lectures by actively engaging students in applied analysis, interpretation, and judgment (Lynn, 1999; Yin, 2009). It is also notable that case studies are not only effective but also an affordable and easily accessible way to bridge theory and practice. They allow students and practitioners to explore real-world fiscal challenges, evaluate decision-making under constraints, and develop practical solutions grounded in evidence and context.

In this book, case studies are presented as more than illustrative examples. They serve as analytical labs in which students actively practice budgeting skills. By working through carefully chosen real-world cases, students learn to diagnose fiscal problems, interpret financial and economic data, assess policy alternatives, and formulate sound recommendations.

Narrative cases allow students to understand context and institutional history, while cross cases highlight similarities and differences across jurisdictions. Decision-forcing cases and simulations push students to confront uncertainty and make consequential choices, mirroring the conditions under which budget officers, managers, and elected officials operate.

Case studies promote learning at the highest levels of cognitive engagement. They incorporate judgment, negotiation, ethical reasoning, and strategic thinking. Case-based instruction moves students away from memorization toward knowledge application. It aligns public budgeting education with the professional

DOI: 10.4324/9781003606833-13

competencies expected of graduates in public administration, nonprofit management, and public policy programs. Case studies cultivate practical and interpersonal skills that are difficult to develop through lectures alone. Group-based case analysis promotes collaboration, exposes students to diverse perspectives, and strengthens communication skills essential for budget deliberations and public accountability. Simulations and role-playing exercises further enhance experiential learning by allowing students to assume the roles of public officials, analysts, and stakeholders, thereby deepening their understanding of political dynamics and institutional incentives embedded in the public budgeting process. Instructors serve not as sole transmitters of knowledge, but as facilitators who guide discussion, challenge assumptions, and help students connect theory to practice.

Case studies can also serve as assessment tools, evaluating students' ability to make informed decisions in complex situations, their ethical judgment, and ability to communicate policy-relevant conclusions in a public context. Students may be asked to present case studies in class or create their own cases based on current events, professional experiences, or policy issues they have researched.

Case study development includes the following steps:

1 Identifying a relevant public problem that requires decision-making.
2 Determining which analytical, administrative, financial, or ethical skills will be emphasized.
3 Researching the topic to ensure accuracy and clarity.
4 Writing a compelling narrative that draws students into real-world dilemma.
5 Ensuring the case is realistic, engaging, and appropriately challenging.

Effective sequencing of case study activities with lectures can significantly enhance student learning. The course could begin with lectures to establish a foundational knowledge base and ensure that students understand core concepts. Once this groundwork is in place, narrative case studies can be introduced, providing students with the opportunity to apply what they have learned. As students develop stronger analytical abilities, the instructor can incorporate full-class decision-forcing simulations. At this point, the instructor takes on the role of a facilitator.

Overall, this book includes 27 case studies that are intended to bridge budget theory and practice through real-world stories in narrative cases and role playing in decision-forcing simulation cases. The 27 cases in the book cover various issues related to budget preparation, revenue and expenditure estimates, internal control violations, green budgeting, participatory budgeting, project prioritization in capital budgeting, benefit-cost analysis, credit ratings, debt issuance, economic incentives, fiscal emergencies and bankruptcy, and various other topics.

Twenty-six of the case studies in this book are single cases that examine specific budget situations. Only one case study on the universal school meals program is a multi-case study that evaluates the program in nine states. Eight of these 27 case studies are cross-cases. Two of them examine congestion pricing in London and New York City. Three cases examine embezzlement and internal control violations in Clark County, OH, the City of Nelsonville, OH, and the City of Dixon, IL. Three other cases are on bankruptcy and fiscal emergency in Milwaukee, WI, East Cleveland, OH, and Moffett, OK. Seven of the 27 cases are embedded and address situation from various levels of governance, including department, city, state, and federal. These are the cases of New York congestion pricing, Milwaukee, Moffett, and East Cleveland fiscal emergencies, California "Welcome stranger" case, the case of school closures in Jefferson County Colorado, and a case of budgeting during COVID-19 pandemic in Cuyahoga County, Ohio.

The four decision-forcing cases in this book are structured as simulation games, in which students are assigned different roles and asked to make various budget decisions. These decision-forcing cases cover revenue shortfall situation in Matteson, IL, school closures in Jefferson County, CO, budgeting for vacancies in Cuyahoga County, OH, and ranking of infrastructure projects at the federal level.

References

Lynn Jr, L. E. (1999). *Teaching and learning with cases: A guidebook.* CQ Press.
Yin, R. K. (2009). *Case study research: Design and methods* (4th ed.). Sage.

INDEX

For Product Safety Concerns and Information please contact our EU representative GPSR@taylorandfrancis.com Taylor & Francis Verlag GmbH, Kaufingerstraße 24, 80331 München, Germany